Cuba

WORLD BIBLIOGRAPHICAL SERIES

General Editors:
Robert G. Neville (Executive Editor)
John J. Horton

Robert A. Myers   Hans H. Wellisch
Ian Wallace   Ralph Lee Woodward, Jr.

John J. Horton is Deputy Librarian of the University of Bradford and was formerly Chairman of its Academic Board of Studies in Social Sciences. He has maintained a longstanding interest in the discipline of area studies and its associated bibliographical problems, with special reference to European Studies. In particular he has published in the field of Icelandic and of Yugoslav studies, including the two relevant volumes in the World Bibliographical Series.

Robert A. Myers is Associate Professor of Anthropology in the Division of Social Sciences and Director of Study Abroad Programs at Alfred University, Alfred, New York. He has studied post-colonial island nations of the Caribbean and has spent two years in Nigeria on a Fulbright Lectureship. His interests include international public health, historical anthropology and developing societies. In addition to *Amerindians of the Lesser Antilles: a bibliography* (1981), *A Resource Guide to Dominica, 1493-1986* (1987) and numerous articles, he has compiled the World Bibliographical Series volumes on *Dominica* (1987), *Nigeria* (1989) and *Ghana* (1991).

Ian Wallace is Professor of German at the University of Bath. A graduate of Oxford in French and German, he also studied in Tübingen, Heidelberg and Lausanne before taking teaching posts at universities in the USA, Scotland and England. He specializes in contemporary German affairs, especially literature and culture, on which he has published numerous articles and books. In 1979 he founded the journal *GDR Monitor*, which he continues to edit under its new title *German Monitor*.

Hans H. Wellisch is Professor emeritus at the College of Library and Information Services, University of Maryland. He was President of the American Society of Indexers and was a member of the International Federation for Documentation. He is the author of numerous articles and several books on indexing and abstracting, and has published *The Conversion of Scripts and Indexing and Abstracting: an International Bibliography*, and *Indexing from A to Z*. He also contributes frequently to *Journal of the American Society for Information Science*, *The Indexer* and other professional journals.

Ralph Lee Woodward, Jr. is Professor of History at Tulane University, New Orleans. He is the author of *Central America, a Nation Divided*, 2nd ed. (1985), as well as several monographs and more than seventy scholarly articles on modern Latin America. He has also compiled volumes in the World Bibliographical Series on *Belize* (1980), *El Salvador* (1988), *Guatemala* (Rev. Ed.) (1992) and *Nicaragua* (Rev. Ed.) (1994). Dr. Woodward edited the Central American section of the *Research Guide to Central America and the Caribbean* (1985) and is currently associate editor of Scribner's *Encyclopedia of Latin American History*.

VOLUME 75

Cuba

Jean Stubbs, Lila Haines and Meic F. Haines

Compilers

CLIO PRESS

OXFORD, ENGLAND · SANTA BARBARA, CALIFORNIA
DENVER, COLORADO

British Library Cataloguing in Publication Data

Stubbs, Jean, 1946-
Cuba. – (World bibliographical series; vol. 75)
1. Cuba – Bibliography
I. Title   II. Haines, Lila   III. Haines, Meic F.
016.9'7291

ISBN 1–85109–021–5

ABC-CLIO Ltd.,
Old Clarendon Ironworks,
35A Great Clarendon Street,
Oxford OX2 6AT, England.

———————

ABC-CLIO Inc.,
130 Cremona Drive,
Santa Barbara,
CA 93116, USA.

Designed by Bernard Crossland.
Typeset by Columns Design and Production Services Ltd., Reading, England.
Printed and bound in Great Britain by Bookcraft (Bath) Ltd., Midsomer Norton.

THE WORLD BIBLIOGRAPHICAL SERIES

This series, which is principally designed for the English speaker, will eventually cover every country (and many of the world's principal regions), each in a separate volume comprising annotated entries on works dealing with its history, geography, economy and politics; and with its people, their culture, customs, religion and social organization. Attention will also be paid to current living conditions – housing, education, newspapers, clothing, etc.– that are all too often ignored in standard bibliographies; and to those particular aspects relevant to individual countries. Each volume seeks to achieve, by use of careful selectivity and critical assessment of the literature, an expression of the country and an appreciation of its nature and national aspirations, to guide the reader towards an understanding of its importance. The keynote of the series is to provide, in a uniform format, an interpretation of each country that will express its culture, its place in the world, and the qualities and background that make it unique. The views expressed in individual volumes, however, are not necessarily those of the publisher.

VOLUMES IN THE SERIES

Contents

Contents

Contents

Contents

Contents

Introduction

Cuba, the largest island in the Greater Antilles, lies at the point where the Gulf of Mexico, the Caribbean Sea and the Atlantic Ocean meet. Its nearest large neighbours are Florida (150 km north), Haiti (77 km east), Jamaica (140 km south) and Mexico (210 km west). The Cuban archipelago lies between 19° 49′ and 23° 17′ north, and between 74° 7′ and 84° 57′ west. The national territory, which also includes the Isle of Youth (Isla de la Juventud) and about 1,600 offshore keys, covers an area of 110,992 square kilometres (approximately two-thirds the size of Great Britain). The main island measures 1,250 kilometres in length (approximately east to west) and varies in width from 31 to 191 kilometres from north to south. Situated south of the Tropic of Cancer, Cuba has a subtropical climate, with an average annual temperature of twenty-three degrees centigrade. Rainfall is comparatively high, though there is a dry season from November to April, and the island is affected by hurricanes.

A limestone plain covers almost three-quarters of the island. In the east the dominant feature is the Sierra Maestra mountain range, which includes the country's highest peaks: Turquino (1,974 metres); Cuba (1,872 metres); La Bayamesa (1,730 metres); and Martí (1,722 metres). The highest point in the Guaniguanico range in the westernmost part of the island, composed of the Sierra de los Organos and the Sierra del Rosario, rises to little more than 700 metres. The San Juan peak (1,140 metres) is the highest point in the central Guamohaya (Escambray) mountains.

Cuba has over 200 rivers, of which the longest is the Cauto. Most are short, however, and unsuitable for hydro-electric power. The Zapata peninsula on the south coast includes what is considered to be one of the Caribbean's most ecologically important wetland areas.

Cuba has long generated a degree of interest out of all proportion to its size. This has less to do with its acknowledged beauty, or even its strategic position, than with its perceived economic potential and, in the last four decades of the 20th century, the revolution led by Fidel Castro.

Introduction

Indeed, it was Cuba's economic potential that first led to Western interest in the island and when Christopher Columbus's flotilla 'discovered' Cuba in 1492, it was the prospect of gold that proved the initial attraction. Later, a different kind of treasure, the profits generated by sugar and tobacco, proved irresistible to the Spanish colonizers who ruled Cuba until 1898, only briefly interrupted by the 1762-63 British occupation of Havana. When the Spanish first arrived, they found the island already inhabited by indigenous peoples whom archaeologists have traditionally divided into the Taíno, sub-Taíno, Mayarí, Ciboney Cayo Redondo and Ciboney Guayabo Blanco cultural groups. Early European travellers noted that these groups were at differing stages of development, the Taíno being the most technologically advanced. Never numerous, their communities eventually disintegrated, partly as a result of the greed of the early settlers who exploited them to death in mining and agricultural operations, and partly under the onslaught of European diseases. Their genes, however, clearly live on in some remote rural populations, particularly in the extreme west and east of the island.

Cuba was one of the first Caribbean islands to be settled during Spain's expansionary period in the 16th and 17th centuries. It was not until the second half of the 18th century, however, with the introduction of plantation sugar farming, that the island became of major importance to the Spanish. Cuba rapidly turned into a sugar monoculture, a radical development that is still heavily influencing the economic profile of the island at the end of the 20th century.

During this period of rapid expansion of Spanish colonial control, the slave trade flourished, following its rapid growth during the English occupation of Havana in 1762. Declared illegal by treaties between Spain and Britain in 1817, the trade nonetheless continued until 1835, when a further treaty, combined with stricter Spanish policing, led to its gradual decline and virtual disappearance by the 1860s. Despite this, Spain did not officially abolish slavery in Cuba until 1886.

The 1840s and 1850s saw the island plunged into economic and political crisis as increasing competition from other sugar exporters, such as Jamaica, encroached on its US market for sugar. Within Cuba, a lobby in favour of annexation by the United States grew up among some sugar plantation owners, but this lost support after the defeat of the pro-slavery south in the American Civil War. The majority of the plantation owners then concentrated on seeking reform, while a Cuban independence movement emerged, primarily in the eastern provinces where there were fewer sugar mills and the economy was more vulnerable.

The weakness of the Spanish colonial government during the late 1860s, combined with the economic crisis, fuelled a decade of rebellion in Cuba, which was led initially by plantation owners. First among these was Carlos Manuel de Céspedes who, on 10 October 1868, freed his slaves and issued the 'Grito de Yara', a call to arms influenced by the American Declaration of Independence. This marked the beginning of the Ten Years War (1868-78), Cuba's first war of independence.

In 1869 a Constituent Assembly convened in Guáimaro proclaimed a liberal Constitution, declared an end to slavery, and backed annexation by the USA. New leaders emerged in the course of the struggle, notably the Cuban mulatto, Antonio Maceo, and the Dominican, Maximo Gómez, both of whom were to play a prominent role again in the second war of independence (1895-98).

Despite inflicting a spectacular defeat on the Spaniards in 1875, General Gómez was forced to resign his command, and was thus prevented from carrying out his plan of stopping the flow of revenue to Spain by capturing the rich western provinces. In 1878 as a result of the Treaty of Zanjón, the Spanish offered Cuba the kind of autonomy already offered to Puerto Rico. A faction led by General Maceo rejected this treaty and demanded independence and the abolition of slavery. The general and his followers were defeated and Maceo, Gómez and other leaders went into exile. In the period following the Zanjón Treaty nationalist sentiment coalesced and two distinct trends emerged: the more revolutionary elements formed the Cuban Revolutionary Party in 1892; while the Liberal Autonomist Party was formed with the aim of attaining independence by peaceful means. Though it temporarily gained the support of many Cubans, the latter achieved little, not even universal suffrage when Spain proclaimed it in 1890.

Economically, the period between Cuba's two independence wars was one of modernization, with the building of more efficient sugar mills both in the war-wasted east and in the prosperous west, which had escaped the Ten Years War unscathed. War-ruined plantation owners became suppliers of cane (*colonos*), or sold out completely, often to US business. Ties with the United States, Cuba's principal export market, had already become more important than those with Spain, and this was to be a key factor in US intervention in the final stages of Cuba's second war of independence. Socially, the interwar period saw the polarization and radicalization of the independence struggle, with many former slaves swelling the *independentista* ranks and cementing a socio-economic as well as political agenda.

The Cuban Revolutionary Party founded by José Martí in 1892 became the focus for, and Martí the driving force behind, a new push for independence which was to culminate in the second war of independence (1895-98). Wary of the economic attrition of a prolonged war, and the emergence of military caudillos, Martí planned for a quick victory by means of a mass rebellion involving all regions of the island, backed by resources purchased with funds raised mainly from exiles in the United States. Though the seizure by the US authorities of military supplies gathered in Florida for shipment to Cuba alerted the Spaniards to the seriousness of his intentions, Martí attempted to press ahead with his original plan. Small uprisings in February 1895 were quickly quashed, and in May Martí himself was killed in a confrontation with Spanish forces.

This left the rebel leadership in the hands of the veteran generals Maceo and Gómez. The Spaniards reacted to rebel successes by mounting a war of extermination which sparked international protests to the Spanish government. A newly appointed Captain-General proclaimed Cuban autonomy and appointed several liberals (*autonomistas*) to a new government. However, the rebels refused to recognize the new government and pressure for intervention mounted in the United States.

The first step towards US involvement came in January 1898, with a 'friendly' visit to Havana by the US battleship *Maine*. However, on 15 February an explosion aboard the *Maine* sank the vessel, killing 260 crew members. The US navy was placed on alert and in April, under US pressure, Spain offered a truce which the rebel forces turned down. On 20 April, direct US intervention began and was welcomed and militarily aided by the rebel army. When the US fleet captured Santiago, however, the Cubans were forbidden to enter the city and US troops began to occupy the country. The Cuban forces were excluded from the subsequent peace talks in Paris and on 10 December a treaty was signed ending Spanish rule not only in Cuba, but also in Puerto Rico and the Philippines.

A US military government ruled a devastated island from 1899 to 1902. US capital expanded its presence in the sugar industry and also invested in railways, tobacco, minerals and public utilities. Circumstances in the United States and in Cuba led US President McKinley to decide in favour of fostering a friendly government in Havana. In November 1900, thirty-one delegates representing the then six Cuban provinces met to draw up a constitution, but were confronted in January 1901 with US demands. When it became clear that the choice was between a republic subject to US intervention or no republic, the delegates voted by sixteen to fifteen, the latter led by black parliamentarian Juan Gualberto Gómez, in favour of adding the Platt Amendment (earlier approved by the US Congress) to the Cuban constitution. This amendment ceded to the US government the right to intervene in Cuban affairs.

On 20 May 1902, Tomás Estrada Palma was inaugurated as Cuba's first president. His four-year term of office (1902-6) was a period of economic recovery, and one in which commercial links to the United States were strengthened by a treaty granting Cuban sugar preferential entry to the US market. The citizens of the new republic found themselves caught economically between traditional Spanish commercial dominance and growing US control of the land and the sugar industry. With few economic options open to Cubans, politics became a profitable concern in its own right and corruption was rampant. Not surprisingly perhaps, major strikes rocked Havana's tobacco factories, railroads and docklands in these years.

Estrada Palma's decision to call elections in 1906 did nothing to cleanse the body politic, rather it precipitated a descent into violence. Following an armed rebellion in August 1906, the United States again took control of the island and US troops remained until 1909. In this period, the virtual exclusion of black Cubans from the 20th-century political scene was the backdrop to Cuba's brief period of separatist race politics and the 1912 Oriente race war, with US involvement. A show of US force helped put down another rebellion during the 1917 election campaign, and there was a further US intervention in 1921.

These events took place against a backdrop of spectacularly rising sugar prices on the world market after the First World War, and this led to the rapid expansion and modernization of the Cuban sugar industry. Cheap labour was imported from neighbouring Haiti and Jamaica, as well as other Caribbean islands, thus increasing social and racial tensions. US control of the sugar industry grew, along with Cuban dependence on the US market for imports and exports. The 'dance of the millions', as the period of unprecedented prosperity was known, ended suddenly when sugar prices plummeted, from 22.5 cents per pound in May to 3.75 cents in mid-December 1920. This had devastating consequences for a country that had moved much closer to being a monoculture economy.

The period up to the 1930s was characterized by instability, corruption and increasing government authoritarianism, which, following labour and student unrest, culminated in the dictatorship of General Gerardo Machado. However, in what has gone down in history as the failed revolution of 1933, Machado was ousted and an alliance between revolutionary students and army sergeants brought Fulgencio Batista to centre stage on a nationalistic ticket, backed by the US government. By 1935, all revolutionary uprisings had finally been quelled.

The years that followed were marked by Popular Front politics, with alliances between labour and capital, and Batista stepped down in the 1944 elections. The years 1946-48 witnessed growing Cold War tensions and political corruption again took hold. When a young Fidel Castro was running for election in Havana in 1952, it was a much-changed Batista who seized power once more in a military coup. His repressive rule provoked opposition from student and urban guerrilla groups. One such group attacked the Moncada Barracks in Santiago de Cuba in 1953, with the aim of sparking a nationwide rebellion. The rebellion failed and the insurgents were captured. Many were summarily executed; the remainder were tried and imprisoned but released into exile in 1955. Their leader, Fidel Castro, and a group of eighty-one followers returned to Cuba in December 1956. Though all but twelve were killed in a matter of days, the survivors initiated a guerrilla struggle in the Sierra Maestra mountains that gained increasing popular support and culminated in victory over General Batista's demoralized forces.

The flight of Batista and his close followers on New Year's Eve 1958 left power in the hands of the victorious revolutionaries. Their early priorities – land reform, a literacy campaign, education, health and housing – had been promised in the defence plea delivered by Fidel Castro after the attack on the Moncada Barracks. Though, at least initially, the new government was essentially in the radical Cuban nationalist tradition, their actions set off Cold War alarm bells in Washington.

A series of tit-for-tat expropriations by Havana and sanctions by Washington set US–Cuban relations plunging to a new low. Washington broke off diplomatic relations in January 1961 after Cuba nationalized assets valued at over $1bn belonging to US companies. The US government also backed the abortive invasion attempt by anti-Castro exiles at the Bay of Pigs in April 1961.

In March 1962 the US extended the partial embargo it had imposed on trade with Cuba in 1960 to include all goods. Most analysts agree that it was the breakdown in US–Cuban relations followed by the US embargo that drove Cuba into the Soviet camp and led to Castro's open declaration of a Marxist position. Moscow's decision to intervene when the United States imposed the trade embargo on Cuba is likely to have been motivated by political rather than economic ambitions, given the generous Soviet subsidy made to the island's economy. Whatever the rationale, the combination of Cold War hostility between Moscow and Washington and the heat of historic US–Cuban mutual distrust, almost resulted in a nuclear holocaust. The Cuban Missile Crisis of October 1962, when the United States of America and the Soviet Union brought the world to the brink of nuclear war following Moscow's decision to deploy nuclear warheads near Havana, exemplified Cuba's new place in the world order. It also taught the Cubans that they were peripheral to, if not a pawn in the strategy of the superpowers.

Nevertheless, the western hemisphere's first one-party socialist state went on to become an important player in Third World and Eastern bloc politics. Generous Soviet subsidies and tight central planning were the backdrop to an ambitious experiment in political, economic and social engineering. Cuba, already one of the most urbanized islands of the Caribbean, invested in industrial development, education, and ambitious welfare provision, all of which the 1990s have since seen eroded.

Following the demise of the former Soviet Union, and with it the socialist trading bloc (the Council for Mutual Economic Assistance [Comecon], which Havana joined in 1974), Cuba has again found itself the centre of considerable international attention. Economic hardship has been the dominant concern of the politicians and public alike in Cuba in the 1990s. The stated aim of preserving the main social achievements of the revolution in the face of the collapse of Soviet socialism initially took the form of an economic balancing act with a mainly external focus: attracting inward investment, while developing tourism as a source of convertible currency in place of lost export earnings. On the domestic front, the government declared a 'special period in peacetime', an austerity programme marked by food shortages, cuts in power and public transport, and an attempt to make state enterprises more efficient. By 1993 it had become clear that this course was more likely to destroy the system than to save it: the money supply was raging out of control; subsidies to loss-making industries were soaring; and the black market was thriving as the state sector found itself unable to supply even basic necessities.

The legalization of hard currency use by Cubans announced in 1993 marked a turning point for economic policy. The new direction aimed to: control inflation and bring the illegally circulating hard currency under a degree of state control; reduce the budget deficit; and encourage higher production by allowing wider self-employment, turning state farms into cooperatives, and granting greater autonomy to state enterprises. It also involved creating a more open and supportive environment for foreign investment, an aim which received institutional backing with the passing of a more liberal foreign investment law in September 1995 and the drafting of laws to reform banking and other key economic sectors.

The year 1995 also saw mounting international opposition to US attempts to extend its trade embargo. This took place side-by-side with considerable diplomatic activity by President Castro and other government officials as part of a concerted attempt to strengthen relations with important economic partners, including Latin American and Caribbean nations, the European Union, China, Vietnam and Japan. The future of relations with Washington, however, remained unclear.

Thousands of mainly middle-class Cubans emigrated to Florida and other parts of the USA in the early 1960s, forming the nucleus of a lobby that has ensured Washington's policy towards Cuba has remained cold ever since. The attempt at normalization during the Carter presidency (1977-81) ended with the Mariel boatlift, when some 125,000 Cubans left for the United States. A 1984 migration agreement was suspended by Havana after the US-sponsored Radio Martí began to beam anti-Castro programmes into Cuba.

A new thaw in relations began in 1988 following an agreement on the future of Angola (including withdrawal of Cuban troops), but in 1992, under election-year pressure from the Cuban-American lobby, President Bush closed US ports to ships which had docked in Cuba during the previous six months. In October 1992 Congress passed a bill prohibiting third-country subsidiaries of US companies from trading with Cuba.

A new migration accord was reached in September 1994 in the wake of another exodus which occurred at the depths of Cuba's post-1989 economic decline, when over 30,000 Cubans risked their lives in an attempt to reach the United States on makeshift rafts. However, new US legislation to further tighten the embargo was approved in March 1996, following the shooting down by the Cuban airforce of two planes belonging to Miami Cubans. At the time of writing, however, President Clinton was being asked by Washington's NAFTA partners and by European governments to postpone the implementation of its most controversial clauses, seen as extraterritorial in their scope and in possible breach of international free trade agreements.

So long as US–Cuban relations remain confrontational there is little likelihood of major political change in Cuba. While US President Clinton announced some minor concessions in 1995 he also backed a stricter enforcement of embargo legislation. Although the logic of recent events in Cuba, compounded by the island's need for economic regeneration, suggests that the final years of the 20th century may see deeper economic change and the beginnings of political reform, the future scenario is closely linked to an issue that emerged forcefully a century earlier: relations with the United States of America.

The economy

For most of the revolutionary period central planning and collective ownership of the means of production were Cuba's key economic tenets. More recently there has been a shift away from direct control of production although the state retains ownership of the island's resource base, and the government prioritizes certain sectors and attempts to control the flow of key commodities. Monetary and fiscal instruments of economic policy have gained in importance since being introduced in 1994.

The Gross Domestic Product suffered a cumulative fall of almost thirty-five per cent in the period 1989-94 but began to recover in 1994 and growth was an estimated 2.5 per cent in 1995. The budget deficit was cut from Ps5bn in 1993 to Ps750m in 1995, just three per cent of GDP. This was achieved by price rises, civil service cuts, and other measures aimed at mopping up surplus liquidity.

The United States of America was Cuba's major trading partner prior to the 1959 revolution. In the two decades up to 1989, however, foreign trade was conducted increasingly with the Eastern bloc. Although Western Europe, Japan and China took a significant share at certain times, Eastern Europe accounted for over eighty per cent in 1989. The value of foreign trade totalled some Ps13.5bn in 1989 and although it fell to under Ps3.2bn by 1993, it rose to an estimated $3.6bn in 1995. The period 1989-95 saw a re-orientation in the direction of foreign trade, as well as a shift in its structure. Most significantly, the Commonwealth of Independent States accounted for only twenty per cent of trade in 1993, compared with the seventy per cent with the former Soviet Union in 1989.

Sugar remains the largest commodity export, although the 1994-95 sugar harvest hit an historic low from which it is struggling to recover with the help of expensive Western finance. Other agricultural exports include citrus fruits, tobacco and coffee. Cuba has one of the world's most important nickel and cobalt reserves, and production and exports are now being resurrected in this sector through foreign investment. The island also has small deposits of other minerals. Tourism has developed rapidly in the 1990s with the aid of foreign investment, and earned close to $1bn in 1995, putting it ahead of the traditional top earner, sugar, in gross earnings. However, the island is heavily dependent on oil imports to meet energy needs, although the output from domestic sources has risen in the 1990s, following the introduction of modern technology by Western companies.

The national currency is the peso. The use of the US dollar and other freely convertible currencies by Cubans was legalized in mid-1993, although only the US dollar is in common use. On the black market the peso plummeted against the US dollar in the period 1990-94, but recovered to stabilize at around 25:1 in 1995. A convertible peso, on a par with the US dollar, was introduced in January 1995 and has held its value on the informal market.

Introduction

The Constitution

Cuba has a controversial constitutional history, dating back to the Platt Amendment (see p. xviii). The amendment, which remained in force until 1934, gave the United States of America the right to intervene in Cuban affairs and provided for the establishment of a US naval base at Guantánamo Bay in eastern Cuba which, over ninety years on, is still a bone of contention between the two nations.

In February 1976, seventeen years after Castro led his guerrillas to victory against the Batista regime, a new Constitution was approved by referendum. It enshrined a new institutional framework, the People's Power system of deliberative and administrative assemblies. The first elections under the new system were held the following October. The 1976 Constitution also reaffirmed the socialist nature of the Cuban state (declared by Castro in April 1961), the leading role of the Cuban Communist Party (formed in 1965 from the Popular Socialist Party and the Castro-led 26th July Movement), and the principles of social ownership of the means of production and central planning and control of economic activity. The Constitution was amended in July 1992 to afford protection to foreign investment in Cuba, liberalize the concepts of property and the state's economic role, and to provide limited recognition to private enterprise.

The political system

Cuba is a one-party state but claims to have evolved a political framework facilitating extensive grassroots involvement in decision-making. Its 589-member National Assembly has been directly elected since the Constitution was reformed in 1992, although the complex nomination system still allows the Cuban Communist Party to exercise extensive control over the selection of 'non-party' candidates. The People's Power system of government also embraces 14 Provincial and 169 Municipal Assemblies. The 2,200 km 'special municipality' of the Isle of Youth (Isla de la Juventud) off the southern coast has quasi-provincial status, possibly due as much to the fact that it has been the scene of enclave economic and educational experiments as to its offshore situation. An additional tier of local government, serving communities of around 30,000, was added in 1992; known as People's Councils, these numbered 102 in 1995.

In the period between National Assembly sessions, of which there are two a year, with provision for special sessions, the thirty-member Council of State has legislative powers. Its Council of Ministers and Executive Council (comprising the President, First Vice-President and five Vice-Presidents) exercise executive and administrative functions. The Cuban Communist Party and the Union of Young Communists have special constitutional status and corresponding political strength. In addition, mass organizations of women, small farmers and trade unionists have also been fairly powerful forces at the height of the revolutionary period. They are still accorded an important consultative role, in particular through the so-called 'Workers' Parliaments' which have been convened to discuss the reforms introduced in the 1990s.

Society

While the economic imperative was the driving force that made Cuba the racially and culturally complex society it ultimately became, social factors also generated their own agenda. The successive waves of immigrants from Spain's mainland regions and the Canary Islands have all contributed their speech patterns to the island's language as well as their cultural characteristics. The encounter between these dialects, the now-extinct aboriginal languages and those of the slaves brought from Africa has resulted in a variety of Spanish that is distinctly Caribbean, but with certain unmistakeable phonetic and lexical characteristics of its own.

Somewhat more than half the Cuban population claims Spanish origins, the rest being mainly black or mulatto (mixed race). In the 1790s, a wave of French refugee planters fled, with their retinues of servants and slaves, from a revolution in neighbouring Saint Domingue (today Haiti) to eastern Cuba. It is a region which has experienced a constant flow of immigrants from neighbouring islands, mainly for seasonal agricultural work. In addition, Chinese indentured labourers were brought to Cuba to replace the slaves freed in 1886. There has also been a sprinkling of other European as well as Arab settlers and small-scale Japanese settlements earlier in this century. Immigration continued well into the 20th century, with thousands of Spanish immigrants arriving annually even as late as 1934. The Jewish population, never large, shrank rapidly after the 1959 revolution.

Cuba's population was estimated at over 11 million in 1995, with around seventy-five per cent living in urban areas. The capital, Havana (La Habana), has over 2.1 million inhabitants, with a net growth rate of 17,000 in 1994, a third higher than the annual average over the previous two decades. Average life expectancy in 1992 was 73.5 years for men and 77.4 years for women. The infant mortality rate was 9.4 per thousand live births in 1995, the lowest in Latin

America, and the maternal mortality rate was 3.3 per 10,000 live births. The proportion of elderly people within the total population is increasing, and today over twelve per cent of Cubans are over sixty years of age.

Cuba's health-care system is free at the point of provision. There is one doctor for approximately every 230 people and most inhabitants now have access to the community health-care network which places an emphasis on preventive medicine. Nevertheless, there has been a fall in nutrition levels in the crisis-ridden 1990s. According to official figures, daily per capita consumption of fats dropped by forty per cent in the period 1989-93, average consumption of vitamins A and C by seventy-six per cent and sixty-two per cent respectively, and calcium by nineteen per cent.

Although Cuba's health and education indicators were among the highest in the region even before the 1959 revolution, provision was uneven. One of the revolution's earliest social priorities was a literacy programme, launched in 1961, and an educational infrastructure was built up across the island, allowing mass access to education at all levels. Education is free at all levels and literacy is around ninety-six per cent. Cuba now has forty-six university-level institutions, in which almost 153,500 students (fifty-eight per cent of them women) were registered in the 1994-95 academic year. There is a heavy emphasis placed on the disciplines of science and technology, with a concomitantly strong scientific establishment, whose expertise in areas such as genetic engineering and biotechnology has made the export of health products a useful economic activity. High educational standards are also being used to attract investment. Despite the progress made in this area, the general education system has, through economic necessity, suffered from a severe resource scarcity throughout the 1990s, although no schools have been closed and teacher numbers have been largely maintained.

Culture

Music has been Cuba's main cultural link with the non-Hispanic world. Indeed, Cuban music has deeply influenced the world's musical consciousness in the 20th century, jazz and salsa being genres that spring immediately to mind. There is a growing international appreciation of the variety and wealth of musical traditions in Cuba.

Most other Cuban art forms, however, remain largely undiscovered by English-speakers. Relatively few Cuban authors are well known outside the Spanish-speaking world, and this has led some on the island to believe that in order to gain international recognition it is necessary to become a dissident. While Cuban cinema has won the respect of other film-makers, particularly in Latin America with which it has close and mutually enriching links, it has only recently gained some popular recognition among English-speakers with the nomination of the feature film *Fresa y chocolate* (Strawberry and chocolate) for an Oscar in 1995. The Cuban film industry's recent output has been of extraordinary quality given the serious shortage of resources.

Both Cuba's physical colonial heritage and its ecological riches have received international recognition. UNESCO has named Old Havana and Trinidad as World Heritage Centres and has designated several areas of the island as world biosphere reserves.

The bibliography

Our main emphasis when compiling this volume has been on recent work which is either at the cutting edge of research or covers topics which have received little attention in earlier bibliographies, though we have included some classics which have never been superseded. While attempting to provide the English-speaker with key works of reference in all sectors, we have also aimed to strike a balance between texts in English and Spanish, between often polarized viewpoints and between Cuban and foreign authors, as well as providing access to the views of Cubans on the island and in exile.

The end product is inevitably somewhat uneven. Some areas are better served by book-length texts in English, others by Spanish-language texts or journal articles, some more obscure than others. The overall bias is towards publications in Cuba, the USA and Britain, with a few from Australia, though much has also been published on Cuba in, for example, other Latin American countries, Spain, and the former socialist bloc.

Some eleven million Cubans reside on the island in the mid-1990s, with an estimated two million overseas, over 1.5 million of them in the USA. Cuban-Americans are among the wealthiest immigrant communities in the United States, with a strong intellectual class. The academic work produced by intellectuals of that class, both in Spanish and English, has therefore become a growth industry, swamping intellectual production about the island elsewhere outside Cuba.

On the island, a similar growth in publications took place as a result of the educational and publishing revolution. The output of the latter is primarily in Spanish, though notable works have been translated into English. However, access to these publications abroad has often been difficult and, with the grave problems in publishing in the crisis-hit 1990s, works published in Cuba have become rarer and more inaccessible. A new development which could go some way to alleviating these problems, is the trend towards joint publishing ventures between institutions and individuals in Cuba and overseas publishing houses. There are also welcome signs of a slight upturn in publishing as the country begins to emerge from the depths of the economic crisis.

In the final analysis, the criteria for inclusion are tied up with trends, availability and taste. English-language texts on Cuba are far more numerous on the political and socio-economic aspects of the revolution, US–Cuba relations, and, to a lesser extent, other international relations, and the Cuban-American community. The battle of ideas between Cubans at home and abroad permeates the sections on the revolution and its leaders, especially Fidel Castro, and politics in general. Travel and tourism are fairly well served in English, as well as being less contentious.

There is a vast literature on the history of Cuba, which made this a particularly difficult section to compile. The final selection includes the work of some of Cuba's leading historians and also those reflecting trends in modern historiography. Special attention was paid to 19th- and 20th-century political, social and economic history, and to aspects which are key to an understanding of revolutionary Cuba: the late 19th-century wars of independence and US intervention; the 1930s worker-peasant-student uprising; and the 1950s insurrection. It was impossible to do justice to the wealth of titles published in Cuba, in Spanish, either before or after 1959, especially on Spanish colonialism, US neo-colonialism and dependence, Cuban nationalism and class struggle.

In an attempt to counteract the somewhat artificial pre- and post-1959 divide, certain specialized texts in late modern history have been included under their thematic sections, e.g. agriculture, economy, education, labour and women. Slavery and race also form a separate section. Cuba was one of the last countries in which slavery was abolished (1886) and the recent centenary of that event produced a spate of works. Race is also re-emerging as an issue in the crisis 1990s.

Of necessity, revolution became the umbrella for general texts which touch on a variety of topics spanning politics, economics, sociology and culture. To a certain extent, a case could be made for a new division, post-1989 Cuba, to reflect the fundamental changes occurring as a result of the disappearance of the socialist bloc. A substantial section on finance, trade and investment reflects the recent upsurge of interest in Cuba as an emerging market and a player in its own right on the world economic stage, rather than as an adjunct to the US or Soviet markets.

In certain disciplines there is a rich bibliography in Spanish but a relative paucity of publications in English. This is particularly marked in the case of geography, flora and fauna, prehistory and archaeology, linguistics, science and technology and, to a lesser extent, literature and the arts. It may safely be predicted that future bibliographies will be richer in texts on issues such as the environment, and possibly science and technology, areas in which Cuban activity is just beginning to capture international interest. In the meantime, the reader seriously concerned with pursuing an interest in any of these disciplines could begin by making direct contact with institutions such as the Cuban Academy of Sciences (now part of the Ministry of Science, Technology and the Environment), whose archives contain the fruits of decades of Cuban research.

Acknowledgements

All three compilers have lived and worked in Cuba: Jean Stubbs in 1968-87; and Lila Haines and Meic Haines in 1986-92, and as a result, have first-hand knowledge of the country as well as substantial personal Cuba libraries. We are also, however, indebted to many people and places.

Six librarians willingly shared their knowledge with Jean Stubbs: Jerome Nichol, Librarian of the Center for Cuban Studies in New York; Richard Phillips, Latin American and Caribbean Librarian, University of Florida, Gainesville; Pat Noble, Latin American and Caribbean Librarian in Senate House Library, University of London; Alan Biggins and David Blake, respectively Librarians of the University of London Institutes of Latin American and Commonwealth Studies; and Crispin Partridge, Caribbean Librarian at the University of North London. Valerie Cooper at the Institute of Latin American Studies Library also assisted in locating bibliographical details. Jean Stubbs also consulted works held in the Library of Congress in Washington. Her colleagues and students at the University of North London and her own Anglo-Cuban family were most forebearing and helped keep her on track.

Meic Haines consulted specialized material in branches of the British Library: the British Museum (Natural History) and the Science Reference and Information Service.

Lila Haines was able to draw on the archives of Cuba Business Limited for specialist trade, finance and investment material and other publications by US organizations. The library of University of Wales

Swansea also proved a useful resource. Gerry Hagelberg generously shared his deep knowledge of the sugar industry, and Cuban friends, in particular Carmen González, Niurka Pérez and Mayda Álvarez, gladly responded to last-minute pleas to locate recent Cuban publications.

At ABC-CLIO, Robert Neville was a long-suffering managing editor. Our editor, Sarah Leatherbarrow, in effect became the fourth compiler. She displayed great diligence and efficiency, not only liaising with the three of us to supply missing bibliographical details and annotations, but also seeking them out herself in the Bodleian Library, Oxford, and Senate House, London. She applied her editorial skills to reordering sections, cross-referencing, numbering and indexing. Her input was invaluable in reaching publication.

As a result of the collective work of all involved, and unfolding events, the delay in publishing this work has also had its positive side. In 1991 it was unclear in what direction Cuba would go. In summer 1994, a riot in Havana and the exodus of thousands of rafters attempting to cross the Florida Straits in search of a better life appeared to some to herald the beginning of the end. However, by the end of 1995, it was clear that Cuba had defied the domino theory of collapse and was restructuring its economy, society and international relations. As we write, events such as the February 1996 shooting down of Cuban-American planes flying over Cuban airspace continue to cast doubt on Cuba's future. Nevertheless, there is still hope that the country may enter the 21st century with a stable political system, having embarked on a reconciliation between island and overseas Cubans, and brought about the normalization, to some degree, of relations with its powerful enemy the United States of America.

Lila Haines, Meic Haines, Jean Stubbs
February 1996

The Country and Its People

1 **Area handbook for Cuba.**
 Jan Knippers Black. Washington, DC: US Government Printing Office,
 1976. 550p. bibliog.
Offers comprehensive coverage of a range of topics, including geography, history,
population, economy, agriculture, government, labour, foreign policy, education, culture, trade and the armed forces. Though dated, this volume remains a useful reference
work.

2 **Cuba.**
 Adam Kufeld. New York; London: Norton, 1994. 128p. map.
The 106 photographs contained in this book were taken throughout Cuba in 1991 in
what the photographer says was an attempt to portray everyday life. The solid
introduction by travel writer Tom Miller is perceptive and provides an easy guide to
the politics and history of the country.

3 **Cuba for beginners: an illustrated guide for Americans (and their
 government) to socialist Cuba.**
 Rius. London: Pathfinder, 1970. 153p.
This is a classic work, by the great Mexican cartoonist, with an underlying seriousness
which acts as a counter-balance to his wit. It covers the history of Cuba from its
discovery by Columbus, through colonization by Spain, its independence struggles,
and its status as a quasi-colony of the United States, to its socialist revolution in 1959.
Rius offers a hilarious depiction of Uncle Sam's machinations and misadventures with
the bearded Fidelista guerrillas.

4 **Cuba: a guide to the people, politics and culture.**
Emily Hatchwell, Simon Calder. London: Latin American Bureau,
1995. 75p. map. bibliog. (In Focus Series).

This brief work attempts to provide a potted guide to Cuba, from its history and politics to recent economic change and cultural manifestations. However, accuracy is sometimes sacrificed in pursuit of brevity and a reader-friendly style; for example, the authors miss certain fundamental economic points and trends, and culture is treated in a rather cavalier fashion.

5 **Cuba . . . in pictures.**
Nathan Haverstock. Minneapolis, Minnesota: Lerner Publications,
1987. 64p.

Provides a useful introduction to Cuba, through photographs and graphics, with an accompanying text.

6 **Havana 1933.**
Walker Evans. New York: Pantheon; London: Thames & Hudson,
1989. 111p.

Opening with an introductory essay by Gilles Mora, the remainder of the book is then given over to black-and-white photographs, taken by Walker Evans, depicting various aspects of Cuban life in 1933. The photographs of Cuban people and scenery combine to present a clear impression of Cuban life at the time.

7 **Into Cuba.**
Photographs by Barry Lewis, text by Peter Marshall. New York: Alfred
van der Marck Editions; London: Zena Publications, 1985. 192p. map.

A 'coffee table' book with stunning full-colour photographs taken across the length and breadth of the island. The text and photographs combine to offer a portrait of life in 1980s Cuba in the context of its landscape, history, culture and politics, with chapters on Havana, the tobacco and sugar industries, cattle, the mountains, and the Isla de la Juventud (Isle of Youth). The book's strength undoubtedly lies in the way in which both the photography and prose capture the warmth and vitality of the Cuban people.

8 **Let's visit Cuba.**
John Griffiths. London: Burke, 1983. 96p. map.

Griffiths provides a light introduction to the country, the people and the 1959 revolution, as seen in 1983, in the usual vein of the 'Let's Visit' series. He touches on agriculture, industry, education, health, social and political change, culture, and Cuba and the rest of the world. Striking colour and black-and-white photographs are included.

9 **Old Havana, Cuba.**
Nicolas Sapieha. London: Tauris Parke Books, 1990. 128p. bibliog.

The decayed beauty of Cuba's capital city is portrayed in this volume, from its brightly painted façades to its 1930s and 1940s American cars. The photographs are accompanied by a history of the city, which pays particular attention to the colonial past that shaped much of its architecture.

10   **Portrait of Cuba.**
Wayne S. Smith, edited by James W. Porges.   Atlanta, Georgia:
Turner, 1991. 192p.

Presents an account of Cuba's evolution through pictures and text, beginning with the island's early history, and then covering the revolution and revolutionary régime and finally bringing the story up to date with a consideration of contemporary Cuba and its altered circumstances and uncertain future. Readers may also be interested to look at *Cuba: the land, the history, the people, the culture* (Stephen Williams. [n.p.]: Multimedia Books, 1994).

11   **South America, Central America and the Caribbean 1995.**
London: Europa Publications, 1994. 5th ed. 683p.

Part of the Europa reference series of international surveys and directories on countries in a specific region, this volume covers Latin America and the Caribbean. Part one consists of essays on the political, religious and economic problems of the region, together with a section on the commodities of the area. Research institutes and periodicals with an interest in the region are also listed. Part two provides full details of the main regional organizations concerned with Latin American and the Caribbean. The final part contains separate chapters on each country. Cuba is included in this treatment, covering: facts in brief; history and economy; statistical survey and directory of names, addresses and other information; and brief bibliography.

12   **Visión de Cuba.** (Vision of Cuba.)
Alberto Salazar Gutiérrez, Víctor Pérez Galdós.   Havana: Editora
Política, 1987. 207p.

The facts and figures collected together in this volume provide a good introductory overview of Cuba's geography, history, population, ecology, political and state institutions, national symbols, foreign policy, economic and social development, tourism and individual provinces.

Geography

General

13 The Caribbean islands.
Helmut Blume, translated from the German by Johannes Maczewski,
Ann Norton.   London: Longman, 1974. 464p. maps. bibliog.

First published in 1968, this is a solid study of the physical, economic and social geography of the Caribbean region. The first part offers a general survey of the area, whilst the second part comprises descriptions of each island, with a comprehensive bibliography of materials in English, French, German and Spanish.

14 Middle America, its lands and peoples.
Robert C. West, John P. Augelli.   Englewood Cliffs, New Jersey:
Prentice-Hall, 1976. 2nd ed. 494p. maps. bibliog.

A standard geography of the land, people and resources of Central America and the Caribbean, including Cuba.

Cuba

15 Cuba: official standard names approved by the United States Board on Geographic Names.
United States Department of the Interior, Office of Geography.
Washington, DC: US Government Printing Office, 1957. 113p.

Some 9,000 places and features in Cuba are entered in this volume.

16   **Geografía de Cuba.** (Cuban geography.)
Levi Marrero.   Havana: Tipográficos Alfa, 1951. 736p. bibliog.
One of the standard surveys by a leading geographer, recently deceased and long-resident in Puerto Rico, this volume covers each of Cuba's then six provinces, including their geology, climate, soil, coasts, flora and fauna, population, agriculture, mining, forestry, fishing and economy.

17   **Geografía de Cuba.** (Cuban geography.)
Antonio Núñez Jiménez.   Havana: Pueblo y Educación, 1973. 4 vols.
The author, a leading geographer, examines the major features of Cuban geography, region by region, covering physical geography, natural resources and economic geography.

18   **Geografía y espeleología en revolución.** (Geography and speleology in revolution.)
Havana: Imprenta Central de las Fuerzas Armadas Revolucionarias, 1986. 190p.
Documents, speeches and articles relating to the work of the Cuban Speleology Society are published here by the Cuban Armed Forces' Press.

19   **Geología de Cuba.** (Cuban geology.)
Gustavo Furrazola-Bermúdez.   Havana: Editora del Consejo Nacional de Universidades, 1964. 239p. maps. bibliog.
A geological survey of Cuba, containing information on mineral resources, land formation and water management.

20   **Introducción a la geografía de Cuba.** (Introduction to the geography of Cuba.)
Salvador Massip, Sarah A. Ysalque de Massip.   Havana: [n.p.], 1942. 250p. bibliog.
Two leading geographers of the time provide a survey of Cuba's physical geography, cartography, geological origins, coasts, climate and zoology, which is still relevant today.

21   **Nomenclatura geográfica y toponímica de Cuba.** (Cuban geographical and toponymical names.)
Ernesto de los Rios.   Havana: Biblioteca Nacional José Martí, 1970. 159p.
The author provides a useful catalogue of Cuban geographical names, places, and features.

22 **Nuevo atlas nacional de Cuba.** (New national atlas of Cuba.)
   Foreword by Rosa Elena Simeón. Cuban Academy of Sciences,
   Institute of Geodesy, 1989. [n.p.].

The definitive atlas of Cuba, this was the fruit of a major co-operative effort involving all relevant Cuban specialist institutions. It is divided into the following sections: general and reference; geophysical characteristics; geological constitution; relief; karst; climate; water resources; maritime resources; soils; flora and vegetation; fauna; landscape; population and settlements; social infrastructure; natural resources; agriculture; cattle; forestry; the sugar economy; industry; construction; transport and communications; economic regionalization; foreign trade; the environment; history; and the revolution.

23 **Los recursos climáticos de Cuba, su utilización en la economía
   nacional.** (Cuba's climatic resources, their use in the national
   economy.)
   F. F. Davitaya, I. I. Trusov. Havana: Cuban Academy of Sciences,
   1965. 68p.

A study of climatic conditions in Cuba and their implications for agricultural production.

Regional

24 **Geology and paleontology of Central Camagüey, Cuba.**
   Aart Van Wessem. Utrecht, Netherlands: J. Van Beokhoevn, 1943. 91p.

This is a rare, if dated, work in English on the geology and palaeontology of the central-eastern region.

25 **The high Sierra Maestra.**
   B. E. Fernow. *Bulletin of the American Geographical Society*, vol. 39,
   no. 5 (1907), p. 257-68.

Fernow's description of this mountain region is dated, but still useful. It deals with the topography, geology, climate, plant geography and animal life of the eastern mountain range which for centuries has sheltered fugitives and rebels, including indigenous peoples, runaway slaves, and 19th-century independence and 20th-century revolutionary fighters.

The Caribbean environment.
See item no. 821.

La erosión desgasta a Cuba. (Erosion is wearing Cuba away.)
See item no. 824.

**Geografía del medio ambiente: una alternativa del ordenamiento
ecológico.** (Geography of the environment: an alternative to the ecological
order.)
See item no. 825.

Tourism and Travel Guides

Tourism

26 **Last resorts: the costs of tourism in the Caribbean.**
Polly Patullo, foreword by Michael Manley.   London: Latin America
Bureau, 1996. 220p. bibliog.

The 1959 revolution brought an end to Cuba's growing tourist market and for many
years the island was taken off the tourist map. In the 1990s, however, tourism has
again become an important factor in Cuba's precarious economic survival. The issues
discussed here in a Caribbean context are therefore most pertinent to the Cuban
experience. A well-researched review, this work provides a cost–benefit analysis of
the conflictual short and long-term prospects, including the new eco-tourism and the
ways in which tourism corrupts peoples and cultures.

27 **Tourism development in Cuba.**
Derek R. Hall.   In: *Tourism in the less developed countries.*
Edited by D. Harrison.   London: Halsted Press, 1992, p. 102-20.

Explores the paradox of Cuba's return to the promotion of tourism, in the context of:
Cuba's pre-revolutionary tourist history; the move away from tourism after 1959
under a socialist government; and the return in the 1980s to encouragement of
Western tourists as part of an economic development strategy. See also 'El turismo y
su desarrollo' by Ramón Martín (*Economía y Desarrollo*, no. 106 [Sept.-Oct. 1988],
p. 30-37; no. 107 [Nov.-Dec. 1988], p. 30-39).

28 **Tourism development in transition economies: the Cuba case.**
Françoise L. Simon.   *Columbia Journal of World Business*, vol. 30,
no. 1 (spring 1995), p. 26-40.

Simon's well-documented article discusses the impact of tourism on Cuba's recent
economic and structural development, the foreign investment it has garnered and what
is needed in the future. The author compares Cuban efforts to generate revenue from
international tourism both with those of other transitional economies, from Vietnam to

7

Hungary, and with its more experienced Caribbean neighbours. Simon, who is a Professor of Marketing and International Business at the Columbia Business School, based her article in part on a series of twenty interviews conducted in Havana in January 1995.

29 Tourism in Cuba: a development strategy for the 1990s?
María Dolores Espino. *Cuban Studies*, no. 23 (1993), p. 49-70.

An early asessment of tourism's emerging rôle in Cuba's economic development plans, this paper provides valuable statistics and a useful review of the evolution of the Cuban tourist industry prior to 1990. However, Espino's attempt to analyse the recent phase of the strategy is marred by minor errors and is now outdated.

Travel guides

30 The complete guide to Cuba.
Paula DiPerna. New York: St. Martin's Press, 1979. 275p. 11 maps.

The classic US travel guide to Cuba, and the first to appear after the 1959 revolution when only a few intrepid Americans dared to visit the country, this is dedicated to the hope that goodwill between people affirmed by travellers might outlive the enmity between governments. The guide begins with reference to the small openings in large doors, which are characteristic of Cuban architecture; in itself a small opening, the work was solidly researched, with an empathy for the country and people, and still makes good reading. It has been the basis for many guidebooks since.

31 Cuba.
In: *Baedeker's Caribbean*. Edited by Helmut Linde, translated from the German by James Hogarth. Basingstoke, England: Publishing Division of the Automobile Association, Jarrold & Sons Ltd., 1992, p. 159-201. 2 maps.

The first Baedeker handbook for travellers appeared over 150 years ago, and since then they have been designed to provide updated practical information, as well as taking a look at the relevant country and its people and its culture. The compact chapter on Cuba provides a brief introduction to the country's geography, history, government, economy, transport, population and settlement, as well as a guide to the main cities and towns.

32 Cuba.
In: *Caribbean islands handbook 1996*. Edited by Sarah Cameron, Ben Box. Bath, England: Trade & Travel Publications. 1995. 7th ed, p. 140-84.

Up-to-date information for independent travellers is given on all the Caribbean islands, including Cuba. A new edition is published on 1 September each year, for which the text is updated, based on the editors' personal travels, extensive information from correspondents living in the region, and other varied sources of information in the region and beyond. General chapters cover introductory hints, Miami as a major gateway to the Caribbean, health information, geology, flora and fauna and responsible tourism, whale and dolphin watching, watersports and sailing, scuba diving, windsurfing and walking. Sections on each island cover history, government, economy, culture, flora and fauna, diving and marine life, beaches and watersports, other sports, festivals, excursions and maps.

33 Cuba: an Insight Guide.
Edited by Tony Perrottet, Joann Biondi, photographs by Eduardo Gil, et al. Basingstoke, England: APA Publications (HK) Ltd. (distributed in UK by GeoCenter International UK Ltd), 1995. 283p.

While this work would have benefited from a more thorough weeding out of irritating historical errors, it is nevertheless a delightful read. Among the various contributors, two US journalists long resident in Cuba, Jane McManus and Marge Zimmerman, share their extensive and detailed insider knowledge of the island. Zimmerman, for example, takes the readers on a journey to the other Havana not normally seen by tourists, the rural province with its small towns stretching from north to south across the island. Another US journalist, Larry Luxnor, provides insights gained from his frequent visits to Cuba, and Nobel Prize-winning novelist Gabriel García Márquez's knowledge of Cuba enriches a mainly enjoyable and useful guide.

34 Cuba: official guide.
A. Gerald Gravette. London; Basingstoke, England: Macmillan Caribbean, 1988. 277p. 30 maps.

A glossy UK travel guide endorsed by the Cuban Tourist Board, which provides comprehensive coverage of the country and is profusely illustrated in colour throughout. In addition to travelling tips, general information and advice on where to go and what to see, the book includes chapters on geography, history, politics, culture, economy, and nature. Detailed maps and plans of main towns accompany the text.

35 Getting to know Cuba: a travel guide.
Jane McManus. New York: St. Martin's Press, 1989. 198p.

Described as an easy-to-use handbook for Canadian and American visitors planning a first trip to Cuba, this pocket-size guide is packed with information and colour photographs. It is written by a United States journalist who has lived and worked in Cuba for over twenty years, a good number of them with Cuba's National Institute of Tourism. The guide includes practical information on how to travel to the island (including special United States permissions), and on what a curious traveller, open to understanding another people and culture, can expect from the trip. Information on special-interest tourism (such as health, fishing and hunting) and ten short conversations in Spanish are also provided.

36 Guía turística/tourist guide.
Havana: SI-MAR, 1995. 160p.

This bilingual Spanish–English tourist guide aims to provide a comprehensive view of the country and includes seven articles by Cuban specialists on the sciences, economy, culture and society.

9

37 **Guide to Cuba.**
Stephen Fallon. Chalfont St. Peter, England: Bradt Publications; Old
Saybrook, Connecticut: Globe Pequot Press, 1995. 245p. 42 maps.
bibliog.

The author travels throughout the island, reaching some of the more remote parts by
pedal bike, trying to find a solution to the question 'What is Cuba?' His answer is a
mixture of many different things, but of one thing he is certain: punished for taking a
different path from its powerful northern neighbour, the United States of America,
which has tightened the economic screw, tourism has become Cuba's paradoxical
salvation. As a result, a visit to this troubled jewel of the Caribbean is an interesting,
memorable and rewarding experience.

38 **Hildebrand's travel guide: Cuba.**
Heidi Rann, Peter Geide, translated from the German by Jacqueline
Baroncini. Frankfurt, Germany: Karto & Grafik, 1985. 176p. maps.

This guide was written for the then growing West German tourist trade to Cuba. Much
of the practical information is by now dated but it is well illustrated and contains a
great deal of background information.

39 **Odyssey illustrated guide to Cuba.**
Andrew Coe, photographs by Rolando Pujol. Hong Kong: The
Guidebook Company, 1995. 314p. 13 maps. bibliog.

A guide-book by a British traveller, with maps and many full-colour as well as black-
and-white photographs by a Cuban press photographer. In addition to the usual
sections on background history, geography, and tourist information, there are special
essays on rum, cigars, music, Santería [a syncretic cult] and the US Guantánamo Bay
Naval Base, and excerpts from literary classics.

40 **Tourist guide of Cuba.**
José Antonio Tamargo, Alberto Riaza. Havana: National Tourism
Institute, 1986. 143p.

Constitutes a practical tourist guide, with maps and information for getting around,
and quality colour reproductions.

41 **Travellers survival kit: Cuba.**
Simon Calder, Emily Hatchwell. Oxford: Vacation Work, 1993.
22 maps. 287p.

Carter and Hatchwell present the pros and cons of going to Cuba as an intrepid
individual traveller, with an emphasis on the possibilities and hazards of low-cost
tourism. Unfortunately, the pace of change in the Cuba of the 1990s is so fast as to
have dated much of the practical information and advice only a year or two after
publication. It remains, however, a light, humorous insight to a country which reveals
a tragic yet fascinating blend of burgeoning Western package tourism and crumbling
Eastern-bloc-style socialism. The authors find that its people nonetheless display a
'Cubanness' born of Spanish and African roots.

Dossier: Cuba.
See item no. 235.

Travellers' Accounts

19th century

42   **Cuba with pen and pencil.**
      Samuel Hazard.   Hartford, Connecticut: Hartford, 1871. 584p.
About half of this detailed and illustrated travel account covers the varied aspects of
life in Havana, whilst the remainder consists of the author's travels through rural Cuba
and to provincial capitals.

43   **Due South; or, Cuba, past and present.**
      Maturin M. Ballou.   Boston, Massachusetts: Houghton Mifflin, 1886.
      2nd ed. 316p.
This is a perceptive account, especially of social conditions during the inter-war
period of great upheaval.

44   **Excursión a Vuelta Abajo.** (Excursion to Vuelta Abajo.)
      Cirilo Villaverde.   Havana: Editorial Letras Cubanas, 1981. 246p.
A classic travelogue from the author of the 19th-century Cuban novel *Cecilia Valdés*.
Villaverde graphically captures the social history of the famous cigar tobacco-
producing region of western Cuba in the 1830s and 1840s.

45   **La isla de Cuba en el siglo XIX vista por los extranjeros.** (The island
      of Cuba in the 19th century as seen by foreigners.)
      Juan Pérez de la Riva.   Havana: Ciencias Sociales, 1981. 265p. bibliog.
Cuba's leading historical demographer provides an important critique of the views of
foreigners in their travel accounts of Cuba in the 19th century.

46   **The island of Cuba.**
Alexander von Humboldt, translated from the Spanish with notes and preliminary essay by J. S. Thrasher.   New York: Negro Universities Press, 1969. 2nd ed. 397p. maps.

A classic account originally published in 1856 (Derby & Jackson), this contains hard data and narrative on administration, the economy and slavery. The author travelled through Cuba in the early 19th century, observing and recording local conditions at a time of rapid change on the island.

47   **The island of Cuba: its resources, progress, and prospects.**
Richard Robert Madden.   London: C. Gilpin, 1849. 252p. Reprinted, London: Partridge & Oakey, 1969.

Madden's classic account is particularly thorough in its description of the slave trade and slave conditions in Cuba. The author has since been implicated in the 1844 Ladder Conspiracy (an alleged abolitionist plot which led to the massacre of thousands of blacks and free coloureds by Spanish Government forces).

48   **The Mambí-Land, or, adventures of a *Herald* correspondent in Cuba.**
James O'Kelly.   Philadelphia, Pennsylvania: J. B. Lippincott & Co., 1874. 359p. Translated into Spanish and reprinted, Havana, 1930, 1968 and 1990.

First published as a series of reports in the *New York Herald*, this account appeared in book form two years later, after the author's escape from a Spanish prison. O'Kelly travelled 'the other Cuba', not the slave-holding, sugar-producing Queen of the Antilles, but the unvisited territory of eastern Cuba Libre, or Mambí-Land, in the throes of its Ten Years War of Independence (1868-78). The end-product provides a war-time record of life behind the lines in the insurgent camps. The editions published in Spanish carry the 1930 introduction by Fernando Ortiz on the life and writings of O'Kelly.

49   **Sixty years in Cuba.**
Edward Atkins.   Cambridge, Massachusetts: Riverside Press, 1926. Reprinted, New York: Arno Press, 1980. 362p.

Edward Atkins was a major owner of sugar property in Cuba and held positions of responsibility in the island and the United States. His memoir spans the period 1860-1910, providing information on sugar and finance.

50   **Slaves, sugar and colonial society: travel accounts of Cuba, 1801-1899.**
Edited by Louis A. Pérez, Jr.   Wilmington, Delaware: Scholarly Resources, 1992. 259p. bibliog.

Pérez brings together extracts from rare accounts by foreign visitors to Cuba from the United States, Great Britain, Denmark and Spain. They testify to the fact that 19th-century Cuba was an almost obligatory crossroads for Europeans travelling to the New World and also within easy reach for North Americans. Their perceptive observations cover slavery and the great sugar plantations; Church, state and religion; health, education and charity; rural life and society. They paint a picture of prosperity, turmoil and unrest, at a time when Cubans were confronting the colonial status quo with rapid and radical change.

51 **To Cuba and back: a vacation voyage.**
Richard Henry Dana, Jr.   Boston, Massachusetts: Ticknor & Fields, 1859. Reprinted, Carbondale, Illinois: Southern Illinois University Press, 1966 (edited by C. Harvey Gardiner). 288p.
The author describes general conditions in Cuba, with special emphasis on Havana and Matanzas, observing the customs of urban and rural life.

52 **Travels in the west: Cuba with notices of Puerto Rico and the slave trade.**
David Turnbull.   London: Longman, 1840. Reprinted, New York: Negro Universities Press, 1969; AMS Press, 1973. 574p.
Turnbull was a key British agent in attempting to undermine the slave trade to Cuba as far as Britain was concerned. His account pays particular attention to the condition of slaves and free coloureds, to the situation in Havana, and to mining, sugar, coffee and tobacco.

53 **Viajeras del Caribe.** (Women travellers of the Caribbean.)
Nara Araújo.   Havana: Editorial Arte y Literatura, 1983. 550p. bibliog.
Constitutes a literary critic's contemporary selection of excerpts from letters and diaries written by several women travellers to the various parts of the Caribbean. The volume is especially interesting as it provides a comparative Pan-Caribbean window on the experiences and impressions of those who were often young and travelling alone in times of colonial strictures.

20th century (pre-1959)

54 **Un canario en Cuba.** (A Canary Islander in Cuba.)
Francisco González Díaz.   Havana: Imprenta La Prueba, 1916. 347p.
A travel account which provides an extensive commentary on life in Cuba for the many Spanish immigrants of the time, especially those from the Canary Islands.

55 **Cuba.**
Erne Fergusson.   New York: Knopf, 1946. 308p.
This travelogue incorporates both impressions of and historical sketches on conditions in the provinces at the time of writing.

56   Cuban tapestry.

Sydney A. Clark.   New York: R. M. McBride & Company, 1939. 289p.

Sydney Clark provided one of the better narratives on the social and economic conditions in 1930s Cuba in the wake of depression and the upheavals of the 1920s and early 1930s.

57   El toro: a motorcar story of interior Cuba.

E. Ralph Estep.   Detroit, Michigan: Packard Motor Car Company, 1909. 107p.

In this account the author travels the length and breadth of the island by car, making observations about living conditions in the interior.

58   When it's cocktail time in Cuba.

Basil D. Wood.   New York: H. Liveright, 1928. 284p.

A travel account which takes a look at a lighter side of Cuba, that of the leisure, amusements, sports and recreation of the country's North American community.

20th century (post-1959)

59   Crónicas para caminantes. (Tales for travellers.)

Angel Tomás.   Havana: Editora Política, 1988. 268p.

In these twenty-six essays, the author invites readers to wander around Cuba in the footsteps of characters as diverse as a Nazi spy and a group of Swedish immigrants. Some of the people he meets talk of their beliefs inherited from African ancestors, whilst others speak of their lives before the 1959 revolution, providing insights into various aspects of Cuba's culture and social history.

60   Cuba: a journey.

Jacobo Timmerman, translated by Toby Talbot, with a new foreword by the author.   New York: Picador, 1994. 3rd ed. 130p.

A well-known Argentinian left-winger writes of his disillusionment with Cuba, concluding that ideology distorts the lives of the population. He condemns cultural and intellectual repression and denounces the Cuban government as just another dictatorship. The book was also published by Vintage in 1992 and earlier by Alfred Knopf in 1990.

61   Cuba roja: como viven los cubanos con Fidel Castro. (Red Cuba: how the Cubans live with Fidel Castro.)

Román Orozco, foreword by Manuel Leguineche.   Bogotá, Colombia: Javier Vergara, 1993. 948p.

Cuba roja was edited in conjunction with, and written by the editor of, the Madrid-based publication *Cambio 16*. Orozco was the journal's correspondent in the United

States and Mexico, and stayed for a number of prolonged periods in Cuba, in 1988-93. During this time he travelled extensively throughout the island, using his experience as the basis for this, his first book. It is apparent from the narrative that Orozco loves Cuba but his is no pilgrimage. He immerses himself in its blend of politics and culture, of both Spanish and African origin, as lived by its island and exile peoples in moments of economic crisis and social tension.

62   **A Cuban journey.**
      Lee Chadwick.   London: Dennis Dobson, 1975; Westport,
      Connecticut: Lawrence Hill, 1976. 212p. map.

A sensitive account, with an unabashedly partisan view, this was written by a British traveller with a particular interest in the children of Cuba. The author provides a good background history to the revolution before launching into her diary of impressions of Havana and the countryside – Las Villas, Camagüey and Oriente. She has interesting observations to make on literacy, education, teacher training, rebel youth, children's literature and the arts.

63   **Does Fidel eat more than your father? Conversations in Cuba.**
      Barry Reckord.   New York: Praeger, 1971. 175p.

Drawing on experience from his time spent in Cuba in the late 1960s, Reckord, a Jamaican playwright, writes a light-hearted account, making interesting comparisons between Cuban and anglophone Caribbean approaches to problems.

64   **Driving through Cuba: an east–west journey.**
      Carlo Gebler.   London: Hamish Hamilton. 1988. 294p.

The author of this travel account drove as a tourist around revolutionary Cuba in a car with his wife and daughter. He describes how, for three months, his main preoccupation was trying to function in and understand an alien economy, from the limited perspective of his own cultural background. His story is one of car break-downs and hotel facilities not functioning; of unexpected detours, passengers and conversations; and of anecdotes, chance meetings, mishaps and prejudices.

65   **Havana journal.**
      Andrew Salkey.   London: Penguin, 1971. 316p.

The now deceased Jamaican writer shares his recorded diary, complete with dialogues, of a late 1960s trip to Havana.

66   **In Cuba.**
      Ernesto Cardenal.   New York: New Directions Books, 1974. 340p.

Cardenal, the Nicaraguan poet-priest, and subsequently Minister of Culture under the Sandinista government, wrote about two trips he made to Cuba in 1970 and 1971, when the country was in a state of flux. In his account, he talks with writers, priests, farmers, workers and officials, including Fidel Castro.

67 **In the fist of the revolution: life in a Cuban country town.**
José Yglesias. New York: Pantheon, 1968. 307p. map.

A Cuban American, the author lived for three months in 1967 in the eastern mountain town of Mayarí. In this account he narrates the impact of the Cuban revolution on the town and its people.

68 **In *Granma*'s wake: *Girl Stella*'s voyage to Cuba.**
Frank Mulville. London: Seafarer Books, 1970. 302p. map.

Mulville has made a name for himself by writing about his yachting voyages, often single-handed, all over the world. On this occasion in the late 1960s, he sailed on the small craft *Girl Stella*, with his wife and their two young boys, from their home-town of Maldon in England, to Cuba. It was a first for the revolutionary authorities to give permission for them to sail and dock all around the island.

69 **Inside Cuba.**
Joe Nicholson, Jr. New York: Sheed & Ward, 1974. 235p.

When he wrote this up-beat reflective account, the author, a United States investigative reporter for the *New York Post*, presumed that US–Cuban relations would soon be normalized. Nicholson first arrived in Cuba in 1964 aboard a US destroyer that sailed into the US naval base in Guantánamo. His appetite to see Cuba was whetted, and in 1972, after covering the Allende government in Chile, he flew back to spend six weeks journeying round the island. Nicholson visited many places, interviewed leaders and people, and, while disturbed by collectivist uniformity, found support for Fidel, the equality of the revolution, and the principles of communism.

70 **Return to Havana: the decline of Cuban society under Castro.**
Maurice Halperin. Nashville, Tennessee: Vanderbilt University Press, 1994. 200p. bibliog.

Halperin first visited Cuba in 1935 but was deported. He returned in 1960 at Che Guevara's invitation and went back again in 1962, this time staying for six years and subsequently writing two books. In 1989 he returned yet again, in his eighties, to stay for a month in Varadero. This book reflects his saddened impressions of Cuba thirty years after the revolution.

71 **Six days in Havana.**
By James Michener, photographs by John King. Austin, Texas: University of Texas Press, 1989. 144p. 3 maps.

Words and pictures complement each other in this work, offering views of a city many North Americans might never otherwise see. Residential districts, downtown business and government, the old city, churches, museums, a distillery, outlying coffee and sugar plantations, and Hemingway's old La Vigía estate and Cojímar fishing village are all captured on film. The author talks with some 200 Cubans from all walks of life.

72 **Trading with the enemy: a Yankee travels through Castro's Cuba.**
Tom Miller. New York: Atheneum, 1992. 353p. bibliog.

In this, another of Miller's highly personal travel books, he meanders through the streets of Havana (which 'knew him by his shoes'); travels with his favourite baseball team; and generally pursues his at times idiosyncratic interests around the island. In the process he offers the reader a feel for life in Cuba in the early 1990s, letting a cross-section of personalities, from a grafitti artist to Cuba's best-known cook, pour out their hearts and their opinions.

73 **The youngest revolution: a personal report on Cuba.**
Elizabeth Sutherland.   New York: Dial Press, 1959. 277p.
This sympathetic account of the early days of the revolution particularly praises the social programmes, especially health and education.

Flora and Fauna

General

74 **The cruise of the *Thomas Barrera*: the narrative of a scientific expedition to western Cuba and the Colorado reefs, with observations on the geology, fauna, and flora of the region.**
John B. Henderson. New York: G. P. Putnam's Sons, 1916. 320p. maps.

This account of an expedition provides commentary on the geography, marine features and wildlife of western Cuba.

75 **A naturalist in Cuba.**
Thomas Barbour. Boston, Massachusetts: Little, Brown & Co., 1945. 317p.

Although dated, this illustrated account of a Cuban journey is useful because it provides one of the very few descriptions in English of Cuban flora and fauna.

Flora

76 **Diccionario botánico de nombres vulgares cubanos.** (Dictionary of common Cuban botanical names.)
Juan Tomás Roig y Mesa. Havana: Editorial Científico-Técnica, 1988. 2 vols. bibliog.

An essential work of scholarship, this was first published in 1928 and has subsequently been amplified and updated. The list of some 6,000 of the most common

18

indigenous and introduced plant species growing in Cuba, was compiled by a key figure among Cuban botanists, based on a life's work at the experimental plant station outside Havana. Roig y Mesa catalogues species by common vernacular names, cross-referencing them to regional variants, and providing a detailed description of their characteristics and domestic, medicinal and agricultural uses. There is an index of scientific names and a small number of photographs.

77 **Historia de la botánica en Cuba.** (The history of Cuban botany.)
   José Álvarez Condé. Havana: [n.p.], 1959. 353p. maps.
The text is in both English and Spanish and provides biographies of important botanists in Cuba from the 16th to the 20th centuries.

78 **Mi tesoro es Cuba: joyas de la ciencia y la naturaleza.** (Cuba is my treasure: gems of science and nature.)
   Salvador Capote Llano. Havana: Editorial Científico-Técnica, 1983. 157p. bibliog.
A highly readable yet scientifically rigorous exploration of some of the plant species which contribute to the peculiar character of the Cuban landscape.

79 **Phytogeographic survey of North America; a consideration of the phytogeography of the North American continent, including Mexico, Central America, and the West Indies, together with the evolution of North American plant distribution.**
   John W. Harshberger. Leipzig, Germany: W. Engelmann; New York: G. E. Stechert, 1911. 790p. map. bibliog.
This is an older work but it is especially useful for its comparative bibliographical coverage, listing titles from the 16th to the early 20th centuries.

80 **Plantas medicinales, aromáticas y venenosas de Cuba.** (Medicinal, aromatic and poisonous plants of Cuba.)
   Juan Tomás Roig y Mesa. Havana: Científico-Técnica, 1974. 2nd ed. 949p.
Richly illustrated with colour and black-and-white photographs, this classic compendium contains a Cuban pharmacological bibliography in chronological order (1767-1944) with over ninety titles. Plants are listed alphabetically by their common names and scientific names, scientific synonyms and other vulgar names are provided, along with information on: habitat and distribution; botanical description; parts used; their applications; and a bibliography. A glossary of medical, botanical and pharmaceutical terms used is added, with plants grouped according to their applications (abortifacient, anti-asthmatic, anti-spasm, for example). Medicinal plants are ordered according to the Engler-Gilg. botanical classification and there is an index of Cuban common names and scientific names.

Fauna

81 **Atlas de las mariposas diurnas de Cuba (Lepidoptera: Rhopalocera).** (Atlas of Cuban diurnal butterflies.)
Pastor D. Alayo, L. R. Hernández.   Havana: Editorial Científico-Técnica, 1987. 148p. bibliog.

Provides a detailed description of 194 species of butterfly and their habitats, with an introductory article on the order of Lepidoptera and a history of their study in Cuba. There are forty-nine pages of colour plates.

82 **Birds collected in Cuba and Haiti by the Parish-Smithsonian expedition of 1930.**
Alexander Wetmore.   *US National Museum. Proceedings,* vol. 81, art. 2 (1932), p. 1-40.

Wetmore includes an annotated list of birds found in the two countries.

83 **Descripción de diferentes piezas de historia natural, las más del ramo marítimo.** (Description of various items of natural history, mainly marine in origin.)
Antonio Parra.   Havana: Editorial Academia, 1989. 2 vols.

A bicentennial commemorative set comprising a facsimile edition of the first work ever to be published on Cuban fauna in 1787, and a series of articles on the life and work of its Portuguese author Antonio Parra.

84 **Diccionario multilingüe de especies marinas (español-inglés-francés-alemán-portugués).** (Multilingual dictionary of marine species [Spanish-English-French-German-Portuguese].)
Leonardo Depestre Catony, Eladio Blanco Cabrera.   Havana: Editorial Científico-Técnica, 1987. 80p. bibliog.

The main section consists of an alphabetical list of the scientific names of 543 marine species, each entry giving the most common name in Spanish, English, French, German and Portuguese. There is an index of species names in each of the five languages, referring back to the main list.

85 **Polymita.**
J. M. Fernández Milera, J. R. Martínez Fernández.   Havana: Editorial Científico-Técnica, 1987. 119p. bibliog.

A study of the life-cycle and habitat of six species belonging to the Polymita genus of snail, which is found exclusively in Cuba and is in danger of extinction. There are 126 colour plates and distribution maps.

86   **Sinopsís de los peces marinos de Cuba.** (A summary of Cuba's marine
species.)
Darío J. Guitart.   Havana: Cuban Academy of Sciences, Oceanology
Institute, 1974-78. 4 vols.
A comprehensive guide to the marine species found in Cuban offshore waters,
published over a four-year period and based on extensive research.

Catálogo de plantas urbanas amenazadas o extinguidas. (Catalogue of
threatened or extinct urban plants.)
See item no. 822.

**Diez años de colaboración científica Cuba–RDA (en el campo de la
protección de plantas).** (Ten years of Cuban/East German scientific
collaboration [in the field of plant protection].)
See item no. 823.

**Bibliografía botánica cubana, teórica y aplicada, con énfasis en la
silvicultura (1900-67).** (A Cuban botanical bibliography, theoretical and
applied, with emphasis on forestry [1900-67].)
See item no. 1149.

Prehistory and Archaeology

Prehistory

87 **Agricultura aborigen antillana.** (Caribbean aboriginal agriculture.)
Ernesto E. Tabío. Havana: Ciencias Sociales, 1989. 137p. bibliog.

An ethno-historical monograph which looks at the principal tropical agriculture and irrigation techniques developed and the crops adopted in the Caribbean, particularly Cuba and the Bahamas. The author seeks to trace the origins of these and to assess the influence of various climatological factors on aboriginal settlement patterns. He finds parallels in a far wider geographical area comprising the Amazon Basin and the Caribbean coasts of Colombia and Venezuela.

88 **Las cuatro culturas indias de Cuba.** (The four Indian cultures of Cuba.)
Fernando Ortiz. Havana: Orellano y Cía, 1943. 176p.

This volume examines significant cultural differences between the two major indigenous Ciboney and Taíno peoples.

89 **Cuba before Columbus.**
Mark Raymond Harrington. New York: Museum of the American Indian, 1921. 2 vols. bibliog.

Although dated, this is one of the most comprehensive English-language accounts of pre-Columbian cultures in Cuba. The text is accompanied by illustrations, plates and maps.

90 **Desaparición de la población indígena cubana.** (Disappearance of the Cuban indigenous population.)
Juan Pérez de la Riva. *Universidad de La Habana*, nos. 196-97 (1972), p. 61-84.

Covers the demography of Cuba's indigenous peoples and the demise of their cultures in the early 16th century.

91   **The handbook of South American Indians, vol. 4: the circum-Caribbean tribes.**
Edited by Julian H. Seward.   New York: Cooper Square Publishers, 1963. var. pag. bibliog.

Although this volume, one of a set of seven originally published in 1945 by the Smithsonian Institute, Bureau of American Ethnology, is dated, it remains a basic source for the study of the later ethnography of the Ciboney and Arawak peoples in the Caribbean. Part three covers 'The West Indies' and this includes Cuba. References to Cuba can be found under three sub-sections: The Ciboney; The ethnology of the Ciboney; and The Arawak. Another section 'The ethnography of Cuba' by Adolfo de Hostos appears on p. 542-43.

92   **Prehistoria de Cuba.** (Cuban prehistory.)
Ernesto E. Tabío, Estrella Rey.   Havana: Ciencias Sociales, 1985. 2nd ed. 234p. bibliog.

Follows the periodization traditionally accepted for the indigenous inhabitants of Cuba, dividing them into five cultural groups: Taíno, Subtaíno, Mayarí, Ciboney Cayo Redondo and Ciboney Guayabo Blanco. The authors note the consensus among Cuban scholars that a revision is needed to take account of new findings, though these required further verification at the time of publication.

93   **El taíno de Cuba.** (The Taíno in Cuba.)
José M. Guarch Delmonte.   Havana: Cuban Academy of Sciences, 1978. 263p.

An expert on aboriginal settlements attempts a tentative ethno-historical reconstruction of the lifestyle of the Taíno people in Cuba.

94   **The Taínos: rise and decline of the people who greeted Columbus.**
Irving Rouse.   New Haven, Connecticut: Yale University Press, 1992. 211p.

Focusing on the nearly 7,000-year-long history of the Taíno people in the Caribbean, Rouse discusses questions such as: Who were they?, how did they become dominant in the area? and why did they disappear under European rule?

Archaeology

95   **The archaeology of Cuba.**
Daniel G. Brinton.   *American Archaeologist*, vol. 2, no. 10 (Oct. 1986), p. 17-21.

An older work, which provides a view of archaeological sites and of the archaeological profession in Cuba in 1898.

96 **Arqueología aborigen de Cuba.** (The aboriginal archaeology of Cuba.)
Ramón Dacal Moure, Manuel Rivero de la Calle.   Havana: Editorial
Gente Nueva, 1986. 174p. bibliog.

While this illustrated review of Cuban archaeology is aimed at a non-specialist
readership, it nevertheless provides a clear guide to the discipline in Cuba. It relates
the country's archaeological history, discusses Cuba in the context of Caribbean
migration, and surveys the state of knowledge about the various periods of human
settlement on the island. See also: *Artefactos de concha en las comunidades
aborígenes cubanas* (Shell artefacts in Cuban aboriginal communities) by Ramón
Dacal Moure (Havana: University of Havana, 1978. 114p.) which is an illustrated
description of pre-Columbian artefacts discovered in Cuba.

97 **Caverna, costa y meseta.** (Cavern, coast & tableland.)
Felipe Pichardo Moya.   Havana: Ciencias Sociales, 1990. 152p.
bibliog.

A reprint of a 1943 classic text by one of the founding figures of Cuban archaeology.
Following a substantial introduction which seeks to dissipate the terminological
confusion previously shrouding the distinct ethno-cultural groups who first settled the
island, Pichardo traces the development of the peoples whose habitats are described in
the title. The volume ends with a useful annotated bibliography of the works of
previous historians.

98 **La cerámica taína de Cuba.** (Cuban Taíno pottery.)
José M. Guarch Delmonte.   Havana: Cuban Academy of Sciences,
1972. 78p. bibliog.

This text comprises a detailed account of Taíno pottery based on archaeological work
in eastern Cuba.

99 **The Ciboney culture of Cayo Redondo, Cuba.**
Cornelius Osgood.   New Haven, Connecticut: Yale University Press,
1942. 65p. maps.

A rare study in English of a site of the Ciboney peoples.

100 **Cuba arqueológica.** (Archaeological Cuba.)
Santiago de Cuba: Editorial Oriente, 1978. 271p.

These are the proceedings of a conference on aboriginal culture held in Santiago de
Cuba.

101 **Cuba, dibujos rupestres.** (Cuba, cave drawings.)
Antonio Núñez Jiménez.   Havana: Ciencias Sociales, 1975. 503p.
maps. bibliog.

A study of cave drawings and paintings, in which each site is examined in detail with
accompanying illustrations.

102 **Excavación arqueológica, El Porvenir, Banes.** (Archaeological
     excavation of El Porvenir, Banes.)
     Nilecta Castellano, Milton Pino.   Santiago de Cuba: Editorial Oriente,
     1978. 41p.

The authors describe the excavation of an aboriginal settlement in eastern Cuba, an
area believed to have some of the most important and extensive remains in the
Caribbean.

103 **Historia de la arqueología cubana.** (The history of Cuban
     archaeology.)
     Fernando Ortiz.   *Cuba Contemporánea*, vol. 30, no. 117 (Sept. 1922),
     p. 5-35; no. 118 (Oct. 1922), p. 126-64.

Ortiz offers two articles on the development of archaeology on the island from the
early colonial period up until the early 20th century. The first piece details the
principal archaeologists (both Cuban and non-Cuban) and their work. The second
covers museums, philology and archaeology in the Caribbean.

104 **Introducción a la arqueología de las Antillas.** (Introduction to
     Antillean archaeology.)
     Ernesto E. Tabío.   Havana: Ciencias Sociales, 1988. 176p. bibliog.

Begins with a general survey of the state of archaeological research in the entire
Caribbean region, including Cuba, up to the end of the 1970s. Tabío studies the area's
geography, flora and fauna and climatic conditions, and speculates on the origins of
aboriginal settlers and the most likely migration routes. Subsequent sections deal in
turn with the Bahamas, Jamaica, Hispaniola, Puerto Rico, the Virgin Islands, the
Lesser Antilles and Trinidad, concentrating in each case on the distribution and
settlement patterns of ethnic and cultural groups and the ceramic styles which
characterize them. There is a brief outline of the archaeological investigation
undertaken in each area.

105 **La Manuela: arqueología de un cafetal habanero.** (La Manuela:
     archaeology of a Havana coffee estate.)
     Luciano Bernard Bosch, Víctor Blanco Condé, Alexis Rives Pantoja.
     Havana: Ciencias Sociales, 1985. 142p. bibliog.

The history behind the ruins of La Manuela, a 19th-century coffee plantation based on
slave labour in southern Havana province, is charted in this work. The authors talked
with peasant farmers in the area, studied maps and documents, charted land tenure and
production, and reconstructed the archaeology of the plantation.

History

Regional

106 **The Caribbean: the genesis of a fragmented nationalism.**
Franklin W. Knight.   New York: Oxford University Press, 1978.
251p. maps. bibliog.

This volume offers a pan-Caribbean perspective on a region that has moved from the centre of the Western world to its periphery. The book covers five centuries of economic and social development, from the Spanish Conquest to the present, and examines topics such as: the slave-run plantation economy; the changes in political control over the centuries; the impact of the United States; and the effects of the Cuban revolution on the area. It looks particularly at nation-building and fragmented nationalism and has a separate chapter on Cuba.

107 **De Cristóbal Colón a Fidel Castro: el Caribe, frontera imperial.**
(From Christopher Columbus to Fidel Castro: the Caribbean, imperial frontier.)
Juan Bosch.   Havana: Casa de las Américas, 1981. 343p. bibliog.

Designed to provide a potted modern history of the Caribbean, this book is aimed at a more popular audience. The coveted frontier referred to in the title is the tragic underlying theme to five centuries of imperial pillage and violence, and the resistance of the local peoples to it, from conquest, through slavery, social and political struggle, to incipient nation state. The book contains chapters on a number of themes, such as conquest, uprising, piracy and war, and events such as the Haitian revolution and Cuban independence and revolution.

108 **Encyclopedia of Latin American history and culture.**
Edited by Barbara Tenenbaum. Old Tappan, New Jersey: Charles
Scribner's, 1995. 4 vols.
Over 2,000 individual biographies are contained within this encyclopaedia, along with
a narrative historical survey and series of entries on history, geography, politics,
constitutions, political parties, labour unions and educational institutions.

109 **From Columbus to Castro: the history of the Caribbean.**
Eric Williams. London: André Deutsch, 1970. 576p.
A survey of Caribbean history by the Trinidadian historian who was later to become
Prime Minister of independent Trinidad and Tobago. The main theme running through
the book is supported by an argument outlined in an earlier work on capitalism and
slavery, which links sugar and slavery with the rise of European capitalism and
empire, followed by North American imperialism.

110 **International historical statistics: the Americas 1750-1988.**
B. R. Mitchell. New York: Stockton, 1993. 2nd ed. 960p.
A wealth of historical statistics are provided in this volume, and Cuba is included in
the coverage. Comprehensive information is offered on such topics as population,
labour, agriculture, industry, transport, trade, education and the national finances.

111 **Main currents in Caribbean thought: the historical evolution of
Caribbean society in its ideological aspects, 1492-1900.**
Gordon K. Lewis. Baltimore, Maryland: Johns Hopkins University
Press, 1983. 375p. (Studies in Atlantic History and Culture).
Also published in paperback in 1987 (492p.), this is an ambitious, interpretative
compendium of the history of ideas in the Pan-Caribbean. It emphasizes the unity of
the Caribbean historical experience over and above colonial, political, cultural and
linguistic divides.

Cuba

112 **Cuba between reform and revolution.**
Louis A. Pérez, Jr. Oxford: Oxford University Press, 1988. 504p.
bibliog.
The underlying theme of this work is the ideological duality which has existed over
the past century in competing definitions of *cubanidad*: the liberal constructs of *patria*
and the radical formulations of nationalism. The account provides a fine insight into
the complex and often contradictory socio-political forces at work in Cuban society,
and presents 'the chronicle of a people locked in relentless struggle against the by-
products of their history: against slavery and racism, against inequality and injustice,
against uncertainty and insecurity'. It is especially useful in its treatment of the late
19th century, and draws on the ideas and research of Cuban scholars on the island

whose work, with rare exceptions, has not been translated into English. The end-product has, as it set out to have, 'sabor a Cuba ... sabor a son' (the flavour of Cuba ... the flavour of *son* [a Cuban music form]).

113 **Cuba, economía y sociedad.** (Cuba: economy and society.)
Levi Marrero. Madrid: Editorial Playor, 1971-88. 14 vols. bibliog.

Spanning the history of Cuba from the pre-Columbian period to the present, these volumes represent a major reference work by the late historian-geographer. They contain historical narrative, archival documents, statistical charts and illustrations.

114 **Cuba: economía y sociedad.** (Cuba: economy and society.)
Juan Martínez-Alier, Verena Martínez-Alier. Paris: Ruedo Ibérico, 1972. 254p. bibliog.

This volume brings together the work of two authors, one a Spanish historian and the other a German anthropologist, to provide an analysis of slavery, racism, virginity, machismo and honour in 19th-century Cuba. It also covers: the economy, 1900-58; the national bourgeoisie; the anti-imperialist and anti-proletarian small farmer ideas, 1934-60; the 'land or labour' debate on the peasantry and 1959-60 agrarian reform; and the great economic debate of 1963-65.

115 **Cuba, from Columbus to Castro.**
Jaime Suchlicki. New York: Charles Scribner's, 1974. 242p. bibliog.

Offers a general survey of Cuban history from pre-Columbian times, with the emphasis on 20th-century political history.

116 **Cuba, la perla de las Antillas: actas de las jornadas sobre 'Cuba y su historia'.** (Cuba, pearl of the Antilles: proceedings of the conference on 'Cuba and its history'.)
Edited by Consuelo Naranjo Orovio, Romás Mallo Gutiérrez.
Madrid: Doce Calles/CSIC, 1994. 344p.

Contributions in this volume are written by scholars in Spain, as well as France and Cuba, and cover 19th- and 20th-century Cuba. The book is arranged in four parts: culture; population and society; politics; and the economy. The first section highlights fundamental liberal cultural and scientific institutions of the 19th century (the Jardín Botánico, the Sociedades Económicas de Amigos del País, the Real Sociedad Patriótica de La Habana and the Comisión Real de Guantánamo) and focuses on the anthropological debate around racism in the slavery period. The second part traces post-slavery immigrant groups (Mexicans from Yucatán, Germans, Spaniards and others) and reflects on social banditry. The third concentrates on late 19th-century failed Spanish reforms and incipient Cuban nationhood and national thinking, while the fourth looks at the slave trade, railways and merchant banking.

117 **Cuba: the pursuit of freedom.**
Hugh Thomas. London: Eyre & Spottiswood, 1971. 1,696p. maps. bibliog.

Thomas devotes the first 116 chapters of this epic work to a review of Cuban history, from the 1762 English expedition to capture Havana, to the end of the 1960s. In the second part he analyses the revolutionary period, acknowledging somewhat grudgingly its material achievements, but arguing that the revolution betrayed its principles and became an 'ubiquitous tyranny'. The work contains thirty-two pages of plates. See also Hugh Thomas's *The Cuban revolution* (London: Weidenfeld & Nicolson, 1986. 755p.) which is the third reprint of the first edition (1971) and contains about half the text of *Cuba: the pursuit of freedom*. It covers the period 1952-70 and omits the appendices, glossary and bibliography.

118 **Cuba: a short history.**
Edited by Leslie Bethell. Cambridge, England; New York; Melbourne: Cambridge University Press, 1993. 172p. bibliog.

This work brings together chapters on Cuba from volumes three, five and seven of *The Cambridge history of Latin America*, a multi-volume work spanning five centuries. Four historians cover four periods (c. 1750-1860; c. 1860-1930; c. 1930-59; and post-1959) to provide a useful economic, social and political history of modern Cuba.

119 **Essays on Cuban history: historiography and research.**
Louis A. Pérez, Jr. Gainesville, Florida: University Press of Florida, 1995. 318p.

The first section of this three-part series of essays deals with key themes in 19th- and 20th-century Cuban history, including the US interventions of 1898, Cuban emigration to the USA, Protestant missionary activity, and the development of the Cuban armed forces after 1959. The second section looks at trends in the historical literature itself, while the third offers a guide to some of the larger research collections, including the Cuban National Archives, missionary manuscript collections, and US government records.

120 **Historia de Cuba.** (History of Cuba.)
Dirección Política de las Fuerzas Armadas Revolucionarias. Havana: Instituto Cubano del Libro, 1971. 624p. 3rd ed. bibliog.

One of the most in-depth overall histories of Cuba, this volume begins with the pre-Columbian period and conquest and works through early and late colonization, to the 20th-century United States occupation and 1933 revolution. One great strength of the book is the revisionist treatment of 19th-century slavery and abolition, reformism and insurrection and the frustrated republic of the early 20th century.

121 **Historical dictionary of Cuba.**
Jaime Suchlicki. Metuchen, New Jersey: Scarecrow Press, 1988. 368p. map. bibliog. (Latin American Dictionaries, no. 22).

Adheres to the usual general format for Scarecrow's historical dictionaries, providing a lengthy dictionary section of terms, events, personalities and other relevant information on Cuba, followed by an extensive bibliography.

122 **A history of the Cuban nation.**
Ramiro Guerra y Sánchez, et al., translated under the general direction
of James J. Mailia. Havana: Editorial Historia de la Nación Cubana,
1958. 10 vols. bibliog.

This multi-volume collaborative endeavour is a standard general reference work by
some of the principal Cuban historians of the period. It deals chronologically with
prehistory, the colonial period, independence struggles and the republic, and
thematically with literature, art, theatre, foreign policy, economics, education, law,
architecture and labour.

123 **Manual de historia de Cuba.** (Manual of Cuban history.)
Ramiro Guerra y Sánchez. Havana: Ciencias Sociales, 1980. 6th ed.
720p.

Originally published in 1938, this volume comprises a five-section overview of Cuban
history from the Spanish conquest to 1930. The author aims to render in accessible
narrative a re-interpretation of major events and developments in Cuban history:
economic conditions, social and political institutions, foreign influences; and historical
dates and figures.

124 **What happened in Cuba?**
Robert Freeman Smith. New York: Twayne, 1963. 360p. bibliog.

A collection of documentary sources which are strong on US–Cuban diplomatic
history but also cover economy, politics and military affairs, over the period 1783-
1962.

Provincial and local

125 **Baracoa, apuntes para su historia.** (Baracoa: historical notes.)
José Ignacio Castro. Havana: Editorial Arte y Literatura, 1977. 132p.
bibliog.

Castro presents a narrative of the history of one of the oldest cities in Cuba. The
account is particularly valuable for the wealth of information it contains on the 19th
century.

126 **The beginnings of Havana.**
Irene A. Wright. *Hispanic American Historical Review*, vol. 5, no. 3
(Aug. 1922), p. 498-503.

Though dated, this is one of the few Cuban local history accounts to be written in
English. In it the author attempts to dispel the long-standing confusion as to the
founding and early history of Havana (1514-50).

127 **Camagüey (Biografía de una provincia).** (Camagüey [Biography of a province].)
Mary Cruz del Pino.   Havana: El Siglo XX, 1955. 261p. bibliog.

Part of a series on the former six provinces of Cuba, this detailed study of Camagüey covers political, military, economic and cultural history over the colonial period and up until the 1950s. Companion volumes are: Julio Le Riverend on Havana; Emeterio Santovenia on Pinar del Río; Francisco Ponte Domínguez on Matanzas; Rafael Rodríguez Altunaga on Las Villas; and Juan Jérez Villareal on Oriente.

128 **Crónicas de Santiago de Cuba.** (Chronicles of Santiago de Cuba.)
Emilio Bacardí Moreau.   Madrid: Gráficas Breogán, 1972. 10 vols.

A detailed chronology of major events in Cuba's second city and eastern capital, from early colonization until 1898. It was first published as three volumes in Santiago de Cuba in 1925.

129 **Cuban rural society in the nineteenth century: the social and economic history of monoculture in Matanzas.**
Laird W. Bergad.   Princeton, New Jersey: Princeton University Press, 1990. 425p. bibliog.

Bergad has produced an excellent and rare regional study in English, based on regional archival documentation, of the rise and fall of Matanzas as the 19th-century sugar region of colonial Cuba. It provides an account of the society constructed around the sugar industry in four epochs: the sugar frontier of Matanzas before the railroads (1800-37); monoculture *par excellence* (1837-78); monoculture transformed through war and emancipation (1878-95); and war and independence (1895-1900). An analysis is made of élite family histories, major demographic trends of the slave population, cash flows and patterns of slave manumission, the demise of the planter class, and post-emancipation solutions to land settlement and labour.

130 **Es Santiago de Cuba.** (This is Santiago de Cuba.)
Havana: Editora Política, 1984. 129p.

An illustrated introduction to eastern Cuba's principal city, with an emphasis on its revolutionary history. The work contains Fidel Castro's speech marking the twenty-fifth anniversary of the 1959 revolution.

131 **La fidelísima Habana.** (Most faithful Havana.)
Gustavo Eguren.   Havana: Editorial Letras Cubanas, 1986. 424p. bibliog.

Gustavo Eguren is a well-known contemporary novelist. In this volume he has compiled a year-by-year history of Havana from 1508 to 1899, in the form of quotations from newspaper articles, letters and the writings of novelists and travellers. The text is lavishly illustrated with engravings and photographs.

132 **Guantánamo.**
Regino E. Boti.   Guantánamo: Imprenta de El Resumen, 1912. 87p.

Traces the origins and development of the eastern city of Guantánamo, emphasizing political and administrative developments, soon after the United States Naval Base was located there.

133   **La Habana: ciudad antigua.** (Havana: antique city.)
Eusebio Leal Spengler.   Havana: Editorial Letras Cubanas, 1988.
123p. bibliog.

In this publication the historian of Havana introduces the reader to the old city and port. He includes a chronology of events, from the arrival of Columbus in 1492 to the birth of José Martí in 1853, and reproductions of 18th- and 19th-century prints.

134   **Havana: portrait of a city.**
Juliet Barclay, photographs by Martin Charles, foreword by Eusebio Leal Spengler, introduction by Francisco de Bortón y Escasany.
London: Cassell, 1993. 224p.

Four hundred years of Havana's history (1492-1900) are covered in this volume, for which the author consulted archival resources in Havana, Madrid and London, with a unique use of visual primary sources as the basis for description. The book evidences not only old buildings, palaces and churches, but also costumes, colours, sounds, smells, food, music, religion and people. The photographs are beautiful and recapture the city's rich history.

135   **Historia de Cuba.** (A history of Cuba.)
Ricardo V. Rousset.   Havana: Librería Cervantes de Ricardo Velasco, 1918. 3 vols.

All six of Cuba's former provinces (there are now fourteen) are represented in this older historical survey. Two regions are covered per volume, with an entry for each municipality.

136   **Historia de Trinidad.** (A history of Trinidad.)
Francisco Marín Villafuerte.   Havana: Jesús Montero, 1945. 405p.

Trinidad, on the central south coast, is one of Cuba's oldest towns, and one of the best preserved. This account is particularly detailed on the 17th to 19th centuries, covering the town's settlement, ecclesiastical history, wars of independence, and social and cultural history.

137   **Memoria histórica de Cienfuegos y su jurisdicción.** (Historical record of Cienfuegos and its jurisdiction.)
Enrique Edo.   Havana: Ucar, García y Cía, 1953. 821p.

Of encyclopaedic proportions, this detailed study of the city and its environs over three centuries, from the 1520s to the 1880s, is especially strong on 19th-century politics, economy, administration, religion, society, culture and education.

138   **Sugar and social change in Oriente, Cuba, 1898-1946.**
Robert R. Hoernal.   *Journal of Latin American Studies*, vol. 8, no. 2 (Nov. 1976), p. 215-49.

Traces fifty years of socio-economic change, brought about by the impact of the large sugar estates on local communities and culture.

Spanish colony

139 **Cuba in the 1850s: through the lens of Charles DeForest Fredricks.**
Robert M. Levine. Gainesville, Florida: University Press of Florida,
1990. 86p.
These previously unpublished photographs capture a moment when Cuban society was
on the verge of social, economic and technological modernization.

140 **Cuba, 1753-1815: crown, military, and society.**
Allan J. Kuethe. Knoxville, Tennessee: University of Tennessee
Press, 1986. 213p. map. bibliog.
A study of how the Bourbon reforms and English occupation of Havana in 1762
contributed to the growth and development of a sense of Cuban nationhood.

141 **The early history of Cuba, 1492-1586.**
Irene A. Wright. New York: Macmillan, 1916. 390p. map.
Based on original archival research, this remains one of the few English-language
accounts of political development, public administration and international rivalries in
the early colonial period.

142 **Félix Varela 1788-1853.**
Eusebio Reyes Fernández. Havana: Editora Política, 1989. 125p.
bibliog.
This study of Félix Varela, which is one of a recent spate of publications in Cuba on
the early 19th-century Cuban thinker-reformer, was published in 1989, at a time when
Cuban intellectuals were spearheading the move away from Marxism-Leninism to a
more autochthonous form of Cuban social and political thinking. One aspect traces
Cuban nationalism from Félix Varela through José Martí to Fidel Castro. There are
chapters on Varela's early and later years, Varela the philosopher and the religious
thinker.

143 **Félix Varela: su pensamiento político y su época.** (Félix Varela: his
political thinking and his times.)
Olivia Miranda. Havana: Ciencias Sociales, 1984. 137p. bibliog.
Father Varela's writings strongly influenced the development of Cuban revolutionary
philosophy, and continue to provide a focus for debate on what should be the guiding
principles for future Cuban social policy. This analysis discusses the emergence of
Varela's philosophy in the context of the economic and social currents of the period
1790-1830.

144 **Seis ensayos de interpretación histórica.** (Six essays of historical interpretation.)
Rafael Duharte Jiménez. Santiago de Cuba: Editorial Oriente, 1983. 110p. bibliog.

These thought-provoking essays present an interpretation of key themes in Cuba's 19th-century history, concerning the free coloureds, creole inferiority, nationalist thinking, and black and caudillo fears.

145 **The siege and capture of Havana, 1762.**
Edited by David Syrett. London: Navy Records Society, 1970. 355p. maps.

A collection of correspondence, naval communiqués, official orders and ledgers of events reflecting the English planning, preparation and assault against Havana in 1762.

146 **Torn between empires: economy, society, and patterns of political thought in the Hispanic Caribbean, 1840-1878.**
Luis Martínez-Fernández. Athens, Georgia; London: University of Georgia Press, 1994. 333p. bibliog.

This study draws heavily on archival sources in North America and meets a significant need for an English-language synthesis on the crucial years of the mid-19th century for the territories of the Hispanic Caribbean: Cuba, Puerto Rico and the Dominican Republic. Divided into two chronological parts, 1840-60 and 1861-78, the latter receiving the major impact of the American Civil War, the book's comparative focus falls on the underlying balance-of-power transformations, within the common heritage of insularity, colonialism and slavery. Cuba features prominently throughout, and the author highlights two powerful elements in its history of this period: first, the Creoles' acute race consciousness (a case in point is the Cuban 'Africanization scare'), which was often exploited by imperial interests vying for their allegiance; and second, the United States' growing economic interests in the region, which existed earlier and was stronger than is often recognized.

Independence and US intervention

147 **Ámbito de Martí.** (Concerning Martí.)
Guillermo Zendegui. Havana: Sociedad Colombista Panamericana, Fernández y Cía, 1957. 224p. 4 maps.

A richly documented and illustrated account of the involvement of Cuban Independence leader José Martí in Cuba as well as in Europe (France and Spain) and the Americas (United States, Mexico, Venezuela, Costa Rica, Jamaica, Haiti and the Dominican Republic).

148 **The American image of the Cuban insurgents in 1898.**
Joseph Smith. *Zeitschrift für Anglistik und Amerikanistik*, vol. 40
(1992), p. 319-29.
During US Congress debates in 1898 there was some discussion of what members saw
as the brave Cuban patriots' fight against Spanish misrule of the island and it was
considered whether the United States should militarily intervene in Cuba. After
intervention, Congress began to perceive the insurgents as a rabble and a threat to law
and order, thereby justifying the withholding of independence until 1902.

149 **Atlas histórico-biográfico José Martí.** (Historico-biographical atlas
of José Martí.)
Havana: Instituto Cubano de Geodesia y Cartografía and Centro de
Estudios Martianos, 1983. 128p. maps. bibliog.
Modelled on a similar atlas produced on Lenin in the then Soviet Union, geographers
and Martí specialists worked together to produce this atlas containing an abundance of
full-colour maps, accompanied by text and photographs, charting the life and times of
José Martí. Maps include the European colonial world; US territorial expansion; Cuba
in the 18th and 19th centuries (political, economic and demographic aspects); Martí's
Havana and deportation; Martí's travels and the first independence war; Martí's
landing in the second war and his subsequent death; and the ambit of Martí's legacy in
the Americas, Europe and the 1959 Cuban revolution.

150 **Bolívar y la independencia de Cuba.** (Bolívar and the independence
of Cuba.)
Francisco Pérez Guzmán. Havana: Editorial Letras Cubanas, 1988.
195p.
Traces the influence of Bolívar's thinking on the revolutionary movements in Cuba
during the early 19th century, with a social, economic and political overview of Cuban
colonial society.

151 **Cuba between empires, 1878-1902.**
Louis A. Pérez, Jr. Pittsburgh, Pennsylvania: University of
Pittsburgh, 1983. 490p. bibliog.
A seminal text on Cuba's struggles for independence, carrying the analysis through
the years of the first US military occupation. This was a crucial period in defining the
future course of 20th-century Cuban history. Pérez explains, with authority, how
Cuban separation from Spain was compromised by the US military occupation and
subsequent economic and political dependency.

152 **Cuba no debe su independencia a los Estados Unidos.** (Cuba does
not owe its independence to the United States.)
Emilio Roig de Leuchsenring. Havana: Ediciones la Tertulia, 1960.
155p.
Comprises two main essays: 'The Cuban people won their own independence' and
'The US state was always the enemy of Cuban independence'. Roig belonged to an
intensely nationalist generation of Cuban historians determined to revindicate Cuba's
own history of struggle, especially *vis-à-vis* the all-pervasive US neo-colonial

presence. This study, which was first published in 1950, was specifically written to counteract the notion that Cuba owed its independence from Spain to the United States.

153　**España y Cuba: 1868-1898: revolución burguesa y relaciones coloniales.** (Spain and Cuba: 1868-1898: bourgeois revolution and colonial relations.)
Aurea Matilde Fernández.　Havana: Ciencias Sociales, 1988. 243p.

The history of the ties between the colony of Cuba and metropolitan Spain is a topic little researched by either Spanish or Cuban historians and this work attempts to redress the balance. Fernández lectures in Spanish history at the University of Havana.

154　**Inside the monster: writings on the United States and American imperialism by José Martí.**
José Martí, edited by Philip S. Foner.　New York; London: Monthly Review Press, 1975. 386p.

Cuba's 19th-century independence leader José Martí was both a man of action and a prolific writer, leaving forty volumes of his collected writings, including poetry and journalistic articles. For the last fifteen years of his life, Martí lived in the United States, earning his living by writing for the Latin American and United States press. He is still a character of great significance in the Americas and yet is little known in the English-speaking world even now, a century since his death. Foner rendered the invaluable service of making key works available in English for the first time, conveying the progression of Martí's thinking on the United States, from his initial belief in American ideals of freedom and democracy to his growing recognition of the failure of the late 19th-century United States to live up to those ideals. The collection includes essays that read beautifully and are still exciting, fresh and prophetic today.

155　**José Martí, architect of Cuba's freedom.**
Peter Turton.　London: Zed Press, 1986. 157p. bibliog.

Turton presents a concise introduction in English to the life and thought of José Martí, the prolific writer and political leader whose 19th-century influence on Cuba is matched only by that of Fidel Castro in the 20th. This is a lucid exploration of the influence of Krausism on Martí and of the evolution of Martí's own views on Cuban independence, on Latin America, and on the United States. His central concerns are still very much living issues today, thereby giving long overdue recognition to a figure who is little known outside Cuba, and even less so in the non-Spanish-speaking world.

156　**José Martí in the United States: the Florida experience.**
Edited by Louis A. Pérez, Jr.　Tempe, Arizona: Arizona State University, Center for Latin American Studies Press, 1995. 114p.

An anthology of essays to mark the centenary of the death of the Cuban independence leader José Martí, examining his experience among the important 19th-century Cuban community in Tampa. There are contributions from E. Collazo Pérez, N. Hewitt, A. Lugo Ortiz, N. R. Mirabal, A. A. Ronda Varona, C. N. Ronning, I. A. Schulman, L. G. Westfall, and J. Yglesias, with an introduction by Pérez and preface by K. L. Stoner.

157   **José Martí, mentor of the Cuban nation.**
      M. Kirk.   Gainesville, Florida: University Press of Florida, 1983.
      212p. bibliog.
A comprehensive examination of the works of José Martí and his thinking on political, social and economic issues, morality and revolution.

158   **José Martí, revolutionary democrat.**
      Edited by C. Abel, N. Torrents.   London: Athlone Press, 1988. 238p.
      bibliog.
Essays on Martí by Cuban, British, European and North American scholars from a conference held in London are collected together in this volume. The themes covered include Martí's literary and journalistic writing, his ideology and his active role in promoting the revolutionary ideal.

159   **Lawless liberators: political banditry and Cuban independence.**
      Rosalie Schwartz.   Durham, North Carolina: Duke University Press,
      1989. 297p.
Schwartz views the Cuban struggle for independence as a political movement led primarily by individuals, both élite and bandit. Her account largely covers white individuals in 19th-century Havana province, who were no moral heroes and whose support she does not see as being rooted in the times.

160   **Lords of the mountain: social banditry and peasant protest in
      Cuba, 1878-1918.**
      Louis A. Pérez, Jr.   Pittsburgh, Pennsylvania: University of Pittsburgh
      Press, 1989. 267p.
The author examines the late 19th- and early 20th-century rural social dislocation caused in Cuba by rapid economic change, which produced an abundance of rural bandits. Individual bandits appear rarely in the study, which focuses largely on social structures and social change, with an emphasis on eastern Cuba in the period after the independence wars, bringing important considerations of race to the fore.

161   **Our America.**
      José Martí, edited by Philip S. Foner.   New York: Monthly Review
      Press, 1977. 448p.
Contains essays, speeches, correspondence and journalistic articles written by José Martí, with special reference to Latin America and Cuban independence.

162   **El pensamiento vivo de Máximo Gómez.** (The living ideas of
      Máximo Gómez.)
      Compiled by Bernardo García Domínguez.   Santo Domingo, Cuba:
      CEDEE, 1991. 228p.
This compilation brings together writings from the years 1870-1905, including letters, autobiographies and notes often jotted down in dangerous and clandestine moments. Together, they bring to light lesser-known facets of the thought of the Dominican-born, 19th-century Cuban independence general, such as his notion of familial love, his inner personality, and his vision of freedom and sovereignty for all peoples.

163 **Pluma y machete.** (Pen and machete knife.)
Ramón Roa. Havana: Instituto Cubano del Libro, 1969. 418p.

A posthumous collection of writings by Ramón Roa, who fought in and wrote about Cuba's independence wars of the late 19th century. It includes Roa's most famous, 100-page account of his experiences in the war, 'On foot and barefoot' (1890), along with his other prose and verse of the time which was published in Havana, and in revolutionary publications edited in Paris and New York. Some personal correspondence is also included.

164 **The Spanish-Cuban-American War & the birth of American imperialism, 1895-1902.**
Philip S. Foner. New York: Monthly Review Press, 1972. 2 vols.

A comprehensive account of the second Cuban war of independence of 1895-98, which placed Cuba firmly back in the Spanish-American equation. The author follows this with a consideration of the first US occupation of Cuba in 1899-1902.

165 **The 'Splendid Little War' of 1898: a reappraisal.**
Joseph Smith. *History*, no. 258, vol. 80 (Feb. 1995), p. 22-37.

This well-researched article assesses some shocking administrative shortcomings and military deficiencies in the United States war effort. Rather than one of American glory, the story is portrayed as a complicated clash between myth and reality in American attitudes and responses to foreign policy issues.

Republic

166 **Un análisis psicosocial del cubano, 1898-1925.** (A psychosocial analysis of the Cuban, 1898-1925.)
Jorge Ibarra. Havana: Ciencias Sociales, 1985. 344p.

Contains nine essays on the socio-cultural history of the early Cuban republic, covering such topics as literature and the arts, folklore and crime.

167 **El antimperialismo en la historia de Cuba.** (Anti-imperialism in Cuba's history.)
Olga Cabrera. Havana: Ciencias Sociales, 1985. 237p.

A collection of writings selected by a contemporary Cuban political and labour historian. Viewed together, the writings by key figures in Cuba's history demonstrate a clear thread in over a century of anti-imperialist thinking: Manuel de Céspedes; José Martí; Antonio Maceo; Máximo Gómez; Vicente Mestre Amabili; Manuel Sanguily; Salvador Cisneros Betancourt; Julio César Gandarilla; Enrique José Varona; Julio Antonio Mella; Rubén Martínez Villena; Antonio Guiteras; Emilio Roig de Leuchsenring; Raúl Roa; Blas Roca; and Fidel Castro.

168   **Cuba under the Platt Amendment, 1902-1934.**
       Louis A. Pérez, Jr.   Pittsburgh, Pennsylvania: University of Pittsburgh
       Press, 1986. 401p. bibliog.

This is a thorough study of the impact of US involvement in Cuba on politics,
government and the social structure.

169   **La expansión territorial de los Estados Unidos: a expensas de
       España y los países hispanoamericanos.** (The territorial expansion of
       the United States: at the expense of Spain and the Hispano-American
       countries.)
       Ramiro Guerra.   Havana: Editorial Nacional de Cuba, 1964. 502p.

From the outset, Ramiro Guerra approaches 19th- and 20th-century Cuban history as
one of tragic contradictions: prosperity on the basis of plantation slavery and its
abolition and independence from Spain undermined by the new colonizer, the United
States. This is a classic Cuban account of US–Cuba relations, from the Monroe
Doctrine and Manifest Destiny through Wall Street and the Good Neighbour Policy,
which situates the long-standing nationalist strand of Cuban thinking.

170   **A history of the Cuban Republic.**
       Charles E. Chapman.   New York: Macmillan, 1927. 685p. maps.
       bibliog.

A standard English-language text, this concentrates largely on Cuban political and
foreign policy issues in the early years of the Republic. It was prepared in collaboration with the US State Department and Embassy.

171   **Intervention, revolution and politics in Cuba, 1913-1918.**
       Louis A. Pérez, Jr.   Pittsburgh, Pennsylvania: University of Pittsburgh
       Press, 1978. 198p. bibliog.

In this study of the period of the Menocal government, the author analyses the
economy during the First World War, and party politics in pluralistic times for Cuba,
with Liberal opposition to Conservative rule.

172   **University students and revolution in Cuba, 1920-1968.**
       Jaime Suchlicki.   Coral Gables, Florida: University of Miami Press,
       1969. 177p. bibliog.

A historical survey of university student involvement in national politics from the
1920s to the 1950s.

1930s revolution

173 **Crónica del año 33.** (Chronicle of the year '33.)
Enrique de la Osa.   Havana: Ciencias Sociales, 1989. 157p.

The author, de la Osa, was an eye-witness to the events in Cuba during 1933 that led to the downfall of the Machado dictatorship. In this well-written and researched account, he includes short biographies for the main protagonists.

174 **Cuba 1933: prologue to revolution.**
L. E. Aguilar.   Ithaca, New York: Cornell University Press, 1972. 256p. bibliog.

This is a detailed standard English-language study of late 1920s and early 1930s Cuba. It charts the deteriorating economic conditions in the country; developments within the various sectors of Cuban society reacting to both depression and the increasing political repression of the Machado régime; and US diplomacy.

175 **La revolución del 30 se fue a la bolina.** (The lost '30s revolution.)
Raúl Roa.   Havana: Instituto Cubano del Libro, 1969. 320p.

A compilation of texts written over the years by Raúl Roa, a key participant in the 1930s revolution. The collection ends with a 1968 interview with him reflecting back over his life and the continuity between the 1933 and 1959 revolutions. Also of interest may be *Raúl Roa: Canciller de la dignidad* (Raúl Roa: a dignified foreign minister) (Havana: Ciencias Sociales, 1986. 391p.) which is primarily a compilation of the major speeches of Raúl Roa.

176 **La revolución del 30: sus dos últimos años.** (The 1930s revolution: the last two years.)
José A. Tabares del Real.   Havana: Ciencias Sociales, 1975. 3rd ed. 375p. bibliog.

Based on extensive primary archival research and interview material, this consititutes a detailed history of the structural crisis of Cuban neo-colonial society and the revolutionary process of 1934-35. The author places a special focus on the Caffery-Batista-Mendieta government of 1934-35 and the revolutionary general strike of March 1935.

177 **La revolución del 33.** (The 1933 revolution.)
Lionel Soto.   Havana: Ciencias Sociales, 1977. 3 vols.

A detailed account of the struggle which culminated in the overthrow of General Machado in 1933. The first volume traces the historical antecedents up to the assassination of Julio Antonio Mella. The second volume homes in on the intensified struggle until the flight of Machado. The third volume considers the political manoeuvring which took place after Machado's fall to wrest victory from the revolutionary forces, and follows events up to the 100-day government which dealt the death blow to the 1933 revolution.

178 **Revolution and reaction in Cuba, 1933-1960: a political sociology from Machado to Castro.**
Samuel Farber. Middletown, Connecticut: Wesleyan University Press, 1976. 283p. bibliog.
A historical study of the Cuban revolution and Castro's rise to power. The author examines the evolution of political and social groupings emerging from the 1930s and their role in events in the 1950s. Emphasis is placed on the Cuban class structure and the influence of the 1933 revolution in forming the attitudes and institutions of the later revolution. The Castro revolution is categorized as Bonapartist, in that it had a revolutionary leadership not responsive to any one class but manipulative of all.

1950s insurrection

179 **The Auténtico Party and the political opposition in Cuba, 1952-1957.**
Charles D. Ameringer. *Hispanic American Historical Review*, no. 55 (May 1985), p. 327-51.
An account of mainstream opposition to the Batista government.

180 **Camilo: señor de la vanguardia.** (Camilo: lord of the vanguard.)
William Gálvez. Havana: Ciencias Sociales, 1988. 574p.
Gálvez presents a military biography of Camilo Cienfuegos, who had risen to the rank of chief of staff of the Cuban Rebel Army by the time he disappeared on a flight from Camagüey to Havana in October 1959. He was also one of the twelve survivors of the *Granma* landing in eastern Cuba in 1956. This is essentially a history of the invasion of central Cuba in 1959, in which Cienfuegos led a column, along with Ernesto Guevara. The biography reproduces Cienfuegos' writings and includes transcripts of his recorded speeches.

181 **The Cuban insurrection, 1952-1959.**
Ramón Bonachea, Marta San Martín. New Brunswick, New Jersey: Transaction, 1973. 450p. maps. bibliog.
Examines the part played by revolutionary organizations and leaders, arguing that the victory over Batista was due as much to urban resistance as to rural guerrilla warfare.

182 **La cueva del muerto.** (Dead Man's Cave.)
Marta Rojas. Havana: Unión de Escritores y Artistas de Cuba, 1983. 225p.
Constitutes a narrative reconstruction of events during the week of 26 July-1 August 1953 following the attack on the Moncada Garrison in Santiago de Cuba, which has been heralded as the start of the Cuban revolution. This is the story based on testimonies of local people involved when Fidel Castro and other assailants were on the run in the Sierra Maestra mountains.

183 **De Tuxpan a La Plata.** (From Tuxpan to La Plata.)
Havana: Editora Política, 1985. 243p.

This military history of the 26th July Movement describes the preparations and training of the eighty-two expeditionaries who set sail for Cuba on the *Granma* from Tuxpan, Mexico, in November 1956. The account ends with the first major victory at La Plata in February 1957.

184 **Fidel Castro's political strategy.**
Marta Harnecker. New York: Pathfinder, 1987. 157p.

Harnecker tells the story of how Fidel Castro forged a revolutionary strategy to bring down the US-backed Batista dictatorship in 1959, using the letters, documents and speeches of Fidel Castro and others leaders of the 26th July Movement.

185 **Financing Castro's revolution, 1956-1958.**
Alfred L. Padula, Jr. *Revista / Review Interamericana*, no. 8 (summer 1978), p. 234-46.

Through a detailed analysis of the financing of the armed struggle in Cuba, the author demonstrates that the larger share of donations came from the middle class.

186 **El juicio del Moncada.** (The Moncada trial.)
Marta Rojas. Havana: Ciencias Sociales, 1988. 357p.

A young journalism graduate from Santiago de Cuba, Rojas reported on the aftermath of the 1953 attack on the Moncada Garrison and the trial of the captured survivors. She was the only journalist present when Fidel Castro was sentenced and gave his historic 'History will absolve me' defence plea. The book is based on her notes made at the time and on interviews in subsequent years. It is an enlarged, revised reprint of *La generación del centenario en el juicio del Moncada* (The generation of the centennial at the Moncada trial), and includes a complete list of the assailants, official police and medical documents, the text of Fidel Castro's plea, and archival photographs.

187 **Moncada: memories of an attack that launched the Cuban revolution.**
Haydée Santamaría, translated and introduced by Robert Taber, with an afterword by Roberto Fernández Retamar. Secaucus, New Jersey: Lyle Stuart, 1980. 118p.

Haydée Santamaría and Melba Hernández were the only women who took part in the 1953 attack on the Moncada Garrison. In this account, based on a talk given to University of Havana students in 1967, Santamaría provides a rare glimpse in English into the attack in which she lost her brother and fiancé. See also *Moncada Tania the unforgettable guerrilla.* Edited by Marta Rojas, Mirta Rodríguez Calderón (New York: Random House, 1971. 212p.).

188 **¡Presente! Apuntes para la historia del movimiento estudiantial cubano.** (Present! Notes for a history of the Cuban student movement.)
Juan Nuiry Sánchez.   Havana: Ciencias Sociales, 1988. 277p.

The greater part of this work describes the activities of the Federation of University Students (FEU), when its president was José Antonio Echeverría. The author was FEU vice-president (1955-56) and took part in the historic attack on Radio Reloj in March 1957 in which Echeverría lost his life.

189 **Recuerdos del Moncada.** (Memories of the Moncada.)
Mario Lazo Pérez.   Havana: Editora Política, 1987. 190p.

First published in 1979, this is a readable and informative memoir of one participant's account of the attack on the Moncada Garrison in Santiago de Cuba in July 1953. The author tells about his childhood, his revolutionary involvement, how the attack was carried out, and how he avoided capture.

190 **Time was on our side.**
Mario Mencía.   Havana: Editora Política, 1982. 283p.

Describes in detail the events which took place in the 1950s while Fidel Castro and the other survivors of the attack on the Moncada Garrison were imprisoned on the Isle of Pines. The text includes articles published in *Bohemia* magazine on the twenty-fifth anniversary of their release from prison and provides insights into Fidel Castro's understanding of the situation, and the way in which he planned and directed the struggle against the Batista government.

191 **The unsuspected revolution: the birth and rise of Castroism.**
M. Llerena.   Ithaca, New York: Cornell University Press, 1978. 323p.

A memoir of the armed struggle conducted against the Batista régime by one who was an early supporter and later opponent of Fidel Castro.

192 **The winds of December.**
John Dorschner, Robert Fabricio.   East Rutherford, New Jersey: Coward, McCann & Geoghgan, 1980. 552p. bibliog.

The authors present a detailed political, diplomatic and military chronicle of the last month of the armed struggle against the Batista régime in 1958. The account was based on US State Department documents and over 200 interviews with pro- and anti-Batista participants and eyewitnesses, including Fidel Castro.

Old Havana, Cuba.
See item no. 9.

Excursión a Vuelta Abajo. (Excursion to Vuelta Abajo.)
See item no. 44.

The Mambí-Land, or, adventures of a *Herald* correspondent in Cuba.
See item no. 48.

Sixty years in Cuba.
See item no. 49.

Antonio Maceo, apuntes para una historia de su vida. (Antonio Maceo: biographical notes.)
See item no. 358.

Antonio Maceo: the 'bronze titan' of Cuba's struggle for independence.
See item no. 359.

Revista de la Biblioteca Nacional José Martí. (The José Martí National Library Review.)
See item no. 1105.

Country Profile: Cuba.
See item no. 1109.

Anales del Caribe. (Annals of the Caribbean.)
See item no. 1115.

Historiography in the revolution: a bibliography of Cuban scholarship, 1959-1979.
See item no. 1152.

Revolution

1960s

193 **Background to revolution: the development of modern Cuba.**
Edited by R. F. Smith. New York: Alfred A. Knopf, 1966. Reprinted, Huntington, New York: Krieger, 1979. 244p. bibliog.

Essays on a broad range of topics are collected in this volume to provide an introductory background to the Cuban revolution. This includes political and economic history, slavery and race, class structure, and US–Cuba relations.

194 **Cuba: anatomy of a revolution.**
Leo Huberman, Paul M. Sweezy. New York; London: Monthly Review Press, 1960. 2nd ed. 208p. map.

The first edition of this classic, early, quasi-academic, quasi-journalistic account of the Cuban revolution was published in June 1960 after the authors, two American socialists, had spent three weeks in Cuba in March of that year. A second expanded edition appeared in the November, following a further three-week trip in September-October. The intervening months were crucial ones in terms of the hardening US reaction to Cuba, with US oil companies in Cuba refusing to refine Soviet oil and the US government cutting the Cuban sugar quota. This account describes the background to and making of the revolution.

195 **Cuba: the economic and social revolution.**
Dudley Seers, Andrés Bianchi, Richard Jolly, Max Nolff. Chapel Hill, North Carolina: University of North Carolina, 1964. 432p.

Contains four lengthy essays, one on the economic and social background of the revolution, and the other three on education, agriculture, and industry in the early years.

196 **Cuba en el tránsito al socialismo (1959-63).** (Cuba on the road to socialism [1959-63].)
Carlos Rafael Rodríguez.   Mexico City: Siglo Veintiuno Editores SA, 1978. 233p.

One of Cuba's leading Marxist intellectuals analyses the events leading up to the Cuban revolution. An appendix discusses the agrarian reform implemented by the revolutionary government, justifying it in terms of the social conditions which, he argues, made the revolution necessary.

197 **Cuba in revolution.**
Edited by Rolando E. Bonachea, Nelson P. Valdés.   Garden City, New York: Doubleday & Company, 1972. 544p.

Over twenty articles by North Americans and Cubans, both in Cuba and in exile, are brought together in this publication. They cover a broad range of topics, from the 1950s insurrection to economic policy, sugar production, labour, health, education, culture, and bureacracy.

198 **Cuba: tragedy in our hemisphere.**
Maurice Zeitlin, Robert Scheer.   New York: Grove Press, 1963. 316p.

A sympathetic account of the revolution in the early years, with a brief historical overview and great detail on the years 1959-62.

199 **Inside the Cuban revolution.**
Adolfo Gilly, translated from the Spanish by Félix Gutiérrez.
New York: Monthly Review Press, 1964. 88p.

This journalistic account is based on the author's experiences living among the Cuban people in 1962 and 1963. It takes a look at the internal situation in Cuba at the time and considers the most important forces at work. It is striking how many of the key issues raised are still relevant today.

200 **Listen yankee: the revolution in Cuba.**
C. Wright Mills.   New York: McGraw Hill, 1960. 192p. bibliog.

A passionate defence of the Cuban revolution which captures the radical nature of the early revolution.

201 **M-26, the biography of a revolution.**
Robert Taber.   New York: Lyle Stuart, 1961. 348p.

The author of this early account of the revolutionary struggle was a United States correspondent who lived among the guerrilla fighters of the 26th July Movement.

202 **Revolution in the revolution: armed struggle and political struggle in Latin America.**
Régis Debray, translated by Bobbye Ortiz. New York: Monthly Review Press; Harmondsworth, England: Penguin, 1967. 126p.

This is the French intellectual Debray's classic attempt to develop a new theory of revolutionary struggle from the Cuban experience, in which armed guerrillas would play a vanguard role.

203 **Sartre on Cuba.**
Jean-Paul Sartre. Westport, Connecticut: Greenwood, 1974. 160p.

Reprinted from the 1961 Ballantine edition, this is a now classic early account of the Cuban revolution, seen through the eyes of the leading French existentialist on a short visit to the island. Sartre reflects on Havana as a city; sugar, landowners and agrarian reform; inequality and injustice of the kind that brought revolution to Cuba; the principled revolutionary 'beards'; and Che Guevara.

204 **Socialism in Cuba.**
Leo Huberman, Paul M. Sweezy. New York; London: Monthly Review Press, 1969. 221p.

The authors return to Cuba, ten years after their first account of the Cuban revolution (see item no. 194), to study the ways in which the revolutionary government attempted to transform the economy and society of Cuba, substituting itself for the market as the guide and engine of economic and social development. Huberman and Sweezy look at education, health, economic diversification, the private sector, incentives, resources and technology. As Marxists, they found much to admire, but they also deal in detail with many failures and mistakes. An interesting final chapter suggests that the régime's paternalistic political style and tendency to shut off political debate may prove injurious in the long run.

1970s

205 **Cuba: the making of a revolution.**
Ramón Eduardo Ruiz. New York: W. W. Norton, 1970. 190p. bibliog.

A classic Mexican-authored account of the Cuban revolution from a nationalistic standpoint. It takes as its point of departure the Cuban paradox of a relatively rich country which underwent a major social cataclysm, attempting to explain why it was relatively rich Cuba and not its poverty-stricken neighbours which rose in revolution. Ruiz traces Cuba's bitter-sweet sugar history, the 19th-century roots of Cuban nationalism and José Martí, the 20th-century lost opportunity and return of the old order, Cuban-style socialism, and the revolution in the making.

206 **Cuba: the second decade.**
Edited by John Griffiths, Peter Griffiths. London: Writers & Readers
Cooperative, 1979. 271p.

Aimed at the general reader, this publication provides an overview of the first twenty
years of the revolution, dealing with political, economic, social and cultural questions.
Seeking to convey a sense of the day-to-day experience of Cuban life as well as an
analysis of the underlying issues, the contributions discuss issues ranging from
People's Power in its infancy and the 1970s economy and planning, to the elderly,
women and the family, sports, education, and the arts.

207 **The Cuban way.**
Richard Hart. London: Caribbean Labour Solidarity, 1978. 54p. map.

Two decades of the Cuban revolution are covered in this report by a Jamaican
socialist, trade unionist and historian. Long a scholar of Cuba, in the field of
Caribbean history and politics, Hart lectured in 1977 at the University of Havana on
Jamaican history and wrote this personal, first-hand account on his return to Britain.

208 **Is Cuba socialist?**
René Dumont. London: André Deutsch, 1974. 159p.

The French socialist-agronomist was invited to Cuba as an economic adviser. In this,
the second of two studies on Cuba, Dumont examined the early period of Cuban
socialism, the guerrilla movement, the successful revolution and centralized planning.
He found much to criticize: managerial privilege; dependence on the Soviet Union;
and concentration of power in the hands of Castro and the military. He presented his
criticism as constructive, saddened as he was to see the triumph of liberation
overshadowed by economic disorder.

209 **Revolutionary change in Cuba.**
Edited by Carmelo Mesa-Lago. Pittsburgh, Pennsylvania: University
of Pittsburgh Press, 1971. 544p.

An early work by the Cuban American scholar who went on to become the dean of
Cuban Studies in Pittsburgh. The book consists of eighteen articles separated into
three sections (polity, economy and society). The first covers power and the
Communist Party and the influence of foreign powers. The second deals with central
planning, trade relations and labour, and the third homes in on education, religion and
the arts.

210 **Venceremos Brigade: young Americans sharing the life and work
of revolutionary Cuba.**
The Venceremos Brigade. New York: Simon & Schuster, 1971.
412p.

A fascinating compilation of diary entries, letters, interviews, tapes, essays, poetry and
photographs by young radical Americans, members of the first 1970 Venceremos work
brigade in Cuba. The excitement and energy, alongside the indiscipline, boredom and
physical fatigue are the backdrop to a description of what they learnt about themselves
and about the revolution.

1980s

211 Cuba: a different America.

Edited by Wilber A. Chaffee, Jr., Gary Prevost. Totowa, New Jersey: Rowman & Littlefield, 1989. 181p.

The essays collected in this volume are based on fieldwork carried out in Cuba by the various contributors, and present vignettes and commentaries on broad aspects of Cuba, some of which have undergone rapid transformation. As a whole, the compilation demonstrates the ways in which the revolution has changed the lives of ordinary Cubans, principally for the better in the opinion of the authors, and created a consciousness very different from elsewhere in the Americas. The collection predicts that Castro, with the support of his people, will accommodate radical change, and calls most of all for the United States to understand rather than condemn Cuba.

212 Cuba libre: breaking the chains?

Peter Marshall. Boston, Massachusetts: Faber & Faber, 1987. 300p.

This is a sympathetic British view, based on travel through post-1959 Cuba, with a background of Cuba's history since colonial days.

213 Cuba: politics, economics and society.

Max Azicri. London; New York: Pinter, 1988. 276p.

Part of the 'Marxist Regimes' series of thirty-six country-based, multidisciplinary volumes which assess the successes and failures of the application of Marxist doctrine to society. Including basic data on topics such as history and political traditions, social structure, the political system, the economic system, and domestic and foreign policies, this serves as a good introduction to Cuba in the late 1980s.

214 The Cuba reader: the making of a revolutionary society.

Edited by Philip Brenner, William Leogrande, Donna Rich, Daniel Siegel. New York: Grove Press, 1989. 564p.

This reader was compiled with a US audience in mind, in an attempt to close the seemingly unbridgeable political, economic and socio-cultural gap between the United States of America and Cuba. The collection represents a good introductory source for academics and general readers looking for an overview of three decades of the Cuban Revolution, from 1959 to 1989, with some reference to the pre-1959 period. It contains extracts from older classic works such as Martí's *Our America* and Castro's *History will absolve me*, as well as the writings of other major Cuban figures, and key US scholars writing about Cuba.

215 Cuba: the test of time.

Jean Stubbs. London: Latin American Bureau, 1989. 142p. bibliog.

Striking a balance between the accessible and the scholarly, this work provides an introduction to contemporary Cuba through the 1988 prism of a system in confusion and crisis, and on the brink of a major transformation. The reader is guided through Cuba's collectivist development, revolutionary ethos and popular politicization, as a build-up to the country's overriding need in the 1990s to adapt to the changing world economy and polity. This involves a mental as well as political adjustment. Cuba's nationalism and Third Worldism are seen as key to understanding the 'logic' of non-capitulation and survival of the revolution against all odds.

216 Cuba: twenty-five years of revolution, 1959-1984.
Edited by Sandor Halebsky, John M. Kirk. New York: Praeger, 1985. 466p.

Presents a retrospective account of two and a half decades of revolution, with articles on education, medicine, nutrition, women, religion, culture and the arts, economy and labour, foreign policy and historiography. See also *Cronología: 25 años de revolución* (Chronology: 25 years of revolution), edited by Carina Pino-Santos Navarro (Havana: Editora Política, 1987. 395p.). This provides a useful chronology of the most important events and decisions of the 1959-83 period. A similar publication is *Cronología de la revolución: 1984-89* (Chronology of the revolution: 1984-89), edited by Elsa Pérez Guerra and Minerva Hernández Fhan (Havana: Editora Política, 1991. 241p.).

217 The Cuban revolution, 25 years later.
Hugh Thomas, Georges A. Fauriol, Juan Carlos Weiss. Boulder, Colorado: Westview, 1984. 69p. map.

This is a highly critical reappraisal of the Cuban revolution, which challenges the Havana government's claims of success in areas such as education, culture and the economy.

218 Revolutionary Cuba.
Terence Cannon. Havana: Editorial José Martí, 1981. 279p. bibliog.

Writing for fellow Americans, Cannon uses Cuban source materials, in the form of books, magazines, archives and interviews, to impart a Cuban vision of the revolution and the world Cubans helped change. Part one reconstructs the history of 1950s insurrection contextualized in the 19th-century independence struggles and the 1933 revolution. Part two charts the events of the early years after the 1959 revolution, while part three covers the issues of education, health, labour and government as the revolution 'matured' through its second decade.

219 Socialist Cuba: past interpretations and future challenges.
Edited by Sergio Roca. Boulder, Colorado: Westview, 1988. 253p.

Contains thoughtful and provocative essays on economic and political topics, foreign relations, demographic change, race relations and religion. Three essays in particular should be highlighted: Jorge Pérez López who provides an empirical study of Cuba's hard currency–Soviet oil re-export trade; Rhoda Rabkin examines party policy-making and implementation; and Carmelo Mesa-Lago offers a critique of the return of ideology in the rectification campaign.

1990s

220 Back from the future: Cuba under Castro.

Susan Eva Eckstein. Princeton, New Jersey: Princeton University
Press, 1994. 286p.

The author traces Cuba's retreat from the utopian communism of the 1960s, through
the transition to socialism of the 1970s and 1980s, to the socialist autarky of the
1990s. Eckstein challenges totalitarian models of communism, detailing the ways in
which global and economic dynamics, along with forces in civil society, have shaped
Cuban economic and social policy, and political structures. This work adopts an
informed approach, which refuses to resort to simplistic political conclusions in order
to explain complex societal problems. The author charts various policy changes that
have occurred, and discusses the gulf between the political ideology of the régime and
the reality of political life. Highlighting the growing power of popular action to sway
policy, Eckstein shows the extent to which Castro has taken account of such action
and thus adopted a more pragmatic political policy. She concludes by calling on
Washington to work with rather than against Castro for political change.

221 Conflict and change in Cuba.

Edited by Enrique A. Baloyra, James Morris. Albuquerque, New
Mexico: University of New Mexico Press, 1993. 347p.

Focuses on the direction of conflict and change in Cuban society following the impact
of Soviet reform. Part one introduces the topic with articles by Alfred Padula and
Baloyra. In part two Marifeli Pérez-Stable, Sergio Roca and Phyllis Greene Walker
look at the state and its leader, while part three contains contributions by Peter
Johnson on the intelligentsia, Juan M. del Águila on dissidence, and Damián
Fernández on youth. Finally, part four concludes with essays by W. Raymond Duncan
on US–Cuban relations and J. Richard Planas, Baloyra and Roberto Lozano on the
impact of Soviet reforms.

222 Cuba: adapting to a post-Soviet world.

Special issue of *NACLA Report on the Americas*, vol. 29, no. 2
(Sept./Oct. 1995), p. 6-56. (Available from NACLA, PO Box 77,
Hopewell, Pennsylvania, 16650-0077, USA).

As well as containing contributions from several well-known Cubanologists, this
special report includes interviews carried out in Cuba by a team from the North
American Congress on Latin America, a non-profit-making research organization. It
provides an excellent introduction for the general reader to some of the major
repercussions of Cuba's post-1989 economic crisis. The examinations of US policy
towards Cuba and the changing role of the Cuban-American community provide
valuable pointers to possible developments in US–Cuban relations. Four foreign
personalities reflect on what Cuba has meant and now means to them. Perhaps most
useful of all are the nine testimonies from Cubans living on the island which help the
outsider understand the debate taking place on Cuba's future.

223   **Cuba after the Cold War.**
Edited by Carmelo Mesa-Lago.   Pittsburgh, Pennsylvania: University of Pittsburgh Press, 1993. 383p.

A compilation of articles by ten influential scholars specializing on Cuba, viewed in a Central and South America context, after the fall of communism and the transition to a market economy in Eastern Europe. Major themes concern the impact on Cuba of the collapse of the USSR, implications for the Cuban and regional left, Cuba's strategies for confronting the crisis, and future scenarios of political and economic transformation in Cuba.

224   **Cuba after thirty years: rectification and the revolution.**
Edited by Richard Gillespie.   London: Frank Cass, 1990. 188p.

Comprising a selection of papers from a conference of *The Journal of Communist Studies*, this volume marks the thirtieth anniversary of the Cuban revolution, and focuses on developments of the 1980s. Written at a time of liberalization in the communist world, it analyses Cuba's retreat from reform and re-assertion of revolution with 'rectification' in the comparative context of the broader communist movement and Latin American revolutions. The volume covers Latin American and Soviet relations, the economy, the military and the Communist Party, cinema and ideology.

225   **Cuba: la agenda democrática.** (Cuba: the democratic agenda.)
Haroldo Dilla Alfonso, et al.   *Revista/Review Interamericana*, vol. 22, nos. 3-4 (autumn/winter 1992). 126p.

This special issue of the journal is devoted entirely to Cuba, comprising articles by leading Cuban social scientists living in Cuba and committed to socialism. Juan Valdés Paz discusses Cuba's Latin American and Caribbean policy in the 1990s, Santiago Pérez covers the end of special relations between the USSR and Cuba, Aurelio Alonso Tejada writes on political participation and religious faith and Gerardo González Núñez examines Cuba and the world market. Other essays are: Verónica Loynaz Fernández on Cuba, Europe and Latin America; Rafael Hernández on the USA and Cuba; and Haroldo Dilla Alfonso on the democratic agenda and the re-articulation of political consensus in Cuba.

226   **Cuba at a crossroads: politics and economics after the Fourth Party Congress.**
Edited by Jorge F. Pérez López.   Gainesville, Florida: University Press of Florida, 1994. 300p. bibliog.

These scholarly essays take as a point of departure the October 1991 Fourth Party Congress of Cuba's Communist Party which marked the beginning of efforts to redefine policies in light of the loss of Soviet bloc markets and subsidies. The essays deal with important areas currently under scrutiny: politics and mass organizations; international relations; labour relations; and specific aspects of the country's survival strategy. Although written before the reform process was stepped up in 1993-94 many of the contributions in this work presage them, and provide some statistics which are otherwise hard to obtain.

227   **Cuba: el desafío del cambio.** (Cuba: the challenge of change.)
       Madrid: Institute for European–Latin American Relations (IRELA),
       1990. 54p. (Dossier no. 27).

Prepared as Cuba plunged into crisis, this publication contains sections covering rectification, continuity of political power and opposition, and possible scenarios of economic change. Annexes include resolutions of the European Parliament and international bodies on Cuba and the official Cuban response to human rights allegations.

228   **Cuba: dilemmas of a revolution.**
       Juan M. del Águila.   Boulder, Colorado; San Francisco; Oxford:
       Westview, 1994. 3rd ed. 222p. bibliog.

The third edition of this concise and comprehensive introduction to contemporary Cuba provides new material on the impact of the collapse of Eastern bloc communism, which left the revolution more vulnerable than ever. The situation within the Communist Party, the armed forces, and major élites and institutions is analysed as economic and political difficulties deepened. The author argues that the economic reforms are at odds with Marxist ideology and that the failure to liberalize suggests the régime is seriously concerned about the emergence of political dissidence and opposition.

229   **Cuba en crisis.** (Cuba in crisis.)
       Edited by Jorge Rodríguez Beruff.   San Juan, Puerto Rico: Editorial
       de la Universidad de Puerto Rico, 1995. 218p.

An essential study for understanding the critical situation in Cuba in the 1990s. The work is characterized by a balance of analysis and perspective and contains contributions by Cubans living in and away from the island. Santiago Pérez, Gerardo González Núñez, Haroldo Dilla Alfonso and Ana Teresa Vincentelli, all researchers at the Havana Centre for Study of the Americas, focus on the economy, the People's Power system of government, the end of the Soviet–Cuba alliance, Cuba and the world market, and Cuba and the Caribbean. Cuban-Americans Jorge Domínguez, Marifeli Pérez-Stable and Nelson Valdés look at alternative Cuban political traditions and future scenarios. The Puerto Rican-Cuban, Jorge Rodríguez Beruff, contributes an introductory 'Whither Cuba?'.

230   **Cuba: facing change.**
       NACLA Report on the Americas, vol. 24, no. 2 (Aug. 1990), p. 13-48.

This NACLA report on Cuba captured the beginning of the process of change and economic deterioration and includes an essay on Fidel Castro by the Nobel Prize-winning novelist Gabriel García Márquez.

231   **Cuba in transition: crisis and transformation.**
       Edited by Sandor Halebsky, John M. Kirk, with Carollee Bengelsdorf,
       Richard L. Harris, Jean Stubbs, Andrew Zimbalist.   Boulder,
       Colorado: Westview, 1992. 244p.

Addresses the 1990s crisis facing Cuba's political system, economy and society, following the disintegration of the former Soviet bloc, and considers the dilemma facing Cuba's leaders and people committed to the revolution's goals and ideals: the need for reform. The work focuses on participatory democracy, economic prospects, and Cuban life, emphasizing issues of race, class, gender and age.

232 Cuba looks to the year 2000.

Marc Frank. New York: International Publishers, 1993. 225p.

Drawing on his experience of living and working in Cuba from 1984 to 1991, Frank, a US journalist, attempts to convey what Cuban socialism looks like from the inside, why it has survived and how Cubans have adjusted to the new world order. Written from a sympathetic stance and in an accessible style, the book best captures the social achievements of 1980s Cuba, the devastating effects of the end of Eastern bloc socialism compounded by the stepped-up US blockade and hostility, and the mind-set of Cuba up to 1990 with Guevarist rectification. However, a book claiming to look to the future would have done better to start, rather than end, with the criticism voiced in the 1990s about the internal running of the economy and social services and the hopes of a major political shake-up.

233 Cuba: talking about the revolution.

Conversations with Juan Antonio Blanco by Medea Benjamin.
Melbourne, Australia: Ocean Press; San Francisco: Global Exchange, 1993. 105p.

A frank discussion on the 1990s situation in Cuba in question-and-answer format between a Cuban and a North American, each director of a non-governmental organization in their respective countries. Blanco heads the Félix Varela Centre for the study of ethics and politics in Havana, and Benjamin is director of Global Exchange, a San Francisco-based organization promoting international people-to-people ties. Blanco argues for Cuba's moral stand with the poor of the earth, and the prevalence of the socialist ethic of being over the capitalist ethic of having.

234 Cuban communism: 1959-1995.

Irving Louis Horowitz. New Brunswick, New Jersey: Transaction, 1995. 8th ed. 873p.

Called by some the Bible of Cuban studies, this compendium of articles is now in its eighth edition. The volume is divided into sections on history, society, politics, economics and the military, and well over half is new material dealing especially with 1990s changes in the alignment of world geopolitical forces, profound adjustments in Cuba, and prospects for a further erosion or dismantling of the Castro régime. Horowitz's main theme concerns the staying power of dictators and illegitimate régimes despite crisis and delegitimation.

235 Dossier: Cuba.

Annales des Pays d'Amérique Latine et des Caraïbes, nos. 11-12 (1992), special issue.

A collection of five essays, brought together in a special section of the *Annales*, which are published yearly by ASERCCA/CREALC. Two focus on political and ideological issues facing 1990s Cuba (Roberto Spíndola and Antoni Kapcia); one provides an economic overview (Miguel Alejandro Figueras and Sergio Plasencia); one is on tourist development (Eduardo Klinger Pevida); and the last reviews the Cuban security question from the 1962 Missile Crisis to the 1980s.

236 **Revolutionary Cuba and the end of the Cold War.**
David C. Jordan. Lanham, Maryland: University Press of America,
1993. 284p. bibliog.

This study seeks to analyse the effects on Cuba of the end of the Cold War and the break-up of the former Soviet Union. Jordan begins by discussing the rise of Cuban nationalism in recent years, the legacy of José Martí and the interpretation of Marxist-Leninist thought in Cuba. He then considers the links which were established with the Soviet Union in 1959 and examines relations with the United States, including the Missile Crisis and the peace initiatives proposed by Carter. With the collapse of communism in the Eastern bloc Cuba found itself in an isolated and precarious position and Jordan considers the possible future outcomes for the revolutionary régime.

237 **Transformation and struggle: Cuba faces the 1990s.**
Edited by Sandor Halebsky, John M. Kirk, with the assistance of
Rafael Hernández. New York: Praeger, 1990. 291p.

This reader defies the existing narrow definitions of policy and politics by established and new scholars, both Cuban and North American, some of whom display greater depth than others, but whose contributions remain at best bland. The collection attempts to portray a Cuba facing the 1990s with a burst of increased vigour: economic rectification, political liberalization and social advancement. Its more upbeat linear projections were inevitably eclipsed by the severe external and internal dislocation, with the collapse of Soviet–Cuban relations, renewed pragmatism and nationalism.

The youngest revolution: a personal report on Cuba.
See item no. 73.

Che Guevara and the Cuban revolution, writings and speeches of Ernesto Che Guevara.
See item no. 269.

Remaking the public sphere: women and revolution in Cuba.
See item no. 380.

Socialism and feminism: women and the Cuban revolution.
See item no. 382.

Women and the Cuban revolution.
See item no. 385.

Women's equality and the Cuban revolution.
See item no. 387.

Women's rights and the Cuban revolution.
See item no. 388.

Cuba, 1953-1978: a bibliographical guide to the literature.
See item no. 1159.

The Cuban revolution of Fidel Castro viewed from abroad: an annotated bibliography.
See item no. 1160.

The Cuban revolution: a research-study guide (1959-1969).
See item no. 1161.

The Cuban revolutionary war, 1953-1958: a bibliography.
See item no. 1162.

Cuban studies since the revolution.
See item no. 1163.

Revolutionary Cuba: a bibliographical guide.
See item no. 1165.

Biographies, Memoirs and Collected Writings

Fidel Castro

Biographies and studies

1960s and 1970s

238 **Castroism: theory and practice.**
Theodore Draper. New York: Praeger, 1965. 263p.

The sequel to the author's earlier *Castro's revolution, myth and realities* (Praeger, 1962), this is an interpretative analysis of Fidel Castro's thinking, in the context of a discussion of Marxism-Leninism, the class origins of the revolution and economic policies. A central thesis for Draper is that of the revolution betrayed, that is, a nationalist movement turning communist.

239 **The early Fidel: roots of Castro's communism.**
Lionel Martin. Secaucus, New Jersey: Lyle Stuart, 1978. 272p.

Written by a US reporter based in Cuba since the early 1960s, this remains an interesting account of the early Fidel Castro. Present in 1961 when Castro proclaimed the socialist character of the revolution, the author set out to establish when Castro became a socialist but found little to substantiate Fidel's own version, which claimed that by the time he left university in 1950 he was a Marxist-Leninist dreaming of a socialist Cuba. This study explores previously little-known facts about Castro's relationships with Marxists at university and points to the Marxist content of Castro's pre-revolution speeches, letters, manifestos and articles.

Biographies, Memoirs and Collected Writings. Fidel Castro. Biographies and studies. 1980s

240 **Fidel Castro.**
    Herbert L. Matthews.   New York: Simon & Schuster, 1969. 382p.
    bibliog.

A sympathetic biography in which the New York reporter who interviewed Fidel Castro behind the lines in the 1950s revolutionary insurrection traces the political career of the Cuban leader from the early 1950s through the 1960s.

1980s

241 **Castro: a biography of Fidel Castro.**
    P. Bourne.   London: Macmillan, 1986. 332p.

This mainly sympathetic portrait of Castro attempts to analyse his political development in psychoanalytical terms, paying particular attention to his early years and the insurrection period. The author, a psychiatrist and former adviser to US President Carter, emphasizes Castro's allegedly difficult early relationship with his father, suggesting this was the driving force of his actions.

242 **Family portrait with Fidel.**
    Carlos Franqui, translated from the Spanish by Alfred MacAdam.
    London: Jonathan Cape, 1980. 262p.

A leading revolutionary figure who left Cuba in the mid-1960s presents a dramatic account of intrigues and factions in the early revolutionary government; an intimate psychological and political portrait of Fidel Castro; and insider testimony on domestic and foreign policy in the early years of the revolution.

243 **Fidel Castro y la revolución cubana.** (Fidel Castro and the Cuban revolution.)
    Carlos Alberto Montaner.   Barcelona, Spain: Plaza & Janes, 1983. 281p.

Montaner's essay is sharply critical of Castro's leadership. He pays little attention to the question of genuine support for Castro in Cuba but painfully explores the régime's less tolerant sides with regard to intellectual life, religion, sexuality, race, and freedom of political expression and association.

244 **Fidel: a critical portrait.**
    Tad Szulc.   London: Hutchinson, 1986. 585p. bibliog.

Purported to be the only biography written with the active co-operation of Fidel Castro, this is the work of the US journalist who broke the 1961 Bay of Pigs story for the *New York Times*. Based on in-depth interviews with Castro and other leading figures of the Cuban revolution, plus bibliographical and archival research and stays on the island, the study recounts detailed stories of Castro's life and career, including conspiracies, battles, victories and defeats, as well as Castro's personal views and private moments, including his relationship with his son, Fidelito. This is not a biography Castro himself is reputed to like.

245   **The taming of Fidel Castro.**
Maurice Halperin.   Berkeley, California: University of California
Press, 1981. 345p.

The sequel to the author's earlier study *The rise and decline of Fidel Castro, an essay in contemporary history* (Berkeley: University of California Press, 1974. 380p.), this completes the account of the first decade of the revolution by covering the years 1964-68. It also includes a prologue recapitulating ground covered in the first volume, an assessment of the failed ten million-ton sugar harvest of 1970, and an epilogue summarizing changes in the second decade. Lesser-known topics covered include the Oscar Lewis case in 1969, and Castro and the Jews.

246   **A totally free man: the unauthorized autobiography of Fidel
Castro.**
John Krich.   New York; London; Toronto; Sydney; Tokyo: Simon &
Schuster, 1981. 171p.

Fidel Castro has proved intensely guarded about his private life. In this fictitious 'autobiography', he talks non-stop into a tape recorder, reviewing the events of his life, from his privileged origins and Jesuit school days to his close relationship with Ernesto Che Guevara. The result is a surreal multi-dimensional tragicomedy that bears some but not a lot of relation to reality.

1990s

247   **Castro.**
Sebastian Balfour.   London: Longman, 1995. 2nd ed. 198p. bibliog.
(Profiles in Power Series).

This is more than a personal biography. It sets out to examine the historical context in which Castro emerged as a national and international statesman and the ideological base on which the new Cuban state was founded. It situates Castro's political ideas more firmly in Cuba's radical nationalist tradition than in Marxism-Leninism. This in turn is located in the wave of Third World nationalism harnessing state socialism for independence and development. The work also highlights the latter years of Castro's rule in the crisis 1990s, with changing perceptions of Cubans about their leader and the succession question. This second edition brings the analysis up to date in the post-communist world.

248   **Castro's Cuba, Cuba's Fidel.**
Lee Lockwood.   Boulder, Colorado; San Francisco; Oxford:
Westview, 1990. 379p. bibliog.

The interview that forms the backbone to this account took place in 1965. The book was then first published by Macmillan in 1967, and in paperback by Random House/Vintage Press in 1969. The Westview edition includes a new chapter, in which the author examines some of the important topics Castro dealt with in the 1965 interview, in the light of the passage of twenty-five years, especially world rejection of socialism in favour of multi-party politics and free-market economies. Lockwood's interview remains one of the most insightful and enduring accounts.

Biographies, Memoirs and Collected Writings. Fidel Castro. Biographies and studies. 1990s

249 **Castro's final hour: the secret story behind the coming downfall of communist Cuba.**
Andrés Oppenheimer. New York: Simon & Schuster, 1993. 2nd ed. 474p.

Key incidents at the heart of this account (the trial and execution of Cuban General Ochoa on a drugs charge, the US invasion of Panama, the loss of Nicaragua as an ally, and the demise of the Eastern bloc) are told with interesting and entertaining, if not always accurate, detail. The conclusions are altogether serious: Oppenheimer opines that Castro is paranoid, brutal and megalomaniac and that his, and the revolution's end are near. However, events failed to bear out this final epithet, leaving an account that obscures rather than helps reveal the forces and dynamics shaping Cuba.

250 **An encounter with Fidel.**
Gianni Miná. Melbourne, Australia: Ocean Press, 1991. 273p.

Castro himself joked that this marathon interview of fifteen straight hours, carried out in 1987 for Italian television, set a record. This published version of the interview has a personal introduction by the Colombian Nobel Prize-winner Gabriel García Márquez on Fidel and his craft of the word. Castro reflects on his country and his own role in the Cuban revolution and discusses human rights, culture, sports, health and religion. He speaks of Khrushchev, Kennedy and the 1962 Cuban Missile Crisis; US–Cuban relations in the Reagan and Bush years; Gorbachev and the Soviet Union; debt, dependence and the Third World; and, for the first time, his own relationship with Che Guevara.

251 **Face to face with Fidel Castro: a conversation with Tomás Borge.**
Fidel Castro, interviewed by Tomás Borge, translated by Mary Todd. Melbourne, Australia: Ocean Press, 1993. 181p.

Fidel Castro talks candidly on a fascinating range of subjects with fellow revolutionary and 'comandante' Tomás Borge, the only surviving member of the founding nucleus of the Sandinista National Liberation Front of Nicaragua. The book is both personal and political as Castro reflects back over his own life, the cataclysmic events of his lifetime, figures such as Che Guevara and John Kennedy, topics such as neo-liberalism, democracy, human rights and homosexuality.

252 **Fidel Castro.**
Robert E. Quirk. New York; London: W. W. Norton & Company, 1993. 898p.

Claims to tell the full story of Castro's rise to power, his régime, his allies and his adversaries: that of an ambitious man steering his small nation on a doomed course in the midst of international rivalries and world revolution. Written with the conviction of a Castro detractor, it is a good-gossip read but lacking in original source material and sound historical analysis. Borrowing extensively from previous biographies, secondary myth and half truths about a man who has kept his private life a jealously guarded secret, the book shores up a simplistic portrait of a self-adulating, power-seeking Castro.

253   **Fidel! Castro's political and social thought.**
       Sheldon Liss.   Boulder, Colorado: Westview, 1994. 246p. bibliog.
Less a biography than a narrative of Fidel's attempt to build socialism in Cuba, the underlying premise is that to understand Fidel one needs to understand the history of Cuba and Latin America as well as the philosophical underpinnings of Marxism-Leninism. There are few studies that do both. Cuban Marxism is analysed less as a defined doctrine than as a product of the political and social thought and praxis of Fidel Castro, described as already a Marxist in his worldview by 1950, though also firmly inscribed in the radical Latin American and Cuban tradition.

254   **Guerrilla prince: the untold story of Fidel Castro.**
       Georgie Anne Geyer.   Boston, Massachusetts: Little, Brown & Co., 1991. 462p. bibliog.
A highly critical, and at times sensational, unauthorized biography of Castro by a US journalist, this probes his personal life and discusses his central role in world politics. The author concludes that Castro the revolutionary became a paranoid dictator.

Speeches and writings

255   **Building socialism in Cuba: our power is that of working people.**
       Fidel Castro, edited by Michael Taber.   New York: Pathfinder, 1987. 367p. (Fidel Castro Speeches, vol. 2, 1960-82).
First printed in 1981, these speeches span over two decades of efforts, under Fidel Castro's leadership, to transform Cuba into a socialist society. They provide a useful guide to the evolution of Castro's thinking from his earliest years in power through critical moments such as the Missile Crisis and the shift towards a Soviet-style centrally planned economy.

256   **Fidel Castro: nothing can stop the course of history.**
       Fidel Castro, interviewed by Jeffrey M. Elliot, Mervyn M. Dymally. New York; London: Pathfinder, 1986. Reprinted, 1988. 258p.
In an interview with two left-wing journalists from the United States, the Cuban leader speaks about US–Cuban relations, Cuba's role in opposing apartheid rule in South Africa, the overthrow of the Bishop government in Grenada and the Latin American foreign debt.

257   **Fidel Castro speaks.**
       Edited by M. Kenner, J. Petrás.   London; Harmondsworth, England: Penguin, 1972. 426p. bibliog.
Sixteen of Castro's most important speeches for the period 1959-68 are collected here and divided into four sections: radicalization of the revolution to 1961; revolutionary struggle in Latin America; characteristics of the Cuban road to communism; and goals of the Cuban revolution.

Biographies, Memoirs and Collected Writings. Fidel Castro. Speeches and writings

258   **In defence of socialism.**
       Fidel Castro, edited by Mary-Alice Waters.   New York: Pathfinder,
       1989. 142p. maps. (Fidel Castro Speeches, vol. 4).

In four major speeches delivered on the 30th anniversary of the Cuban revolution, Castro outlines his position on economic and social issues, arguing that progress is possible without capitalism. He also discusses Cuban policy in southern Africa.

259   **Revolutionary struggle 1947-1958: selected works of Fidel Castro.**
       Edited by Rolando E. Bonachea, Nelson P. Valdés.   Cambridge,
       Massachusetts: MIT Press, 1972. 471p. bibliog.

An invaluable collection of the translated speeches, articles and statements of Fidel Castro from his days as a student at the University of Havana to the triumph of the revolution. An introductory essay places the collection in context.

260   **War and crisis in the Americas.**
       Fidel Castro, edited by Michael Taber.   New York: Pathfinder, 1985.
       249p. (Fidel Castro Speeches, vol. 3, 1984-85).

These speeches cover a period in which Cuba and the United States were at logger-heads in Central America and the Caribbean, and the foreign debt was a burning issue for the region.

261   **The world economic and social crisis: its impact on the**
       underdeveloped countries, its somber prospects and the need to
       struggle if we are to survive.
       Fidel Castro Ruz.   Havana: Publishing Office of the Council of State,
       1983. 224p. bibliog.

Reproduces the report made to the Seventh Summit Conference of the Movement of Non-Aligned Countries held in Delhi in 1983, by the then outgoing president of the movement, Fidel Castro. The report covers commodities and trade problems, monetary and financial questions, agriculture and food, industrialization and economic development, transnational corporations, the energy crisis, co-operation among and quality of life in underdeveloped countries, arms build-up and development. It ends with an action plan for what is described as one of the worst economic crises in world history.

62

Che Guevara

Studies

262 **Che Guevara en el presente de la América Latina.** (Che Guevara in present-day Latin America.)
Pedro Vuskovic, Belarmino Elqueta.   Havana: Casa de las Américas, 1987. 148p.

This winner of the 1987 Casa de las Américas award focuses on Ernesto Che Guevara's thought and life as a key influence in 1960s Cuba and the transition to socialism, and compares Cuba with Chile and Nicaragua.

263 **Che, el socialismo y el comunismo.** (Che, socialism and communism.)
Fernando Martínez Heredia.   Havana: Casa de las Américas, 1989. 185p. bibliog.

This study took the Ernesto Che Guevara special prize awarded by the Casa de las Américas in 1989. The author argues the relevance of Che's political thinking on socialism and communism as a way forward for Cuba.

264 **Con el Che por Sudamérica.** (With Che through South America.)
Alberto Granado.   Havana: Editorial Letras Cubanas, 1989. 265p.

A tale of Che Guevara's travels through South America in 1951 told by his travelling companion.

265 **The death of Che Guevara.**
Jay Cantor.   New York: Alfred A. Knopf, 1983. 578p.

A novel improvising and inventing the life and death of Ernesto Che Guevara. Part one opens in 1965 with Guevara on the Isle of Pines for a period of self-criticism, writing his autobiography before leaving for Bolivia. In Part two, it is his bodyguard who returns from Bolivia to complete the tale.

266 **Un hombre bravo.** (A brave man.)
Adys Cupull, Froilán González.   Havana: Editorial Capitán San Luis, [n.d.]. 416p.

The authors spent ten years investigating Che's life, during which time they set up schools of Che Guevara studies in the Universities of Santiago and Santa Clara, and undertook travels of their own to retrace the steps of the great man from Argentina through Cuba to Bolivia. A tribute to Che, the work is divided into five sections containing chronological entries of major events and writings, and includes facsimiles of original documents.

Biographies, Memoirs and Collected Writings. Che Guevara. Memoirs and writings

267 **Mi hijo el Che.** (My son Che.)
Ernesto Guevara Lynch. Havana: Editorial Arte y Literatura, 1988. 431p.

An anecdotal biography of Ernesto Che Guevara (Argentina, 1928-67), written by his father. It recounts Che's infancy, childhood, adolescence and young adulthood, and includes many early photographs.

Memoirs and writings

268 **The Bolivian diary of Ernesto Che Guevara.**
Ernesto Che Guevara, introduction by Mary-Alice Waters. London; New York: Pathfinder, 1995. 467p. maps.

Presents the day-by-day chronicle of the 1966-67 guerrilla struggle in Bolivia by one of the central leaders of the Cuban revolution and examines the campaign to forge a continent-wide revolutionary movement. This new edition introduces excerpts from the diaries and accounts of other participants in the Bolivian campaign, as well as documents written by Guevara in Bolivia, and a 1968 introduction by Fidel Castro.

269 **Che Guevara and the Cuban revolution, writings and speeches of Ernesto Che Guevara.**
Ernesto Guevara. Sydney: Pathfinder/Pacific & Asia, 1987. 413p.

One of the most complete English-language collections of Guevara's works, this volume includes articles and speeches on the Cuban revolutionary war and Cuba's efforts to develop the economy in the face of US hostility, forge a new social consciousness in a society building socialism, and support freedom struggles throughout the world. See also *Episodes of the Cuban revolutionary war 1956-58* by Ernesto Che Guevara, introduction by Mary-Alice Waters (New York: Pathfinder, 1996. 483p. 3 maps. illus.).

270 **Che: a memoir by Fidel Castro.**
Edited by David Deutschmann. Melbourne, Australia: Ocean Press, 1993. 165p.

Fidel Castro writes of his relationship with his comrade-in-arms and close political collaborator, in the early years of the Cuban revolution. The work includes a detailed account of their last days together in Cuba, as well as a frank assessment of Guevara's ill-fated Bolivian mission. A chronology and glossary are included, as are 24 pages of photographs.

271 **Che Guevara: a new society, reflections for today's world.**
Ernesto Che Guevara, edited by David Deutschmann. Melbourne, Australia: Ocean Press, 1991. 234p.

An anthology of Ernesto Guevara's speeches and writings on the political, economic and social process of the transition to socialism: from political sovereignty, economic planning and independence; through bureaucratism, culture and medicine; to his ideology of socialism and man in Cuba. The volume includes an introductory 1987 speech by Fidel Castro on the relevance of Che's ideas twenty years on.

272 **Che, sierra adentro.** (Che, in the mountains.)
Froilán Escobar, Félix Guerra. Havana: Editora Política, 1988. 366p.

A collection of reminiscences by former combatants revealing the character and exploits of Ernesto Che Guevara from the landing of the *Granma* in December 1956 to the invasion of central Cuba in 1958 led by Che and Camilo Cienfuegos.

273 **Guerrilla warfare.**
Ernesto Guevara. Harmondsworth, England: Penguin, 1969. 143p.

Guevara's classic writings on the guerrilla *foco* theory and guerrilla warfare are contained in this volume. In it Guevara evaluated and systematized the tactics which toppled the Batista dictatorship in Cuba in 1959. What has been described as 'the cold precision of Guevara's style' reportedly made this required reading for counter-insurgency experts as well as the Third World guerrillas who were the target audience.

274 **The motorcycle diaries: a journey around South America.**
Ernesto Che Guevara, translated by Ann Wright. London: Verso, 1995. 155p.

No attempt is made here to paint a hero's perfection, but rather the portrait of a young man from a middle-class Argentinian family developing a social conscience on a journey of revelation through Latin America. Written when he was twenty-three years old, these diaries reveal a sensitive, compassionate youth who identified with the poor and the downtrodden, although he makes some less than politically correct references in passing to homosexuals and blacks. See also *Roll over Che Guevara: travels of a radical reporter* by Marc Cooper (London: Verso, 1994. 291p.).

275 **Reminiscences of the Cuban revolutionary war.**
Ernesto Che Guevara. New York: Monthly Review Press, 1968. 287p.

A memoir detailing questions of guerrilla warfare tactics and organization, leadership and strategy, during the period of the Cuban revolutionary war of 1956-58 when Guevara was with the Cuban Rebel Army.

276 **Venceremos: the speeches and writings of Ernesto Che Guevara.**
Edited by John Gerassi. London: Weidenfeld & Nicholson, 1968. 606p.

Contains most of Guevara's speeches and writings from 1956 to 1967. They range from accounts of guerrilla combat to analyses of political and economic themes and include his farewell letter to Fidel Castro.

Encyclopedia of Latin American history and culture.
See item no. 108.

Félix Varela 1788-1853.
See item no. 142.

Félix Varela: su pensamiento político y su época. (Félix Varela: his political thinking and his times.)
See item no. 143.

Atlas histórico-biográfico José Martí. (Historico-biographical atlas of José Martí.)
See item no. 149.

José Martí, architect of Cuba's freedom.
See item no. 155.

José Martí, mentor of the Cuban nation.
See item no. 157.

José Martí, revolutionary democrat.
See item no. 158.

Camilo: señor de la vanguardia. (Camilo: lord of the vanguard.)
See item no. 180.

Antonio Maceo, apuntes para una historia de su vida. (Antonio Maceo: biographical notes.)
See item no. 358.

Antonio Maceo: the 'bronze titan' of Cuba's struggle for independence.
See item no. 359.

Cuba's freedom fighter, Antonio Maceo: 1845-1996.
See item no. 360.

Guillermo Sardiñas: el sacerdote comandante, testimonio. (Guillermo Sardiñas: the priest-commander, testimony.)
See item no. 438.

Cuba's internationalist foreign policy, 1975-80.
See item no. 585.

Alfredo López: maestro del proletariado cubano. (Alfredo López: master of the Cuban proletariat.)
See item no. 785.

Esbozo biográfico de Jesús Menéndez. (Biographical sketch of Jesús Menéndez.)
See item no. 793.

Who's who in Latin America: part VII, Cuba, Dominican Republic and Haiti.
See item no. 1141.

Island Population

Demography

277 Age structure, fertility swings and socioeconomic development in Cuba.
Sergio Díaz-Briquets. In: *Socialist Cuba: past interpretations and future challenges.* Edited by Sergio Roca. Boulder, Colorado: Westview, 1988, p. 159-74.

This analysis of Cuban demographic patterns and projections to the year 2025 is presented in comparative perspective, with the United States, Argentina and Colombia. Thus, the boom 1960s and bust 1970s and 1980s Cuban cycle is compared with the post-Second World War cycle in the United States. The author highlights the resulting demographic strains and resource needs, including issues such as rising 1980s crime rates among an increasing cohort of young male adults.

278 Cuban population estimates, 1953-1970.
Lowry Nelson. *Journal of Inter-American Studies and World Affairs*, vol. 12, no. 3 (July 1970), p. 392-400.

Discusses Cuban population growth, emphasizing fertility and emigration as they affect demographic trends.

279 Densidad de población y urbanización. (Density of population and urbanization.)
Junta Central de Planificación (Central Planning Board). Havana: Instituto Cubano del Libro, 1975. 85p.

Uses the results of the 1970 census to contrast urban and rural population densities, making comparisons with earlier censuses and projecting future growth. A second section compares historical urbanization trends and provides data on growth rates, the size of urban centres and planned developments.

280 **La fecundidad en Cuba.** (Fertility in Cuba.)
Luisa Álvarez Vázquez. Havana: Ciencias Sociales, 1985. 183p.

In this study the demography of Cuba is explored through fertility, in its biological and social aspects, notably standard of living and occupation. An initial section evaluates the reliability of available demographic studies and statistics and takes a historical overview of fertility up to the 1959 revolution and the decade of the 1960s. The author then looks at the 1970s in detail, before proceeding to outline future projections and policy implications.

281 **La población de Cuba.** (The Cuban population.)
Centro de Estudios Demográficos. Havana: Ciencias Sociales, 1976. 236p. maps.

A comprehensive work dealing with major demographic trends, including population growth, fertility, mortality, internal migration and foreign immigration, labour force characteristics, race, and population projections. Intended principally for the general reader, this work is one of the most complete studies available on Cuban demography, although it is now dated.

282 **The population of Cuba: the growth and characteristics of its labour force.**
Lisandro Pérez. *Columbia Journal of World Business*, vol. 30, no. 1 (spring 1995), p. 58-65.

Analyses Cuba's demographic profile, emphasizing the characteristics of its labour force that can be expected to influence dynamic change. Pérez concludes that the labour force is likely to be a positive factor as a market economy emerges, given its low dependency ratio, high level of education and the value placed on entrepreneurship.

283 **La revolución demográfica en Cuba.** (The demographic revolution in Cuba.)
Raúl Hernández Castellón. Havana: Ciencias Sociales, 1988. 219p.

Contains a wealth of facts and figures on Cuban demography, in the context of the theory of demographic revolution.

Spanish

284 **Guerra, migración y muerte (el ejército español en Cuba como vía migratoria).** (War, migration and death [the Spanish army in Cuba as a means of migration].)
Manuel R. Moreno Fraginals, José J. Moreno Masó. Barcelona, Spain: Ediciones Jucar, 1992. 162p. bibliog.

Abundant archives on the Spanish army and colonial wars testify to the existence of emigrant soldiers in Cuba, to the extent that the island, like Puerto Rico, was virtually planned on a military basis. Throughout the 17th and 18th centuries, more soldiers than civilians left Spain for Cuba, and in the 19th century, there were over 600,000. This book explores the war- and peace-time lives of these soldiers, from their involvement in Cuba's sugar boom to their relations with white, black and mulatto city women, and their creole offspring.

285 **Nación e inmigración: los españoles en Cuba (ss. XIX y XX).** (Nation and immigration: the Spanish in Cuba [19th and 20th centuries].)
Jordi Maluquer de Motes. Barcelona, Spain: Ediciones Jucar, 1992. 190p. bibliog.

A well-researched statistical and interpretative analysis of two centuries of Spanish immigration into Cuba, during the 19th century when it was a Spanish colony and after its independence from Spain in the 20th century. Painstaking archival work in Spain, Cuba and Puerto Rico, as well as secondary source material, forms the basis of a regional breakdown of the origins and destination of migrants, their occupations and their characteristics as a group.

286 **Las remesas de los emigrantes españoles en América: siglos XIX y XX.** (Remittances of Spanish emigrants in the Americas: 19th and 20th centuries.)
José Ramón García López. Barcelona, Spain: Ediciones Jucar, 1992. 211p. bibliog.

Based on banking, business, personal, legal and official documentation, this study provides a well-researched overview of the extent and nature of remittances sent back to Spain from émigrés in the Americas. In this, émigrés in Cuba played a substantial role.

African

287 **El barracón y otros ensayos.** (The slave yard and other essays.)
Juan Pérez de la Riva. Havana: Ciencias Sociales, 1975. 529p.

This is a landmark demographic analysis of the component parts of Cuba's population over a period of time: Spanish and French-Haitian settler migration; forced migration of African slaves; 19th-century Chinese indentured labourers; and 20th-century Caribbean seasonal workers. Also included are classic interpretative essays treating the island with two histories (Cuba east and west), population and development, the reliability of demographic statistics, Havana and Pinar del Río.

288 **Blacks in colonial Cuba, 1774-1899.**
Kenneth F. Kiple. Gainesville, Florida: University Press of Florida, 1976. 115p. bibliog.

Constitutes a detailed compilation of census data on blacks, both free and slave, including many tables from the main population censuses taken between 1774 and 1899.

Caribbean

289 **Azúcar e inmigración 1900-1940.** (Sugar and immigration 1900-40.)
Rolando Álvarez Estévez. Havana: Ciencias Sociales, 1988. 290p. bibliog.

Based on documentary and testimonial sources, this account goes beyond a 'shortage of labour' explanation for the influx of Caribbeans, especially Jamaican and Haitians, brought in to work the eastern US-owned sugar plantations of 20th-century Cuba. It looks at the context of Cubans' resistance to work on the plantations; establishment economics and ideology of the insertion of Caribbean labour; and the struggles associated with seasonality, discrimination and ultimately deportation.

290 **Caidije.**
Jesús Guanche, Dennis Moreno. Santiago de Cuba: Editorial Oriente, 1988. 139p. bibliog.

In 1976 a study was made of a small settlement of Haitian immigrant sugar workers in Minas municipality, Camagüey province. This account of the study begins with a general overview of economic migration in the first three decades of this century. It then describes the project's findings relating to the material culture and spiritual and social life of the immigrant canecutters in the 1920s and 1930s.

291 **Jamaican migrants and the Cuban sugar industry, 1900-1934.**
Franklin W. Knight. In: *Between slavery and free labor: the Spanish-speaking Caribbean in the nineteenth century*. Edited by Manuel Moreno Fraginals, Frank Moya Pons, Stanley L. Engerman. Baltimore, Maryland: Johns Hopkins University Press, 1985, p. 94-114.

An estimated 35,000 Caribbean seasonal migrant workers were brought to work on the US-owned sugar plantations in eastern Cuba in the early years of this century. This article charts the patterns of outmigration from Jamaica and examines the characteristics of the migrants. It also provides biographies of three Jamaican 'survivors' of the 1920s community, and assesses the impact of the migration.

292 **A note on Haitian migration to Cuba, 1890-1934.**
Mats Lundahl. *Cuban Studies*, vol. 12, no. 2 (July 1982), p. 21-36.

A useful introductory article examining the relationship between economic and domestic pressures in Haiti and patterns of Haitian worker migration to Cuba.

Other

293 **Chinese contract labour in Cuba, 1847-1874.**
Mary Turner. *Caribbean Studies*, vol. 14, no. 2 (July 1974), p. 66-81.

Drawing heavily on demographic data, this article examines the introduction of Chinese indentured labour in mid-19th century Cuba.

294 **The Dutch and Cuba, 1609-1643.**
Irene A. Wright. *Hispanic American Historical Review*, vol. 9 (Nov. 1921), p. 547-634.

Examines the impact of Dutch corsairs and traders on Cuba.

295 **French colonization in Cuba, 1791-1809.**
William R. Lux. *The Americas*, no. 29 (July 1972), p. 57-61.

Lux presents an overview of the French contribution to Cuba after the Haitian revolution of 1791-1804.

296 **Idéologie et ethnicité: les Chinois Macao à Cuba, 1847-1886.**
(Ideology and ethnicity: the Macao Chinese in Cuba, 1847-86.)
Denise Helly. Montreal, Canada: Les Presses de l'Université de Montréal, 1979. 345p. bibliog.

This is a detailed study of Chinese indentureship in Cuba, with particular reference to sugar production and slavery.

297 **A study of the Chinese in Cuba, 1847-1947.**
Duvon C. Corbitt. Wilmore, Kentucky: Ashbury College Press, 1971.
142p. bibliog.

A monograph tracing the history of the Chinese in Cuba, from the indentured labourers of the mid-19th century to successful 20th-century merchants and professionals.

298 **Tropical diaspora: the Jewish experience in Cuba.**
Robert M. Levine. Gainesville, Florida: University Press of Florida, 1993. 416p.

The author traces the 20th-century passage of several thousand Jewish people through Cuba and charts the arrival of Sephardic and Ashkenazi Jews, from the beginning of the century to the 1930s. On their way to the United States, many nonetheless integrated into social clubs and some became prominent radical political activists; anti-semitic feeling never really took root and the community numbered some 4,000. The second wave of war refugees from Hitler were often looked down on by earlier settlers who were Spanish-speaking and well on their way to becoming middle class. The new arrivals assimilated less and moved on, leaving an older Jewish community that intermarried and integrated. With the revolution, there was an exodus of ninety-five per cent of the Jews to the United States and Israel, leaving other prominent Jewish communists to join the Castro government.

Un canario en Cuba. (A Canary Islander in Cuba.)
See item no. 54.

Azúcar y población en las Antillas. (Sugar and population in the Caribbean.)
See item no. 751.

Overseas Population

United States: pre-1959

299   Afro-Cubans in exile: Tampa, Florida, 1886-1984.
Susan D. Greenbaum.   *Cuban Studies*, vol. 15, no. 1 (winter 1985),
p. 59-72.

One of the few studies to deal with the emigration of black Cubans to the United
States, this article raises important broader questions of both a historical and
contemporary nature. It charts the history of Afro-Cubans in the segregationist US
South of the 1900s, and describes the forming of the Martí-Maceo Union, which is
still in existence.

**300   The Cuban experience in the United States, 1865-1940: migration,
community, and identity.**
Gerald E. Poyo.   *Cuban Studies*, vol. 21 (1991), p. 19-36.

This article provides a rare overview of the Cuban experience in the United States
from the mid-19th to the mid-20th centuries. Poyo charts their history from émigré
communities to immigrant centres with a Cuban-American identity.

301   La emigración cubana en Estados Unidos, 1868-1878. (The Cuban
emigration to the United States, 1868-1878.)
Rolando Álvarez Estévez.   Havana: Ciencias Sociales, 1986. 168p.
bibliog.

Traces the emergence and growth of US-Cuban émigrés during Cuba's first war of
independence, focusing on the social origins of the various communities, their
contribution to the independence struggle, and their dispersal at the end of the war.

302 **Key West: cigar city U.S.A.**
L. Glenn Westfall.   Key West, Florida: Historic Key West
Preservation Board, 1984. 72p.

On rare occasions historians can make an impact on a locality. One such historian is
Westfall, who restored to Key West its Havana cigar past. Beautifully illustrated with
fine cigar labels, as well as views and personalities of the key's Cuban heyday, the
book traces the 1870s to 1930s growth and decline of the cigar and Cuban presence in
the area. It was a period interspersed with the political turbulence of Cuban
nationalism and labour unrest and natural disaster in the form of fire and hurricane.

303 **Tampa Bay History – a centennial history of Ybor City.**
Tampa Bay History, vol. 7, no. 2 (fall/winter 1985). 175p. special
issue.

A special issue of the *Tampa Bay History*, this was published for the centenary of the
founding of Ybor City in Florida, as a town in its own right based on the Cuban cigar
industry. Though quickly incorporated into Tampa, the immigrant Cuban community
which formed its population long remained a city within a city. Florida-based scholars
chart the early history of Ybor City and its Cuban migrants, drawing on archival
material and on personal recollections of Ybor City residents. Articles cover local
entrepreneurs, immigrant co-operative societies, cigar worker struggles, cigar label
art, and include documentation on Afro-Cubans as well as reminiscences of a cigar
reader and baseball player.

304 **With all, and for the good of all: the emergence of popular
nationalism in the Cuban communities of the United States,
1848-1989.**
Gerald E. Poyo.   Durham, England; London: Duke University Press,
1989. 182p. bibliog.

This meticulously researched study brings together a wealth of original material on the
history of the exile Cuban communities in the United States, raising key questions as
to the scope and nature of Cuban nationalism abroad. It traces the long-standing roots
and traditions of Cubans in the USA, especially the more radical popular nationalism
among Florida's 19th-century Cuban émigré tobacco communities. The study also
discusses the fears and divisions which feed reformism, separatism, liberalism,
annexationism, abolitionism, anarchism, socialism, militarism and incipient nationhood. It deals with José Martí, founder of the Cuban Revolutionary Party, whose skills
as a nationalist orator and organizer enabled him to address issues of social change
within the independence ideal, and thereby tap the community's great diversity. The
account ends as Martí's vision is truncated by US occupation and involvement in the
economy and polity of the nascent Cuban Republic.

United States: post-1959

305 La aculturación de la comunidad cubana en los Estados Unidos.
(The acculturation of the Cuban community in the United States.)
Juan Valdés Paz. *Cuadernos de Nuestra América*, vol. 4, no. 7
(Jan.-June 1987), p. 160-218.
A Cuban reading of secondary studies conducted in the United States, outlining the
process of acculturation of the Cuban-American community.

306 The Americans: Latin American and Caribbean peoples in the United States.
Rubén Rumbault. In: *Americas: new interpretative essays.*
Edited by Alfred Stepan. Oxford: Oxford University Press, 1992,
p. 273-307.
Situates the notable Cuban presence in the United States, from the 19th century to the
present, in the context of histories and patterns of settlement of peoples from Latin
America and the Caribbean, differentiating in terms of class, occupation and language.

307 The assimilation of Cuban exiles.
Eleanor Rogg. New York: Aberdeen Press, 1974. 241p. bibliog.
Approximately one-tenth of Cuban immigrant household heads were surveyed in 1968
for this study of Cuban exiles' 1960s cultural adjustment and assimilation in West
New York, New Jersey. The study, which includes statistical tables and copies of the
questionnaires, provides useful comparison with other studies conducted in Miami and
Indianapolis.

308 City on the edge: the transformation of Miami.
Alejandro Portes, Alex Stepick. Berkeley, California: University of
California Press, 1993. 281p. map. bibliog.
An analysis of the urban sociology and political economy behind the transformation of
Miami from an anglo backwater and tourist-retirement land into the nation's Cuban-
American dominated, intensely immigrant, and significantly Spanish-speaking, world
city. Based on a wealth of historical documentation, surveys, interviews, press
accounts and original research, the study reconstructs the story of the rich Cuban
émigrés of the 1960s who built a prosperous 1970s enclave, into which successive
waves of 1980s Cuban, Nicaraguan and Haitian refugees flooded, pushing out native
African-Americans and a shrinking anglo population. In the embittered clash of
politics, race, culture, class and language, Miami is depicted as a city on the edge of
the future, for good and ill.

309 **Contra viento y marea: jóvenes cubanos hablan desde su exilio en Estados Unidos.** (Against all odds: young Cubans talk from exile in the United States.)
Grupo Areíto.   Havana: Casa de las Américas, 1978. 258p;
Mexico City: Siglo XXI, 1978. 185p.

A landmark in its time, this book is based on fifty testimonies of young Cuban Americans returning to Cuba and reflecting upon their own radicalization. It shows the disenchantment and alienation of double exile and torn loyalties.

310 **Cuban Americans: masters of survival.**
José Llanes.   Cambridge, Massachusetts: Abt Books, 1982. 229p.

The author created fifty-eight composite characters out of interviews with Cuban-Americans of the post-1959, pre-1980, Mariel waves of exiles, and linked narrative in their own words, to provide an 'insider' account of the exile experience.

311 **Cubans in exile: disaffection and revolution.**
Richard R. Fagen, Richard M. Brody, Thomas J. O'Leary.   Stanford, California: Stanford University Press, 1968. 161p.

A survey of the early post-revolutionary Cuban migration of 1959 and the early 1960s, focusing on social origin, professional background, racial composition and income.

312 **The exile: Cuba in the heart of Miami.**
David Rieff.   London: Vintage Books, 1994. 2nd ed. 220p.

Centred on the experiences of a well-to-do Cuban-born couple who left the island before 1970, and their first-generation American son, this books provides some interesting insights into a group of immigrants who rejected assimilation and succeeded in imposing their culture and mores on the city that took them in. It tends to be repetitive and anecdotal rather than analytical, and no epilogue was added after the 1992 edition to take account of the the emerging dialogue between Cubans on the island and abroad.

313 **Miami.**
Joan Didion.   New York: Simon & Schuster, 1988. 2nd ed. 238p.

Didion presents a prose journey through the complex and dramatic reality of Cuban Florida and Miami, the prosperous 'second city' of Cuban exiles. She guides the reader through stories of 'guerrilla discount' hotels and Father's Day specials at gun shops, depicting a disturbing world of money-making, drugs and arms running. The end-product is a portrait of the underlying violence and charge of a city of extremes of wealth and a clash of cultures: white anglo, black, and Hispanic Cuban.

314 **Retrato del Mariel: el ángulo socioeconómico.** (Portrait of Mariel: the socio-economic angle.)
Rafael Hernández, Redi Gomis.   *Cuadernos de Nuestra América*, vol. 3, no. 5 (Jan.-June 1986), p. 124-51.

Analyses the socio-economic profile of the Cubans who left the island for the USA in the 1980 Mariel boatlift. The authors find that the group consisted of considerable anti-social elements for whom the US consumer market was a significant point of attraction.

315 **US Cuban policy and the Cuban community question.**
Rafael Hernández. *Line of March*, no. 18 (fall 1985), p. 9-27.

A special issue of papers from a 1984 Havana seminar on US minority communities included this study of the Cuban situation, written after the 1980 Mariel exodus, which created a new setback in the growing relations between islanders and the émigré community. The paper provides a retrospective rundown of US–Cuban relations and the immigration cycle, in the context of blockade, national security, ideological warfare, human rights and terrorism.

316 **With open arms: Cuban migration to the United States.**
Féliz Roberto Masud-Piloto.   Totowa, New Jersey: Rowman & Littlefield, 1988. 148p. bibliog.

An exceptional study of the Cuban migration experience since 1959 from a historian's perspective, this includes an initial chapter on the history of migration before 1959.

317 **World cities in the Caribbean: the rise of Miami and San Juan.**
Ramón Grosfoguel.   *Review*, vol. 17, no. 3 (summer 1994), p. 351-81.

Grosfoguel takes a world systems approach to urbanization in the Caribbean, in the context of global logics of world cities, and applies this to San Juan and Miami which he sees as symbolic showcases of US Cold War politics. The article charts the capital flowing into the two cities in the post-1973 capitalist restructuring, and in each case highlights the Cuban connection. The author builds on previous work demonstrating the very favourable geopolitical environment in which Cubans found themselves in the United States, as opposed to other immigrant groups, contrasting especially with the Haitian experience.

Other

318 **La colonia cubana de París 1895-1898.** (The Cuban community in Paris 1895-1898.)
Paul Estrade.   Havana: Ciencias Sociales, 1984. 383p.

Based on archival sources in Paris, Madrid and Havana, as well as oral testimony, this account delves into the world of the Cuban community in France at the time of Cuba's second war of independence. It highlights the work of Ramón Betances, Vicente Mestre Amábile and Domingo Figarola-Caneda, in addition to the political manoeuvrings of the French bourgeoisie and popular support in France for Cuba's independence.

319 **Cuba y la defensa de la república española (1936-1939).** (Cuba and
the defence of the Spanish Republic [1936-1939].)
Instituto de Historia del Movimiento Comunista y de la Revolución
Socialista de Cuba. Havana: Editora Política, 1981. 303p. maps.
bibliog.

Documents Cuban solidarity with the anti-fascist struggle in Spain in the form of the
oral testimony of those involved and through available documentation. Compiled by a
team of researchers under Ramón Nicolau González, a leading protagonist in the then
clandestine Cuban Communist Party, the volume comprises forty-six testimonial
accounts, twenty documents, a list of known Cuban fighters (those killed in action and
those who lived to tell their story) and photographs of the protagonists in action in
Spain.

320 **Los cubanos en Puerto Rico: economía étnica e identidad cultural.**
(Cubans in Puerto Rico: ethnic economy and cultural identity.)
José Cobas, Jorge Duany. San Juan, Puerto Rico: University of
Puerto Rico Press, 1995. 252p. bibliog.

This book looks at how Cuban immigrants adapted to life in Puerto Rico by
specializing in small-scale retailing and professional services. The authors categorize
the Cuban community in Puerto Rico as a typical 'intermediate group' on a par with
the Jews in Western Europe or the Chinese in Southeast Asia. Their economic
experience, argue the authors, has heavily influenced their cultural identity and social
relations, though cultural and linguistic similarities between the immigrants and their
hosts have helped soften possible social isolation and ethnic persecution.

321 **Los que volvieron a África.** (Back to Africa.)
Rodolfo Sarracino. Havana: Ciencias Sociales, 1988. 269p. bibliog.

Taking up the story in the 1840s, when slavery was widespread, and carrying it as far
as the 1980s and the Angola War, the author reconstructs a moving, personal account
of two sides of a family history, on the basis of interviews, correspondence and other
documentary evidence provided by present-day family members living in Lagos,
Nigeria, and Matanzas, Cuba. The two sides of the family know of each other only
through photographs and letters, which are full of the simple, intimate details that
people tend to write in letters all over the world. Theirs is a family divided by events
of epic proportions, and the account raises important questions about the 19th-century
return to Africa movement and the historical roots of Cuba's involvement in the
continent.

**Neither golden exile nor dirty worm: ethnic identity in recent Cuban-
American novels.**
See item no. 869.

Bibliography for the Mariel-Cuban diaspora.
See item no. 1155.

**Cubans in the United States: a bibliography for research in the social
and behavioral sciences, 1960-1983.**
See item no. 1156.

Slavery and Race

General history and culture

322 The African presence in Cuban culture.
Miguel Barnet, foreword by Antoni Kapcia.   Coventry, England:
University of Warwick, 1986. 16p.

Given as the Second Walter Rodney Memorial Lecture at the University, this presents
a brief overview of the African ethnic groups that were taken to Cuba, especially the
Bantu, Yoruba and Carabalí, and of the development of a powerful Afro-Cuban
culture of resistance in the face of slavery and the colonial plantation system. The
tradition of struggle, belief systems and *cabildos* all contributed to a national identity
comprising African and Spanish elements, and Cuba as an Afro-Latin people.

323 Afro-Cuba: an anthology of Cuban writing on race, politics and culture.
Edited and introduced by Pedro Pérez Sarduy, Jean Stubbs.
Melbourne, Australia: Ocean Press; London: Latin America Bureau,
1993. 309p. bibliog.

This is the only anthology available to the non-Spanish-speaking reader on the black
experience in Cuba through the eyes of the island's writers, scholars and artists. The
articles, mostly written since the 1959 revolution, have been translated from the
Spanish to provide a multi-faceted introduction to the complexities of Cuba's ethnic
history and present, by mixing poetry, fiction, political analysis and anthropology. The
introduction by the authors provides an overview and calls for an ongoing assessment
of race in Cuba.

324 Castro, the blacks and Africa.
Carlos Moore.   Los Angeles: University of California Press, 1989. 476p.

A black Cuban émigré imparts his vision of the revolution as essentially a victory of
the anti-imperialist segment of the white middle class and black Cubans' retreat from
political struggle. Black Cubans were then seduced by Castro's benevolent messianic

leadership without any real race redemption occurring and were recruited for sensitive operations, not least in Africa, to shore up Cuban internationalism. The work culminates with an identification of the common features of Cuba and (apartheid) South Africa, in terms of their isolation and white minority rule in the face of growing black majority demands. Revolutionary Cuba is depicted as both negrophile and negrophobic, and Fidel Castro as a manipulator of race for his personal aggrandizement.

325   **Cómo surgió la cultura nacional.** (The birth of a national culture.)
      Walterio Carbonell.   Havana: Ediciones Yaka, 1961. 131p.
This discussion of the origins of Cuban culture pays particular attention to the Afro-Cuban elements and their influence on the developing nation.

326   **Cuba.**
      Gail McGarrity, Osvaldo Cárdenas.   In: *No longer invisible:*
      Afro-Latin Americans today.   Edited by Minority Rights Group.
      London: Minority Rights Publications, 1995, p. 77-108.
McGarrity and Cárdenas cover Cuba in an anthology which provides a unique country-by-country panorama of Afro-Latin Americans. The authors offer a perceptive overview of modern race history in Cuba, from the late 19th-century rise of the nation, through race relations in the 20th century in pre- and post-revolutionary times. They argue that awareness of race as an issue of major historical and contemporary significance has been suppressed and denied, and highlight the need to monitor the increasing racism of the 1990s.

327   **Flash of the spirit: African & Afro-American art and philosophy.**
      Robert Farris Thompson.   New York: Vintage Books, 1984. 2nd ed.
      317p.
This major work demonstrates how five African civilizations – Yoruba, Kongo, Ejagham, Mande and Cross River – have shaped the aesthetic and social traditions of black people in the Americas. The author, an art historian, demonstrates how this influence can be seen in anthropology, musicology, religion and philosophy, and deals in detail with the Yoruba and Congo influences in Cuba.

The slavery period

328   **Between slavery and free labor: the Spanish speaking Caribbean in**
      the nineteenth century.
      Edited by Manuel Moreno Fraginals, Frank Moya Pons, Stanley L.
      Engerman.   Baltimore, Maryland: Johns Hopkins University Press,
      1985. 292p. maps.
This volume is based on papers presented at the conference on The Problems of Transition from Slavery to Free Labor in the Caribbean, which was held at the Museo

del Hombre Dominicano in Santo Domingo in June 1981. It contains an introductory overview by the editor to the plantations in Cuba, Puerto Rico and the Dominican Republic in the late 19th century. This is followed by four chapters on Cuba: Rebecca Scott on adaptation and challenge in slave society, 1860-86; Fe Iglesias on the development of capitalism in sugar prodution, 1860-1900; Francisco López Segrera on dependency, plantation and social class, 1762-1900; and Franklin Knight on Jamaican migrants in the Cuban sugar industry, 1900-1934.

329 **Burguesía esclavista y abolición.** (The slaveholding bourgeoisie and abolition.)
    María del Carmen Barcia.   Havana: Ciencias Sociales, 1987. 229p.
A Marxist-Leninist history of the Cuban slaveholding class and of the abolition of slavery. The basic thesis posited is that the abolition process and the attitudes of the slaveholding class were coincidental with, and thereby conditioned by, the late development of the plantation system in Cuba. In this, there was a fundamental growing contradiction between the Spanish metropolis, lagging behind its colony in economic development, and Cuba's main US market. Chapters in the book cover theory and analysis, sugar development in 1840-80, the crisis of the slave plantation, and slaveholder positions on the abolition of slavery.

330 **Los cimarrones de Cuba.** (Cuban maroons.)
    Gabino La Rosa Corzo.   Havana: Ciencias Sociales, 1988. 205p.
    bibliog.
A quantitative and qualitative history based on primary sources on maroonage in 19th-century Cuba. Periodization, geographical and gender distribution, repression and the effects of maroonage on the colony are all covered in this study.

331 **Comercio clandestino de esclavos.** (The secret slave trade.)
    José Luciano Franco.   Havana: Ciencias Sociales, 1980. Reprinted, 1985. 400p.
This is a scholarly account, written by one of Cuba's most prolific black historians of slavery and race. The author focuses especially on the clandestine continuation of the trade after it had been internationally prohibited during the early 19th century.

332 **Contribución a la historia de la gente sin historia.** (Contribution to the history of the people with no history.)
    Pedro Deschamps Chapeaux, Juan Pérez de la Riva.   Havana: Ciencias Sociales, 1974. 283p.
The essays reprinted in this important collection were written by a leading black historian and a historical demographer and were originally published in the 1960s. They reflect important historiographical advances on the lives of those people hitherto hidden from 19th-century Cuban history and describe the situation of: the black undertaker, tailor, stevedore, dentist and midwife; urban runaways; African returnee slaves, indentured Chinese labour and the clandestine slave trade. Deschamps Chapeaux in particular builds on previous work on ordinary blacks in the 19th-century economy and journalism.

333   **Cuban palenques.** (Cuban runaway slave communities.)
       Francisco Pérez de la Riva. In: *Maroon societies: rebel slave*
       communities in the Americas. Edited by Richard Price. Baltimore,
       Maryland: Johns Hopkins University Press, 1979, p. 49-59.

An extract from a 1952 Spanish-language publication by a Cuban historian, this
account contains a description of maroon settlements in western and eastern Cuba,
their spatial layout and political organization. Other chapters in the same volume may
also be of interest: 'Maroons and slave rebellions in the Spanish territories' by José
Luciano Franco (p. 35-48); and 'Hunting the maroons with dogs in Cuba' by
Demoticus Philalethes (p. 60-73).

334   **The Cuban slave market, 1790-1880.**
       Laird W. Bergad, Fe Iglesias García, María del Carmen Barcia.
       Chapel Hill, North Carolina: University of North Carolina Press, 1995.
       245p. bibliog.

Bergad, a US historian of Cuba, and Iglesias and Barcia, both Cuban historians, joined
forces to produce this monumental analysis of statistical data, which has been painstakingly culled from Cuban slave archives. The work, which offers a detailed study of
the Cuban slave market, begins with an introductory chapter on prices and the
historiography of slavery. Subsequent chapters cover: the sources and methods of data
collection; the development of African slavery and Cuban economic history; the price
structure of the Cuban slave market; regional variations in Havana, Santiago and
Cienfuegos; and manumission and letters of freedom. The study, which concludes
with a section on comparative perspectives, points to the sensitivity of the slave
market to short-term economic and political variables.

335   **La esclavitud en Cuba.** (Slavery in Cuba.)
       Instituto de Ciencias Históricas. Havana: Editorial Academia, 1986.
       279p. bibliog.

Articles by Cuban historians are brought together in this volume to mark the centenary
of abolition in Cuba. José Luciano Franco writes on the slave trade, Rafael López
Valdés on a periodization of slavery, Fe Iglesias on abolition, Gabino la Rosa on
maroon settlements and Gloria García on slave markets. There is also an evaluation of
archaeological, bibliographical and documentary sources for the study of slavery and
abolition. See also: *A history of slavery in Cuba* by Hubert H. S. Aimes (New York:
Octagon Books, 1967. 298p. bibliog.).

336   **Esclavitud y sociedad: notas y documentos para la historia de la**
       esclavitud en Cuba. (Slavery and society: notes and documents on the
       history of slavery in Cuba.)
       Eusebio Torres-Cuevas, Eusebio Reyes Fernández. Havana: Ciencias
       Sociales, 1986. 274p. bibliog.

Traces the history of slavery in Cuba from the 16th century and Fray Bartolomé de
Las Casas, through the laws of the Indies and the Church, as a backdrop to a detailed
study of 19th-century plantation slavery, a product of capitalist Europe. The study
looks at the radical change in slavery as a mode of production, pro- and anti-slavery
ideas, the crisis of the slaveholding society, and the links between the struggles for
abolition and independence from Spain.

337 **Inglaterra: sus dos caras en la lucha cubana por la abolición.**
(England's two faces in the Cuban struggle for abolition.)
Rodolfo Sarracino.   Havana: Editorial Letras Cubanas, 1989. 224p.
bibliog.

Based on archival sources in the Havana National Archive and National Library and in
the London Public Record Office, the author reveals the dual role played by the British
government in relation to the abolition of slavery in Cuba and interference in
conspiracies on the island.

338 **El negro en la sociedad colonial.** (The black man in colonial society.)
Rafael Duharte Jiménez.   Santiago de Cuba: Editorial Oriente, 1988.
142p.

A study of slavery, runaways and abolition in urban Cuba, with a separate section
focusing on Santiago de Cuba, by a leading contemporary Santiago historian. The
author raises important questions regarding both the considerable scope for, and
limitations placed on, the economic and social mobility of blacks in colonial Cuba.

339 **Odious commerce: Britain, Spain and the abolition of the Cuban
slave trade.**
David Murray.   Cambridge, England: Cambridge University Press,
1980. 423p. bibliog.

Murray provides a well-documented, detailed account of the slave trade in Cuba from
1762 to its suppression in the 1860s. The study builds on the author's earlier work on
the British abolitionists in Cuba, 1833-45. See also: *Spain and the abolition of slavery
in Cuba, 1817-1886* by Arthur F. Corwin (Austin, Texas: University of Texas Press,
1967. 373p. bibliog.).

340 **The overthrow of colonial slavery 1776-1848.**
Robin Blackburn.   London; New York: Verso, 1988. 560p.

Perceptive and informative passages on Cuba, especially the abolitionist impasse, are
contained in this general work on the overthrow of slavery in North America, the
Caribbean and Latin America.

341 **Slave emancipation in Cuba.**
Rebecca Scott.   Princeton, New Jersey: Princeton University Press,
1985. 319p. maps. bibliog.

A pioneering study focusing on the slaves' own contribution to the end of slavery in
Cuba. Using Cuban archival sources, the author examines the process of emancipation
through individual estates and how individual slaves put pressure on slaveholders for
their freedom.

342 **Slave society in Cuba during the nineteenth century.**
Franklin W. Knight.   Madison, Wisconsin: University of Wisconsin
Press, 1970. 228p. maps. bibliog.

Special reference is made to sugar, politics, culture and economic development in this
socio-economic study of the rise and decline of the Cuban slave system.

343 **Slavery in the Americas: a comparative study of Cuba and Virginia.**
Herbert S. Klein. Chicago, Illinois: University of Chicago Press, 1967. 270p.

A comparative study of slavery in the two societies, with an emphasis on the legal system, education, religion, government and status of free coloureds.

344 **Social aspects of Cuban nationalism: race, slavery and the Guerra Chiquita, 1879-1880.**
Ada Ferrer. *Cuban Studies*, no. 21 (1991), p. 37-56.

This article documents the various forms of participation among Afro-Cubans and slaves in the 1879-80 War, and examines reactions to it among the white separatist leadership and the Spanish and Cuban opposition. Ferrer argues that the significant presence of people of colour as leaders and supporters of insurgency and the withdrawal of white sectors heralded the transformation of a nationalist political struggle into a broader movement for social change.

345 **Social control in slave plantation societies: a comparison of St. Domingue and Cuba.**
Gwendolyn Midlo Hall. Baltimore, Maryland: Johns Hopkins University Press, 1971. 166p. bibliog.

Slave policy in the Dominican Republic and Cuba and its effect on society is examined in this monograph in relation to religion, education, law, manumission, and racism as a form of ideological control.

346 **The Spanish colonial government's responses to the pan-nationalist agenda of the Afro-Cuban mutual aid societies, 1868-1895.**
Philip A. Howard. *Revista/Review Interamericana*, vol. 22, nos. 1-2 (1992), p. 151-67.

Bringing to light new documentation from Cuba and Spain on the flourishing Afro-Cuban *cabildos*, or mutual aid societies in cities of Cuba, Howard examines their response to war, and subsequent transformation from African-nation to Pan-Afro-Cuban associations.

347 **Sugar is made with blood: the conspiracy of La Escalera and the conflict between empires over slaves.**
Robert L. Paquette. Middletown, Connecticut: Wesleyan University Press, 1988. 346p.

A vivid and controversial history of the 1844 conspiracy against slavery in Cuba, in the context of a clash of the Spanish and British empires. Drawing on new archival sources, the author questions received wisdom about key figures such as Turnbull and Plácido. The study unravels layers of history, and yet ultimately leaves us with much the same enigma: was the 1844 Ladder Conspiracy real or fantasy? Whatever the answer, the fact remains that it supplied the Spanish colonial government with ammunition enough to massacre the burgeoning black bourgeois and petit-bourgeois classes, as well as rebel slaves.

348 **Temas acerca de la esclavitud.** (Writings on slavery.)
Havana: Ciencias Sociales, 1988. 288p.

A group of both established and young historians worked under the auspices of the Cuban Academy of Sciences to produce a volume commemorating the centenary of abolition. This covered the slave system itself and sources and methods for the study of slavery.

Republic and revolution

349 **Between slavery & free labour: early experiments with free labour and patterns of slave emancipation in Brazil & Cuba.**
Lucia Lamounier. In: *From chattel slaves to wage slaves: the dynamics of labour bargaining in the Americas, 1896-1990.* Edited by Mary Turner. Bloomington, Indiana: Indiana University Press; London: James Currey; Kingston: Ian Randle, 1995, p. 185-200.

Provides a study of the emancipation processes in Cuba and Brazil, in the framework of the broader question the book sets out to answer: Did emancipation improve the lot of slaves? The author explores the similarities and differences in the legal and contractual framework in which former slaves had to learn to operate in the two countries in question.

350 **The black man in Cuban society: from colonial times to the revolution.**
Roberto Nodal. *Journal of Black Studies*, vol. 16, no. 3 (1986), p. 251-67.

Nodal discusses the discrimination suffered by blacks in Cuba between 1780 and 1880. He explains how, despite the 1868-78 Cuban war for independence which united all Cubans, prejudice against blacks in the Cuban Republic after 1902 was made worse by US influence. This ultimately led to the Oriente province rebellion in 1912. Nodal claims that despite the efforts of Fernando Ortiz, racism continued until Fidel Castro's revolution in 1959. Since then, he says, the social position of black Cubans has improved.

351 **Cuba, colour and the revolution.**
David Booth. *Science and Society*, vol. 11, no. 2 (1976), p. 129-72.

This perceptive sociological analysis of the race question in Cuba was unique at the time of writing. The author contends that neither those giving the positive side of the argument nor those offering a negative point of view succeeded in establishing the distinguishing features of racial oppression in Cuba, because they simply reduced the problem to a variant of the North American pattern of racial exclusion. Booth explores subjects such as slavery, racism and nationalism in order to highlight the complexities of the colour-class system in pre-revolutionary Cuba. He notes that although there is a marked absence of black protest organizations, a strong functional African counter-cultural presence exists. It is argued that the uneven revolutionary attack on racism was due not only to material constraints but also to the deficiencies of the political leadership in understanding and addressing private as well as public racism.

352 **Garvey and Cuba.**
Bernardo García Domínguez.   In: *Garvey: his work and impact.*
Edited by Rupert Lewis, Patrick Bryan.   Kingston, Jamaica:
University of the West Indies, Institute of Social and Economic
Research, 1988, p. 299-305.

Cuba was home to several branches of the United Negro Improvement Association, which was founded in the United States by Jamaican-born Marcus Garvey. Garvey himself visited Cuba in 1921, and the movement there recruited from among the wave of Jamaican and other West Indian migrant sugar workers. The author, a researcher from Santiago de Cuba, conducted interviews in five towns and cities in eastern Cuba (Santiago de Cuba, Guantánamo, Banes, Palma Soriano and Morón) and uses oral history to complement archival documentation and newspaper accounts of Garveyism in Cuba.

353 **El negro en Cuba, 1902-1958.** (The black man in Cuba, 1902-1958.)
Tomás Fernández Robaina.   Havana: Ciencias Sociales, 1990. 225p.
bibliog.

Making extensive use of primary and secondary Cuban sources, especially the Cuban press, the author carried out a study of over half a century of black Cubans' struggle against discrimination. He documents key early 20th-century organizations, such as the Central Directorate of Societies of the Coloured Race, the Committee of Veterans and Societies of Colour and the Independent Coloured Party, and also explores the dynamics of class and race politics from the 1930s to the 1950s, spanning the labour movement and political parties. He depicts the expressed black unease with US and Cuban republican politics as legitimately separatist in its opposition to race hostility.

354 **Our rightful share: the Afro-Cuban struggle for equality 1886-1912.**
Aline Helg.   Chapel Hill, North Carolina: University of North
Carolina Press, 1995. 400p.

The author examines the issue of race in Cuban society and politics during the transition from Spanish colony to republic. On the basis of rich archival and secondary source material, the author challenges the myth of racial equality in Cuba, demonstrating how deeply rooted racism was in the period 1886-1912.

355 **El problema negro en Cuba y su solución definitiva.** (The race
problem in Cuba and its definitive solution.)
Pedro Serviat.   Havana: Editora Política, 1986. 197p. bibliog.

A clear exposition of the thinking that informed revolutionary thinking on race by a leading communist militant. Serviat deals with the more integrationist position of Juan Gualberto Gómez in contradistinction to the more separatist ideas of Rafael Serra, Pedro Ivonet and Evaristo Estenoz. He analyses the race position *vis-à-vis* immigrant black Caribbean labour, 1930s and 1940s Communist Party and civil rights movements struggles, and 1940s and 1950s black co-operativism. He sees the revolution as providing the definitive solution to the black problem. See also *Vida y obra de Juan Gualberto Gómez* (Life and work of Juan Gualberto Gómez). Edited by

Angelina Edreira de Caballero (Havana: R. Mendez, 1954. Reprinted Madrid, 1984. 199p.). It incorporates Gomez' *Por Cuba libre* (For Free Cuba) (Havana: Office of the Historian, 1954. 453p.

356 **Race and inequality in Cuba, 1899-1981.**
Alejandro de la Fuente. *Journal of Contemporary History*, vol. 30 (Jan. 1995), p. 131-68.

The aim of this article is to go beyond the bipolar approach to contemporary race relations in Cuba that has been taken by supporters and detractors of the revolution. The author looks at race differentials on the basis of Cuban population statistics, 1899-1980s, concluding that they diminished in key social areas between 1899 and 1930. However, strong inequalities are suggested by fertility and mortality indicators, so that by the 1940s the demographic transition had been completed in these two areas by whites, but not by blacks and mulattos. It is shown that in the post-revolutionary period, race inequalities disappeared in the areas of fertility and mortality, as well as literacy. The article stops short of an attitudinal analysis.

357 **Race in Argentina and Cuba 1880-1930: theories, policies and popular reaction.**
Aline Helg. In: *The idea of race in Latin America, 1870-1940.*
Edited by Richard Graham. Austin, Texas: University of Texas Press, 1990, p. 37-69.

This is an intriguing comparative essay on two racially dissimilar societies involving similar bodies of thought. In the past, as elsewhere in Latin America, leaders in Argentina and Cuba aspired to a closer connection with Europe and North America, where 'scientific' thought condemned non-white races to an inferior category. This in turn jarred with the heterogeneous racial make-up of their societies and growing sense of national identity. Helg charts the Argentinian élites' glorification of whitening to the point of xenophobia with regard to first the Indians and then the Jews, and shows how their ideas were replicated by Cuban élites *vis-à-vis* the black sector of the population.

Leading black figures (biographies and writings)

358 **Antonio Maceo, apuntes para una historia de su vida.** (Antonio Maceo: biographical notes.)
José Luciano Franco. Havana: Ciencias Sociales, 1973. 3 vols. bibliog.

Written by Cuba's leading 20th-century Afro-Cuban historian, this is the bibliography that resurrected Maceo as the brown-skinned revolutionary general and military genius behind Cuba's 19th-century independence wars. The life and times of the hero (1845-96) come alive in a narrative that was extensively researched in Cuba's archives, and formed the backbone of future studies.

359 **Antonio Maceo: the 'bronze titan' of Cuba's struggle for independence.**
Philip S. Foner.   New York: Monthly Review Press, 1977. 339p. map. bibliog.

The standard English-language biography of the outstanding brown-skinned general of Cuba's late 19th-century first and second wars of independence.

360 **Cuba's freedom fighter, Antonio Maceo: 1845-1896.**
Magdalena M. Pando.   Gainesville, Florida: Felicity Press, 1980. 144p. bibliog.

An unabashedly sympathetic biography of Antonio Maceo, focusing mainly on the latter years of his life in the 1890s.

361 **Cultura: lucha de clases y conflicto racial, 1878-1895.** (Culture, class struggle and race conflict, 1878-95.)
Raquel Mendieta Costa.   Havana: Editorial Pueblo y Educación, 1989. 92p.

Viewed in relation to class and race tensions in the period between the two major wars of independence, this is an informative study of the Central Directorate of Societies of People of Colour and key leaders of the battle against racism Juan Gualberto Gómez, Martín Morúa Delgado and Plácido.

362 **Rafael Serra: patriota y revolucionario, fraternal amigo de Martí.**
(Rafael Serra: patriot and revolutionary, fraternal friend of Martí.)
Emilio Roig de Leuchsenring.   Havana: Oficina del Historiador de la Ciudad, 1959. 139p.

A compilation comprising writings on and by Rafael Serra. The collection opens with a 1942 eulogy celebrating the link between Rafael Serra and the patriotic League of Coloured People, and José Martí and the Cuban Revolutionary Party. There follows a section of letters from Martí to Serra, and writings on Serra and his work, in the years 1888-94. The final section includes speeches, declarations and articles by Serra. A more recent study is the one by Pedro Deschamps Chapeaux: *Rafael Serra y Montalvo: obrero incansable de nuestra independencia* (Rafael Serra Montalvo: tireless worker for our independence) (Havana: Unión de Escritores y Artistas de Cuba, 1974. 189p. bibliog.).

The island of Cuba.
See item no. 46.

The island of Cuba: its resources, progress, and prospects.
See item no. 47.

Slaves, sugar and colonial society: travel accounts of Cuba, 1801-1899.
See item no. 50.

Travels in the west: Cuba with notices of Puerto Rico and the slave trade.
See item no. 52.

Blacks in colonial Cuba, 1774-1899.
See item no. 288.

The female slave in Cuba during the first half of the nineteenth century.
See item no. 364.

Marriage, class and colour in nineteenth century Cuba: a study of racial attitudes and sexual values in a slave society.
See item no. 368.

La polémica de la esclavitud: Álvaro Reynoso. (The slavery controversy: Álvaro Reynoso.)
See item no. 851.

El negro en la novela hispanoamericana. (The black man in the Latin American novel.)
See item no. 868.

Sugar's secrets: race and the erotics of Cuban nationalism.
See item no. 879.

The autobiography of a runaway slave.
See item no. 883.

The blacks in Cuba: a bibliography.
See item no. 1157.

Women

Pre-1959

363 Les clubs féminins dans le parti révolutionnaire cubain, 1892-1898.
(Women's clubs in the Cuban Revolutionary Party, 1892-1898.)
Paul Estrade. Paris: L'Equipe de Récherche de l'Université de Paris VIII, 1986. 42p. (Histoires des Antilles Hispaniques, no. 2).
Constitutes a rare, if brief, look at the proliferation and significance of women's revolutionary clubs in the independence war effort of the late 19th century. The author, a French historian of Cuba, documents the clubs in Cuba, the United States (Key West, Tampa, Jacksonville, New York), the Dominican Republic and Mexico.

364 The female slave in Cuba during the first half of the nineteenth century.
Digna Castañeda. In: *Engendering history: Caribbean women in historical perspective*. Edited by Verene Shepherd, Bridget Brereton, Barbara Bailey. London: James Currey; Kingston, Jamaica: Ian Randle, 1995, p. 141-54.
This article is a first approximation of the lives of women under slavery in Cuba. On the basis of archival research in Havana, the author documents 19th-century court cases of abuse against slave women.

365 From the house to the streets: the Cuban women's movement for legal reform, 1898-1940.
K. Lynn Stoner. Durham, North Carolina; London: Duke University Press, 1991. 242p. bibliog.
There is no comparable study in Cuban women's history to this account of how, during the early decades of the 20th century, Cuban women fought and won legal reforms for themselves (including the right to vote in 1934) that were among the most advanced in the world. The author traces the growth of women's organizations and

activism between 1902 and 1940, providing a background on prominent individual women and broader events. The focus is on the feminist history of élite, white women, but Stoner does point to links between them and black, working and peasant women. Also highlighted is the relationship between the 'feminist' struggle and wider political and international upheavals in Cuba's post-colonial transition to a modern state.

366   **Gender constructs of labour in prerevolutionary Cuban tobacco.**
      Jean Stubbs.   *Social and Economic Studies*, vol. 37, nos.1-2 (1988),
      p. 241-69. bibliog.

Attempts to establish gender constructs for the Cuban tobacco history by documenting the extensive, yet often unacknowledged, involvement of women in tobacco agriculture and industry, and in crucial moments of struggle. The article deals especially with concepts such as technology and skill, with the introduction of machinery and the downgrading and feminization of hitherto skilled trades. It also explores the issue of gender in the international and national division of labour, as the changing emphasis of production from cigars to cigarettes again resulted in a feminization of the labour force, undercutting strong male unions, but ushering in a militant women's labour movement with some outstanding leaders.

367   **Historia de una familia mambisa: Mariana Grajales.** (The history
      of a family of independence fighters: Mariana Grajales.)
      Nidia Sarabia, prologue by José Luciano Franco.   Havana: Editorial
      Orbe, 1975. 271p. bibliog.

An exhaustive study using archival documentation and oral history in Cuba and Jamaica on the life of Mariana Grajales, showing her to be an independence fighter in her own right, as well as the mother of the great brown General Antonio Maceo.

368   **Marriage, class and colour in nineteenth century Cuba: a study of
      racial attitudes and sexual values in a slave society.**
      Verena Martínez Alier.   Ann Arbor, Michigan: University of
      Michigan, 1989. 2nd ed. 202p. bibliog.

This is a now classic study in the historical anthropology of inter-racial marriages in 19th-century Cuba, which uses archival records of elopements and parental dissent. Martínez Alier perceptively and imaginatively examines points of rupture in the social order and values based on a rigid racial and sexual hierarchy. From the margins of slave society, she looks at concubinage, seduction, ideals of virginity, virility and honour, and how they are linked to race, class and gender.

369   **La mujer en los cien años de lucha, 1868-1968.** (Women in the one
      hundred years of struggle, 1868-1968.)
      Havana: Comisión de Orientación Revolucionaria del Comité
      Provincial del Partido Comunista de Cuba en La Habana, 1968. 84p.

Brought out to mark the 100 years of struggle since the outbreak of Cuba's first war of independence in 1868, this study highlights stellar women's participation in the struggle: women in the 1868-78 and 1895-98 wars; women's organizations and action against the 1901 Platt Amendment, sexual and occupational discrimination, and the Machado and Batista dictatorships; women's support for the revolution and women's struggles the world over; and the work of the Federation of Cuban Women.

370 **Recuerdos secretos de dos mujeres públicas.** (Secret memories of
   two public women.)
   Tomás Fernández Robaína.   Havana: Editorial Letras Cubanas, 1984.
   105p.

Fernández Robaína presents a testimonial reconstruction of the lives of two former
prostitutes before and after their revolutionary rehabilitation. Personal recollections
are interspersed with newspaper articles, books and documents on the social problem
of prostitution in Cuban society. The pre-revolutionary setting is the brothel under-
world of the Colón and San Isidro red-light districts of Havana, through the
testimonies of Consuelo la Charmé and Violeta.

371 **Social and political motherhood of Cuba: Mariana Grajales Cuello.**
   Jean Stubbs.   In: *Engendering history: Caribbean women in historical
   perspective.*   Edited by Verene Shepherd, Bridget Brereton, Barbara
   Bailey.   London: James Currey; Kingston, Jamaica: Ian Randle, 1995,
   p. 296-317.

This article traces the construction, and variations over time, of the mother myth of
Mariana Grajales Cuello, best known as the mother of Cuba's independence generals
Antonio and José Maceo. Always centring on a motherhood that is heroically self-
abnegating, the myth has oscillated between Catholic and secular, liberal patriotic and
revolutionary, with race as a factor either absent or downplayed. Without new primary
research, it is impossible to distinguish myth from reality. However, the author
suggests an alternative Afro-Cuban myth in which gender as mother-signifier
functions very differently and Grajales becomes both nurturer and warrior.

Post-1959

372 **Cuba.**
   Germaine Greer.   In: *Women: a world report.*   London: Methuen,
   1985, p. 271-91.

Revealing as much about a Western feminist as it does about women in Cuba, this text
is considered a 'classic' in its own right. Greer provides a light-hearted, hopeful quasi-
journalistic piece in which she is almost begrudgingly impressed by the legends of
heroic Cuban women and the achievements in health-care, education and institutionalized rights. At the same time, however, she recognizes Cuban sexual politics as
downplaying women.

373 **Cuba: revolutionizing women, family, and power.**
   Jean Stubbs.   In: *Women and politics worldwide.*   Edited by Barbara
   J. Nelson, Najma Chowdhury.   New Haven, Connecticut: Yale
   University Press, 1994, p. 189-207.

Presents a retrospective assessment of the achievements, limitations and contradictions of policies for Cuban women over a thirty-year period after the revolution.

Stubbs first treats the involvement of women in the revolution and then the struggle for the emancipation of women within the revolution itself. This was achieved through formal participation in the Federation of Cuban Women and other organizations and through employment, but with markedly less success on the domestic and personal fronts.

374 Cuban women confront the future.
Vilma Espín, edited by Deborah Shnookal. Melbourne, Australia: Ocean Press, 1991. 78p.

A unique English-language collection of interviews conducted in 1988 and 1989 with Vilma Espín, who was a key protagonist in the Cuban revolution and the Cuban women's movement. Espín reflects on how women see their gains, the challenges in socialist Cuba, how they are confronting discrimination and prejudice, and how family life is changing. This provides an insider view of the role women have played in the revolution.

375 Focus on women's lives.
Cuba Update (April/June 1995), p. 8-43. (New York: Center for Cuban Studies, 124 West 23rd St, New York, NY 10011).

This collection of short pieces, some of which are excerpts from larger works, attempts to provide a snapshot of the lives of Cuban women today, with an emphasis on the everyday rather than the unusual. The women profiled are not the famous; the experiences of everyday trials could be those of any woman in Cuba today, whatever her educational or social status. The themes discussed include women's changing consciousness and the politics of sexuality in a time of economic crisis.

376 Gathering rage: the failure of twentieth century revolutions to develop a feminist agenda.
Margaret Randall. New York: Monthly Review Press, 1992. 192p.

The author criticizes the failure of socialism in Cuba and Nicaragua to liberate women and develop an autonomous women's arena, and the failure of feminists such as herself to be critical. A North American writer who lived and worked in Cuba during the late 1960s and early 1970s, she conducted interviews with Cuban women all over the island, optimistic about Cuban women's progress under the revolution and socialism, and seeing racism and sexism as fast on their way to becoming things of the past. Here, she reinterprets some of the stories from her earlier works (1974 and 1981) to argue against the paternalism and tokenism of revolution and call for a non-hierarchical, feminist socialism.

377 La mujer en Cuba: familia y sociedad. (Woman in Cuba: family and society.)
Vilma Espín Guillois. Havana: Imprenta Central de las Fuerzas Armadas Revolucionarias, 1990. 266p.

A collection of major speeches and interviews given during 1975-89 by Vilma Espín, president of the Federation of Cuban Women since its founding in 1960, one of the women in the 1950s insurrection, and a leading woman in the Communist Party of Cuba. Issues range across themes that have been central to the revolution and the Federation: the integration of women into the labour force, education, family, health care, national and international politics and feminism.

378 **NWSA Journal.**
Whole issue. vol. 5, no. 3 (fall 1993).

The journal contains several short articles by and about Cuban women: María del Carmen Caño Secado writes on class differences in familial situations; Ann Ferguson on the 1993 women's studies conference at Havana University; Marta Núñez Sarmiento on women workers in non-traditional occupations; Mirta Rodríguez Calderón on the domestic as a conscious political choice in the crisis 1990s; María Isabel Sosa and Clotilde Proveyer reflect on a case-study of attitudes among working women in Havana; Norma Vasallo Barreta and Irene Smith Alayón on rehabilitation programmes among women prisoners; and Esther Velis on the role over the years of the Federation of Cuban Women.

379 **On the problem of studying women in Cuba.**
Carolee Bengelsdorf. *Race & Class*, vol. 1, no. 2 (1985), p. 35-50.

Bengelsdorf makes an attempt to bridge the conceptual gap between, on the one hand, Western feminist views of Cuban women and the socialist revolution, and, on the other, mainstream Federation of Cuban Women views of Western feminism. The author highlights the polarized and static underpinnings of both positions, and explores some of the issues from a socialist feminist stance, and through the prism of the family and women's entry into the labour force. The essay was also reprinted in *Cuban political economy: controversies in Cubanology*. Edited by Andrew Zimbalist. (Boulder, Colorado: Westview, 1988, p. 119-36).

380 **Remaking the public sphere: women and revolution in Cuba.**
Sheryl L. Lutjens. In: *Women and revolution in Africa, Asia and the New World.* Edited by Mary Ann Tétreault. Columbia, South Carolina: University of South Carolina Press, 1994, p. 366-93.

Lutjens applies recent feminist theory on civil society and controversies concerning the dichotomy between public and private to the experience of women in revolutionary Cuba, demonstrating both the separateness and permeability of these two spheres. The article provides a tentative look at the effects of the late 1980s rectification and 1990s special period on women's lives. A version of this article was published in *Latin American Perspectives* (1995).

381 **Sex, gender and revolution: the problem of construction and the construction of a problem.**
Virginia R. Domínguez. *Cuban Studies*, vol. 17 (1987), p. 7-24.

The author opens a series of articles in the same issue by focusing on the reasons for various approaches that have been taken in the United States to study Cuban women, in particular the various liberal, Marxist, and radical feminist paradigms. In a sequel article, Marifeli Pérez-Stable develops these points, to suggest a possible future militancy among women which challenges existing structures and inequalities thus far not addressed by the orthodox Marxism of the revolution and the Federation of Cuban Women on the woman question.

382 **Socialism and feminism: women and the Cuban revolution.**
Nicola Murray. *Feminist Review*, pt. 1, no. 2 (1979), p. 57-73; pt. 2,
no. 3 (1979), p. 99-108.

In this early feminist analysis of the sexual politics of Cuban socialism, Murray
argues that the Cuban revolutionary government chose economic development over
the liberation of women, thereby making their position difficult in terms of production,
reproduction, sexuality and child socialization. She concludes that there are three
major obstacles to women's liberation: a lack of autonomy in a paternalistic state;
machismo; and a reinforced gender division of labour.

383 **Socialist morality, sexual preference, family and state intervention
in Cuba.**
Laura Gotkowitz, Richard Turits. *Socialism and Democracy*, no. 6
(spring/summer 1988).

Using three case-studies (1960s sexual puritanism, the 1975 Family Code, and 1980s
juvenile delinquency), the authors suggest conflicting discourses at work in terms of
public and private, policy and reality. For example, the Family Code is explored in
relation to its conflicting meanings of the family as the key agent of socialization;
narrative of rule governing family life, breakdown and divorce; and conflation of
women's rights with social reproduction.

384 **The 'woman question' in Cuba: an analysis of material constraints
on its resolution.**
Muriel Nazzari. In: *Promissory notes: women in the transition to
socialism.* Edited by Sonia Kruks, Rayna Rapp, Marilyn B. Young.
New York: Monthly Review Press, 1989, p. 109-26.

This essay analyses the position of women in the context of the larger struggle
surrounding economic strategies adopted during Cuba's transition from capitalism to
socialism. It argues that Cuba's adoption in the early 1970s of a system of distribution
based on material incentives and profit perpetuated women's inequality in the home
and the workforce.

385 **Women and the Cuban revolution.**
Edited by Elizabeth Stone. New York: Pathfinder, 1981. 156p.

The speeches and documents reproduced in this book reflect the changes and
awakening of women during the first two decades of the Cuban revolution. The author
provides a brief introduction to colonial and post-colonial pre-revolutionary Cuba, and
highlights the positive endeavours of the revolutionary process of transition where
women are concerned. The first chapter comprises two accounts on the early years by
Vilma Espín, president of the Federation of Cuban Women (FMC), one written in
1961 and one in 1974. Subsequent chapters contain Fidel Castro's speeches to the
FMC in 1966, 1974 and 1980, in addition to the 1975 Communist Party of Cuba
Thesis on the Full Exercise of Women's Equality. The Maternity Law and the Family
Code are reproduced as appendices and the work contains black-and-white
photographs.

386 **Women of Cuba.**
   Inger Holt-Seeland, translated from the Spanish by Elizabeth Hamilton
   Lacoste with Mirtha Quintales, José Vigo. Westport, Connecticut:
   Lawrence Hill & Co., 1981. 190p.

Offers a valuable portrait of six Cuban women, who talk about their work, the past,
the future, their lives in general and how they have changed with the revolution. The
female interviewees include a farm worker and a factory worker, a student Communist
Youth member, a high-born housewife who stayed in the country after the revolution,
and an older black woman whose memories go back to the turn of the century.

387 **Women's equality and the Cuban revolution.**
   Isabel Larguía, John Dumoulin. In: *Women and change in Latin
   America.* Edited by June Nash, Helen Safa. South Hadley,
   Massachusetts: Bergin & Garvey, 1986.

The authors, an Argentinian woman and North American man, who had long been
resident in Cuba at the time of writing, aimed to raise the debate on women's
emancipation to a more theoretical level, both in Cuba and abroad. They draw on the
classic works of Marxism, especially Engels, on the conditions of women under
capitalism and under socialism, and the post-1960s wave of feminist thinking, to
evaluate Cuban praxis. See also 'Women in Socialist Cuba' by Alfred Padula and Lois
Smith, in *Cuba: twenty-five years of revolution, 1959-1984.* Edited by Sandor Halesbsky,
John M. Kirk (New York: Praeger, 1989, p. 79-92).

388 **Women's rights and the Cuban revolution.**
   Julie Marie Bunck. In: *Cuban communism, 1959-1995.* Edited by
   Irving Louis Horowitz. New Brunswick, New Jersey; London:
   Transaction, 1995. 8th ed., p. 427-47.

One of a selection of articles on the different aspects of the Cuban revolution, this
piece puts forward four arguments. The first claims that equality for women was only
a secondary goal of the revolution since Castro was more concerned with increasing
the labour force and production. Second, despite Castro's advocacy of equality, he
himself harboured traditional attitudes toward women. Third, despite the government
and FMC resources ploughed into changing gender attitudes, these remained little
altered. Fourth, the government in effect tolerated and preserved pre-revolutionary
gender attitudes.

Work

389 **Cuban women and work in the U.S. labor force: perspectives on
   the nature of change.**
   Yolanda Prieto. *Cuban Studies*, no. 17 (1987), p. 73-91.

A study based on a survey of Cuban-American women in New Jersey, which argues
that their desire to better their families and maintain or acquire middle-class status led

to even stronger labour force participation rates than in Cuba itself. Prieto's informants are from wealthier sectors of pre-revolutionary Cuba and share a pro-US, anti-Castro ideology, which facilitated their integration into US society and material achievement.

390 **La incorporación y permanencia de la mujer campesina de las cooperativas de producción agropecuaria.** (The incorporation and permanence of the peasant woman in agricultural co-operatives.)
Federación de Mujeres Cubanas. Havana: Estudios de la Mujer, 1991.

Reports on research conducted by the Federation of Cuban Women with the National Association of Small Farmers and Centre for Youth Studies, on the decreasing numbers of women active in the co-operatives. Over 1,000 peasant women and almost 500 men (in and out of co-operatives) were interviewed, with responses highlighting the barriers of women's responsibility for childcare and domestic labour, traditional notions of women's jobs, and the continuing ideology of male superiority.

391 **The Latin American agrarian reform experience.**
Carmen Diana Deere. In: *Rural women and state policy.* Edited by Carmen Diana Deere, Magdalena León. Boulder, Colorado: Westview, 1987, p. 165-90.

An overview article whose central thesis is that most Latin American agrarian reforms have benefited men, since male household heads have been the designated beneficiaries. This is documented on a country-by-country basis, whereby Cuba's 1977 co-operativization programme stands out as the positive exception with twenty-five women beneficiaries. The author then moves on to analyse mechanisms of gender exclusion and argues the case for co-operatives and the importance of women's inclusion as effective co-operative members. An earlier article dealing with Peru, Chile and Cuba, was published in *Women and change in Latin America*, edited by June Nash, Helen Safa (South Hadley, Massachusetts: Bergin & Garvey, 1986).

392 **La mujer rural y urbana: estudios de casos.** (Rural and urban women: case-studies.)
Mariana Ravenet Ramírez, Niurka Pérez Rojas, Marta Toledo Fraga. Havana: Ciencias Sociales, 1989. 207p. bibliog.

In this volume a study is made of the urban and rural integration of women in an agro-industrial complex in Melena del Sur, Havana province, based on oral interviewing, time studies and participant observation. The analysis is woven around the day-to-day stories of three women: a fifty-year-old peasant woman, a co-operative farmworker born after the revolution, and an industrial worker in her thirties. The conclusions reached are mixed as the women and their families talk about work outside and inside the home, socialization of children, political participation and recreation.

393 **Mujeres en empleos no tradicionales.** (Women in non-traditional employment.)
Marta Núñez Sarmiento. Havana: Ciencias Sociales, 1991. 23p.

The findings of a 1988-90 study conducted in a tile factory show women there facing many of the same problems as women in traditional jobs, especially around the double day. Particularly notable was that women on average earned only half the pay of the men due to their lower positions. However, they were highly critical of management, seventy-five per cent of them considering they were ready to take on a leadership position, compared with only twenty-six per cent of the men. Younger women seemed more likely to share domestic chores more equally with their partner.

394   **The myth of the male breadwinner: women and industrialization in the Caribbean.**
      Helen Icken Safa.   Boulder, Colorado: Westview, 1995. 208p. bibliog.

The result of collaborative ethnographic research in Puerto Rico, the Dominican Republic and Cuba, this monograph concentrates on the experience of women textile workers but broadens out the debate to look at crucial changes taking place in the feminization of labour. The study on Cuba was conducted in 1986, in a textile factory outside Havana, and encompassed three generations of women. Survey, life story and participant observation techniques were used to explore the workplace and home life, discussing issues such as: positions in the factory and collective participation; family and kinship patterns; domestic division of labour; and financial and other decision-making.

395   **Women and Cuban smallholder agriculture in transition.**
      Jean Stubbs.   In: *Women & change in the Caribbean*.   Edited by
      Janet H. Momsen.   Kingston: Ian Randle; Bloomington and
      Indianapolis, Indiana: Indiana University Press; London: James
      Currey, 1993, p. 219-31.

Highlights the late 1980s trend toward a rethinking of smallholder agriculture, in the predominance of large-scale state and co-operative agriculture. The author also examines the questions raised by a focus on gender and household in the smallholder sector. Tobacco is used as a case-study, although it is the exception rather than the rule, in that it has remained a primarily smallholding sector. Earlier versions of this article were published in *World development* (vol. 15, no. 1 [1987], p. 41-65) and *Rural women and state policy: feminist perspectives on Latin American agricultural development*, edited by Carmen Diana Deere, Magdalena León (Boulder, Colorado: Westview, 1987, p. 142-61).

396   **Women in rural production and reproduction in the Soviet Union, China, Cuba and Tanzania: socialist development experiences.**
      Elizabeth J. Croll.   *Signs: Journal of Women in Culture and Society*,
      vol. 7, no. 2 (winter 1981), p. 361-74, 375-99.

A comparative attempt to evaluate the degree to which a change in rural relations of production resulted in an erosion of patriarchal authority in the household. It highlights the commonality of experiences in the resilience of a domestic division of labour, overall intensification of women's labour, ideological rather than material explanations for gender inequality, and lack of women's involvement in decision-making. Empirical data is assembled country by country on rural women's labour, domestic division of labour, and women's involvement in decision-making. Cuba proves to be much more urban than the other three, and the study far more qualitative given the relative lack of statistical data available.

Family and fertility

397 Características sociodemográficas de la familia cubana: 1953-1970.
(Socio-demographic characteristics of the Cuban family: 1953-70.)
Niurka Pérez Rojas. Havana: Ciencias Sociales, 1979. 69p.

Compares data from the population censuses of 1953 and 1970, to draw conclusions about changing family patterns. Among the trends highlighted are increasing divorce rates and the incidence of female-headed families.

398 Cuba.
Alfonso Farnós, Fernando González, Raúl Hernández. In: *Working women in socialist countries: the fertility connection.* Edited by Valentina Bodrova, Richard Anker. Geneva: International Labour Office, 1985, p. 197-233.

A statistical account of the interrelationship between changes taking place in the situation of Cuban women and demographic changes, such as marriage, fertility and infant mortality, which in turn impact on the situation of women, in both negative and positive ways. It looks in particular detail at the findings of the 1979 National Demographic Survey, and outlines possible future directions.

399 The Cuban family in the 1980s.
Lois Smith, Alfred Padula. In: *Transformation and struggle: Cuba faces the 1990s.* Edited by Sandor Halebsky, John M. Kirk. New York: Praeger, 1990, p. 175-88.

The authors explore the contradictory impact of the revolution on the Cuban family over three decades. This serves as a backdrop to what has been increasingly identified since the late 1970s as the 'crisis' of the family, with high rates of teenage pregnancy, divorce, and female-headed households. Smith and Padula analyse the nature and effects of revolutionary policies in this regard, and the growing contradiction between a more democratic family and the intensely patriarchal state.

400 Cuban women: changing roles and population trends.
Sonia Catasús, et al. Geneva: International Labour Office, 1988. 123p.

This is a statistical analysis of the changes women have experienced since the 1959 revolution and their effects on declining fertility and infant mortality, as well as patterns of conjugality and abortion and contraceptive use. Research was carried out in three different regions: urban Plaza de la Revolución and suburban Buenavista, both in Havana, and rural Yateras, in eastern Cuba. Most striking was the overall fertility decline which occurred with improved health, education and occupation.

401 **The problems of single motherhood in Cuba.**
Marguerite Rosenthal. In: *Cuba in transition: crisis and transformation.* Edited by Sandor Halebsky, John M. Kirk. Boulder, Colorado: Westview, 1992, p. 161-75.

The author underlines the gap between the norm of the nuclear family set out in the Family Code and the reality of some forty per cent of Cuban families as single-parent and overwhelmingly female-headed. She highlights the problems such families and women face, and the extent to which revolutionary measures have recognized, ameliorated or aggravated those problems. Rising teenage pregnancy rates are discussed in the context of a baby-boom generation replicating patterns of early reproductive activity.

402 **Social policy and the family in socialist Cuba.**
Inés Reca. In: *The Cuban revolution into the 1990s.* Edited by Centro de Estudios sobre América. Boulder, Colorado: Westview, 1992, p. 147-61.

A largely narrative study of family-related issues drawing heavily on 1980s demographic and social surveys concerning issues defined as key variables. The Chilean author, then head of the Group of the Family of the Centre for Social and Psychological Research at the Cuban Academy of Sciences, provides data on the workforce, political leadership, hours of housework, and household arrangements, broken down by generation and gender. The chapter is based on a longer study in Spanish published in Havana in 1990 on family composition, marriage and divorce, household membership, labour force participation, sex education and communication. There is little questioning of the normative, ideal-type, 'complete' (nuclear) family.

Sexuality and sex education

403 **Honor, shame and women's liberation in Cuba.**
Geoffrey Fox. In: *Male and female in Latin America.* Edited by Ann Pescatello. Pittsburgh, Pennsylvania: University of Pittsburgh Press, 1973, p. 274-90.

Fox takes a rare look at male reactions to the changed status of women, through the prism of émigré Cuban men. He singles out male resistance to a redefinition of moral codes in terms of the concepts of honour and shame shaping their machismo, serving to highlight the conflict between traditions and modernity in sex roles and social change.

404 **Sexuality and socialism in Cuba.**
Lois Smith.   In: *Cuba in transition: crisis and transformation.*
Edited by Sandor Halebsky, et al.   Boulder, Colorado: Westview,
1992, p. 177-91.

Smith discusses the sex education campaign of the National Working Group on Sex Education, viewing it as more about revolutionary morality than sexuality. She focuses especially on elements of continuity and change, considering the Church and revolution as watchdogs of public morality, and the encouragement of stable heterosexuality and monogamy to remould a private sphere more consistent with revolutionary public policies for women. As in an earlier article of 1989, Smith highlights both the benefits to women from the health revolution and the continuing patriarchal ideas underlying health provision.

Viajeras del Caribe. (Women travellers of the Caribbean.)
See item no. 53.

La fecundidad en Cuba. (Fertility in Cuba.)
See item no. 280.

Breaking the silences: 20th century poetry by Cuban women.
See item no. 852.

Images of women in pre- and post-revolutionary Cuban novels.
See item no. 864.

Poetisas cubanas. (Cuban women poets.)
See item no. 874.

Cuba: a view from inside: short films by and about Cuban women.
See item no. 994.

Bibliografía de la mujer cubana. (Bibliography of the Cuban woman.)
See item no. 1168.

Languages and Dialects

405 **The Abakuá secret society in Cuba: language and culture.**
Rafael A. Núñez Cedeño. *Hispania*, vol. 71, no. 1 (1988), p. 148-54.
bibliog.

Begins with a brief introduction to the African background of the Abakuá Secret
Society and an overview of the origins of black people in Cuba. The author then
tackles the linguistic influence of Abakuá, questioning whether it is a rule-governed
vernacular, a pidgin, or some other form of language. He provides details of research
carried out into the language and presents the results. The appendix contains the
questionnaire administered to participants in the research.

406 **Algunas consideraciones sobre *Patois cubain* de F. Boytel Jambu.**
(Some thoughts on F. Boytel Jambu's *Patois cubain*.)
Edited by Isabel Martínez Gordo. Havana: Editorial Academia, 1989.
70p.

A previously unpublished early 20th-century text, this was discovered in the museum
at the restored La Isabelica coffee plantation at Gran Piedra outside Santiago de Cuba.
In an extensive introduction the editor, Martínez Gordo, stresses the text's deficiencies
as a work of scholarship and questions Boytel Jambu's basic assertion of the existence
of a 'Cuban creole'. This, he claimed, arose from, but was distinct from, the Haitian
creole spoken by the descendants of slaves brought from the neighbouring republic.

407 **Anagó: vocabulario lucumí (El Yoruba que se habla en Cuba).**
(Anagó: Lucumí vocabulary [The Yoruba spoken in Cuba].)
Lydia Cabrera, prologue by Roger Bastide. Miami, Florida:
Ediciones Universal, 1986. 326p.

Ordered alphabetically, this lexicon reveals the meaning of words and phrases used in
Cuba which speak of beliefs, attitudes, conduct, personality, family, culture, and
above all continuity and change through Middle Passage, slavery and beyond. It is a
testimony to Afro-Cuban linguistic resistance. There are also companion volumes on
Abakuá, Bantú and Ñáñigo vocabulary.

408   **Apuntes para la historia de la lingüística en Cuba.** (Notes for a
history of Cuban linguistics.)
Rodolfo Alpizar Castillo.   Havana: Ciencias Sociales, 1989. 190p.
bibliog.

An historical survey of the writers and extant documents dealing with the peculiarities
of Cuban Spanish. Particular attention is paid to Pedro Espinola's *Memoir on defects
of pronunciation . . .* (1795); a catechism (early 1790s) written for first generation
African slaves; and Esteban Pichardo's pioneering *Dictionary of Cuban provincial-
isms* (1836).

409   **Autosegmental phonology and liquid assimilation in Havana
Spanish.**
James W. Harris.   In: *Selected papers from the XIIIth linguistic
symposium on romance languages.*   Edited by Larry D. King,
Catherine A. Maley.   Amsterdam: John Benjamins Publishing
Company, 1983, p. 127-48. (Current Issues in Linguistic Theory,
vol. 36).

Harris presents a detailed discussion of the complexities of liquid assimilation in the
Cuban dialect *habanero*, with examples of speech patterns.

410   **Bibliografía comentada de estudios lingüísticos publicados en
Cuba, 1959-1980.** (Annotated bibliography of linguistic studies
published in Cuba, 1959-80.)
Iraída López-Iñíguez.   *Cuban Studies*, vol. 13, no. 1 (winter 1983),
p. 41-68.

Includes over 200 works on linguistics published during the first two decades after the
revolution in Cuba. The author deals with grammar, phonetics, syntax, semantics,
lexicography, and dialects.

411   **Consideraciones acerca del vocabulario cubano.** (Thoughts on
Cuban vocabulary.)
Leonardo Depestre Catony.   Havana: Ciencias Sociales, 1985. 58p.

This is a list of some of the most frequently heard, distinctively Cuban, popular and
vulgar expressions, with explanations and examples. It is accompanied by brief essays
on sporting vocabulary and the influence of English on Cuban vocabulary, particularly
during the years of US domination.

412   **El consonantismo en Cuba.** (Pronunciation of consonants in Cuba.)
J. Vitelio Ruiz Hernández, Eloina Miyares.   Havana: Ciencias
Sociales, 1984. 140p. bibliog.

The work is divided into two sections entitled 'Descriptive Linguistics' and
'Prescriptive Linguistics'. The first section comprises a detailed phonetic analysis of
the peculiarities of consonant pronunciation found in Cuban popular speech. The
second half gives an account of efforts undertaken in schools during the 1970s to
correct 'defective' non-standard pronunciation of consonants.

413 **Cuba: del 'acere' al 'chow'.** (Cuba: from 'buddy' to 'chow'.)
Eduardo de Benito. In: *La palabra americana* (American talk).
Santiago de Chile: Los Andes, 1992, p. 71-86.

This beautifully illustrated book is based on a series of twelve BBC Latin American
Service radio programmes and provides a colourful study of the evolution of the
various colloquialisms and adaptations in the Spanish-American language. The author
analyses the apposition of dependence and independence in defence of Cuban Spanish,
and looks in particular detail at the Africanisms.

414 **Current trends in the investigation of Cuban and Puerto Rican
phonology.**
T. D. Terrell. In: *Spanish in the United States: sociolinguistic
aspects.* Edited by Jon Amastae, Lucía Elias Olivares. Cambridge,
England; New York: Cambridge University Press, 1982, p. 47-70.

Terrell examines the differences between Cuban and Puerto Rican Spanish and that
spoken in other areas of Latin America. She looks at the four main areas of interest in
Cuban and Puerto Rican speech, namely: the aspiration and deletion of 's' at the ends
of words and syllables; velarization and deletion of 'a' at the ends of words and
syllables; the lateralization of 'r' at the ends of words and syllables; and the
velarization and devoicing of 'r' and the intervocalic trilled 'rr'. Terrell concludes that
much more research on how languages change still needs to be carried out.

415 **De lo popular y lo vulgar en el habla cubana.** (Popular and vulgar
expressions in spoken Cuban.)
Carlos Paz Pérez. Havana: Ciencias Sociales, 1988. 228p.

The author offers a linguistic discussion of the origins and usage of popular and vulgar
Cuban expressions, with a glossary and bibliography.

416 **Diccionario cubano de términos populares y vulgares.** (Dictionary
of Cuban popular and vulgar expressions.)
Carlos Paz Pérez. Havana: Ciencias Sociales, 1994. 192p.

A series of alphabetical lists, divided into twenty-one thematic areas (such as dress,
money, death and Afro-Cuban rituals), of contemporary popular expressions and
marginal slang, accompanied by explanations and examples of usage. The introduction
discusses the historical influences which have played a part in the development of
modern Cuban Spanish.

417 **Diccionario de cubanismos más usuales: como habla el cubano.**
(Dictionary of the most frequent Cubanisms: how Cubans speak.)
José Sánchez-Boudy. Miami, Florida: Ediciones Universal, 1978.
429p.

This survey of modern popular usage is unusual in that it also seeks to include items
peculiar to the speech of the Cuban exile community in the United States.

418 **Diccionario provincial casi razonado de vozes y frases cubanas.**
(Dictionary of Cuban provincial terms and expressions.)
Esteban Pichardo. Havana: Ciencias Sociales, 1985. 640p.

Originally published in 1836, this was the first dictionary to deal with the vocabulary
of a specific Latin American country. Four editions, each more wide-ranging than the
last, were published in Pichardo's lifetime. The entries consist of frequently extensive
articles which provide the origins, as well as the meanings of the alphabetically listed
terms, and list regional variations.

419 **La evolución de los indoamericanismos en el español hablado en
Cuba.** (The evolution of Amerindian elements in the spoken Spanish
of Cuba.)
Sergio Valdés Bernal. Havana: Ciencias Sociales, 1986. 188p.
bibliog.

The author provides a detailed analysis of the processes at work in the adoption and
gradual evolution of Amerindian vocabulary within the Spanish spoken in Cuba.

420 **Felipe Poey, lingüísta.** (Felipe Poey, linguist.)
Rodolfo Alpizar Castillo. Havana: Ciencias Sociales, 1984. 206p.
bibliog.

An account of the life and wide-ranging achievements of the pioneering Franco-Cuban
naturalist, anthropologist and linguist, Felipe Poey y Aloy (1799-1891) is followed by
a selection of his writings on linguistic topics.

421 **Fraseología y contexto.** (Phraseology and context.)
Antonia María Tristá. Havana: Ciencias Sociales, 1988. 195p.

A study of phrases in Cuban Spanish is made in this work, accompanied by a listing of
over 300 Cuban-Spanish phrases, providing definitions and examples of contemporary
usage.

422 **El habla popular cubana de hoy.** (Contemporary popular Cuban
speech.)
Argelio Santiesteban. Havana: Ciencias Sociales, 1985. 526p.

Some of the most characteristic, popular and vulgar items of vocabulary and expressions to be heard in Cuba today are to be found in this alphabetical list, written by a
popular journalist for a non-academic audience. Humorous and informative, it
includes examples of usage, often from contemporary fiction, and where applicable
provides information on other Spanish-speaking countries where the items also occur.

423 **Las lenguas del Africa subsahara y el español de Cuba.**
(The languages of Sub-Saharan Africa and Cuban Spanish.)
Sergio Valdés Bernal. Havana: Editorial Academia, 1987. 112p.
bibliog.

Presents an account of the linguistic groups to which the African slaves brought to
Cuba belonged, and considers the socio-religious processes whereby elements of their
languages were assimilated into the Spanish spoken on the island.

424 **Markedness and a Cuban dialect of Spanish.**
Jorge M. Guitart. Washington, DC: Georgetown University Press,
1976. 90p.

Guitart begins with an overview of the theory of 'markedness', before moving on to
consider the educated Spanish of Havana and its commonalities with other Spanish-
American and Cuban dialects. He discusses various aspects of markedness, such as the
neutralization of certain elements of speech, and examines Postal's theory of
markedness (1968). Finally the author proposes a theory of relative markedness,
analysing the phonetic neutralization phenomena of *habanero*, or educated Spanish of
Havana, in the light of relative markedness.

425 **Noun-phase pluralization in the Spanish of Cuban Mariel entrants.**
Diane Ringer Uber. *Hispanic Linguistics*, vol. 3, nos. 1-2 (1989),
p. 74-88.

The Spanish spoken by Cuban entrants into the United States on the 1980 Mariel
boatlift is analysed in this study.

426 **Nuevo catauro de cubanismos.** (New catalogue of Cubanisms.)
Fernando Ortiz. Havana: Ciencias Sociales, 1985. 526p. bibliog.

Originally published in 1923, this is a classic work of Cuban lexicographical studies
by the leading Cuban ethnographer. Expanding on the work of his predecessor
Esteban Pichardo, Ortiz defines, illustrates the usage and offers explanations of the
origins of thousands of items of Cuban vocabulary.

427 **Palabras del trasfondo: estudio sobre el coloquialismo cubano.**
(Words from the undercurrent: study of Cuban colloquialism.)
Virgilio López Lemus. Havana: Editorial Letras Cubanas, 1988.
414p.

A study of the colloquial use of language in the work of contemporary Cuban poets.

428 **The use of English and Spanish among Cubans in Miami.**
Isabel Castellanos. *Cuban Studies*, vol. 20 (1990), p. 49-63.

One of several articles on Cuban Spanish, as spoken by Cubans in Miami and as used
in the Afro-Cuban religions.

Religion

General

429 Expresiones religiosas existentes en Cuba. (Religious manifestations existing in Cuba.)
Daysi Fariñas, et al.   Havana: Editorial Academia, 1990. [n.p.].

This overview of religious practice in modern Cuba provides a guide to Christian churches and organizations, the Ecumenical Council, Judaism and the various syncretic cults in Cuba.

430 Fidel & religion.
Conversations with Frei Betto.   Melbourne, Australia: Ocean Press, 1990. 268p.

Based on interviews lasting twenty-three hours and carried out over four days in 1985 between Fidel Castro and a Brazilian priest, this is unique on two counts: Castro's reminiscences about his childhood years and education in religious schools, and the meeting of two worldviews – Marxism and Christianity. Each held his ground, firm in his own convictions, yet with a mutual understanding of morality, ethics and the need for unity in defence of the poor in the fight for a better world. Betto recounts his visit to Cuba, and Castro reflects on the experience and challenges of the Cuban revolution, and relations between the Communist Party of Cuba and the Church. Also published in Cuba as *Fidel and religion: talks with Frei Betto* (Havana: Publications of the Council of State, 1987. 535p.) and in the United States as *Fidel and religion: Castro talks on revolution and religion with Frei Betto* (Introduction by Harvey Cox. New York: Simon & Schuster, 1988. 313p.).

431 Religion in Cuba today: a new church in a new society.
Edited by Alice Hageman, Philip E. Wheaton.   New York: Association Press, 1971. 317p.

A sympathetic account of religion and Church–state relations in the early years of the revolution, including interviews with leading figures of various religious organizations in Cuba and official Church statements. This compilation of articles encompasses history, theology and biblical mission.

432 **La religión en la cultura.** (Religion in culture.)
Jorge Ramírez Calzadilla, et al. Havana: Editorial Academia. 1990.

This ambitious work brings together a wide range of research into religious expression in Cuba. It attempts to cover the Cuban cultural and historical context of Catholicism, Protestantism, African religions, Spiritism and Pentecostalism, and takes a valuable look at religious practices in rural Cuba.

433 **Salvation through Christ or Marx: religion in revolutionary Cuba.**
Margaret E. Crahan. In: *Churches and politics in Latin America.*
Edited by Daniel H. Levine. Beverly Hills, California: Sage, 1980,
p. 238-66.

Crahan deals with the Catholic, Protestant and Afro-Cuban religions in Cuba. She provides a background survey of pre-revolutionary Cuba which points to the weakness of institutional Christianity before 1959, as well as outlining official discouragement of religious practice in the first two decades of revolution.

Catholicism

434 **El amor todo lo espera: mensaje de la conferencia de obispos católicos de Cuba.** (Love hopes all things: message from the conference of Catholic bishops in Cuba.)
The Cuban Catholic Bishops. Havana: Havana Diocese, Cuban Catholic Church, 1993. 8p.

This pastoral message from the Catholic bishops of Cuba, calling for dialogue and fraternal relations between Cubans at home and abroad, was directed at politicians as well as practising Catholics. It focused on Cuba's deepening economic, social and moral dilemmas and sparked heated debate in the media in Cuba and the United States.

435 **Between God and the Party: religion and politics in revolutionary Cuba.**
John M. Kirk. Tampa, Florida: University of South Florida Press,
1989. 231p.

This monograph charts the historical rise, decline and resurgence of the Catholic Church. From a powerful colonial institution which assimilated the idea of slavery, the Church came to lack any broad constituency and, after 1902, was denied constitutional recognition. The study's principal concern is the post-1959 process of deterioration in Church–state relations through to the rapprochement of the 1980s. It underscores the personal, generational and class nature of the immediate post-revolutionary confrontation, and the latter-day *modus vivendi* with a socialized and radicalized new theology, which helps explain the remarkable resurgence of Church popularity and fortunes.

436 **The Catholic faith and revolution in Cuba: contradictions and understanding.**
Aurelio Alonso Tejada. In: *Transformation and struggle: Cuba faces the 1990s.* Edited by Sandor Halebsky, John Kirk, with Rafael Hernández. New York: Praeger, 1990, p. 219-33.
Traces the history of Church–state relations from the 1950s up to Fidel Castro's high-profile meetings with religious leaders in Brazil and Havana. The author argues that while the Cuban revolution has only been in conflict with two religious institutions (the Catholic Church and Jehovah's Witnesses) discrimination has been more generalized.

437 **The Church and socialism in Cuba.**
Raúl Gómez Treto, translated by Phillip Bergman. Maryknoll, New York: Orbis Books, 1988. 151p.
Written for the Latin American Church History Commission by a leading Cuban lay Catholic, this is one of the best accounts of Church–state relations in the post-1959 period, with an outline of the general situation of the Church before 1959. From a vantage point of relatively harmonious relations, the author, himself sympathetic to the revolution, ably charts a periodization as disconcertion (1959-60), confrontation (1961-62), evasion (1963-67), re-encounter (1968-78), and dialogue (1979-85). He discusses the growing 1960s differences between the institutional Church's Euro-centric and anti-revolution stance and younger Catholics' recognition of the revolution's commitment to equality, health and education, in line with the new social concerns of the Latin American Church.

438 **Guillermo Sardiñas: el sacerdote comandante, testimonio.**
(Guillermo Sardiñas: the priest-commander, testimony.)
Yolanda Portuondo. Havana: Editorial Cultural Popular, 1987. 257p.
Sardiñas (1914-64) was the first priest to join the rebel army in the Sierra Maestra as a non-combatant. This biography is based on the testimony of people who knew him.

439 **Iglesia y esclavitud en Cuba.** (Church and slavery in Cuba.)
Javier Laviña. *America Negra*, no. 1 (June 1991), p. 11-29.
The initial accord between Church and property became strained with the 19th-century sugar boom, as clergy in chapels built on the sugar estates found themselves between colonial state, master and slave. The author documents how the clergy were increasingly called upon to christianize the slaves, which was perceived as a means of ensuring their docility.

440 **International and national aspects of the Catholic Church in Cuba.**
Jorge I. Domínguez. *Cuban Studies* (1989), vol. 19, p. 43-60.
An analysis of Church–state relations in Cuba over three decades, this article focuses on the tensions between national and international factors which have helped shape the relationship. It pays particular attention to the second half of the 1980s when

relations appeared to be warming, examining the documents of the 1986 Catholic Congress and the government's response, and noting a slowly emerging détente.

Protestantism

441 Baptists in western Cuba: from the wars of independence to revolution.
Harold Greer.   *Cuban Studies*, vol. 19 (1989), p. 61-77.

This article traces the history of Baptists in western Cuba from their beginnings in colonial times to the present day. It discusses the warm reception Baptists received in Cuba during the anti-Spanish period and considers the work they did there. The numbers of Cubans joining the denomination grew rapidly, so that by the early years of the Castro revolution they were at their greatest. Greer explains that although Baptists at first supported the revolution, they soon began to suffer restrictions and in 1965 over fifty of their leaders were arrested. Today, however, relations with the Cuban government are the best they have been since 1965.

442 The Cuban church in a sugar economy.
John Merle Davis.   New York: International Missionary Council, 1942. 144p.

A dated, but informative, study of US Protestant missionary work in Cuba, examining ways in which the evangelical churches might better integrate on the island.

443 Methodism's first fifty years in Cuba.
Sterling Augustus Neblett.   Wilmore, Kentucky: Ashbury Press, 1976. 303p. bibliog.

The period in which Methodism established itself as one of the most successful Protestant denominations in 20th-century Cuba forms the subject matter of this informative work. It provides information on churches, missions, schools, and clinics between 1899, when an American political and military presence was first established in Cuba, and 1949.

444 Visiting Quakers in Cuba at Easter 1994: reflections from a group of British Quakers.
Compiled by Marigold Best.   London: Quaker Peace & Service, 1994. 32p.

A light yet thoughtful and introspective report of a two-week visit to Cuba by British Quakers, with an eye to welfare provision in the current crisis. The visit was hosted by the Cuban Ecumenical Council and Cuban Quakers in Havana and eastern Cuba.

Afro-Cuban religions

445 **African religious influences in Cuba, Puerto Rico and Hispaniola.**
George Brandon. *Journal of Caribbean Studies*, vol. 7, no. 2
(winter 1989); no. 3 (spring 1990), p. 201-31. bibliog.

Brandon presents a clear and systematic discussion of the historical and contemporary
presence of African religious influences in three Caribbean countries. He pays
particular attention to Santería, the Afro-Cuban syncretic religion. Another larger
work by Brandon covering the spread of Santería in the New World, and published by
Indiana University Press in 1993, is *Santería from Africa to the New World*.

446 **Afro-Cuban religion in exile: Santería in South Florida.**
Stephan Palmié. *Journal of Caribbean Studies*, vol. 5, no. 3 (1986),
p. 171-79.

An anthropological enquiry into the spread of Santería to middle-class, white, Cuban
American South Florida. The author suggests the need to look more closely at Santería
as an Afro-Cuban religious system, rather than its inadequate categorization as a
symbol for ethnic identification, psychological defence, and an alternative therapy for
a dislocated community.

447 **Hablen paleros y santeros.** (Let the Palo and Santería priests speak.)
Tomás Fernández Robaina. Havana: Ciencias Sociales, 1994.

Based on interviews conducted during the 1980s, this is an important contribution to
the growing body of literature on Afro-Cuban religions. In this work the practitioners
of two of those religions, Palo and Santería, reveal the beauty and strength of
conviction of their beliefs and ethics. They also discuss their rituals and their concerns
in modern-day Cuba.

448 **Legends of Santería.**
Migene González-Wippler. St. Paul, Minnesota: Llewelyn
Publications, 1994. 274p. bibliog.

González-Wippler has collected together some fifty *patakines* (stories) about the
orishas, or deities, of the Santería religion, as told by three of the cult's priests.

449 **Los llamados cultos sincréticos y el espiritismo.** (The so-called
syncretic cults and spiritism.)
Aníbal Argüelles, Ileana Hodge. Havana: Editorial Academia, 1991.
[n.p.].

This is the result of research into the cults introduced into Cuba by African slaves:
Regla de Ocho (Santería); Regla Conga (or Palo Monte); Regla Arará; Ganga; Vudú;
and the Abakuá Secret Societies. In addition to this it covers the various
manifestations of spiritism, which have been particularly vibrant during important
moments in history, such as the 19th-century wars of independence. The work
includes antecedents of these cults, their emergence and evolution under Cuban
conditions, internal links, structure and functioning, as well as a sociological analysis
which attempts to assess their social significance.

450 **El Monte: Igbo, Finda, Ewe Orisha, Vititi Nfinda.**
Lydia Cabrera.   Miami, Florida: Colección del Chicherekú, 1986. 564p.
First published in Havana in 1954, this is subtitled 'Notes on the religions, magic, superstitions and folklore of black Cubans and the Cuban people'. It is heralded as the classic work of a prolific author. Herself phenotypically white Cuban, Cabrera painstakingly documents the extensive African heritage which permeates the whole of Cuba, in tribute to black Cuba and at the same time sensitizing her fellow white Cubans to their own African influences. The study contains invaluable sections on plants and their medical use. See also: *¿Sincretismo religioso? Santa Bárbara – Changó* by Natalia Bolívar and Marco López Cepero (Havana: Editorial Pablo de la Torriente, 1995), which argues that transculturation has occurred between Afro-Cuban religions and Catholicism.

451 **Orin Orisa: songs for selected heads.**
John Mason.   New York: Yoruba Theological Archministry, 1992. 402p.
For twenty-five years John Mason was intrigued by the fact that Cubans, Afro-Americans and Puerto Ricans were moved to dance and sing to hundreds of songs they had memorized but whose words they didn't understand. A Yoruba priest, he himself was moved to transcribe and translate over 550 Yoruba songs as he knew them to be sung, or as they were given to him, mainly from Cuba but more recently also in the United States, invoking some twenty-five orisa (orisha) or deities. In this way, the Yoruba voice and heritage could be heard and appreciated.

452 **Los orishas en Cuba.** (The orishas in Cuba.)
Natalia Bolívar.   Havana: Fundación Pablo Milanés, 1994. 2nd ed.
301p. bibliog.
A revised and expanded edition of a book published in 1990 that rapidly sold out in Cuba. It was the first of its kind to narrate in popularized, mini-encyclopaedic form the myths, legends and attributes of the Santería orishas (orisas) or deities. The book is divided into gatekeeper orishas, orishas of creation, nature, motherhood, water, fire, divination, health and death, and includes a glossary. This is the product of many years of study by an author who was curator of the Havana Fine Arts, Napoleonic and Numismatic Museums.

453 **Reglas de Congo: Palo Monte Mayombe.**
Lydia Cabrera.   Miami, Florida: Ediciones CR, 1979. 225p.
While the Bantu people of Africa, known as Congo in Cuba, were numerous, they found less acceptance in Cuba than other immigrant groups. They were generally feared and distrusted, and their secret rituals seen as evil. This narrative is based on the stories told to Cabrera by Cubans of Congo descent, reconstructing a history of oppression and marginality, accommodation and resistance, and religious beliefs and conduct which, like all others, speak both good and evil.

454 **The Santería experience.**
Migene González-Wippler.   St. Paul, Minnesota: Llewelyn
Publications, 1992. 2nd ed. 365p. bibliog.
The author recounts her own experiences as a researcher and initiate of Santería. The work was first published in 1989.

455　**Santería – the religion: a legacy of faith, rites, and magic.**
Migene González-Wippler.　St. Paul, Minnesota: Llewelyn
Publications, 1994. 2nd ed. 400p. bibliog.

First published in 1989 by Harmony Books (Washington, DC), this is a comprehensive introduction to the beliefs and rites of this syncretic cult which evolved in Cuba from a fusion of Catholicism with the beliefs of African slaves.

456　**El sistema religioso de los afrocubanos.** (The religious beliefs of the
Afro-Cubans.)
Rómulo Lachateñere, selection of texts and prologue by Isaac Barreal.
Havana: Ciencias Sociales, 1992. 414p.

This volume comprises a major trilogy of works by the late leading Cuban scholar of Yoruba-based Santería in Cuba: 'Oh, mío Yemayá!', 1938; 'Manual de Santería', 1942; and 'El sistema religioso de los Lucumí y otras influencias africanas en Cuba' (The religious beliefs of the Lucumí and other African influences in Cuba), part published in article form in 1939-46 and 1961, and part unpublished. Ten further articles are also included.

457　**Sobre muertos y dioses.** (On dead men and gods.)
Joel James Figarola.　Santiago de Cuba: Ediciones Caserón, 1989.
85p.

The author outlines the principles and philosophy underlying Afro-Cuban belief systems, highlighting conscience, honesty, creativity, social quality, and national solidarity in the conduct, thinking and ritual of believers and practitioners. A key concept is that of multiple representation of forces in existence, and the nurturing of the living by the gods and the dead.

458　**El vodú en cuba.** (Vodun in Cuba.)
Joel James, José Miller, Alexis Alarcón.　Santo Domingo, Dominican
Republic: CEDEE, 1992. 348p. bibliog.

Written by three Cuban researchers from the Casa del Caribe in Santiago de Cuba and published in the Dominican Republic, this study establishes vodun as a significant belief system in eastern Cuba. The authors situate this in the context of 200 years of immigration from nearby Haiti, but also trace the evolution of Cuban syncretic forms. The study contains detailed descriptions of ceremonies, beliefs, divinities, attributes, ritual food and drink, and provides a glossary of terms.

459　**Walking the night: the Afro-Cuban world of Santería.**
Raúl Canizares.　Rochester, Vermont: Destiny Books, 1993. 148p.
bibliog.

The author, a practitioner in Florida, describes Santería as the faith of thinking people responding to an evolving, and often hostile, diaspora environment. He argues that it is the product less of syncretism than of dissimulation, the conscious, deliberate use of Catholicism to allow the practice of African-origin beliefs. The book provides a background history and descriptive overview, dispelling myths and disinformation. It incorporates life stories and narrative, describes the use of herbs and plants, and concludes with reflections on Santería as a world religion.

The Abakuá secret society in Cuba: languages and culture.
See item no. 405.

Law and religion in Marxist Cuba: a human rights inquiry.
See item no. 572.

Herencia clásica: oraciones populares ilustradas por Zaída del Río.
(Classic heritage: popular prayers illustrated by Zaída del Río.)
See item no. 948.

Religion and politics in revolutionary Cuba: a bibliographical guide.
See item no. 1158.

Social Conditions

460 About youth.
Fidel Castro. Havana: Organizing Committee of the Eleventh World Festival of Youth and Students, 1978. 296p.

This compilation of Fidel Castro's speeches to and about the young people of Cuba, made from 1959 to December 1976, provides insights into the evolution of his thinking, and hence of government youth policy. Castro's September 1959 address sets the scene; made during the handing over of a military barracks for use as a school, it stresses the interrelationship between education, young people's right to enjoy life, and their duty to be good revolutionaries. See also: 'Youth and the Cuban revolution: notes on the road traversed and its perspectives' by Juan Luis Martín (*Latin American Perspectives*, vol. 18, no. 2 [spring 1991], p. 95-100).

461 Children in Cuba: twenty years of revolution.
Federación de Mujeres Cubanas. Havana: Ciencias Sociales, 1979. 129p.

An account of two decades of Cuban revolutionary policy and provision for the education, health, social welfare, culture and recreation of children. The introduction places the rights of children within the context of the Universal Human Rights Declaration, and the aspiration of life, health, and material and spiritual welfare for all under the Cuban socialist system. The book first covers the 1961 literacy campaign, followed by: the consolidation of a national education system; the achievements made in health-care and health education; the special programmes instituted for physically and mentally disabled, orphaned and abandoned children; cultural, sports and other institutions.

462 Code on children and youth.
Havana: Ciencias Sociales, 1978. 88p.

This illustrated English-language translation of Law no. 16 (1978) covers: general provisions; shaping a communist personality in the young; participation and initiative among school children, students and working youth; duty to defend the homeland; and youth policy related to culture, physical education and recreation.

463 **Cuba.**

Jill Hamberg. In: *Housing policies in the socialist Third World.*
Edited by Kosta Mathey. London: Mansell, 1990, p. 35-70.

Hamberg presents a well-researched study of housing provision in revolutionary Cuba, with background information on pre-revolutionary times. The article considers urban growth, housing construction and technology, housing distribution, tenure and security, self-built housing, and microbrigades. It draws attention to the fact that housing remains one of the country's most pressing problems, all the more so as other problems receded with the massive investments in economic, educational and health-care facilities over and above housing. Several earlier versions were also published, including the monograph *Under construction, housing policy in revolutionary Cuba.* (New York: Center for Cuban Studies, 1986. 36p.).

464 **El Cubano se ofrece.** (The Cuban introduces himself.)

Iván Cañas. Havana: Ediciones Unión, 1982. [n. p.]. photographs.

Constitutes a photographic record of a small Cuban town, Caibarién, during the sugar harvest in 1970. The photographs and Reynaldo González's introduction capture something of the atmosphere of a watershed year when, though the sugar harvest was a record 8.5 million tonnes, the failure to reach the over-ambitious target of ten million tonnes eventually led to recriminations and a rethink of economic policy.

465 **Cubans.**

Lynn Geldof. London: Bloomsbury, 1991. 358p. bibliog.

In this rare, and mostly successful, attempt to document the views and day-to-day culture of contemporary Cubans, Geldof, who worked in Cuba as a journalist between 1985 and 1989, engages her subjects in conversations which often evince poignant, quirky, thoughtful or humorous observations on Cuban life. Her cast of characters includes a young single mother and an ex-socialite, an alienated young gay man and an establishment cultural figure who later defected, and several known and unknown exiles. Her interviews with academics pursue the implications of Soviet reforms for Cuba's future, the changing trade relationship with the USSR, US–Cuban relations, and youth alienation.

466 **Encuesta de trabajadores rurales 1956-57 realizada por la
Agrupación Católica Universitaria.** (Survey of rural workers
1956-57 carried out by the Catholic University Group.)
Agrupación Católica Universitaria. *Economía y Desarrollo,* no. 12
(1972).

One of the few pre-1959 surveys of socio-economic conditions in Cuba is reproduced in this issue. Long a classic reference, but subject to questioning by some US Cubanologists in recent years, this remains a useful source of information about the social conditions of the rural poor in 1950s Cuba. The survey's findings were among the sources quoted by the Castro-led revolutionaries to justify their far-reaching social reforms after 1959.

467   **Everything within the revolution: Cuban strategies for social development since 1960.**
Thomas C. Dalton.   Boulder, Colorado: Westview, 1993. 178p.
bibliog.

Dalton provides a welcome departure from development measured by economic growth rather than social development, and looks specifically at the creation of institutions and services providing for growth within the social sector, in terms of education, health, and welfare. The study attempts to set these in a comparative framework, taking in both Western modernist and post-modernist thinking and what Dalton describes as the cyclical swings of reformism and retrenchment in East European socialism. Vital to the analysis is his focus on scientific norms and the techniques of intervention and control. This includes psychoanalytic theory, in the transition from the 1960s period of mobilization and redistribution to 1970s institutionalization and regularization.

468   **Living the revolution: an oral history of contemporary Cuba.**
Oscar Lewis, Ruth M. Lewis, Susan M. Rigdon.   Urbana, Illinois: University of Illinois, vol. 1: 'Four men', 1977. 538p.; vol. 2: 'Four women', 1977. 443p. bibliog.; vol. 3: 'Neighbours', 1978. 581p.
bibliog.

These three volumes were published after the death of Oscar Lewis, who headed a team of anthropologists carrying out fieldwork in 1969-70 on the effects of the Cuban revolution among the poor, on what Lewis identified as 'the culture of poverty'. In the foreword to volume one, his widow Ruth Lewis explains how he died shortly after the Cuban government stopped the work and he had to leave the island. The volumes contain rare ethnographical details on the lives of men, women and families living in neighbourhoods of Havana, cutting across race, class and gender parameters, at a unique time of rapid change and upheaval.

469   **Microbrigadas and participation in Cuba.**
Roberto Segre.   In: *The scope of social architecture.*   Edited by
C. Richard Hatch.   New York: Van Nostrand Reinhold, 1984,
p. 349-60.

The author, an Argentinian and long-term resident in Havana, subsequently extended this study and published a monograph in Spanish on pre- and post-1959 housing in Cuba.

470   **No free lunch: food and revolution in Cuba today.**
Edited by Medea Benjamin, Joseph Collins, Michael Scott.   San Francisco: Institute for Food and Development Policy, 1984. 240p.

This is a thoughtful and insightful book from the Food First development lobby in the United States. It provides a highly readable account of the social and food policy of the revolution over a twenty-five-year period. Based on first-hand experience and research, the study takes a candid and balanced look at the successes and failures of food and farming realities, discussing and analysing the positive and negative lessons of Cuba's attempts to end hunger. A decade later the issues raised – rationing, co-operatives and the farmers' markets – are all the more pertinent.

471 **The people of Buenaventura: relocation of slum dwellers in postrevolutionary Cuba.**
Douglas Butterworth. Urbana, Illinois: University of Illinois Press, 1980. 157p. bibliog.

Through an ethnographic study of people from a working-class district of Havana who were rehoused after 1959, Butterworth provides a wealth of detail on family life before and after the revolution.

472 **Recent trends in Cuban housing policies and the revival of the microbrigade movement.**
Kosta Mathey. *Bulletin of Latin American Research*, vol. 8, no. 1 (March 1989), p. 67-81.

An analysis of the microbrigade experiment whereby people from all walks of life worked voluntarily in the construction sector, building housing and public works. Versions of this article also appeared in: *Trialog* (1988), *Netherlands Journal of Housing and Environment Research* (1989) and *Habitat International* (1989).

473 **La seguridad social en Cuba.** (Social security in Cuba.)
Félix Argüelles Varcárcel. Havana: Ciencias Sociales, 1989. 142p.

The author provides an explanation of social security legislation in Cuba, with useful appendices on the evolution of social assistance, current legislation, and the provisions of Law 24 of 1979 covering incapacity, maternity and retirement provisions.

474 **Social control and deviance in Cuba.**
Luis Salas. New York: Praeger, 1979. 398p. bibliog.

An objective treatment by a writer who left Cuba as a child and returned in 1979. He acknowledges many of the revolution's material achievements but questions the impact on the population. Salas argues that an understanding of the nature of deviance and social control is essential to the study of Marxist societies, especially in Cuba where the means adopted for social control and the instilling of the new 'socialist morality' were at the crux of the ideology adopted in the quest for the 'New Man'. Coverage includes chapters on: juvenile delinquency; common crime; sexual deviance; suicide; the role of the judiciary system; the police as a social control mechanism; CDR-grassroots control; regulation of socialist labour; and the use of sanctions and incentives.

475 **Social equity, agrarian transition and development in Cuba, 1845-90.**
Jean Stubbs. In: *Welfare, poverty and development in Latin America*. Edited by Christopher Abel, Colin M. Lewis. Basingstoke, England; London: Macmillan, 1993, p. 281-95.

This article focuses on agrarian policy in the socialist development state and considers the debate around social equity versus economic efficiency, one rendered all the more urgent by Cuba's economic crisis of the 1990s.

476 **Tiempo para no olvidar.** (A time that must not be forgotten.)
Photographs by José Tabío, introduction by Félix Pita Rodríguez.
Havana: Editorial Letras Cubanas, 1985. [n. p.]. photographs.

A posthumous collection of photographs taken before 1959 by a revolutionary
photographer and film-maker, with an introduction by the novelist Félix Pita
Rodríguez. Concentrating on the most poverty-stricken sectors of the population, they
provide a useful record of some of the social conditions which nurtured the revolution.

Due South; or, Cuba, past and present.
See item no. 43.

Excursión a Vuelta Abajo. (Excursion to Vuelta Abajo.)
See item no. 44.

Cuban tapestry.
See item no. 56.

Cuba.
See item no. 526.

Gays under the Cuban revolution.
See item no. 527.

Family code: law no. 1289, 1975.
See item no. 551.

Analysis of research on the Cuban family 1970-87.
See item no. 1166.

Annotated bibliography on the topic of the family.
See item no. 1167.

Health

477 **Apuntes históricos relativos a la farmacia en Cuba.** (Historical notes on Cuban pharmacy.)
Manuel García Hernández, Susana Martínez Fortún y Foyo.
Havana: Ministry of Public Health, 1967. 73p.

A study of the practice of pharmacy, pharmaceutical training and professional organizations in Cuba, from the colonial period up to the 1950s.

478 **La atencion médica en Cuba hasta 1958.** (Health-care in Cuba up to 1958.)
Roberto E. Hernández. *Journal of Inter-American Affairs*, vol. 11, no. 4 (Oct. 1969), p. 533-57.

Argues that the pre-revolutionary health-care system in Cuba was capable of providing adequate medical attention and looks at hospital care provision and the training, number and distribution of medical practitioners.

479 **Cuba as a world medical power: the politics of symbolism.**
Julie Feinsilver. *Latin American Research Review*, vol. 24, no. 2 (1989), p. 1-34. bibliog.

Feinsilver analyses Cuba's health record in a political context, examining the government's use of its health achievements to enhance its international prestige.

480 **The Cuban health-care system: responsiveness to changing population needs and demands.**
Sarah Santana. *World Development*, vol. 15, no. 1 (1987), p. 115-29.

Focuses on the changing Cuban health profile over the twenty-five years since the revolution, based on the principles of health care as a people's right, a responsibility of the state, and an integral part of social and economic development. The author charts the stages from primary health-care and epidemiological control in the 1960s, building the national health system in the 1970s, to 1980s tertiary and community care. Santana emphasizes the responsibility and accountability within the system.

481 **Cuban medicine.**
Ross Danielson. New Brunswick, New Jersey: Transaction, 1979. 247p. bibliog.

This detailed account provides a historical survey of medicine in Cuba, as well as the transformation in Cuban medical training and health provision, especially the organization of rural and primary medical care, in the first decade and a half of revolution. The author discusses the socio-economic cost of the rapid expansion of provision. See also 'Medicine in the community' by the same author, in *Cuba: twenty-five years of revolution, 1959-1984.* Edited by Sandor Halebsky, John M. Kirk (New York: Praeger, 1985, p. 45-61).

482 **The development of high technology and its medical applications in Cuba.**
Manuel Limonta Vidal, Guillermo Padrón. *Latin American Perspectives*, vol. 18, no. 2 (spring 1991), p. 101-13.

The director of the Havana-based Genetic Engineering and Biotechnology Centre discusses the policies and results of the Cuban government's commitment to advanced research and high technology in the state health-care system.

483 **Different roads to a common goal: the lowering of infant mortality rates in Latin America.**
José F. Betancourt. *Revista Geográfica*, no. 107 (Jan.-June 1988), p. 49-66. bibliog.

Reviews the history of the infant mortality rate in Chile, Costa Rica and Cuba, arguing that it is possible to alleviate health, nutritional and educational problems before other socio-economic problems are eliminated.

484 **Fertility determinants in Cuba.**
Paula E. Hollerbach, Sergio Díaz-Briquets. Washington, DC: National Academy Press, 1983. 242p.

An informed and informative discussion of the fertility levelling off in the early 1980s, in which baby-boom / baby-bust trends in revolutionary Cuba are explained in socio-economic and aspirational terms. The first was the product of income redistribution, economic growth and the provision of services, and the second, the result of factors such as high levels of education and employment, low levels of consumption and housing shortage.

485 **El folclor médico de Cuba.** (Medical folklore in Cuba.)
José Seoane Gallo. Havana: Ciencias Sociales, 1984. 896p.

Detailing popular prescriptions, beliefs and superstitions, this fascinating book was researched in Camagüey province in 1961 and 1962. It provides such interesting details as twenty-seven ways to ease ear aches, thirty-three ways to cure eye strain, and twenty-three cures for impotence.

486 **Fundamentación para un nuevo enfoque de la medicina en la comunidad.** (The basis for a new approach to community medicine.)
Cuban Ministry of Health.   Santo Domingo, Dominican Republic: Universidad Autónoma de Santo Domingo, 1977. 43p.

Provides an explanation of the thinking behind Cuba's community health programme, which has since been developed as an actively preventive system reaching most of the island's inhabitants.

487 **Healing the masses: Cuban health politics at home and abroad.**
Julie Feinsilver.   Berkeley, California: University of California Press, 1993. 307p.

This is the most comprehensive and objective work available on the Cuban medical system. It examines in depth the policy context in which the Cuban government decided to spend heavily not just on medical care but also on advanced research. While questioning shortcomings, Feinsilver acknowledges the exceptional achievements.

488 **Health and revolution in Cuba.**
Nelson P. Valdés.   *Science & Society*, vol. 35, no. 3 (autumn 1971), p. 311-31.

The author compares health provision in pre- and post-1959 Cuba over a range of variables, including nutrition, mortality, housing and the prevention and treatment of disease.

489 **Health, health planning, and health services in Cuba.**
Vicente Navarro.   *International Journal of Health Services*, vol. 2, no. 3 (summer 1972), p. 397-432.

Looks at the impact on mortality patterns of the equalization of health resources provision.

490 **The health revolution in Cuba.**
Sergio Díaz-Briquets.   Austin, Texas: University of Texas Press, 1983. 227p.

Health conditions in Cuba in the 20th century are surveyed in this work, with particular emphasis placed on the decline of mortality rates. There is a brief discussion of post-1959 achievements in health-care.

491 **Investigaciones de personalidad en Cuba.** (Research on personality in Cuba.)
Havana: Ciencias Sociales, 1987. 288p.

A collection of articles by Cuban psychologists on personality and motivation, group communication, personality and profession.

492   **La leyenda de Antoñica Izquierdo.** (The legend of Antoñica Izquierdo.)
      Tania Tolezano García, Ernesto Chávez Álvarez.   Havana: Ciencias
      Sociales, 1987. 188p.

Based on contemporary newspaper accounts, documents and over 100 oral interviews, this is a fascinating study of a water healer who became famous nationwide in the 1930s for her miracle cures in poverty-stricken rural Pinar del Río. She died in the Havana insane asylum in 1945. The Cuban film *Water days* is based on her life.

493   **Medical applications of high technology in Cuba.**
      Manuel Limonta Vidal, Guillermo Padrón.   In: *The Cuban revolution
      into the 1990s.*   Edited by Centro de Estudios sobre América.
      Boulder, Colorado: Westview, 1992, p. 163-74.

Discusses how Cuba, unlike many other developing Third World countries, has achieved a high level of medical and scientific development. Topics discussed include: the government programme of disease prevention; the training of staff and financing health-care services; the inauguration of institutions such as the Centro Nacional de Investigaciones Científicas and the Centro de Ingeniería Genética y Biotecnología; the results achieved by such centres; and statistics, such as numbers of personnel and hospitals.

494   **La medicina popular de Cuba.** (Popular medicine in Cuba.)
      Lydia Cabrera.   Miami, Florida: Ediciones Universal, 1987. 270p.

Presents a study of popular Cuban medicine through the ages, covering: doctors and healers of the past; the practice of offering up prayers to the gods to ward against illness and disaster; the development of medicine in Cuba in colonial times; 19th-century Cuban medicine, including rules and practices implemented, yellow fever and the cholera epidemic of 1833; 19th-century public health and the care of the young; 19th-century doctors and medicine, both secret and authorized; Afro-Cuban medicine and the spiritual side of healing; natural medicine in Cuba; and a selection of recipes for herbal remedies. Cabrera also includes an index of Cuban medicinal plants, both indigenous and imported.

495   **Médicos y medicinas en Cuba: historia, biografía, costumbrismo.**
      (Doctors and medicine in Cuba: history, biography, customs.)
      Emilio Roig de Leuchsenring.   Havana: Cuban Academy of Sciences,
      1965. 269p. bibliog.

An important collection of essays on the history of Cuban medicine and medical practices, with biographical sketches of such prominent Cuban physicians as Tomás Romay, Juan Guiteras and Carlos Finlay. The volume includes a section on folk medicine.

496   **The nutriture of Cubans: historical perspective and nutritional
      analysis.**
      Antonio M. Gordon, Jr.   *Cuban Studies*, vol. 13, no. 2 (summer 1983),
      p. 1-34. bibliog.

Compares the nutritional status of Cubans in the 1970s with that of populations in various Third World countries, before comparing the then current Cuban nutritional status with that prevailing before the 1959 revolution. Generalizing from sparse data, the author concludes that it is not possible to establish that Cuban nutriture was worse before the revolution, though it does appear to be better than that in other Third World countries. See also 'Cuba's food distribution system' by Joseph Collins and Medea Benjamin, in *Cuba: twenty-five years of revolution, 1959-1984*. Edited by Sandor Halebsky, John M. Kirk (New York: Praeger, 1985, p. 62-78).

497 Will Cuba's wonderdrugs lead to political and economic wonders?
Julie Feinsilver. *Cuban Studies*, vol. 22 (1992), p. 79-114.

Explores and evaluates Cuba's commitment to the development and export of biotechnology and pharmaceutical products in order to save the revolution from economic ruin. Feinsilver explains how, despite its success in this area, Cuba's export potential is hampered by its inability to compete with multinational companies, its disregard for patents and the US embargo.

Plantas medicinales, aromáticas y venenosas de Cuba. (Medicinal, aromatic and poisonous plants of Cuba.)
See item no. 80.

Biociencias en Cuba 1994-95. (Life sciences in Cuba 1994-95.)
See item no. 714.

The health-care market in Cuba.
See item no. 733.

Avances Médicos de Cuba. (Cuban Medical Advances.)
See item no. 1127.

Revista Cubana de Administración de Salud. (Cuban Journal of Health Administration.)
See item no. 1128.

Revista Cubana de Medicina. (Cuban Journal of Medicine.)
See item no. 1129.

Revista Cubana de Medicina Tropical. (Cuban Journal of Tropical Medicine.)
See item no. 1130.

Politics

1960s

498 Crítica a la época y otros ensayos. (Criticism of the era and other essays.)
José Antonio Portuondo.   Santa Clara, Cuba: Universidad Central de Las Villas, 1965. 311p.

This collection of political essays from one of Cuba's leading political figures, situates the Cuban revolution in the context of world revolution and socialist humanism and looks at the intellectual (as both creative writer and political thinker) and revolution in Cuban history.

499 Cuba: Castroism and communism, 1959-1966.
Andrés Suárez.   Cambridge, Massachusetts: MIT Press, 1967. 266p.

A detailed study of the early radicalization of the revolution and the Cuban transition to socialism, in the context of domestic and foreign politics.

500 Prologue to the Cuban revolution.
Robin Blackburn.   *New Left Review*, vol. 21 (Oct. 1963), p. 52-91.

Blackburn's incisive article still stands today as the class analysis of the origins of the 1959 revolution. It highlights the weakness of the Cuban bourgeoisie at the same time as demonstrating the broad base of middle-class, worker, peasant and student support for revolution.

501 The transformation of political culture in Cuba.
Richard R. Fagen.   Stanford, California: Stanford University Press, 1969. 271p.

Fagen produced an important early sympathetic contribution to an understanding of the process of change in political culture being effected in Cuba in the 1960s transition to socialism. Special attention is paid to the 1961 literacy campaign, the

125

schools of revolutionary instruction, and the Committees for the Defense of the Revolution.

1970s

502 **Cuba: order and revolution.**
Jorge I. Domínguez. Cambridge, Massachusetts: Harvard University Press, 1978. 682p. maps. bibliog.

The bulk of the contents, in this monumental work on 20th-century politics in Cuba, covers the post-1959 period. Part one looks at the pre-revolutionary periods, 1902-33 and 1933-58, and the breakdown of the political system. Part two on government through centralization deals with the new society, economy and government; and part three focuses on the political process and change: public policy; agrarian conflict and peasant politics; and political culture.

503 **Guerrillas in power: the course of the Cuban revolution.**
K. S. Karol. New York: Hill & Wang, 1970. 624p.

Written by an authority on the Chinese revolution, this is a lengthy and controversial political critique of the early Cuban revolution from the left. Much attention is paid to the 1930s antecedents of revolution, the role of the Communist Party, and developments in the 1950s and 1960s.

1980s

504 **Cuba: the revolution in peril.**
Janette Habel, translated from the French by Jon Barnes. London: Verso, 1989. 241p. bibliog.

Analyses the challenges and perils which faced Cuba in the 1980s as its revolution came under the greatest threat to its existence since the 1961 Bay of Pigs invasion and 1962 Missile Crisis. While not underestimating the external pressures on the small island state, Habel details the malaise within Cuban society caused by the limits on popular participation and the absence of a properly functioning socialist democracy. These have contributed to an ossified political order and the alienation of the young. Habel concludes by calling for a bold new policy of revolutionary democracy.

505 **Marxistas de América.** (Marxists of the Americas.)
Havana: Editorial Arte y Literatura, 1985. 465p.

A compilation of articles on culture and society by four leading Marxists of Latin America in the early 20th century: Cubans Julio Antonio Mella and Juan Marinello, along with Peruvian José Carlos Mariátegui and Argentinian Aníbal Ponce. Mercedes Santos Moray introduces all four contributors and underlines their relevance as forerunners to the thinking of the Cuban revolution. Thirty-five extracts of writings by Mella are included and eighteen by Marinello.

506 **Palabras en los setenta.** (Words at seventy.)
Carlos Rafael Rodríguez. Havana: Ciencias Sociales, 1984. 201p.

Rodríguez won the 1940 elections in Cuba on the Communist Party ticket, joined the insurrection in the 1950s, and went on to become a key revolutionary leader. This volume contains speeches and an interview he gave in 1983, and was published in honour of his seventieth birthday.

507 **Roots of revolution: radical thought in Cuba.**
Sheldon B. Liss. Lincoln, Nebraska; London: University of Nebraska Press, 1987. 269p. bibliog.

Liss presents a sympathetic account of the history of Cuban radicals and Cuban radicalism from the 1840s to the 1959 revolution. Summarizing the vast literature on the subject, the author provides an exposition of Cuban radicals' thoughts on their nation's protracted struggle for independence. This includes their beliefs about ethics, morality, religion, social mobility, politics and aesthetics, as well as their views on Cuban–US relations.

508 **Secret report on the Cuban revolution.**
Carlos Alberto Montaner. New Brunswick, New Jersey: Transaction, 1981. 284p. bibliog.

The report begins with a brief analysis of Batista's régime, before presenting the 'true story of the Cuban revolution'. This is followed by a discussion of the revolutionary government in Cuba. Successive chapters treat different aspects of Cuban life, such as religion, race, women, culture, perceptions of sexuality, human rights, the Cuban exodus, US/CIA involvement, and US–Cuban policy.

509 **Transición socialista y democracia: el caso cubano.** (Socialist transition and democracy: the Cuban case.)
Fernando Martínez. *Cuadernos de Nuestra América*, vol. 4, no. 7 (Jan.-July 1987), p. 76-115.

In an analysis of democracy in the Cuban revolution, Martínez focuses on the contradictions of socialist transition and the late 1980s period of rectification. Other publications which may be of interest are: *Cuba: continuity and change* by Jaime Suchlicki and Damián J. Fernández (Miami, Florida: University of Miami, Institute of Interamerican Studies, 1985. 190p.); and *Cuba: el estado marxista y la nueva clase* (Cuba: the Marxist state and the new class) by Ariel Hidalgo (Miami, Florida: General Printing, 1988).

1990s

510 **Caribbean revolutions and revolutionary theory: Cuba, Nicaragua, Grenada.**
Brian Meeks. Basingstoke, England: Macmillan Caribbean, 1993. 210p. bibliog.

The Cuban, Nicaraguan and Grenadian revolutions are compared in this work, drawing on the thoughts of theoreticians such as J. S. Mill and Theda S. Skocpol. Emphasis is placed on the conditions which facilitated the making of these revolutions, the social forces which led the process, and the role of human agency in creating and using revolutionary openings to effect positive changes in history. An expert on Grenada, the author deals with the Grenadian revolution in much more detail than either Nicaragua or Cuba. However, the Cuba chapter focuses on state-building, mass mobilization and limited disentrenchment over three decades of revolution.

511 **Cuban politics: the revolutionary experiment.**
Rhoda P. Rabkin. New York: Praeger, 1991. 233p. bibliog.

Rabkin has attempted a fair approach to the mixed political record of the Cuban revolution, which has reduced the extremes of wealth and poverty in the island, but restricted freedoms and generated exodus. The main areas considered are the genesis of the Castro régime, Fidel-style communism between 1959 and 1970, institutionalization in 1970-86, socialism and sugar, foreign policy, rectification, and the costs and trade-offs of revolution. Also by Rhoda Rabkin is 'Cuban political structure: vanguard party and the masses' in *Cuba: twenty-five years of revolution, 1959-1984.* Edited by Sandor Halebsky, John M. Kirk (New York: Praeger, 1985, p. 251-69).

512 **The Cuban revolution in crisis: from managing socialism to managing survival.**
Frank Fitzgerald. New York: Monthly Review Press, 1994. 239p. bibliog.

In this review of the revolutionary period, Fitzgerald examines the important years up to the late 1980s, plus the post-1989 'Special period', in an attempt to answer some of the most often asked questions about Cuba: Can the revolution survive and who will succeed Castro? In the process of analysing the emergence of new social groups, he expands the body of knowledge on post-1959 social developments.

513 **The Cuban revolution: origins, course, and legacy.**
Marifeli Pérez-Stable. New York: Oxford University Press, 1993. 236p.

Pérez-Stable challenges the teleology of the radical interpretation of Cuban history – that revolution was inevitable – and applies historical sociology to unfulfilled liberal visions of sovereignty and social justice. Central to the analysis is the fragile hegemony of the 'economic classes' and the strength of the 'popular classes', and Castro's refusal to compromise the revolution of the latter to appease the former and the United States: the symbiosis of Fidel-*pueblo* (people) and Fidel-*patria* (homeland). The work's controversial affirmation is that the Revolution ended in 1970.

514   **Island in the storm: the Cuban Communist Party's Fourth Congress.**
       Edited by Gail Reed.   Melbourne, Australia: Ocean Press, 1992. 200p.
The blueprint of Cuba's strategy for survival, as it emerged from the most critical meeting in the revolution's history, this was edited by the only foreign journalist who attended the 1992 Fourth Congress of the Cuban Communist Party. The volume contains Fidel Castro's opening and closing speeches, Congress resolutions, and a listing of the new Party leadership. See also: *First Congress of the Communist Party of Cuba: memoirs* (Havana: Department of Revolutionary Orientation of the Central Committee of the Communist Party of Cuba, 1976, 380p. [Speeches and documents]).

515   **Political change in Cuba: before and after the exodus.**
       Antoni Kapcia.   London: University of London, Institute of Latin American Studies, 1995. 33p. (Occasional Paper, no. 9).
Departing from the events of summer 1994, when tens of thousands of Cubans risked their lives on makeshift craft to escape a society seemingly on the brink of collapse, Kapcia asks how deep the crisis was in the first place, whether it was a Cuban or a US crisis, and what it said about the wider crisis of the Cuban revolution. The latter is the main focus of the study, in which the author argues that various social, economic and political factors suggest that the system may be capable of reforming itself rather than collapsing.

516   **Political leadership in Cuba: background and current projections.**
       Georgina Suárez Hernández, translated by Aníbal Yáñez.   *Latin American Perspectives*, vol. 18, no. 2 (1991), p. 55-68.
Reviews the Cuban revolution of 1959 and describes the subsequent development of the nation's revolutionary political leadership. Noting Cuban political traditions, the author examines the establishment of a single Marxist party within the socialist structure built up in the previous three decades. She suggests that, although political problems continue to exist, there is a clear understanding among the highest levels of the Cuban Communist Party that 'popular participation in the nation's various social arenas is essential to the foundations of democracy'.

517   **Political parties of the Americas, 1980s to 1990s: Canada, Latin America, and the West Indies.**
       Edited by Charles D. Ameringer.   Westport, Connecticut: Greenwood, 1992. 697p.
A useful reference work, designed to complement and update the earlier two-volume work edited by R. J. Alexander (*Political parties of the Americas*. Westport, Connecticut: Greenwood Press, 1982. bibliog.). Each chapter surveys a particular nation or political unit and contains a general essay, bibliography, listing and summary sketch of parties. A similar work containing a chapter on Cuba is *The twenty Latin Americas* (Marcel Niedergang, translated from French by Rosemary Sheed. Harmondsworth, England: Pelican, 1969, p. 311-54 [vol. 2]).

518   **Utopia unarmed: the Latin American left after the Cold War.**
       Jorge G. Castañeda. New York: Vintage Books, 1994. 498p.

The author presents a perceptive study that documents the story behind the Latin America left after thirty years of Cold War. A Mexican political scientist, Castañeda combines insider accounts of intrigue, armed struggle and power with prognosis of the left's continuing relevance on a continent with high levels of destitution and social inequality. Cuba looms large throughout.

Army politics

519   **A problemas viejos soluciones nuevas: el perfeccionamiento empresarial en el MINFAR.** (New solutions for old problems: improving business efficiency in the MINFAR.)
       General Julio Casas Regueiro, Armando Pérez Betancourt, Berto González Sánchez, José Cazanas Reyes, Raúl Lazo.   Havana: Editora Política, 1990. 112p.

Analyses the results of an experiment which introduced what amounted to Western-style management into an armed forces factory, and later to other military-run industries. Carried out in co-operation with the labour and finance ministries, this was part of the 'rectification of errors' programme championed by the Cuban Communist Party in 1985-86, and was expected to have a major impact on industry in general. Though the economic crisis that followed the collapse of the socialist bloc intervened, the approach outlined here has been influential in making the military a force to be reckoned with in the Cuban economy.

520   **Army politics in Cuba, 1898-1959.**
       Louis A. Pérez, Jr.   Pittsburgh, Pennsylvania: University of Pittsburgh Press, 1976. 240p. bibliog.

This study explores the historical emergence and growth of the Cuban army from its inception under the two US occupations of 1898-1902 and 1906-9, through its development as a major political force, to its defeat in the 1956-59 revolutionary war.

521   **Civil–military relations in Cuba: party control and political socialization.**
       William Leogrande.   *Studies in Comparative Communism*, vol. 11, no. 3 (autumn 1978), p. 278-91.

The article examines the relationship between the Revolutionary Armed Forces and civilian political organizations, especially the Cuban Communist Party.

522 **Cuba and the revolutionary myth: the political education of the Cuban Rebel Army, 1953-1963.**
C. Fred Judson. Boulder, Colorado: Westview, 1984. 295p. bibliog.
The author sees the history of the Rebel Army during the 1950s as formative to the new post-1959 armed forces.

523 **Cuba: Havana's military machine.**
John Hoyt Williams. *The Atlantic*, vol. 262, no. 2 (Aug. 1988), p. 18-23.
The author provides a brief summary of military institutions with a discussion of Cuba's military relationship with the Soviet Union in 1988.

524 **Cuba's armed forces: from triumph to survival.**
Richard L. Millett. Washington, DC: Georgetown University, 1993. 8p. (Cuba Briefing Papers, no. 4).
Traces the historical development of Cuba's armed forces (FAR), arguing that ambiguities in its role were sharpened in the 1980s and suggesting that a UN peacekeeping role could ease tensions. The author barely touches on the FAR's economic role, however, which weakens but does not negate his argument that the FAR is unique among Latin American armed forces.

525 **Institutionalization and civil–military relations in Cuba.**
Jorge I. Domínguez. *Cuban Studies*, vol. 6, no. 1 (Jan. 1976), p. 39-65.
In a detailed analysis of the role of the armed forces and institutionalization of the revolution, Domínguez examines changing civil–military relations and the social, economic and political role of the military.

Gay and lesbian politics

526 **Cuba.**
Stephan Likofsky. In: *Coming out.* Edited by Stephan Likofsky. New York: Pantheon Books, 1992, p. 82-101.
The article takes an historical look at gay and lesbian subculture and Cuban policy and considers recent transformations on the island. It documents the twists and turns of policy since the revolution; criticizes the gender egalitarianism based on hetero-sexuality; discusses family and marriage; and promotes the view articulated in sex education of homosexuality as normal and inevitable in any society.

527 **Gays under the Cuban revolution.**
Allen Young. San Francisco: Grey Fox Press, 1981. 112p.

The repression of homosexuality in Cuba is the focus of this book by a former supporter of the Cuban revolution. With one chapter on homophobia before the revolution, Young nonetheless argues that homophobia since 1959 is not of its own Latin American heritage but originates from European international communism, that is, it is an import from the Soviet Union. Much of the text consists of interviews with émigrés who left Cuba on the 1980 Mariel boatlift.

528 **Homosexuality, homophobia and revolution: notes towards an understanding of the Cuban lesbian and gay male experience, part 1.**
Lourdes Argüelles, B. Ruby Rich. *Signs: Journal of Women in Culture and Society*, vol. 9, no. 4 (1984), p. 683-99.

This balanced discussion is based on research conducted in 1979-84 in Cuba and in Cuban émigré enclaves in the United States, Puerto Rico, Mexico and Spain with the aim of beginning to understand the nature and dynamics of the Cuban gay experience. The authors conclude that, despite dramatic improvements, the lives of gays and lesbians were still circumscribed by outdated conceptions of homosexuality and by the memory of the notorious UMAP labour camps in which gays were incarcerated in the early 1970s.

529 **Machos, maricones, and gays: Cuba and homosexuality.**
Ian Lumsden. Philadelphia, Pennsylvania: Temple University Press, 1995. 288p.

An historically based, first-hand account of homosexuality in Cuban society and culture, in which the author links the contemporary treatment of male homosexuality with pre-revolutionary prejudices and preconceptions and contrasts significant improvements over recent years with widespread misconceptions. Lumsden links homophobia with machismo and broader issues of race, religion and gender. He documents the controversy over HIV/AIDS sanatoriums and deals sensitively with the differential experience of being publicly and privately gay in Cuba.

530 **Sexual politics in Cuba: machismo, homosexuality, and AIDS.**
Marvin Leiner. Boulder, Colorado: Westview, 1994. 184p.

Part of an ongoing study of social and educational changes in Cuba, this covers the early heady days of the 1959 revolution to the 1990s in crisis. The focus is on sex education in the context of the changing role of women in Cuba and the worldwide spread of AIDS. Leiner explores the interrelated issues of gender equality, machismo and homosexuality as they affected the progress of sex education and Cuba's response to AIDS.

Social control and deviance in Cuba.
See item no. 474.

Fresa y chocolate. (Strawberry and chocolate.)
See item no. 999.

Country Profile: Cuba.
See item no. 1109.

Cuadernos de Nuestra América. (Notebooks of Our America.)
See item no. 1117.

Cuba Socialista. (Socialist Cuba.)
See item no. 1118.

Political and economic encyclopaedia of South America and the Caribbean.
See item no. 1140.

Administration and
Government

531 **Bodies of People's Power.**
National Assembly of People's Power. Havana: National Assembly
of People's Power, 1981. 46p.

This provides a clear guide to the structure of the Cuban system of government. For
later amendments, see: *República de Cuba: ley electoral* (Republic of Cuba: electoral
law), published by the National Assembly of People's Power (Havana: Ediciones
Entorno, 1992. 64p.), which offers the text of Cuba's electoral law as amended in
1992, when direct elections to the national parliament were introduced. Also of
interest are: *Extraordinary circumstances bring people together: Cuban electoral
process (November 1992-March 1993)* by Nora Madan, et al. (Havana: Editora
Política, 1993. 70p.), which is a collection of writings by Cuban journalists explaining
the legislation governing Cuban elections and their application in the period leading
up to the February 1993 elections; *Elecciones en Cuba: ¿farsa o democracia?*
(Elections in Cuba: farce or democracy?), edited by Mirta Muñiz (Melbourne: Ocean
Press, 1993. 172p.); and 'The organs of people's power and the Communist Party:
the nature of Cuban democracy' by Archibald R. M. Ritter, in *Cuba: twenty-five years of
revolution, 1959-1984.* Edited by Sandor Halebsky, John M. Kirk (New York:
Praeger, 1985, p. 270-90).

532 **IV Congreso del PCC.** (Fourth Congress of the Cuban Communist
Party.)
Communist Party of Cuba. Caracas: Editorial Abre Brecha, 1991.
186p.

The Fourth Party Congress, held in 1991, witnessed landmark debates on the future
directions of Cuba and the speeches, documents and resolutions contained in this
volume are the result of this. Similar publications exist for the first, second and third
congresses of 1975, 1980 and 1985.

533 **Cuba: dictatorship or democracy?**
Marta Harnecker, translated from the Spanish by Patrick Greanville.
Westport, Connecticut: Lawrence Hill, 1980. 239p.

Working with a team of sociologists and writers, Harnecker, a Chilean journalist, assembled documentary evidence for this sympathetic account of a revolutionary form of grassroots participatory democracy. It documents people's post-1959 participation in factories, as lay judges in the courts, in mass discussions of laws and in neighbourhood block committees, which acted as a lead-in to government by the people in the then newly formed electoral and parliamentary system of national, regional and municipal assemblies of People's Power. There are also chapters on the armed forces and the central state administration apparatus.

534 **Cuba in the 1970s: pragmatism and institutionalization.**
Carmelo Mesa-Lago. Albuquerque, New Mexico: University of New Mexico, 1978. 200p. bibliog.

During the 1970s efforts were made in Cuba to separate government functions and set up an electoral system of popular power. These efforts are examined here in the context of economic diversification, increased economic efficiency and productivity, and the democratization of labour organization.

535 **Cuba: the institutionalisation of the revolution.**
Cuban Studies, vol. 6, nos. 1-2 (Jan.-July 1976), special issue.

Contains articles by: Nelson P. Valdés on revolution and institutionalization; Jorge I. Domínguez on institutionalization and civil–military relations; a thoughtful piece by Irving Louis Horowitz on authenticity and autonomy in the Cuban experience; Ed González on the party and People's Power; Leonel Antonio de la Cuesta on the Cuban socialist constitution; and Marifeli Pérez-Stable on institutionalization and the workers' response.

536 **Cuba: nueva división político-administrativa.** (Cuba: new political-administrative division.)
Reynold Rassi. Havana: Editorial Orbe, 1981. 157p.

Detailed social, economic and political information is provided, based on 1977 figures broken down for the new political-administrative division of the country. This involved increasing the number of provinces from six to fourteen, and re-organizing their corresponding municipalities, plus the special municipality of the Isle of Youth.

537 **Cuba's local governments: an experience beyond the paradigms.**
Haroldo Dilla Alfonso, Gerardo González, Ana T. Vincentelli. *Cuban Studies*, vol. 22 (1992), p. 151-72.

This article is based on a three-year study conducted by researchers from the Havana-based Center for Study of the Americas, as part of a regional project co-ordinated by the Centre for Research on Latin America and the Caribbean of the University of York in Toronto, Canada. The article is unique in that it involves fieldwork on leadership and participation in Cuban municipalities in a period of severe economic crisis, electoral and local government reform, with limited political decentralization. It is one of several articles based on a longer monograph published in Spanish in Havana. The authors pose key questions on the future of participative democracy in Cuba.

538 **Formación y desarrollo del estado socialista en Cuba.** (Formation and development of the socialist state in Cuba.)
Olga Fernández Ríos. Havana: Ciencias Sociales, 1988. 256p.

This represents a bold attempt from within the framework of Cuban Marxism-Leninism of the 1980s to explore the general and the particular in the process of destruction of the bourgeois state and the growth and consolidation of the socialist state in Cuba. The focus in the early stages of the Cuban revolution is on the Rebel Army as the genesis of the revolutionary-democratic dictatorship. The author rejects the notion of a duality of power in the early months of 1959, seeing them rather as the period of transformation into the dictatorship of the proletariat and the state of a new type. The state as it evolves is then analysed over the years 1961 to 1976, with the founding of the system of People's Power and its relations with the Communist Party of Cuba.

539 **The problem of democracy in Cuba: between vision and reality.**
Carolee Bengelsdorf. New York: Oxford University Press, 1994. 229p. bibliog.

Drawing on twenty years of first-hand research in Cuba, especially in densely populated, dilapidated Central Havana, Bengelsdorf examines the paradoxical relationship between socialism and democracy in theory and practice. She argues that the Cuban revolution tried, but failed, to fulfil the democratic promise of Marxism. Her analysis of that failure shows how centralizing impulses won out over the vision of decentralization, with a consequent abrogation of civil society and refusal to consider alternative channels for democratic expression. See also *Democracia en Cuba* (Democracy in Cuba) by Carlos Méndez Tovar (Havana: Editorial José Martí, 1995. 179p.).

540 **Report on the October 1986 municipal elections in Cuba.**
Peter Roman. *Socialism and Democracy*, vol. 5 (fall/winter 1987), p. 89-102.

The 1986 elections were the first to be held nationally since the 1959 revolution. This first-hand report on municipal elections that year, based on personal observations and interviews with Cubans, provides an account of the structure of the Organs of Popular Power, municipal assemblies and election day, and the Communist Party role.

541 **Republic of Cuba.**
Juan Manuel del Águila. In: *World encyclopedia of political systems and parties*, vol. 1. Edited by George E. Delury. New York: Facts on File, 1987, p. 240-48.

Provides a simple breakdown of the political organization of Cuba, with brief explanatory paragraphs on: the government in general terms; the executive; the legislature; the judiciary; regional and local government; and the electoral system. This is followed by an overview of the Cuban Communist Party and its history, organization, policy, membership, financing and leadership. Águila then presents a brief discussion of the mass organizations, such as the Union of Communist Youth, in which citizens are encouraged to take part, and finally makes reference to the opposition to Castro's régime and the government's success in controlling it.

542   **State organization in Cuba.**
Domingo García Cárdenas.   Havana: Editorial José Martí, 1986. 134p.
The author was among those who contributed to the creation of the organs of People's Power and the structure of Cuba's socialist state. In this unpretentious descriptive book he outlines their most significant aspects, covering the main objectives for the relative decentralization which took place, such as the intention to increase decision-making at the municipal level within the framework of the system of People's Power. The book contains chapters on the background and organization of the state, the electoral system, central state organization and state organization in the provinces and municipalities.

543   **Statutes of the Communist Party of Cuba.**
Havana: Political Publishing House, 1981. 40p.
Statutes adopted by the First Congress of the Communist Party of Cuba in 1975 are reproduced here, with the modifications agreed by the Second Congress in 1980.

Constitution and Legal System

544 Case 1/1989: end of the Cuban connection.
Havana: Editorial José Martí, 1989. 445p.

In 1989, the trial of Division General Arnaldo Ochoa took place. He was accused along with Antonio de la Guardia, Amado Padrón, Jorge Martínez and others of drug trafficking, abuse of power and corruption, and this had serious international ramifications. In this compilation of source material, chapters cover their arrest, the internal and international implications, the legal situation, the trial hearings, the verdict and the executions. The volume contains transcripts of the trial, as well as Council of State statements, including that of Fidel Castro, ratifying the sentences.

545 Código de trabajo. (Labour code.)
Comité Estatal de Trabajo y Seguridad Social. Havana: República de Cuba, 1985. 108p.

Contains the labour regulations passed by the Cuban parliament in December 1984.

546 Constitución de la República de Cuba. (Constitution of the Republic of Cuba.)
National Assembly of People's Power. Havana: Editora Política, 1992. 59p.

The amendments to the Constitution approved in July 1992 are contained in this document. Of particular interest are: Article eight which guarantees religious freedom; Article fifteen defining state property; Article eighteen on foreign trade; and Article twenty-three recognizing the right of non-State enterprises to own property.

547 Constitution of the Republic of Cuba.
Ministry of Justice. Havana: Editorial Orbe, 1977. 43p.

The text of the first socialist constitution, which came into effect in 1976 following a national referendum.

548 **Criminal justice in Cuba.**
National Lawyers Guild. New York: National Lawyers Guild, June 1988. 21p.

Undertaken by a team of nine US lawyers, this report on prison conditions and the treatment of prisoners in Cuba, reviews Cuba's prison system in the larger context of the criminal justice system and reforms since 1959. The report draws on first-hand research and investigation by the team in Cuba.

549 **Delitos contra la seguridad del estado.** (Crimes against state security.)
Abel Enrique Hart Santamaría. Havana: Ciencias Sociales, 1988. 176p. bibliog.

Written by a Cuban lawyer, this informative account traces the evolution of the concept of 'crimes against state security' in the context of international and Cuban history. The author also pays particular attention to the revolutionary government's position on political and counter-revolutionary crime from the 1960s to the 1980s and considers how the present penal code deals with 'crime against the state'.

550 **La detención y el aseguramiento del acusado en Cuba.** (The detention and security of the accused in Cuba.)
Jorge Bodes Torres. Havana: Ciencias Sociales, 1988. 297p.

A detailed account of the procedures and provisions in Cuba's legal system governing the treatment of those accused of perpetrating crimes. Despite changes during the revolutionary period, the system continues to be non-adversarial, which is Cuba's Spanish and French Napoleonic legacy. The author is a law professor and former Cuban prosecutor.

551 **Family code: law no. 1289, 1975.**
Republic of Cuba. Havana: Editorial José Martí, 1984. 51p.

Reproduces Cuban legislation regulating marriage and the mutual duties and rights of couples, including: property rights; the relations between parents and children; alimony; and the protection of children and incapacitated adults.

552 **Foreign investment law.**
Ministry of Foreign Investment and Economic Cooperation, Republic of Cuba. Havana: Editora Política, 1995. 27p.

This is the official text of the foreign investment law passed by Cuba's National Assembly in September 1995, which revised the legal framework for investment and also repealed Decree-Law no. 50 of 1982, the main basis on which economic associations with foreign capital had been formed hitherto. Innovative features include the provision for one hundred per cent foreign ownership, permission for foreign capital to invest in real estate, and the establishment of free trade zones. See also other reform laws, including: Decree-Law 140 (13 August 1993) on the depenalization of the possession of foreign currency; Decree-Law 141 (8 September 1993) on self-employment; Decree-Law 142 (28 September 1993) on the Formation of Basic Units of Cooperative Production; Decree-Law 149 (4 May 1994) on the confiscation of property and income acquired through illegal means; the Law on creation of a taxation system, approved by the National Assembly on 4 August 1994; Decree-Law 191 (19 September 1994) legalizing the free sale of agricultural produce in markets outside the state distribution system; and the Mining Act, approved by the National Assembly in December 1994, regulating foreign involvement in mineral resources.

553 **Justice and law in Latin America: a Cuban example.**
Francisco José Moreno. *Journal of Inter-American Studies and World Affairs*, vol. 12, no. 3 (July 1970), p. 367-78.

This examination of the revolutionary trials held immediately after the overthrow of Batista in 1959 concludes that, in the Latin American tradition, the demand for justice prevailed over the dictates of law.

554 **Memorias de un juez y periodista cubano.** (Recollections of a Cuban judge and journalist.)
Waldo Medina. Havana: Editorial Pablo de la Torriente, 1988. 94p.

Between 1927 and 1956 Medina (1900-86) was first a journalist and subsequently a judge. This memoir provides an insight into the legal profession during these years which witnessed both the Machado and Batista dictatorships.

555 **Prevención del delito y tratamiento del delincuente en Cuba revolucionaria.** (The prevention of crime and treatment of delinquents in revolutionary Cuba.)
Víctor L. Kautzman Torres. Havana: Ciencias Sociales, 1988. 194p. bibliog.

With a grounding in theory and based on documentary and statistical research, the author outlines the Cuban experience of crime prevention since the 1959 revolution, looking at policy, implementation and treatment. Special attention is paid to the changes in the Cuban judicial system, and there is a detailed case-study of Camagüey province.

556 **Revolution and criminal justice: the Cuban experiment, 1959-1983.**
Adele G. van der Plas, translated from the Dutch by Peter Mason.
Amsterdam: CEDLA, 1987. 328p.

This study traces how the profound changes in post-1959 Cuba were reflected in the basic administration of justice. The author begins by describing the informal, experimental tribunals which took place in the 1960s in town and countryside, in which justice was administered by lay judges chosen by, and from amongst, the people. The volume shows how, during the 1970s, these were integrated into a new system of judicial organization, institutionalized by, and through, the state, with increasing professionalization.

557 **Revolution in the balance: law and society in contemporary Cuba.**
Debra Evenson. Boulder, Colorado: Westview, 1994. 235p. (Latin American Perspectives Series, no. 14).

Presents a well-documented overview of the Cuban legal system and the ways in which law and society intersect over thirty-five years of revolution. This is the product of more than four years' fieldwork by an American professor of law, who had the co-operation of both the National Union of Cuban Jurists and the Library of the Supreme Court of Cuba. Of particular interest is the unsteady footing of the Cuban legal profession and institutions. It was first necessary to adapt to the unfamiliar terrain of socialism from the 1960s to 1980s, and then, in the 1990s, to accommodate changes in economic law and to modernize the criminal justice and judicial system as Cuba adjusted to the world capitalist system.

558 **Thirty years of Cuban revolutionary penal law.**
Raúl Gómez Treto. *Latin American Perspectives*, vol. 18, no. 2
(spring 1991), p. 114-25.

A lawyer who practised both before and after the 1959 revolution describes the evolution of the legal system under socialism. He argues that the severity of the penal code was influenced by both broad social conditions and the strength of the perceived outside threat to the nation.

559 **United States economic measures against Cuba: proceedings in the United Nations and international law issues.**
Edited by Michael Krinsky, David Golove. Northampton,
Massachusetts: Aletheia Press, 1993. 377p.

A compilation of documentary materials relating to the US economic embargo on trade with Cuba, this traces the history of the embargo, its purposes and effects, and places the issue in the context of international law.

Code on children and youth.
See item no. 462.

Revista Cubana de Derecho. (Cuban Journal of Law.)
See item no. 1126.

Human Rights

General

560 Americas Watch Report.
New York: Americas Watch. irreg.

Americas Watch produces periodic reports on human rights violations. Recent reports on Cuba include: 'United States: dangerous dialogue revisited: threats to freedom of expression in Miami's exile community' (Nov. 1994); 'Cuba: stifling the dissent in the midst of crisis' (Feb. 1994); '"Perfecting" the system of control' (Feb. 1993); 'Tightening the grip: human rights abuses in Cuba' (Feb. 1992); 'Behind a sporting façade, stepped-up repression' (Aug. 1991); 'Cuba: attack against independent associations' (Feb. 1991); 'Cuba: pro-democracy activists to stand trial' (June 1990); 'Cuba: jailing the human rights movement' (March 1990); and 'Human rights in Cuba: the need to sustain the pressure' (Jan. 1989).

561 Amnesty International Report.
London: Amnesty International. annual.

A comprehensive yearly human rights report which covers every country in the world, including Cuba. Amnesty International also produces special reports on human rights violations. Recent reports on Cuba include: 'Cuban "rafters" – pawns of two governments' (Oct. 1994); 'Cuba: hundreds imprisoned for "dangerousness"' (Feb. 1994); 'Cuba: silencing the voices of dissent' (Dec. 1992); 'Cuba: prisoners of conscience' (Jan. 1992); 'Cuba: the human rights situation' (Dec. 1990); 'Cuba: recent developments affecting the situation of political prisoners and the use of the death penalty' (Sept. and Jan. 1988); 'Cuba: arrests of human rights activists' (Oct. and Jan. 1987); and 'Political imprisonment in Cuba' (Jan. 1988; Nov. 1986).

562 **Cuba and human rights: devil or angel?**
Karen Wald. Washington, DC: National Council on United
States–Cuban Relations, 1988. 22p.

The author, a US journalist based in Cuba, was commissioned by the Council to analyse the debate on the human rights situation in Cuba, taking into consideration the Cuban perspective. Wald outlines a broad approach, encompassing the Cuban emphasis on collective social and economic rights and the US emphasis on political liberties.

563 **Cuba and the rule of law.**
International Commission of Jurists. Geneva: H. Studer, 1962. 267p.

Presents a critical examination of the first three years following the 1959 revolution, covering: constitutional law and criminal legislation; press, travel and religious freedom; and offences against property. The report condemns Cuba as a totalitarian régime.

564 **Fidel Castro: los derechos humanos 1959-1988.** (Fidel Castro: human rights 1959-88.)
Edited by Fabio Raimundo Torrado. Havana: Editora Política, 1989. 233p.

Contains a selection of the Cuban leader's pronouncements on human rights over three decades. For other accounts from a Cuban revolutionary perspective, see: *Human rights in Cuba* (Havana: José Martí Publishing House, [n. d.]. 60p.) which contains an interview with Fidel Castro and an anonymous discussion of the Cuban Constitution's human rights provisions; *Fidel Castro: talks with US and French journalists, July – August 1983* (Editora Política, 1983. 58p.); and *Iglesias y creyentes en Cuba socialista* (Churches and believers in socialist Cuba) by Doria González (Havana: Editorial Cultura Popular, 1987. 84p.), which is an attempt to set the record straight, from a Cuban revolutionary point of view, on religious expression and Church–state relations.

565 **Human rights and freedom.**
In: *The Cuba reader: the making of a revolutionary society.* Edited by Philip Brenner, William M. Leogrande, Donna Rich, Daniel Siegel. New York: Grove Press, 1989, p. 211-54.

A dossier of extracts, this draws material from: Margaret Crahan on the freedom of worship, critical of the Cuban churches' lack of vitality for a religious rebirth; John Spicer Nichols on the freedom of the press, charting flexibilities and openings within censorship and control; and reports by the Organisation of American States Inter-American Commission on Human Rights, Amnesty International and the Institute for Policy Studies.

566 **Human rights and United States policy toward Latin America.**
Lars Schoultz. Princeton, New Jersey: Princeton University Press, 1981. 421p. bibliog.

A lengthy appraisal of US human rights policy in Latin America, situating pre- and post-revolutionary Cuba within the hemispheric context.

143

567 **Human rights in Cuba.**
United States of America Congress, House of Representatives,
Committee on Foreign Affairs, Subcommittee on Human Rights and
International Organizations. Washington, DC: US Government
Printing Office, 1984. 123p.

The transcript of the June 1984 hearings on human rights in Cuba is reproduced here.
It contains critical testimonies from the State Department, Cuban exiles, Amnesty
International and Americas Watch. See also *Human rights in Castro's Cuba*
(Washington, DC: US Department of State, Bureau of Public Affairs, 1986. Special
report, no. 153).

568 **Human rights in Cuba: an experimental perspective.**
Juan Clark, Angel De Fana, Amaya Sánchez. Miami, Florida: Saeta
Ediciones, 1991. 122p. bibliog.

In this text, a Cuban-American sociologist, a former Cuban political prisoner and a
Venezuelan sociologist berate the Cuban revolution for alleged abuse of the rights
contained in the United Nations Declaration of Human Rights.

569 **Human rights in Cuba: initiating the dialogue.**
Wayne S. Smith. Washington, DC: Center for International Policy,
1995. 7p. (Special issue of the International Policy Report.)

This brief report of a seminar 'Definitions of Human Rights', held in Havana in March
1995, highlights the main areas of agreement and divergence which emerged in the
first official encounter between US and Cuban legal and human rights experts. They
included the alleged dichotomy between the need for public order and the protection
of human rights, and the question of a broader definition of human rights to include
social, economic and cultural as well as political and civil rights. All Cuban
participants believed that their country had been targeted as a human rights violator
for political, rather than humanitarian, reasons. The paper concludes with short reports
of interviews conducted after the seminar with the presidents of Cuba's National
Assembly and Supreme Court, and a leading dissident.

570 **Human rights in Cuba: politics and ideology**.
Tony Platt, Ed McCaughan. In: *Transformation and struggle: Cuba
faces the 1990s*. Edited by Sandor Halebsky, John M. Kirk, with
Rafael Hernández. New York: Praeger, 1990, p. 67-82.

The authors outline the Reagan administration's use of human rights to justify its
antagonism towards Cuba, and chart the Cuban record on collective and individual
human rights. They challenge the 'tropical gulag' view and call for an easing of
tensions between Cuba and the United States and for improved human rights.

571 **Human rights questions: human rights situations and reports of
special rapporteurs and representatives; situation of human rights
in Cuba.**
United Nations. New York: United Nations, 1994. 22p.

This report prepared by Carl-John Groth for the UN reiterates the findings of earlier
reports, namely that the major problems with respect to civil and political rights in

Cuba are related to discrimination on political grounds and the lack of freedom of expression and association.

572 **Law and religion in Marxist Cuba: a human rights inquiry.**
Margaret I. Short, with a foreword by Marcos Antonio Ramos.
Miami, Florida: University of Miami, North-South Center, 1993. 209p.
bibliog.

Short attempts to treat the topic of religious freedom in Cuba in more depth than has hitherto been the case and with a more balanced perspective. The study covers the period between the Cuban revolution and the recent events in Eastern Europe and points to the limitations on religious freedom and violations of civil liberties in the first thirty years of revolution in Cuba. In particular, Short looks at the wide-ranging opinions on Christian participation in the political and revolutionary processes, examines the legislation in place before the 1992 Constitutional reforms and the changes that have taken place since, aimed at lessening constraints against believers. She includes excerpts from interviews with Fidel Castro and surveys legislation and international human rights organizations' reports. Appendices containing various documents on human rights and a chronology of events in Cuba, 1492-1962, are included.

573 **The politics of psychiatry in revolutionary Cuba.**
Charles J. Brown, Armando M. Lago. New Brunswick, New Jersey;
London: Transaction, 1991. 217p.

The authors claim that, while Soviet psychiatric abuse was the focus of world condemnation, Cuba escaped unscathed thanks to its successful public relations campaign portraying its psychiatric institutions as models for other developing nations. They attempt to correct the record with case histories and reprints of US media reports on the topic. In his introduction, former Soviet political prisoner Vladimir Bukovsky describes the Cuban situation as 'not yet a political abuse of psychiatry' but rather 'a bad imitation' of the Soviet use of psychiatry for political ends.

574 **Situación de los derechos humanos en Cuba.** (The human rights situation in Cuba.)
José Pérez Novoa. Geneva: Cuban Delegation to the UN Human Rights Commission, 1993. 12p.

This speech by Cuba's ambassador to the forty-ninth period of sessions on the UN Human Rights Commission outlines the official Cuban position on human rights in the country. In it, the ambassador rejects in the name of his government the 'imposition' of a special human rights regulator, alleging that the proposal was part of a political vendetta. Similar submissions have been made to other sessions of the commission. See also: *In its legitimate defense: Cuba at the Human Rights Commission 1992* by Raúl Roa Kourí (Havana: Editoria Política, 1992. 78p.), which contains documents relating to the debate on human rights at the 1992 session of the UNHRC.

Case testimonies

575 **Against all hope: the prison memoirs of Armando Valladares.**
Armando Valladares, translated by Andrew Hurley. Sevenoaks,
England: Hodder & Stoughton, 1987. 532p.

The Cuban who was later appointed United States ambassador to the United Nations
Human Rights Commission recounts his prison experiences and efforts to regain his
freedom. Described as the story of a man who refused to deny his principles, who was
crippled by imprisonment and who testified to the awful truth about Castro's political
prisons, the account was subseqently discredited when it was learnt that the author had
been a member of the Batista police, imprisoned for sabotage, walked out of jail and
was swiftly given US citizenship to become US Ambassador to the United States
Human Rights Commission. See also item no. 579. Also of interest are the testimonies
of two other Cubans: *The marks of birth* by Pablo Medina (Farrar, Straus & Giroux,
1994); and *Twenty years and forty days: life in a Cuban prison* by Jorge Valls (1986).

576 **Cuba: the unfinished revolution.**
Enrique G. Encinosa. Austin, Texas: Easkin Press, 1988. 215p.

A compilation of twenty-three personal accounts of men and women who rebelled,
suffered and sacrificed because of their opposition to the Castro régime. Among the
better known are Angel Cuadra and Jorge Valls. Another book which will be of
interest is: *Freedom flights: Cuban refugees talk about life under Castro and how they
fled his regime* by Llorin Phillipson and Rafael Llerena (New York: Random House,
1980. 201p.). Published just after the Mariel boatlift, and coinciding with Castro's
leadership of the Third World Non-Aligned Movement, this book contains interviews
conducted in 1976-79 with Cubans living in New York and Miami. It paints a wholly
negative picture of Castro and the Cuban revolution.

577 **General del Pino speaks: an insight into élite corruption and
military dissension in Castro's Cuba.**
Rafael del Pino. Washington, DC: Cuban-American National
Foundation, 1987. 66p.

Published by the leading anti-Castro organization in the United States, this statement
by the highest-ranking Cuban defector alleges corruption in the government and the
armed forces. He speaks of political opposition to Cuba's involvement in Africa and
of tension between the political and military leaders in Cuba.

578 **Harnessing the intellectuals: censoring writers and artists in
today's Cuba.**
Carlos Ripoll. New York: Cuban-American National Foundation,
Freedom House, 1985. 59p.

Viewed from the perspective of a writer who had been in exile since 1960, this
provides an historical overview and contemporary account of the mass media, artistic
creation and theory versus practice in Cuba, and case-studies of two Marxist
dissidents: Ariel Hidalgo and Ricardo Bofill.

579 **Shading light: the Valladares case.**
Danilo H. Figueredo. In: *Intellectual migrations: transcultural contributions of European and Latin American émigrés.* Madison, Wisconsin: University of Wisconsin, Memorial Library, SALALM Secretariat, 1987, p. 231-42.

In this paper given at a seminar on the acquisition of Latin American library materials in Berlin in 1986, Figueredo attempts to assess the evidence presented by the Cuban government against Armando Valladares (see also item no. 575) and to place the case in its political context.

580 **The tiger and the children: Fidel Castro and the judgement of history.**
Roberto Luque Escalona, translated by Manuel A. Tellechea. New Brunswick, New Jersey: Transaction, 1992. 212p.

This is an attempt to argue that history will not absolve Fidel Castro. Freedom House clarifies that the author is not a persecuted figure or a famous dissident, nor is this a prison memoir, but rather the personal and damning testimony of a Cuban still free in spirit. The text, however, has little of interest, and sits uneasily between history, journalism and existential meanderings.

581 **Wings of the morning.**
Orestes Lorenzo. New York: St. Martin's Press, 1994. 346p.

The memoirs of a Cuban airforce pilot who defected to the United States in 1991. Lorenzo looks back over his life, growing up in revolutionary Cuba, and talks of his time in Angola, his escape from Cuba by fighter plane and his return to collect his wife and children.

Foreign Relations

General

582 **Cuba in the world.**
Edited by C. Blasier, Carmelo Mesa-Lago. Pittsburgh, Pennsylvania: University of Pittsburgh Press, 1979. 343p. bibliog.

A collection of essays on Cuban foreign policy, including theoretical issues and relations with the United States, Soviet Union and Latin America.

583 **Cuba: the international dimension.**
Georges A. Fauriol, E. Loser, foreword by Irving L. Horowitz. New Brunswick, New Jersey: Transaction, 1990. 449p.

The central thread of this anthology is that, from being a central player in the Americas as a result of the revolution, Cuba in the 1990s risks becoming an irrelevant anachronism. Contributions from Jaime Suchlicki, William Ratliff, Gillian Gunn, Michael Mazarr, Jorge Pérez López and Juan M. del Águila, among others, discuss shifts and new dimensions in Cuba's relations with the former Soviet Union, the United States, Latin America, Africa, the Middle East and Asia.

584 **Cuba's international relations: the anatomy of a nationalistic foreign policy.**
H. Michael Erisman. Boulder, Colorado: Westview, 1985. 203p.

This is a general study, which highlights Cuba's 1970s policy of globalism in foreign policy and its impact on the Non-Aligned Movement, the United States and the Soviet Union. A central argument is that aspects of Cuban globalism have been obscured by charges of Havana acting as a surrogate of the Soviet Union.

585   **Cuba's internationalist foreign policy, 1975-80.**
Fidel Castro, edited by Michael Taber.   New York: Pathfinder, 1984.
2nd ed. 391p. (Fidel Castro Speeches, vol. 1).

As well as Castro's speeches on Angola, Nicaragua, Vietnam and other foreign policy
issues, this collection includes an essay by the novelist Gabriel García Márquez on
Cuban involvement in Angola. It was first published in 1981.

586   **Cuba's ties to a changing world.**
Edited by Donna Rich Kaplowitz.   Boulder, Colorado: Lynne
Rienner, 1993. 261p. maps.

Focuses on Cuba's relations with the rest of the world, including a discussion of the
alliance between Cuba and the former Soviet Union. It provides useful introductions
to Havana's relations with Japan, Africa, the Middle East in the aftermath of the Gulf
War, Brazil and the Central American and Caribbean nations, often neglected in
favour of the United States and other major countries.

587   **Cuban foreign policy confronts a new international order.**
Edited by H. Michael Erisman, John M. Kirk.   Boulder, Colorado:
Lynne Rienner, 1991. 241p. bibliog.

A collection by United States, Cuban, Canadian and British scholars, this provides a
welcome departure from the 'super-power approach' to Cuban foreign policy. It
situates Cuba within the small-island geopolitical syndrome of needing to maximize
international 'political space'. Topics discussed include: the triangular relationship
between Cuba, the Soviet Union and the United States; Cuba's involvement in Africa
and Latin America; the country's role as mediator in Third World conflicts and the
export of educational revolution; and relations with Western Europe and Canada.
These discussions reveal essentially Cuban strategies of international flexibility in
adapting to the new international order.

588   **To make a world safe for revolution: Cuba's foreign policy.**
Jorge I. Domínguez.   Cambridge, Massachusetts: Harvard University
Press, 1989. 365p.

A wealth of documentary evidence is taken from varied and conflicting sources, and
backed up by extensive interview material. This is used to paint a 'behind the scenes'
picture of how, from 1959 to 1988, the small country of Cuba assumed the foreign
policy of a more important power. The author argues that the guiding principle,
beyond that of sheer survival, was one of deep hostility to the United States and global
imperialism, coupled with adroit manoeuvring within policies of non-alignment and
foreign relations of austerity. He states that, poised between super-power hegemony
and autonomy, militancy and pragmatism, Cuba (prior to 1988) based its foreign
policy on a managed relationship with the Soviet Union, on support for other
revolutionary movements and states, on the reconstruction of relations with capitalist
countries, and on diplomacy in the Americas and the Third World.

Missile Crisis

589 The crisis years: Kennedy and Khrushchev, 1960-1963.
Michael R. Beschloss. New York: HarperCollins, 1991. 816p.

This gripping narrative, which has a fabulous cast of characters, reads like a political novel of the years 1960-63, explaining how and why the 1962 Missile Crisis ever happened, at least from the United States and Soviet sides. Based on interviews with US and Soviet officials and freshly declassified American and Soviet documents, Beschloss offers us the first comprehensive history of the relationship between two proud, vulnerable and legendary leaders, John F. Kennedy and Nikita Khrushchev. Cuba barely comes into the story, which is highly indicative of the superpower view of a crisis fought over Cuban soil.

590 Cuba on the brink: Castro, the Missile Crisis, and the Soviet collapse.
James G. Blight, David A. Welch, Bruce J. Allyn. New York: Pantheon, 1993. 509p.

This book is based on discussions which took place involving important surviving players in the 1962 Cuban Missile Crisis. Previously secret or debated aspects of the crisis came to light in a series of conferences held from 1987 onwards, the first of which took place in Hawk's Key, Florida (1987) and was addressed by Kennedy administration veterans. The second conference, held in Harvard, involved Soviet participants, while Cubans took part in the Moscow conference. The fourth took place in Antigua and at the fifth, held in Havana, Fidel Castro, the only survivor of the three 1962 heads of state, contributed to the discussion. Other works arising from the conference are: *On the brink: Americans and Soviets re-examine the Cuban Missile Crisis* by James Blight, David A. Welch, Bruce J. Allyn; *The shattered crystal ball: fear and learning in the Cuban Missile Crisis* by James G. Blight, foreword by Joseph S. Nye, Jr. (Lanham, Maryland: Littlefield Adams Quality Paperbacks, 1992. 199p.); *Back to the brink: proceedings of the Moscow conference on the Cuban Missile Crisis, Jan. 27-28, 1989*. Edited by Bruce J. Allyn, James G. Blight, David A. Welch (Cambridge, Massachusetts: Harvard University, Centre for Scientific and International Affairs; Lanham, Maryland: University Press of America, 1992. 223p. [CSIA Occasional Paper, no. 9]); and 'Four days with Fidel: a Havana diary' by Arthur Schlesinger, Jr. (*The New York Review*, 26 March 1992, p. 22-28).

591 The Cuban Missile Crisis, 1962: a National Security Archive documents reader.
Laurence Chang, Peter Kornblugh. Washington, DC: National Security Archive and The New Press, 1992. 415p. bibliog.

This is the document-by-document account of the confrontation that brought the world to the brink of nuclear war. Compiled by the National Security Archive, a non-profit organization, it includes the correspondence between Kennedy and Khrushchev, minutes of executive committee meetings, and CIA papers planning to overthrow Fidel Castro, as well as a full chronology of the events surrounding the crisis. The book is complemented by a microfiche set containing over 15,000 pages of government documentation pertaining to the events surrounding the Cuban Missile Crisis.

592 **The Cuban Missile Crisis revisited.**
Edited by James A. Nathan.   New York: St. Martin's Press, 1992.
302p.

This book commemorates the thirty years that have elapsed since the 1962 Missile Crisis. It owes a debt to the American National Security Archive, whose aims are openness and transparency in the foreign policy and defence processes, and to newly opened records of the American, former Soviet and Cuban governments. James Nathan provides an introductory revisionist outline of the strategy of coercive diplomacy into which the Cuban Missile Crisis fell, after which contributors study various aspects of the crisis, including the Washington view and the Cuban view, and the Kennedy–Khrushchev letters.

593 **In the eye of the storm: Castro, Khrushchev, Kennedy and the Missile Crisis.**
Carlos Lechuga.   Melbourne, Australia: Ocean Press, 1995. 220p.

A personal account by Cuba's ambassador to the United Nations at the time of the October 1962 Missile Crisis, along with key documents and letters of the three countries involved. This is a welcome addition to existing accounts which are skewed heavily to the United States and the then Soviet Union.

594 **The missiles of October: the declassified story of John F. Kennedy and the Cuban Missile Crisis.**
Robert Smith Thompson.   New York: Simon & Schuster, 1992. 395p.

This re-examination of hitherto classified documents reaches conclusions that challenge previously held beliefs. In a book that reads like a political thriller, Smith Thompson argues that US President Kennedy knew there were nuclear missiles in Cuba by March 1962, long before the official warning, and that he appeared to be planning a full-scale invasion of Cuba for late 1962.

Soviet Union

595 **El fin de la URSS y Cuba.** (The end of the USSR and Cuba.)
Santiago Pérez.   *Revista / Review Interamericana*, vol. 102, nos. 3-4 (autumn/winter 1992), p. 24-36.

Offers a Cuban view on the economic, political and strategic impact of first *perestroika* and then the break-up of the Soviet Union on Cuba. The article was later reproduced in *Cuba en crisis* (edited by Jorge Rodríguez Beruff. University of Puerto Rico Press, 1995. 218p.).

596 **Opportunities and dangers of Soviet–Cuban expansion: towards a pragmatic U.S. policy.**
Richard J. Payne, with a foreword by Roger Fisher. Albany, New York: State University of New York Press, 1988. 261p. bibliog.

With a view to prescribing workable alternatives to enhance the effectiveness of US foreign policy, the author looks at the nature of the Soviet–Cuban relationship and their objectives in the Third World. He pays particular attention to the Horn of Africa, Afghanistan, Nicaragua, Southern Africa and the Commonwealth Caribbean, and suggests that US foreign policy has foundered on its preoccupation with the ideological contest with communism and with military force as its main policy instrument.

597 **Raíces de las relaciones cubano soviéticas.** (The roots of Cuban– Soviet relations.)
Ángel García, Piotr Mironchuc. Havana: Ciencias Sociales, 1988. 185p.

Traces the history of relations between Cuba and the Soviet Union and during the times of Tsarist Russia.

598 **Las relaciones económicas Cuba–URSS, 1960-1985.** (Cuba–USSR economic relations, 1960-1985.)
José Luis Rodríguez. *Temas de Economía Mundial*, no. 17 (1986), p. 7-33.

The author of this article was the deputy-director of the Centre for International Economic Research at the time of writing, and is now Minister of the Economy. He provides an overview of Soviet–Cuban commercial relations during an important quarter century of rapprochement between the two countries.

599 **La revolución de octubre y la revolución cubana.** (The October revolution and the Cuban revolution.)
Havana: Editora Política, 1987. 296p.

Contains selections from speeches made between 1977 and 1986, mainly by Fidel Castro, concerning the Soviet Union, its leaders and activities. Published to commemorate the seventieth anniversary of the October revolution, the emphasis is on friendship and solidarity between Cuba and the USSR.

600 **Soviet–Cuban alliance: 1959-1991.**
Yuri Pavlov. New Brunswick, New Jersey: Transaction, 1994. 272p. bibliog.

A former Soviet foreign service official from the 1960s writes about many features of the origins and break-up of the Soviet–Cuban relationship, from the 1962 Missile Crisis through the late 1980s. The account includes material not available elsewhere including discussions with US and Cuban officials during the latter years of Gorbachev's presidency. See also *And the Russians stayed: the Sovietisation of Cuba. A personal portrait* by Nestor Carbonell (New York: William Morrow & Co., 1989. 384p.).

601 **Soviet foreign policy and Latin America.**
Sergo Mikoyan. *The Washington Quarterly*, vol. 13, no. 3 (summer 1990), p. 179-91.
Analyses the policy of the then Soviet president Gorbachev towards Latin America, including Cuba, in the context of a new, non-ideological, non-class approach and the practical implications for the Soviet economy and politics. See also: *The Communist challenge in the Caribbean and Central America* by Howard J. Wiarda, Mark Falcoff, Ernest Evans, Jiri and Virginia Valenta (Washington, DC: American Enterprise Institute for Public Policy Research, 1987. 249p.).

602 **The Soviet Union and Cuba.**
Peter Shearman. London: Routledge & Kegan Paul, 1987. 103p.
(Chatham House Papers, no. 38).
Attempts to uncover the underlying patterns to the Soviet–Cuban connection which contributed to, or caused a number of US–Soviet crises, from the 1962 Missile Crisis, the 1970 Cienfuegos submarine issue and the 1979 mini-crisis of the Soviet combat brigade, to Cuba's internationalist involvement in Latin America, Africa and Asia. It is argued that Cuba was largely an autonomous actor in international affairs, although there clearly was bilateral influence between the two countries. See also: 'The Soviet Union and the Caribbean' edited by Paul Sutton, in *Europe and the Caribbean* (London; Basingstoke, England: Macmillan, 1991, p. 149-72).

603 **The Soviet Union and Cuba: interests and influence.**
W. Raymond Duncan. New York: Praeger, 1985. 220p. bibliog.
This chronological survey examines the policy options involved in the development of bilateral relations from the early stage of the revolution to the 1970s. See also: *The Soviet brigade in Cuba: a study in political diplomacy* by David D. Newsom (Bloomington, Indianapolis: Indiana University Press, 1987. 122p.).

604 **The USSR and the Cuban revolution: Soviet ideological and strategical perspectives, 1959-1977.**
Jacques Levesque, translated from the French by Deanna Drendel Leboeuf. New York: Praeger, 1978. 215p. bibliog.
This analysis approaches the Cuban question from a Soviet perspective, drawing out the ideological and strategic rationale involved in the emergence of a close alliance.

United States

605 **Backfire, the CIA's biggest burn.**
Ron Ridenour. Havana: Editorial José Martí, 1991. 174p.
Ridenour tells the story behind the double agents (twenty-six Cubans and one Italian) who infiltrated the CIA for Cuba's Department of State Security, and who told their story in 1987. He includes verbatim testimonies of three of the agents and summaries

of the others, revealing their work in averting CIA anti-Cuba actions. These included sabotage, chemical-biological warfare, and US underestimation of the Cuban revolution.

606   **The Bay of Pigs: the invasion of Cuba by Brigade 2506.**
      Haynes Johnson, et al.   London: Hutchinson, 1965. 368p.

In April 1961, 1,500 Cuban exiles, recruited, trained, equipped and transported by CIA agents, attempted a suicidal invasion of Cuba. This is the story of their hardship and betrayal.

607   **Bush on Cuba: selected statements by the president.**
      Foreword by Vice-President Dan Quayle.   Washington, DC: Cuban-American National Foundation, 1991. 68p.

A compilation of George Bush's comments on Cuba from 1971, when he was US ambassador to the United Nations, to 1991, when he was US president. While too brief to be considered a guide to policy, this collection does provide an insight into thinking on Cuba during the Cold War and up to the late 1980s, when US policy makers believed that socialism had been defeated.

608   **The closest of enemies.**
      Wayne Smith.   New York; London: W. W. Norton & Company, 1987. 308p.

A fascinating personal and diplomatic account of US–Cuba relations since 1957 is provided in this work by a US diplomat who was involved in the daily implementation of Cuban policy until his resignation in 1982. His informative insider story spans a career from junior foreign service officer to the first head of the US Interests Section in Havana, when partial diplomatic relations were renewed with Cuba in 1977 under the Carter administration. Taking early retirement because of his disillusionment with US policy, especially under Reagan, Smith provides a critique that is both intimate and provocative in its political stance, in which he displays a 'feel' for the internal dynamics of Cuba, the country, the people, the revolution and Castro.

609   **Contesting Castro.**
      Thomas G. Paterson.   New York: Oxford University Press, 1994. 352p.

Examines United States policy toward Cuba and Castro since the 1950s with the acumen of a US diplomatic historian. The author focuses on what he sees as ill-informed, self-defeating US policy, which is disdainful of Cuban sovereignty. He deals with the Cuban ambivalence towards an imitation of US ways but also their feelings of rejection and rebellion. Paterson views the 1950s insurrection as a clash between Cuban nationalism and US hegemony, and asks why a superpower not only failed to prevent the loss of a long-dependent weaker state only 100 miles away but also misjudged Castro, the charismatic revolutionary leader. A blend of journalism and academic analysis, with a US bibliographical bias, the strength of this work lies in the detail culled from US archival sources.

610 **Cruel and unusual punishment: the U.S. blockade against Cuba.**
Mary Murray. Melbourne, Australia: Ocean Press, 1993. 117p.

Murray takes the reader through Cuba's perspective on the blockade, as seen by a United States journalist in Cuba. The book includes the Cuban argument which was put to the United Nations, and documents evidence of the US campaign to canvas international support for its continuing cold war against Cuba, and of international figures and organizations speaking out against the blockade.

611 **Cuba in transition: options for US policy.**
Gillian Gunn. New York: Twentieth Century Fund, 1993. 100p.

Chapters one and two of this publication evaluate Cuban–US relations before Castro came to power and relations from 1959 to the present under different United States administrations. Gunn then moves on to discuss the Cuban economic collapse and the relatively small changes that have occurred in US policy towards Cuba since the Soviet demise. She examines the effects of economic deterioration on Cuba's politics and looks at the policy debate taking place in the United States over how to react to changes in Cuba. Gunn concludes by considering the consequences of increased US pressure and suggests new ways to approach the problem.

612 **The Cuban revolution and the United States: a chronological history.**
Jane Franklin. Melbourne, Australia: Ocean Press, 1989. 280p.

A detailed chronology of developments involving Cuba and the United States, from the 1959 triumph of the Cuban revolution through to 1990. Based on wide research, it covers famous events not in isolation but as part of a continuum of developments, some less dramatic or more obscure. The work provides an overview of Cuba–US relations and a comprehensive index enabling the reader to follow issues and subjects (trade and travel, migration and diplomacy, for example), correlate events and trace the activities of particular individuals. This is an invaluable resource for scholars, teachers, journalists, legislators, and those with an interest in international relations.

613 **Data, reflections and discussion on the current situation in Cuba.**
Standing Commission on International Relations. Havana: Republic of Cuba, National Assembly of People's Power, 1994.

This declaration of the Standing Commission outlines US military threats, radio and television aggression and migratory aggression, along with dissidents and human rights campaign support. In response, it calls for the US to change to a policy that is conducive to Cuban development.

614 **From confrontation to negotiation: U.S. relations with Cuba.**
Philip Brenner. Boulder, Colorado: Westview, 1988. 118p. bibliog.

Brenner provides an introduction to US–Cuba relations in the 1980s, with a background overview from 1898 to 1980. He highlights the assumptions, goals and continuities in US policy and offers a clear picture of the issues driving the two countries, around which any discussions of normalization of relations would revolve. A proposed workable alternative to US policy, taking into account the fundamental concerns of both countries, is included.

615 **El gobierno de EE.UU. contra Cuba: revelaciones de la agresión.**
(The US government versus Cuba: revelations of aggression.)
Havana: Ediciones Entorno, 1992. 74p. bibliog.
A team of Cuban scholars analyse the increasing US 1990s aggression towards Cuba,
which consisted of the economic blockade; financing of internal and external opposi-
tion; migration as a political weapon; and radio and television propaganda.

616 **Guantánamo: the bay of discord.**
Roger Ricardo.   Melbourne, Australia: Ocean Press, 1993. 58p. map.
This history of the US military base at Guantánamo, Cuba, outlines the arguments of
both the US and Cuban governments. It documents alleged violations of Cuban territory
originating in the US base and includes the text of the Breckenridge Memorandum and
the Platt Amendment, the key documents in the debate.

617 **The Havana inquiry.**
Hans Magnus Enzensberger, translated by Peter Mayes, introduction
by Martin Duberman.   New York: Holt, Rhinehart & Winston, 1970.
229p.
A documentary play based on the trial testimony of returning Cubans taken prisoner at
the Bay of Pigs fiasco. The saviour of free elections, tired revolutionary, turncoat
agent, mercenary priest, prophet of a third way and a murderer, all tell stories of
motivation, deception and self-deception.

618 **Imperial state and revolution: the United States and Cuba,
1952-86.**
Morris H. Morley.   Cambridge, England: Cambridge University Press,
1987. 571p.
A compelling piece of scholarship, which draws on personal interviews, declassified
documents and other primary sources. It is the most comprehensive analysis to date of
the Kennedy and Johnson administrations' efforts to isolate revolutionary Cuba, and
of US Congress and American business response to White House policy.

619 **Island under siege: the US blockade of Cuba.**
Pedro Prada.   Melbourne, Australia: Ocean Press, 1995. 57p.
A short discussion by a Cuban journalist which gives a reasonably accurate
introduction to what he, like most Cubans, calls the US blockade of the island. The
book includes a chronology, a reprint of Cuban Foreign Minister Robaina's June 1993
letter to the UN Secretary General setting out the Cuban estimate of the embargo's
effect and an interview with US lawyer Michael Krinsky who has long specialized in
embargo law.

620 **The secret war: CIA covert actions against Cuba 1959-1962.**
Fabián Escalante.   Melbourne, Australia: Ocean Press, 1995. 200p.
The former head of Cuban state security provides new evidence on Cuba's
confrontation with US intelligence, and links between the mafia, the Cuban exile
community and the CIA.

621 **Semper Fidel: America and Cuba, 1766-1988.**
Michael J. Mazaar. Baltimore, Maryland: The Nautical and Aviation
Publishing Company of America, 1988. 521p. bibliog.

Based almost exclusively on the body of US writing on Cuba, this account of US–Cuba relations borrows much from a 'great figures' approach to history, and is punctuated with quotes from the leading protagonists, such as Columbus, Monroe, Lincoln, McKinley, Martí, Kennedy and Nixon, as well as Aristotle, Cicero, Burke, Marx, Machiavelli, Nietzsche, Hitler and Mao. Mazaar argues against the ideological bromide of analysts on the right and left, and tells a story of political and diplomatic confrontation and blundering, in which the two key trends 'on a collision course' were US dominance of Cuban affairs and the rise of Cuban nationalism.

622 **Subject to solution: problems in Cuban–US relations.**
Edited by Wayne S. Smith, Esteban Morales Domínguez. Boulder,
Colorado; London: Lynne Rienner, 1988. 158p.

These essays resulted from meetings between Cuban and US scholars during 1985, 1986 and 1987, in which foreign policy and bilateral problems between the two countries were discussed for the first time and suggestions made as to how the two governments could resolve or reduce them, should they wish to do so. Part one covers the Cuban–Soviet alliance, Central America, Latin America and the Caribbean, Africa, and the United Nations. Part two focuses on economic and commercial issues in bilateral relations (including the US trade embargo), the Guantánamo naval base, surveillance overflights, and radio interference. See also *Cuba and the United States: will the Cold War in the Caribbean end?* edited by Joseph S. Tulchin, Rafael Hernández (Boulder, Colorado: Lynne Rienner, 1991. 145p.).

623 **To speak the truth: why Washington's 'Cold War' against Cuba doesn't end.**
Fidel Castro, Ernesto Che Guevara, translated by Michael Taber,
Michael Baumann. New York; London; Montreal; Sydney:
Pathfinder, 1992. 232p.

A new English-language translation of four speeches delivered to the United Nations by Fidel Castro and Ernesto Che Guevara in 1960, 1964 and 1979. Under focus in all four is the character, history and centrality of United States commerce and foreign policy in relation to Cuba, Latin America and the rest of Washington's empire. The discussion covers the instability, inequities and explosive social conflicts of a disintegrating world order.

624 **The United States and the origins of Cuban revolution: an empire of liberty in an age of national liberation.**
J. R. Benjamin. Princeton, New Jersey: Princeton University Press,
1990. 235p. bibliog.

Traces the history of US–Cuban relations from the colonial era to the 1959 revolution and its aftermath, including the US-financed Bay of Pigs invasion of Cuba. Benjamin concludes that the United States never resolved the dilemma posed by its contradictory needs to both stabilize and change Cuba.

625 **U.S.–Cuban relations in the 1990s.**
Edited by Jorge I. Domínguez, Rafael Hernández. Boulder, Colorado: Westview, 1989. 324p.

A juxtaposition of the, at times sharply, divergent treatments of US–Cuban relations in the 1990s is achieved in this account by pairing together US and Cuban scholars writing on six broad topics. These six topics cover: the thirty-year overview (encompassing the possibility of dialogue); questions of national security (pessimistic in seeing how conflict might be overcome); South West Africa (the success story of a negotiated solution); Latin America (success versus lack of success in both US and Cuban policy); economic relations (as they are unimportant or important to the United States); and international law (as a common framework for substantive agreements between the two governments).

626 **ZR rifle: the plot to kill Kennedy and Castro.**
Claudia Furiati. Melbourne, Australia: Ocean Press, 1994. 180p.

Thirty years after the death of Kennedy, Cuba opened its classified files, revealing new evidence leading to the discovery of those who really killed the President. Supported by extensive use of Cuban State Security Department materials and an exclusive interview with Cuba's chief of counterintelligence, Brazilian journalist and film-maker Furiati constructs the story of how and why the CIA, through those involved in its anti-Cuba operations, along with anti-Castro exiles, planned and orchestrated the Kennedy assassination.

Latin America and the Caribbean

627 **América Latina y el Caribe en los noventa.** (Latin America and the Caribbean in the nineties.)
Juan Valdés Paz. *Revista/Review Interamericana*, vol. 202, nos. 3-4 (autumn/winter 1992), p. 11-23.

Summarizes the Cuban perspective on the positions adopted in Cuban foreign policy towards Latin America and the Caribbean in the 1990s. Paz views them as coherent and autochthonous in the broader hemispheric context.

628 **El caribe en la política exterior de Cuba: balance de 30 años 1959-1989.** (The Caribbean in Cuban foreign policy: summing up three decades, 1959-89.)
Gerardo González Núñez. Santo Domingo: Ediciones Cipros, 1991. 95p. bibliog.

The study was written as Cuba was on the verge of reintegration into the Caribbean with the collapse of the Eastern European communist bloc and its special relations with it. A Havana-based Cuban scholar of Caribbean politics and Cuban–Caribbean relations, the author provides an informed and informative overview of three decades, from Cuba's regional isolation to initially selective political rapprochement (with Jamaica, Guyana, Suriname and Grenada) and latterly its moves to economic reintegration. The commonality of economic problems and uneasy proximity and dominance of the United States underlies the pragmatism, flexibility and co-operation for Cuba across the regional political spectrum.

629 Cuba and the new Caribbean economic order.
Ernest H. Preeg, with Johnathan D. Levine. Washington, DC: Center for Strategic and International Studies, 1993. 94p. (CSIS Significant Issues Series, vol. 15, no. 2).

A primarily economic analysis, this includes quantitative projections for the Cuban economy under alternative policy assumptions and political scenarios. The author argues that the inevitable path for Cuba is re-integration within the Caribbean–North American region, but asks how and when.

630 Cuba and Nicaragua: a special relationship.
Gary Prevost. *Latin American Perspectives*, vol. 17, no. 3 (summer 1990), p. 120-37. bibliog.

This overview of relations between the two countries focuses in particular on Cuban aid to the FSLN (the Sandinista guerrillas) after 1979. Contrary to popular perception and the US position, says Prevost, Cuba had a moderating influence on the Nicaraguan revolutionaries.

631 Cuba, Castro and the Caribbean: the Cuban revolution and the crisis in the Western conscience.
Carlos Alberto Montaner. New Brunswick, New Jersey: Transaction, 1985. 116p.

The book begins with a basic chronology of Cuban–US relations up until the revolution in 1959. The author then takes a look at Latin America in general and the influence exerted in the area by other nations, before analysing the concept of Cuban nationalism and the way in which it is bound up with the United States. Montaner considers Cuba's culture and the island's future in relation to its history, and discusses how, in his view, Cuba has become a dictatorship. He also examines the ideology of José Martí and attempts to place Cuba in a Caribbean context.

632 Cuba y la integración de América Latina y el Caribe: génesis del pensamiento integracionista. (Cuba and the integration of Latin America and the Caribbean: genesis of integrationist thought.)
Eduardo Klinger Pevida. Santo Domingo: Promolibro, 1995. 145p.

The thought and action of Simón Bolívar are the points of departure for this analysis of Latin American and Caribbean integration. The author depicts this as being diametrically opposed to 20th-century United States interventionism, viewing contemporary integrationism in that vein. He sees the thinking of Cuba and Fidel Castro as very much in keeping with it.

633 The Cuban revolution and Latin America.
Boris Goldenberg. New York: Praeger, 1965. 376p.

After outlining the history of Cuba in the 20th century Goldenberg examines the impact of the 1959 revolution on Latin America and discusses possible further influences.

634 **The gorrion tree: Cuba and the Grenada revolution.**
John Walton Cotman. New York; Berlin; Bern; Frankfurt; Paris;
Vienna: Peter Lang, 1993. 272p. bibliog.

This is a pioneering and provocative analysis of Cuba's aid to the New Jewel
Movement's revolution in Grenada between 1979 and 1983. Based on confidential
Cuban and Grenadian documents and eleven months' fieldwork in Grenada, it details
the activities of Havana's overseas aid workers, and the overall impact of Cuban
civilian and military aid programmes in Grenada. The author sheds light on the
position Cuba took over the October 1983 collapse of the regime, with the murder of
its leader Maurice Bishop, and subsequent US invasion.

635 **Latin American perspectives on the Cuban transition.**
Boris Yopo. Washington, DC: Georgetown University, 1993. 8p.
(Cuba Briefing Papers, no. 3).

The author, the Director of Studies at the Chilean foreign ministry's diplomatic
academy, argues that Latin American governments are concerned that turmoil in Cuba
could create regional instability.

636 **The new Cuban presence in the Caribbean.**
Barry B. Levine. Boulder, Colorado: Westview, 1983. 247p.

Several aspects of Cuba's relationships within the Caribbean region are dealt with in
this work: cultural and political rivalry with the US; the Latin American communist
parties; and relations with specific countries, including Nicaragua, Mexico, Panama,
Venezuela and the English-speaking Caribbean islands.

637 **La política de la revolución cubana hacia América Latina y el
Caribe: notas para una periodización.** (The policy of the Cuban
revolution toward Latin America and the Caribbean: notes for a
periodization.)
Luis Suárez Salazar. *Cuadernos de Nuestra América*, vol. 3, no. 6
(July-Dec. 1986), p. 137-80.

It is argued that Cuba's Latin American and Caribbean foreign policy demonstrates
some continuity, in that it seeks regional unity, with independence and social justice.
The periods outlined in this study are: reinsertion (1959-62); isolation (1962-70);
rapprochement (1970-79); and consolidation (1979-).

638 **A tropical *perestroika*? Cuba, the Soviet Union and the Caribbean.**
Anthony Bryan. *Caribbean Affairs*, vol. 2, no. 2 (April-June 1989),
p. 92-103.

Analyses Cuban overtures to CARICOM countries in the form of an appeal to
'historic commonality' and 'historic obligation' to work together. This was intended
to follow a Cuban strategy that appeared to be low-profile with respect to political
activists and high-profile at government and trade level.

639   **Under the Eagle: U.S. intervention in Central America and the Caribbean.**
Jenny Pearce.   London: Latin America Bureau, 1981. 273p. bibliog.
Written and published at a time when the Caribbean basin was one of the most volatile areas of the world, this study concentrates on events which have taken place since the Cuban and El Salvador revolutions. These are analysed in the context of the history, motivations and contemporary manifestations of United States supremacist policy in the region, through direct and indirect military intervention, alliances with local oligarchies and economic domination. US policy is seen as leaving a legacy of poverty, repression and underdevelopment, causing social and political unrest, and actively suppressing the struggle for social justice and self-determination of those living 'under the eagle'.

Europe

640   **Cuba/España. España/Cuba: historia común.** (Cuba/Spain. Spain/Cuba: a common history.)
Manuel Moreno Fraginals.   Barcelona, Spain: Crítica, 1995. 310p.
Cuba's best-known historian looks afresh at 400 years of Cuban history, drawing out the cultural and economic factors which led to the heightened social tensions and eventual political independence from Spain. The fact that this did not occur until 1898 meant that continued mass emigration and the firming of relations caused Cuba to remain the most Spanish of the Latin American nations, a not unimportant factor in the new wave of Spanish economic interest in Cuba in the 1990s.

641   **The fractured blockade: West European–Cuban relations during the revolution.**
Edited by Alistair Hennessy, George Lambie.   Basingstoke, England: Macmillan Caribbean, 1993. 358p. bibliog.
The basic argument behind this collection of articles is Western Europe's willingness to trade with Cuba and its critical role in the survival of the revolution. British, Cuban and US scholars document how Western Europe never endorsed the US policy of blockade, with national case-studies on Britain (Leyland Motors), France and Spain. The book concludes with the suggestion that Western Europe in the 1990s may be destined to play a similarly crucial role to the one it played in the 1960s, facilitating the régime's transition.

642   **The relationship between the European Community and Cuba.**
Wolf Grabendorff.   In: *Cuba's ties to a changing world.*   Edited by Donna Rich Kaplowitz.   Boulder, Colorado; London: Lynne Rienner, 1993, p. 89-116.
Traces relations between the Community and Cuba, noting that the EC never defined a clear political strategy on Cuba, but reacted to certain political events as they occurred. Cuba's ties to the Eastern bloc were also viewed as a major obstacle to the

normalization of relations. Grabendorff outlines the main factors in Cuban relations with Spain, Germany and France, and provides useful economic data.

643 **Spanish foreign policy in the Caribbean.**
Jean Grugel. *European Review of Latin American and Caribbean Studies* (Amsterdam), vol. 50 (June 1991), p. 135-53. bibliog.

A very useful review and analysis of Spanish foreign policy in the 1990s, this article examines the opportunities for, and obstacles to, closer economic ties with Cuba in particular, as well as the Dominican Republic and Puerto Rico.

Africa

644 **Angola and Namibia: changing the history of Africa.**
Edited by David Deutschmann. Melbourne, Australia: Ocean Press, 1993. 175p. maps.

This book provides a background to events in the 1970s and 1980s, when over 300,000 Cubans helped defend Angola from repeated South African invasions. Included are contributions from Colombian writer Gabriel García Márquez, as well as Cubans Jorge Risquet, and Fidel and Raúl Castro.

645 **Cuba and Africa: thirty years of solidarity.**
Armando Entralgo, David González López. In: *Cuban foreign policy confronts a new international order.* Edited by H. Michael Erisman, John M. Kirk. Boulder, Colorado: Lynne Rienner, 1991.

This essay reviews Cuban involvement in Africa, including its participation in the Angolan war and the events leading to peace. The authors state that Cuba's African policy was based on opposition to colonialism, racism and neo-colonialism; support for anti-imperialist unity among African States; and the desire to establish diplomatic relations and mutually beneficial co-operation. But the latter aim was frustrated by the fact that Cuba lacked the capacity to trade on a large scale with Africa or to finance development projects. An earlier version appeared in *U.S.–Cuban relations in the 1990s.* Edited by Jorge I. Domínguez, Rafael Hernández (Westview, 1989. 324p.).

646 **Cuba's policy in Africa, 1959-1980.**
William Leogrande. Berkeley, California: University of California, Institute of International Studies, 1980. 82p.

After a brief introduction to Cuban foreign policy in general, the author devotes separate chapters to: Cuban–Soviet relations; Cuban policy in Africa, 1959-75; Cuban involvement in Angola, 1965-79; relations with Ethiopia, 1977-79; and future possibilities of Cuban involvement in Africa. Leogrande then places Cuban foreign policy in a global context, considering the Movement of the Non-aligned Nations, Soviet policy and the US response.

647 **Cuban internationalism in sub-Saharan Africa.**
Sergio Díaz-Briquets. Pittsburgh, Pennsylvania: Duquesne University
Press, 1989. 211p. bibliog.

Following a general overview of Cuba's relations in Africa, the author presents a
wide-ranging analysis of Cuba's involvement in various African countries, but in
particular Angola. He considers the views of Cubans at home towards the policy of
internationalism and the different ways in which the Cuban presence was evident.

648 **Por qué somos internacionalistas.** (Why we are internationalists.)
Eloy Concepción. Havana: Ciencias Sociales, 1987. 200p.

Concepción spent three years in Angola as a journalist. Here, he offers background
information and reports on his impressions and observations on the situation in
Angola, with a focus on South African, United States and Cuban intervention.

Middle East

649 **Castro, Israel and the PLO.**
David J. Kopilow. Washington, DC: Cuban-American National
Foundation, 1984. 44p.

A description of Cuban policy toward Israel and the Palestine Liberation Organization by CANF, an anti-Castro organization in the United States.

650 **Cuba's foreign policy in the Middle East.**
Damián J. Fernández. Boulder, Colorado; London: Westview, 1988.
160p. bibliog.

This thorough review of a less studied area of Cuba's international relations begins
with a detailed overview of foreign policy issues in the period 1959-85. It goes on to
examine Middle East relations by country, placing special emphasis on Libya.
Fernández concludes that, while the Middle East viewed Cuba mainly as an agent of
Soviet interests, and its presence in the area in effect complicated the situation,
Havana was actually trying to mediate inter-Arab conflicts. It also provided military
and paramilitary services such as training in Soviet weaponry.

651 **Cuban–Israeli relations: from the Cuban revolution to the new
world order.**
Allan Metz. *Cuban Studies*, vol. 23 (1993), p. 113-34.

Metz explains how, despite the cool relations existing between Cuba and Israel at the
time of writing, relations between 1959 and 1967 were good. He describes the gradual
deterioration which took place after this date and which continued until 1973 when
relations were severed. Cuba remained a severe critic of the Israeli government until
the late 1980s, when relations became slightly better. Although there are signs of a
rapprochement, Metz proposes several reasons why it will be difficult to improve the
situation further in the near future.

652   **US hands off the Mideast! Cuba speaks out at the United Nations.**
Fidel Castro, Ricardo Alarcón.   New York: Pathfinder, 1990. 81p.
Contains the text of the two Cuban leaders' speeches on the Iraq/Kuwait conflict, in which they decry Washington's war moves and call for peace and cooperation.

Cuba en crisis. (Cuba in crisis.)
See item no. 229.

Fidel Castro: nothing can stop the course of history.
See item no. 256.

War and crisis in the Americas.
See item no. 260.

Law and religion in Marxist Cuba: a human rights inquiry.
See item no. 572.

CubaInfo.
See item no. 1081.

A bibliography of United States–Latin American relations since 1810.
See item no. 1150.

Cuba–U.S. relations: a survey of twentieth century historiography.
See item no. 1151.

Economy

Pre-1959

653 **Caminos para el azúcar.** (Rails for sugar.)
Oscar Zanetti, Alejandro García. Havana: Ciencias Sociales, 1987.
417p. 7 maps. bibliog.
A superb account of the history of the railways from their introduction into Cuba in the mid-19th century up until after the 1959 revolution. Zanetti and García indicate how important the railways were, both to the 19th-century sugar revolution under Spanish colonial rule and to the early 20th-century sugar expansion under US monopolies, and go on to analyse working conditions and labour struggles. Beautifully illustrated, this is the product of years of team research, based on primary source material.

654 **Características fundamentales de la economía cubana.**
(Basic features of the Cuban economy.)
Julián Alienes Urosa. Havana: Banco Nacional de Cuba, 1950. 406p.
bibliog.
The Cuban economy receives a thorough analysis in this work, which focuses mainly on the 1930s and 1940s, with particular attention paid to the problems of economic growth, sugar productivity, population, natural resources, capital accumulation, industry, imports and exports.

655 **Cuba: capitalismo dependiente y subdesarrollo, 1510-1959.**
(Cuba: dependent capitalism and underdevelopment, 1510-1959.)
Francisco López Segrera. Havana: Ciencias Sociales, 1981. 288p.
bibliog.
López Segrera presents an analysis of Cuban economic history in the context of the international economic system, establishing seven historical phases: the *encomienda*, 1510-50; the *hacienda*, 1550-1700; the breakdown of autonomous development, 1700-62; the plantation, 1762-1880; from colonialism to neo-colonialism, 1880-1902; imperialism, 1902-34; and dependent capitalism, 1934-59.

656 **Cuba: tierra indefensa.** (Cuba: defenceless land.)
Alberto Arredondo. Havana: Editorial Lex, 1945. 490p. bibliog.
A survey of economic history from pre-Columbian times up to the revolutionary upheavals of the 1930s, this work covers all the key sectors of the economy: sugar; tobacco; livestock; coffee; banking and finance.

657 **Cuban railroads, 1830-1868: origins and effects of progressive entrepreneurialism.**
Gert J. Oostindie. *Caribbean Studies*, vol. 20, nos. 3-4 (1988), p. 24-45.
Oostindie discusses the origins of the railway in Cuba in the 1830s, noting its development through 1868, the colonial government and private initiatives promoting the railway, and the network of tracks within Cuba.

658 **Economic history of Cuba.**
Julio Le Riverend, translated by María Juana Cazabón, Homero León. Havana: Ensayo Book Institute, 1967. 277p. bibliog.
Translated and revised since it was first published in 1956, this is a standard Cuban textbook, covering the island's economic history from aboriginal times to the early revolutionary period. Key sections are: agrarian and industrial structure, from the Spanish conquest of Cuba through colonial economy, 1510-1659; the slave economy, 1659-1886; and the imperialist phase, 1886-1958, broken down into pre- and post-1934, when the economy went into stagnation. There is a brief chapter on the early revolutionary years.

659 **Historia económica de Cuba.** (Economic history of Cuba.)
Heinrich Friedlaender. Havana: Ciencias Sociales, 1978. 2 vols. bibliog.
Originally published in 1944, this is a classic work on the economic history of Cuba. Volume one covers 1642-1868, the period from Cuba's colonization by Spain up to the outbreak of the first war of independence. This is divided into phases: the colonial system, 1642-1700; the new colonial system, 1700-63; mercantilism, 1763-89; sugar predominance, 1790-1815; and prosperity, 1815-68. Volume two covers the more recent period, again in phases: doctrine, 1868-1900; and supercapitalism, 1900-38.

660 **Industrial Cuba: being a study of present and industrial conditions, with suggestions as to the opportunities presented in the island for American capital, enterprise and labour.**
Robert P. Porter. New York: Arno Press, 1976. 428p. maps.
A reprint of the 1899 edition, this provides exhaustive information on the state of the Cuban economy in the aftermath of the 1895-98 independence war, covering: banking; tariffs; commerce; agriculture; forestry; mining; and transport. It is a poignant reminder of the similarities between the economic dilemmas facing Cuba a century ago and those facing the nation in the 1990s.

661 **Los monopolios norteamericanos en Cuba: contribución al estudio de la penetración imperialista.** (North American monopolies in Cuba: contribution to the study of imperialist penetration.)
Havana: Instituto Cubano del Libro, Ciencias Sociales, 1973. 313p.

Articles based on primary research and conducted by Cuban and East German scholars using documents from nationalized US monopolies, are collected together in this publication. Jesús Chía looks at the soap and perfume industry, focusing on the US companies Colgate-Palmolive and Procter and Gamble and Cuban companies Crusellas y Cía and Sabatés. Jurgen Kuczynski, Dieter Baudis, Gloria García and José A. Piñera look at Esso Standard Oil, the Cuban Electric Company, and the American and Foreign Power Company. María de los Ángeles Ayón focuses on the labour movement in the electric monopoly and Horst Handke and Elli Morhmann consider US public relations.

662 **Our Cuban colony.**
Leland Hamilton Jenks. New York: Vanguard Press, 1928. 341p.

Now a classic critical study of the US dominance of Cuba, this book focuses mainly on the growth of the US economic presence in the late 19th and early 20th centuries. The text contains a wealth of data on US investments in sugar, transport, utilities, banking and mining.

663 **Report on Cuba.**
International Bank for Reconstruction and Development. Baltimore, Maryland: Johns Hopkins University Press, 1951. 1,052p. maps.

One of the most comprehensive reports ever published on the Cuban economy, this is an essential reference for anyone researching the Cuban economy prior to the 1959 revolution. It documents the findings and recommendations of a 1950 economic and technical mission to Cuba organized by the International Bank for Reconstruction and Development in collaboration with the Cuban government. Book one summarizes the mission's diagnosis of Cuba's problems and outlines its major recommendations. In Book two the main features of the economy and resources available for development are examined. Book three reviews the question of production, examining agriculture, industry, mineral resources and applied research with a special focus on the problems of the sugar industry. Books four to seven look in greater depth at aids to production, human problems, administration and finance, while the final sections are devoted to examining international economic relations, development strategy, and technical problems and possibilities.

664 **The United Fruit Company: un caso de dominio imperialista.**
(The United Fruit Company: a case-study of imperialist domination.)
Edited by Alejandro García, Oscar Zanetti. Havana: Ciencias Sociales, 1976. 450p. bibliog.

A history of the US United Fruit Company's involvement in Cuba up until its nationalization in 1960. It deals with the company's social impact and the labour movement which arose in response to its presence.

Post-1959

General

665 **Cambios estructurales en la economía cubana.** (Structural change in the Cuban economy.)
Miguel A. Figueras. *Cuadernos de Nuestra América*, vol. 9, no. 19 (July-Dec. 1992), p. 82-100.

Figueras summarizes the economic scenario inherited by the Cuban revolution, particularly the problem of over-specialization in sugar. He analyses the changes in agriculture over the thirty years since 1959, arguing that Cuba achieved greater agro-industrial integration in that period. It is shown that Cuba also developed the manufacture of capital goods, metal products and spare parts to the point where those sectors accounted for one-sixth of gross non-sugar industrial production.

666 **Capitalism and socialism in Cuba, a study of dependency, development and underdevelopment.**
Patricia Ruffin. Basingstoke, England: Macmillan, 1990. 212p. bibliog.

Details the social, political and economic forces affecting Cuba's prospects for development under both capitalism and socialism. Part one looks at pre-1959 capitalist dependency and underdevelopment in the context of Cuba and the United States. Part two analyses socialist development and dependency in the context of Cuba and the Soviet Union.

667 **Crítica a nuestros críticos.** (Critique of our critics.)
José Luis Rodríguez. Havana: Ciencias Sociales, 1988. 125p.

Rodríguez defends the development record of the Cuban economy and society against Cuban-American 'Cubanologist' critics and their argument that socialism is unviable and undemocratic. Cuban development since 1959 is contrasted in a more favourable light with other countries of Latin America, and Costa Rica in particular. It is argued that, taking into account social indicators such as health and education, Cuba outperformed her neighbours.

668 **Cuba's financial crisis: the secret report from the National Bank of Cuba.**
Washington, DC: Cuban-American National Foundation, 1985. 83p.

This is a report which the publisher claims was submitted to Cuba's Western creditors in February 1985 as part of the government's efforts to reschedule the convertible currency foreign debt. The contents were allegedly unknown to the Cuban public. The report details the state of the economy in 1984, the balance of payments and foreign debt in convertible currency, and the proposed measures to increase and diversify trade with creditor countries. See also other Banco Nacional de Cuba reports (e.g. item no. 730).

669 **Cuba's socialist economy: towards the 1990s.**
Edited by Andrew Zimbalist. Boulder, Colorado; London: Lynne
Rienner, 1987. 188p.

These essays provide an overview of, and are broadly sympathetic to, the economic performance of the first three decades of the revolution. The compilation covers patterns of development between 1959 and 1985, agricultural policy and development, gender issues in contemporary tobacco farming, and the performance of the sugar industry from 1981 to 1985. Industrial growth between 1965 and 1984; capital goods production (1958-85); the health-care system (1959-86); workers' incentives (1959-86); the resolution of worker–management conflicts; planning in the mid-1980s; and hard-currency debt and trade (1959-84) are also covered. The text was first published as an issue of *World Development* (vol. 15, no. 1 [Jan. 1987]).

670 **The Cuban economy: dependency and development.**
Edited by Antonio Jorge, Jaime Suchlicki. Coral Gables, Florida:
Institute of Interamerican Studies, University of Miami, 1989. 134p.

This account develops the thesis of Cuban post-revolutionary dependency on the Soviet Union. There are separate chapters on various aspects of the economy.

671 **The Cuban economy: measurement and analysis of socialist performance.**
Andrew Zimbalist, Claes Brundenius. Baltimore, Maryland: Johns
Hopkins University Press, 1989. 240p.

On the basis of extensive first-hand research and interviews in Cuba, the US and Swedish authors arrive at new estimates of economic growth and changes in the economic structure. They explore the conflict between consumer needs and capital goods industries, examine how workers are motivated with limited material incentives, and assess Cuba's dependence on sugar exports and Soviet aid.

672 **Cuban political economy: controversies in Cubanology.**
Edited by Andrew Zimbalist. Boulder, Colorado; London: Westview,
1988. 240p. bibliog.

This volume extends the boundaries of political economy to the economic trade-offs from Cuba's Third World internationalism and the role of women in Cuban society. It also includes analytical essays that challenge some conventional views on the strength of the post-1959 Cuban economic base; the reliability of Cuban statistics; the planning process; Cuba's dependence on the Soviet Union; and growth rates and structural change.

673 **The economic development of revolutionary Cuba: strategy and performance.**
Archibald R. M. Ritter. New York: Praeger, 1974. 373p. bibliog.

Four aspects of economic strategy and performance are scrutinized for the period 1959-72: income distribution; employment; economic growth; and economic dependence.

674 **The economy of socialist Cuba: a two-decade appraisal.**
Carmelo Mesa-Lago. Albuquerque, New Mexico: University of New
Mexico Press, 1981. 235p.

A thorough overview of the first two decades of the revolutionary economy, in which
the focus is on attempted economic growth, diversification and independence, along
with employment, income distribution and social services.

675 **Measuring Cuban economic performance.**
Jorge Pérez López. Austin, Texas: University of Texas Press, 1987.
202p.

Presents a re-estimation of Cuban national income growth from 1965 to 1982 by an
adjustment of Cuban official constant-price national-income series using a proxy
Guatemalan price set. The result is a powerful downward estimate of aggregate
growth indexes.

676 **Revolution and economic development in Cuba.**
Arthur MacEwan. London; Basingstoke, England: Macmillan, 1981.
265p. bibliog.

McEwan's analysis of two decades in the course of the Cuban economy examines the
relationship between political participation and economic development. He focuses on
agriculture and agrarian development policy, in conjunction with overall development
strategy, state organization, education and labour motivation. Writing from a Marxist
perspective, the author emphasizes the relationship between economic events and
social classes, in both the pre-1959 and post-1959 periods.

677 **Revolutionary Cuba: the challenge to economic growth with
equity.**
Claes Brundenius. Boulder, Colorado: Westview, 1984. 216p.
bibliog.

This comprehensive analysis of Cuba's social and economic evolution from 1959 to
1980 was also the first attempt to evaluate quantitatively the revolution's impact on
economic growth, employment, income distribution and the fulfilling of basic social
needs. Brundenius draws primarily on previously unpublished statistical information
collected on visits to Cuba from 1973. He also places the revolution in a historical and
comparative perspective with references to the 1933-58 period and to two other Latin
American development models: post-1964 Brazil and Peru from 1968 to 1980.

678 **A study on Cuba.**
Cuban Economic Research Project. Coral Gables, Florida: University
of Miami Press, 1965. 774p.

A voluminous work on the Cuban economy from colonial times up until the early
revolutionary period, containing detailed statistical information.

1960s

679 **Che Guevara: economics and politics in the transition to socialism.**
Carlos Tablada. New York: Pathfinder, 1990. 2nd ed. 286p. bibliog.
First published in 1989 and also produced in French and Spanish, this work looks at Ernesto Che Guevara's contributions to the debate on socialist economic management while he was a member of the Cuban government, 1959-66. It includes a discussion of the Marxist concept of politics as concentrated economics, budgetary finance and economic accounting systems in a socialist economy, and views the function of economic planning as the principal organizer of a socialist economy. Tablada also examines the concepts of voluntary work and moral incentives so closely identified with Guevara.

680 **Datos sobre una economía en ruinas, 1902-1963.** (Data on an economy in ruins, 1902-63.)
José M. Illán González. Miami, Florida: [n.p.], 1964. 2nd ed. 160p.
This study is primarily an indictment of the mismanagement of economic planning and production in the first five years of the revolution. The pre-1959 section concentrates mainly on the 1950s Cuban economy.

681 **The economic transformation of Cuba: a first-hand account.**
Edward Boorstein. New York: Monthly Review Press, 1968. 302p.
Boorstein, a Marxist economist, worked for several important Cuban institutions, including the National Bank and the Ministry of Foreign Trade, and had some input into the development of economic policy. This is his first-hand account of economic developments in Cuba in the early 1960s.

682 **Man and socialism in Cuba: the great debate.**
Edited and with an introduction by Bertram Silverman. New York: Atheneum, 1971. 382p.
A collection of articles connected with the great economic debate of 1962 to 1965 on the fundamental problems facing Cuban socialism in transforming the old order. The debate focused on the role of money and the market, material and moral incentives, theory and practice, ethics and necessity, and social conscience. The articles are written by the key protagonists in the debate: Ernesto Che Guevara, Charles Bettelheim and Ernest Mandel, with Joaquín Infante, Luis Álvarez Rom, Alexis Codina, Alberto Mora, Miguel Cossío, and Marcelo Fernández Font. There is an introduction by Silverman placing the debate in context, and an epilogue by Fidel Castro.

1970s

683 **Economic aspects of Cuban involvement in Africa.**
Sergio Roca. *Cuban Studies*, vol. 10, no. 2 (July 1980), p. 55-79.
In this attempt at an economic cost–benefit analysis of Cuban commitment to Africa in the 1970s, particularly in Angola and Ethiopia, Roca finds that the main benefits were

increased leverage with the USSR and earnings from technical personnel. On the negative side, expenses were incurred in the form of domestic opportunity costs in fishing, transportation, social services, construction and leadership commitment to economic tasks, the loss of hypothetical aid from Western sources and postponement of normalization of relations with the USA.

684 **Final report of the Cuban claims program.**
In: *Annual Report to Congress.* Washington, DC: Foreign Claims Settlement Commission of the United States, 1972.

Contains details of those compensation claims made by US nationals in respect of property expropriated by Cuba and accepted by the US Congressional investigatory commission.

1980s

685 **Los cambios en la política económica y los resultados de la economía cubana (1986-89).** (Changes in economic policy and the results of economic policy in Cuba [1986-89].)
José Luis Rodríguez. *Cuadernos de Nuestra América*, vol. 9, no. 19 (July-Dec. 1992), p. 63-81.

The author, who was later appointed minister for finance (1992-95) and the economy (1995-), argues that Cuba has always maintained flexible and self-critical positions which have allowed it to amend the mistakes it has made and try out new experiences. He maintains that after 1986 a number of measures were implemented to eliminate errors and negative tendencies and a set of social programmes were launched alongside a new style of work. Rodríguez stresses that in a particularly complicated scenario, industrialization continues to be a central development goal, and that all sectors of the economy, except agriculture, transport and communications, experienced positive growth in value terms compared with the first half of the previous five-year period.

686 **Cuban socialism: rectification and the new model of accumulation.**
James E. Petras, Morris H. Morley. In: *Cuba in transition: crisis and transformation.* Edited by Sandor Halebsky, John Kirk. Boulder, Colorado: Westview, 1992, p. 15-36. (Latin American Perspectives Series, no. 9).

A shrewd analysis of the late 1980s rectification, which the authors see as a transition from an inward-oriented consumer economy to an outward-looking export economy, with international liberalization legitimated at home by populist measures and moral exhortations. Castro walks the tightrope between external market accommodation and internal cutbacks, attempting to spread the burden equally.

1990s

687 **Are economic reforms propelling Cuba to the market?**
Carmelo Mesa-Lago.   Miami, Florida: North-South Center
Publications, 1994. 86p.

In order to answer the question posed in the title of this short but tightly argued book,
the author examines the available estimates of the extent and effects of economic
decline in Cuba since the collapse of Eastern European socialism in 1989. He studies
Cuba's attempts to find new sources of credit and oil and new trading partners, and
analyses the reforms enacted between July 1993 and May 1994. Mesa-Lago's
conclusion is 'not yet and not very fast', although his analysis might have been
tempered if he had been writing after the largely successful implementation of new
monetary and fiscal policies in 1994 and the later changes in mining, banking and
investment laws.

688 **Aspectos estructurales de la economía cubana.** (Structural aspects of
the Cuban economy.)
Miguel A. Figueras.   Havana: Ciencias Sociales, 1994. 181p.

A very useful review of the evolution of the Cuban economy, its resources, structure
and performance up to the 1990s. The discussion covers key questions such as
agricultural policy and industrialization, the sugar industry, the policy of developing a
science-based high-technology sector, and foreign trade. Figueras, an economist who
has been deputy minister of the sugar industry and first deputy minister of planning,
argues for a very much more diversified economy and the creation of an effective
national saving capacity as a major source of investment capital.

689 **Balancing economic efficiency, social concerns and political
control.**
Gillian Gunn.   Washington, DC: Georgetown University Press, 1994.

A succinct appraisal of three key aspects of the 1990s reform process, namely,
economic efficiency, social welfare, and political control. It is published in the Cuba
Briefing Paper Series quarterly publication of The Cuba Project, a unit of the Center
for Latin American Studies at Georgetown University, designed to serve decision-
makers and analysts interested in Cuba.

690 **Cuba after communism.**
Eliana Cardoso, Ann Helwege.   Cambridge, Massachusetts:
Massachusetts Institute of Technology, 1992. 148p.

The authors of this incisive analysis of Cuba's economic record argue that the more
quickly the island moves to a market economy, the better. They propose a series of
reforms to ease the transition to capitalism, including a Marshall Plan-style aid programme. Suggesting that shock therapy would be good for Cuba, they also agree that
the wisest move the United States could make would be to end the trade embargo and
pursue a constructive role in facilitating transition.

691 **Cuba and the future.**
Edited by Donald E. Schulz. Westport, Connecticut: Greenwood, 1994. 194p. bibliog.

Nine leading Cubanologists contribute to this collection of papers presented at a round-table at the US Army War College organized by the United States Strategic Studies Institute. They address the causes and nature of Cuba's critical circumstances, probable outcomes, and implications for the United States and, in particular, for the US Army. The overall conclusion is that the Castro régime may well survive. From an economic perspective the most salient conclusion is that the US trade embargo is counterproductive.

692 **Cuba: apertura económica y relaciones con Europa.**
(Cuba: economic opening and relations with Europe.)
Edited by Instituto de Relaciones Europeo–Latinoamericanas (Institute of European–Latin American Relations, IRELA). Madrid: IRELA, 1994. 278p.

Key economic and political actors in Cuba and Europe were involved in a conference held in Havana in December 1993, of which these are the proceedings. A consensus view of economic change emerges: the 1990s marked an economic opening to the world economy in the face of continuing US embargo, with growing economic trade and co-operation between Cuba and Europe. However, major differences are registered regarding political conditionality and concepts of democracy and human rights.

693 **Cuba: la reestructuración de la economía, una propuesta para el debate.** (Cuba: the restructuring of the economy, a proposal for discussion.)
Julio Carranza Valdés, Luis Gutiérrez Urdaneta, Pedro Monreal González. Havana: Ciencias Sociales, 1995. 211p. bibliog.

An earlier version of this work was presented to the Cuban government in April 1994. It has now been expanded and updated to take into account events up to January 1995, as well as criticisms arising during the debate the original work generated. It is this debate which gives the book its particular relevance in the history of Cuban economic thought. In it the authors review the country's recent economic history and the proposals for an economic transition originating outside Cuba, before moving on to discuss the conceptual considerations for economic reconstruction. They then outline a three-stage reform programme: restoration of financial equilibrium and efficiency; transition to a regulated market; and decentralization of the economy. The authors express loyalty to the concept of Cuban socialism but take a pragmatic approach to market-oriented reforms. The appendices include listings of reform studies in other countries with implications for Cuba and of specific reform proposals for Cuba, as well as discussion of a managerial experiment in the Armed Forces' enterprises, inflation, and monetary policy.

694 **Cuba: los retos de la economía.** (Cuba: the challenges to the economy.)
Julio Carranza Valdés. *Cuadernos de Nuestra América*, vol. 9, no. 19 (July-Dec. 1992), p. 131-58.

One of the first Cuban analyses of the structural adjustments needed to meet the challenges of reinsertion into the 1990s post-Cold War world economy.

695   **Cuba's economic and management policy response to the changing global environment.**
Susan Brandwayn.   *Public Administration and Development*, vol. 13 (1993), p. 361-75.
The author, a member of the Transnational Corporations and Management Division of the United Nations Department of Economic and Social Development, assesses the institutional reforms in the exporting sector of Cuba's state enterprises and planning system and the prospects for the economy in the 1990s in an increasingly difficult situation. In considering the system's ability to move quickly forward from basic management training to structural change, she stresses: the adaptability of Cuban managers, who have shown themselves to be highly retrainable; and Cuba's considerable resource endowment, including human capital and investment in scientific and technical research and development.

696   **Cuba's second economy: from behind the scenes to center stage.**
Jorge F. Pérez López.   New Brunswick, New Jersey: Transaction, 1995. 172p.
This analysis of the changes taking place in Cuba focuses primarily on domestic factors in order to explain the present economic crisis. Unlike many studies of Cuba which tend to treat the island as uniquely different from other socialist countries and divorce post-1990 events from their historical context, the author of this work places Cuba's 1990s reform process in the wider context of post-1959 policy-making and compares it with the experiences of other centrally planned economies. A weakness lies in the author's failure to refer to what is occurring in China and Vietnam, the two countries with which Cuba most often compares its own reform process, and the downgrading of politics as a factor shaping Cuban economic decisions.

697   **The Cuban economy in a changing international environment.**
José Luis Rodríguez.   *Cuban Studies*, vol. 23 (1993), p. 33-48.
Discusses the effects of the demise of the socialist bloc on the Cuban economy and considers how the development of tourism and exports can only partially counter this. Rodríguez suggests, however, that Cuba has the power to survive the crisis and recover, on the basis of the strategy put forward at the Fourth Congress of the Cuban Communist Party.

698   **El desafío económico de Cuba.** (The economic challenge for Cuba.)
Carlos Lage Dávila.   Havana: Ediciones Entorno/UFO SA, 1992. 73p.
Cuban vice-president Carlos Lage, one of the architects of Cuba's economic reform programme, speaks about major economic issues, the state of the economy at that point in time (November 1992) and the social implications of economic reforms.

699   **La economía cubana: los desafíos de un ajuste sin desocialización.**
(The Cuban economy: the challenge of adjustment without loss of social cohesion.)
Aurelio Alonso.   *Cuadernos de Nuestra América*, vol. 9, no. 19 (July-Dec. 1992), p. 159-74.
A Cuban economist discusses the difficulties of making the economic adjustments necessary to emerge from Cuba's 1990s crisis without destroying the Cuban

revolution's social achievements. This would cause a collapse of the social cohesion which has allowed the Castro government to survive for thirty-five years.

700 **Estrategía de desarrollo económico en Cuba.** (Economic development strategy in Cuba.)
José Luis Rodríguez.   Havana: Ciencias Sociales, 1990. 341p. bibliog.
One of Cuba's leading economic thinkers analyses the problems, failures and successes of the revolutionary government's economic development strategy in each of its main phases. He recognizes that, despite advances, the revolution did not succeed in overcoming inherited structural deformations and argues that external financial equilibrium must be re-established for the development strategy then being pursued to succeed. The work contains a very useful chronology of the most significant economic events to take place between 1959 and 1986, as well as comprehensive statistics.

701 **The foreign assistance requirements of a democratic Cuba: a first approximation.**
José F. Alonso, Armando M. Lago.   London: La Sociedad Económica, 1994. 63p.
The first in a series of occasional papers, this projection by Cuban Americans considers alternative economic settings: the 'Nicaraguan' or 'partial privatization' option; full privatization with membership of the Caribbean Basin Initiative; and full privatization with eventual entry into the North American Free Trade Agreement. The authors' prognosis supports the unfettered free-market route as the most beneficial for Cuba. They express greater optimism regarding the prospects for sugar, nickel and biotechnology, but are more cautious on tourism, industrial exports, construction and real estate development.

702 **Informe sobre la economía de Cuba.** (Report on the Cuban economy.)
G. Zuikov, O. Paniushkina, A. Mijailov, M. Tregubenko.   Madrid: Fundación Liberal José Martí, 1992. 190p.
Presents a report on the Cuban economy as it appeared to four (then) Soviet researchers, some of whom formerly lived in Cuba. Prepared at the invitation of an anti-Castro exile group, the work offers a snapshot of the economy on the point of collapse due to overdependence on trade with the socialist bloc.

703 **The sociological impact of rising foreign investment.**
Gillian Gunn.   Washington, DC: Georgetown University, The Cuba Project, 1993. 16p. (Cuba Briefing Paper Series, no. 1).
This short discussion of the question 'Is foreign investment undermining the Cuban socialist system?' includes the first published case-study of how a non-tourism joint venture – a Havana shipyard – prepared for the arrival of foreign capital and coped with the effect on the workforce. Gunn also examines the ramifications of tourism development and includes interviews with a cross-section of personnel in joint venture hotels.

704 **UNDP: country programme Cuba 1992-96.**
United Nations Development Programme. Havana: UNDP, 1992.
29p.

The twelve projects funded in Cuba by the UNDP cover food production, export of traditional products and the broadening of non-traditional production such as biotechnology, sugar-cane derivatives and electronics, reflecting Cuban development priorities.

705 **Waiting for change: adjustment and reform in Cuba.**
Manuel Pastor, Jr., Andrew Zimbalist. *World Development*, vol. 23, no. 5 (May 1995), p. 705-20.

Noting the failure of Cuba's initial attempts to survive the collapse of trade with the former socialist bloc and the continuing US embargo, the authors put forward a new strategy based on the rapid privatization of state assets. This, they argue, should absorb the monetary overhang, widely distribute assets and control and protect the social safety net that has characterized the Cuban economy.

706 **Winds of economic change in Havana.**
Jacques de Groote, Frank Moss. *Cuba Business* (London), vol. 8, no. 2 (1994), p. 3-8.

An almost verbatim version of the official International Monetary Fund report prepared following an informal International Monetary Fund visit to Cuba in November 1993 at the invitation of the National Bank of Cuba. Though the visit was described as unofficial, the document is important as a record of the IMF's first assessment of Cuban economic conditions since Cuba's withdrawal from that institution in 1964.

Last resorts: the costs of tourism in the Caribbean.
See item no. 26.

Tourism development in transition economies: the Cuba case.
See item no. 28.

Tourism in Cuba: a development strategy for the 1990s?
See item no. 29.

The island of Cuba.
See item no. 46.

Sixty years in Cuba.
See item no. 49.

Cuban tapestry.
See item no. 56.

Dossier: Cuba.
See item no. 235.

In defence of socialism.
See item no. 258.

A problemas viejos soluciones nuevas: el perfeccionamiento empresarial en el MINFAR. (New solutions for old problems: improving business efficiency in the MINFAR.)
See item no. 519.

Cuba and the new Caribbean economic order.
See item no. 629.

Country Report: Cuba, Dominican Republic, Haiti, Puerto Rico.
See item no. 1096.

Boletín de Información sobre la Economía Cubana. (Bulletin of Information about the Cuban Economy.)
See item no. 1108.

Country Profile: Cuba.
See item no. 1109.

Cuestiones de la Economía Planificada. (Questions of Planned Economy.)
See item no. 1110.

Economía y Desarrollo. (Economics and Development.)
See item no. 1111.

La Sociedad Económica. (The Economics Society.)
See item no. 1112.

Tribuna del Economista. (The Economist Tribune.)
See item no. 1113.

Cuadernos de Nuestra América. (Notebooks of Our America.)
See item no. 1117.

Political and economic encyclopaedia of South America and the Caribbean.
See item no. 1140.

Finance, Trade and Investment

Pre-1959

707　**Cuba: its resources and opportunities.**
　　Pulaski F. Hyatt, John T. Hyatt.　New York: J. S. Ogilvie Publishing
　　Company, 1898. 226p.

Two US consular agents in Cuba provide a detailed account of natural, economic and employment conditions in Cuba after the war of independence. This is an interesting text from a century ago, when the United States was seeking to encourage investment in Cuba.

708　**Cuba: the pearl of the Antilles.**
　　Ramón Bustamante.　St. Louis, Missouri: Foreign Publishing
　　Company, 1916. 267p. map.

This book comprises a descriptive guide to Cuba for early 20th-century businessmen and investors, with information on currency, weights and measures, cable and mail rules, tariffs, credit availability, and transport to and within Cuba.

709　**El Grupo Rockefeller actúa.** (The Rockefeller Group in action.)
　　Rodolfo Sarracino.　Havana: Ciencias Sociales, 1987. 233p. bibliog.

Chronicles US interference in the Cuban economy during the 1930s, with particular reference to banking and finance. Sarracino also looks at British relations with Cuba in the same period, arguing that UK monopolies attempted to include Cuba in their Caribbean sphere of influence.

710　**Investment in Cuba.**
　　United States Department of Commerce. Bureau of Foreign Commerce.
　　Washington, DC: US Government Printing Office, 1956. 200p. maps.

Compiled as a basic compendium of information for US businessmen, this volume contains information on all aspects of the economy, and strong sections on business law, labour law, and the investment climate.

711 **Monetary problems of an export economy: the Cuban experience, 1917-1947.**
Henry Christopher Wallich. Cambridge, Massachusetts: Harvard University Press, 1950. 357p. bibliog.

One of the most detailed studies in 20th-century Cuban economic history to have a focus on monetary and currency issues.

Post-1959

712 **Antología.** (Anthology.)
Raúl León Torras. Havana: Ciencias Sociales, 1988. 204p.

Torras's most important economic writings are arranged in three sections in this anthology: foreign trade; sugar; and international finance. This last aspect was at the crux of much of Torras's thinking, highlighting tensions between the USA, Japan and West Germany, and between them and the developing countries. He argues that the latter's foreign debt is not only unpayable but that its very perdurance endangers the world financial system as we know it today. University of Pennsylvania-trained Torras, now deceased, once served under Che Guevara and was for many years head of the National Bank of Cuba.

713 **Back in business: Canada–Cuba relations after 50 years.**
John M. Kirk, Peter McKenna, Julia Sagebien. Ottawa: Canadian Foundation for the Americas, 1995. 30p.

Reviews fifty years of relations between Canada and Cuba, with an emphasis on the economic advantages for both sides. The authors argue that Canadian companies have a marked advantage over their US neighbours in trading with Cuba, but suggest the need to clear away the 'ideological cobwebs' that have hampered analysis.

714 **Biociencias en Cuba 1994-95.** (Life sciences in Cuba 1994-95.)
Havana: Biomundi Consultoría, 1994. 2nd ed. 185p. (Available from: Biomundi Consultoría, calle 200 no. 1922 e/19 y 21, Atabey Playa, Ciudad de La Habana. Aptdo. postal 16015, la Habana 11600).

This fully cross-referenced guide to Cuban scientific institutions and the biotechnology and health-care industry, includes details of key staff and facilities and brief descriptions of commercially traded products. It is also available on a 3.5-inch disk. Related Biomundi publications include: *Guía para negocios: la bioindustria en Cuba* (Business guide: the bioindustry in Cuba) (Havana: Biomundi Consultoría, 1995. 150p.).

715 **Boletín Económico ICE: Cuba.** (Economic Bulletin of the Foreign Trade Institute: Cuba.)
Madrid: Spanish Trade and Tourism Ministry, 1994. 80p.

After presenting an overview of the country, this guide to Cuba describes the development of the economy and its relations and trade with Spain. The legal and institutional framework and the cost of setting up commercial representations are analysed and practical information and lists of useful addresses are included.

716 Business opportunities in Cuba.
Havana: CONAS (Consultores Asociados, SA), 1994. 107p.

Outlines the Ministry of Foreign Investment and Economic Cooperation's policy aimed at stimulating foreign capital participation in the Cuban economy. It lists companies seeking foreign partners by sector and specifies the areas for which a foreign contribution is sought. CONAS also produces brief reports aimed at potential foreign investment partners.

717 C/LAA's Caribbean Basin Commercial Profile.
Cayman Islands, British West Indies; Caribbean Publishing Company;
Washington, DC: Caribbean/Latin American Action, 1994. 262p.

The annual reference source for trade, investment and development in the Caribbean Basin, incorporating the Caribbean Business Directory and Caribbean Basin Databook. The volume contains a Caribbean Basin regional profile, as well as individual country profiles, including facts at a glance, country background, economic summary, government, trade and investment incentives, and examples of foreign business firms with operations in Cuba.

718 Cuba: an assessment of tourism development and opportunities.
Price Waterhouse. Toronto: Cubalink Canada Ltd, 1994. 172p.

Aimed at investors, this report examines business and economic conditions in Cuba and analyses tourism infrastructure and investment opportunities. A useful summary of the legal and fiscal framework existing in 1994 is included.

719 Cuba: business, finance and investment.
London: Euromoney, 1993. 130p.

This documentation from the 1993 London Euromoney Conference contains invaluable English-language abstracts covering key legislation on investment in Cuba. These include: the legal system; approval and registration; accounting and statistics; prices; fiscal obligations; financial; fiscal and customs regulations; arbitration; insurance; labour policy; tourist zones; and environmental protection. Some of the information is redundant following reforms in 1994 and 1995.

720 Cuba creates a new economic model.
London: CARITAG (Caribbean Trade Advisory Group), 1994. 9p.

One of the more recent periodic update reports prepared for the British Overseas Trade Board on the opportunities offered to British business, all of which provide pointers to Cuba's economic restructuring. The 1992 report provides an overview of the restructuring process, the negotiation of joint ventures, tourism and other investment possibilities. The 1993 report outlines the context of new opportunities for British companies. Other CARITAG reports on Cuba include: *Cuba opens its doors to British business* (1992. 20p.); and *Taking commercial advantage of change in Cuba: new opportunities for British companies* (1993. 19p.).

721   **Cuba: emisiones de monedas y billetes 1915-80.** (Cuba: coins and notes issued 1915-80.)

Havana: Museo Numismático del Banco Nacional de Cuba (National Bank of Cuba Numismatic Museum), [n. d.]. 96p.

Explains the national monetary system and describes all coins and notes issued between 1915 and 1980.

722   **Cuba: investment and business.**

Havana: CONAS (Consultores Asociados, SA), 1994. 172p.

This book, which is to be updated regularly, provides practical information about the Cuban economy and the laws and other regulations relevant to foreign trade. It examines Cuba's resources by territory and sector and outlines investment requirements.

723   **Cuba: prospects for reform, trade and investment.**

Gareth Jenkins, Lila Haines.   New York: The Economist Intelligence Unit, 1995. 173p.

Arguing that the Cuban metamorphosis has already begun, this management report commissioned by The Economist Intelligence Unit for its Critical Issues for Latin America Series, combines practical information with an analysis of Cuba's response to the challenge of forced economic change. Part one discusses the political and economic outlook for Cuba, including the impact of US policy, and analyses Havana's economic reform strategy. Part two examines the foreign investment environment and provides information about investment opportunities in the main sectors of the economy: tourism, agribusiness, telecommunications, energy and mining, biotechnology and health-care, information technology and electronics, and industry and construction. Case-studies charting the experience of several large and small foreign investors are included, along with lists of key contacts by sector. See also *Financial Times survey: Cuba* (London: Financial Times, 26 Sept. 1995. 4p.), which offers analytical reports on politics, investment, banking, tourism, sugar, mining and oil. An overview concludes that the economy is beginning to recover, though it is still hampered by various factors, such as the US embargo and continued dependence on a single commodity, sugar.

724   **Cuba's emerging business opportunities.**

Columbia Business School.   *Columbia Journal of World Business*, vol. 30, no. 1 (spring 1995), p. 4-73, 123-28.

Most of this issue is devoted to Cuba and includes articles by leading Cuban specialists on the Cuban market, legal structure, tourism, investment funds, telecommunications, population and Cuba's seaports and airports.

725   **Cuba's seaports and airports: can they handle a post-embargo cargo boom?**

Arlene Alligood.   *Columbia Journal of World Business*, vol. 30, no. 1 (spring 1995), p. 66-73.

Examines the ability of Cuba's air, sea and land transportation systems, its shipping operations and merchant navy to handle a major expansion in trade.

726 **Cuba's telecommunications markets.**
Lila Haines. *Columbia Journal of World Business*, vol. 30, no. 1 (spring 1995), p. 50-57.
Telecommunications was the first sector to benefit from significant liberalization by both the US and Cuban governments. This article analyses the significance of Havana's partial privatization of the state telecoms enterprise and Washington's lifting of the embargo on long-distance telecommunications with Cuba.

727 **Cuban commercial directory 1993/94.**
Havana: Chamber of Commerce of the Republic of Cuba, 1993. 379p.
A guide, in alphabetical order, to Cuban foreign trade enterprises and foreign commercial companies accredited in Cuba. Each entry includes full identification, activities and products traded.

728 **Developing business strategies for Cuba.**
Santiago Fittipaldi. New York: Business International, 1992. 84p.
(Special Report).
With the dissolution of the Soviet Union in the 1990s, Cuba nosedived into economic crisis and it was clear that the economy would have to open up to new world markets to survive. This strategy paper was compiled for The Economist Intelligence Unit/Business International group, with a view to helping companies prepare for the expected opening. Chapters range from the end of socialism and reconstruction of a free-market Cuba to corporate plans for doing business with Cuba, with a focus on the production infrastructure, labour, and tourism.

729 **Doing business with Cuba.**
Havana: Chamber of Commerce of the Republic of Cuba, 1992.
The third printing of a booklet of the same title issued in 1973 and 1985, this has eight chapters, on: general features, foreign trade organization, Cuban customs system, banking system, trade regulations, sanitation and veterinary regulations, and practical information. It describes in detail the Chamber of Commerce and its services, and lists Cuban commercial offices abroad.

730 **Economic report 1994.**
Banco Nacional de Cuba. Havana: Banco Nacional de Cuba, 1995. 35p.
With the publication of this report, the bank resumed its provision of economic information, which was suspended after 1990. The report offers a global and sectoral analysis of the economy and provides an outline explanation of, and data on, foreign trade, domestic finances, exchange rate policy, balance of payments, the foreign debt, the national banking system and economic policy. It includes appendices on GDP, monetary circulation, state budget performance and estimates for 1995, and also marks the first use of the internationally recognized National Accounts System to measure economic activity. Other Banco Nacional de Cuba reports of interest are: *Cuba: foreign debt and its rescheduling process* (December 1986. 16p.), which is an official account of the renegotiation of Cuba's hard-currency foreign debt in 1984 and 1985, the need to renegotiate in 1986 and the forecast for 1987; *Cuba: quarterly economic report* (September 1989. 32p.); and *Cuba: half-yearly economic report* (June 1990. 29p.).

731 **Guía de negocios en Cuba.** (Guide to business in Cuba.)
    Madrid: Banco Exterior de España, 1994. 130p.

A guide to carrying out business in Cuba which describes its economic geography, the form and nature of the government and its economic administration apparatus. Basic economic data are presented as well as a sectoral overview and an analysis of the prospects for economic and financial reform. Also discussed are Cuba's commercial policy, European Union–Cuba trade, the financing of foreign trade operations, investment and insurance.

732 **Guidelines for foreign investors in Cuba.**
    Havana: Ministry of Basic Industry, Cubapetróleo, 1993. 56p.

One of several reports produced for the first oil exploration licensing round in 1993, these guidelines are designed to provide investors with sufficiently detailed information on factors which could influence an initial investment decision. As well as a general country and economic overview, the publication lists Cuban commercial offices abroad and central state agencies. Other reports document the legal framework, financial regulations and other relevant procedures, and a model production sharing contract is included.

733 **The health-care market in Cuba.**
    Cuba Business Research. London: Cuba Business Ltd, 1989. 2 vols.

This comprehensive guide to the Cuban health-care sector was compiled before the collapse of the socialist bloc and therefore lacks an analysis of its effect on the sector and hence the market. Nevertheless, most of the information it contains remains relevant and is presented in a clear, usable format.

734 **Investing in Cuba: problems and prospects.**
    Edited by Jaime Suchlicki, Antonio Jorge. New Brunswick, New
    Jersey: Transaction, 1995. 176p.

Papers presented at the conference of the same title, held in Toronto, Canada in September 1993, are contained in this publication. They cover a range of topics and viewpoints.

735 **New opportunities for US–Cuban trade.**
    Donna Rich Kaplowitz, Michael Kaplowitz. Washington, DC: Johns
    Hopkins University, 1992. 81p.

This study updates and expands the 1988 Johns Hopkins University report 'Opportunities for US–Cuban Trade'. It concludes that US corporations could engage in up to $3 billion worth of trade with Cuba in the first year after the lifting of the US embargo on trade with the island. It also provides an overview of trade in 1959-92, companies which have shown an interest in trading with Cuba and Cuban trade statistics, as well as legal aspects of the US trade embargo and the Cuban Assets Control Regulations.

736 **Oportunidades de negocios en las cinco provincias orientales.**
    (Trade opportunities in the five eastern provinces.)
    Santiago de Cuba: Chamber of Commerce, 1994. 66p.

Prepared for the second meeting of Caribbean business held in Santiago de Cuba in June 1994, this document outlines province-by-province investment needs. It provides a useful guide to the installed industrial capacity in the eastern region of Cuba.

737 **Options for strengthening economic co-operation between Cuba
and the other Latin American and Caribbean countries.**
SELA Permanent Secretariat.   Caracas: SELA (Sistema Económico
Latinoamericano), 1992. 29p.

This report presented to the Latin American Council was drafted in consultation with
the Cuban government with a view to identifying and promoting opportunities for
investment and complementation of production between Cuba and other regional
economies. It argues that the integration of Cuba with the region is a realistic and
feasible means of tackling the difficulties arising from the regional economic crisis
and decreasing international trade. It notes that Cuba faces a unique challenge in being
forced, for the second time, to make far-reaching changes, due to a sudden upheaval in
its external trade relations.

Foreign investment law.
See item no. 552.

**The fractured blockade: West European–Cuban relations during the
revolution.**
See item no. 641.

Business Latin America.
See item no. 1093.

Business Tips on Cuba.
See item no. 1094.

Contactos. (Contacts.)
See item no. 1095.

Cuba Business.
See item no. 1097.

Cuba: Foreign Trade.
See item no. 1098.

The Cuba Report.
See item no. 1099.

Opciones. (Options.)
See item no. 1100.

Industry and Agriculture

Agriculture

738 **La ANAP: 25 años de trabajo.** (ANAP: 25 years of work.)
Adelfo Martín Barrios.   Havana: Asociación Nacional de Agricultores
Pequeños, 1987. 234p.

The author, himself of peasant origin, long active in the peasant movement and a member of the national executive of the National Association of Small Farmers since 1961, provides a lively and informative account of the antecedents and founding of the Association, and the changing issues under focus at six national congresses. This is an essential first-hand account for those wishing to familiarize themselves with the complexities of the non-state sector in a largely state-run economy.

739 **Cuba, agriculture and planning.**
Cuban Economic Research Project.   Coral Gables, Florida: University
of Miami Press, 1965. 325p.

This critical survey of agricultural development and state planning during the early years of the revolution pays particular attention to sugar production, agrarian reform, livestock, and the relationship between rationing and production.

740 **De la finca individual a la cooperativa agropecuaria.** (From the
individual farm to the agricultural co-operative.)
Orlando Gómez.   Havana: Editora Política, 1983. 186p. bibliog.

A compilation of almost 200 articles published in the Cuban daily newspaper *Granma* over the five-year period 1977-82, when the agricultural co-operative movement was under way. Together, the articles provide a solid body of information on a process that mushroomed rapidly, with reportage on policy measures and their implementation, and on the case-study experience of individual co-operatives. See also the older *Hacienda plantations and collective farms* by Juan Martínez-Alier (London: Frank Cass, 1977. 185p. bibliog.).

741 **Household incomes in Cuban agriculture: a comparison of the state, cooperative and peasant sectors.**
Carmen Diana Deere, Ernel González, Niurka Pérez, Gustavo Rodríguez. *Development and Change*, vol. 26, no. 2 (April 1995), p. 209-34.

Presents the results of a 1991 household income survey of the three main groups in Cuban agriculture at that point in time. The survey shows that since 1959 household income levels have improved dramatically in the agricultural sector, with private sector households faring best, while regional difference lessened considerably. It also demonstrates that agricultural households rely on multiple income sources to generate their livelihood rather than being strictly proletarian, collective, or petty commodity producers.

742 **Memorias: V Congreso ANAP.** (Fifth ANAP Congress Documents.)
Asociación Nacional de Agricultores Pequeños. Havana: Editora Política, 1978. 408p.

This compilation of documents from the landmark 1977 Fifth Congress of the National Association of Small Farmers (ANAP) contains speeches by ANAP President José Ramírez Cruz and Cuban President Fidel Castro, along with other Cuban leaders. Congress resolutions include the key document on co-operativization, or third agrarian reform of the Cuban revolution. The book also features interventions from the floor by Cuban delegates, and greetings from foreign guests.

743 **Revolución agraria y cooperativismo en Cuba.** (Agrarian revolution and co-operativism in Cuba.)
Lilia Nahela Becerril Albarrán, Marian Ravenet Ramírez. Havana: Ciencias Sociales, 1989. 207p.

Reviews the development of the farming sector in Cuba, including class formation, agricultural reform, and the role of women and young people. Case-studies of four co-operatives situated in different provinces and specializing in different crops are included.

744 **Rural Cuba.**
Lowry Nelson. Minneapolis, Minnesota: University of Minnesota Press, 1950. 285p. bibliog.

This book resulted from a year of investigation and observation in Cuba, from September 1945 to September 1946. The author first considers the Cuban people as a nation and outlines the problems they face, before studying: the land and climate; settlement patterns; the Cuban land system and its history; different farming methods employed at the time; class structure; the family unit; standard of living; education; and what the future may bring. The book includes appendices containing surveys carried out.

745 **State versus grass-roots strategies for rural democratization: recent developments among the Cuban peasantry.**
Jean Stubbs. *Cuban Studies*, vol. 21 (1991), p. 149-70.

Rural democratization brought material benefits for the Cuban peasantry but it has not reproduced itself as a class. This article suggests a conflict of interests between state and peasantry in the 1990s which demands emphasizing grass-roots rather than state in 'beyond the market' agrarian rethinking.

746 **Toward a periodization of the Cuban collectivization process: changing incentives and peasant response.**
Carmen Diana Deere, Mieke Meurs, Niurka Pérez. *Cuban Studies*, no. 22 (1992), p. 115-49. bibliog.

The economic and political conditions supporting the collectivization process are the focus of this article, which considers how these conditions, and the response of the peasantry, changed over time. The authors argue that, while existing data are inadequate for a conclusive cost–benefit analysis of the policy of promoting co-operative rather than private farming, field studies confirm the policy's basically voluntary nature. They note the tacit acceptance that tobacco and coffee cultivation do not lend themselves to economies of scale and the key challenge of a clearer relationship between centralized state control and co-operative autonomy.

747 **The view from below: Cuban agriculture in the special period in peacetime.**
Carmen Diana Deere, Niurka Pérez, Ernel González. *Journal of Peasant Studies*, vol. 21, no. 2 (Jan. 1994), p. 194-234.

Examines the changes taking place in Cuban agriculture at the local level as a result of the demise of the socialist trading bloc and Cuba's subsequent economic crisis. The dominant theme that emerges is the tendency toward decentralization of Cuba's state farm sector, culminating in the September 1993 decision to form production co-operatives on state land, counterposed to renewed attempts to impose greater state control over peasant producers. Nevertheless, the authors find a good deal of experimentation and heterogeneity in the actual implementation of state policy at local level.

Forestry

748 **Breve caracterización de la actividad forestal en Cuba.**
(Short description of forestry activity in Cuba.)
Havana: Agriculture Ministry, Forestry Research Centre, 1985. 52p. bibliog.

Describes the forested areas in Cuba, forestry development in the period 1959-83, conservation plans and protected areas, and the state of forestry-related industry.

749 **The forests of Cuba.**
Earl Emmett Smith. Cambridge, Massachusetts: Harvard University Press, 1954. 98p.

A descriptive survey of Cuba's principal forest areas in the early 1950s.

Industry

750 **Industrial reform and the Cuban economy.**
Andrew Zimbalist. In: *Industrial reform in socialist countries.*
Edited by Ian Jeffreys. London: Edward Elgar, 1991, p. 92-110.
bibliog.
Cuba's two-pronged economic survival strategy guaranteed basic nutrition and livelihood while implementing reforms aimed at enabling Cuba to participate in the world market. Zimbalist places this strategy in the context of the then ongoing rectification campaign and Cuba's historical experience with economic reform. He argues that recent history has reinforced Fidel Castro's disposition to maintain close control over the reform process. See also the section by Max Nolff (p. 283-338) on industry in *Cuba: the economic and social revolution* (q.v.), edited by Dudley Seers.

Sugar

Pre-1959

751 **Azúcar y población en las Antillas.** (Sugar and population in the
Caribbean.)
Ramiro Guerra y Sánchez, introduction by Manuel Moreno Fraginals.
Havana: Ciencias Sociales, 1976. 4th ed. 279p.
Originally published in 1927, this study of the interaction between the development of the sugar industry and population growth first situates the Cuban case in a wider Caribbean context. It traces the process of land appropriation and division in Cuba and the emergence of the plantation system, and goes on to discuss the economic and social effects of that system. The author argues that the Cuban plantation system was unable to withstand US competition and superior organization, leading to overproduction, economic dependence and Cuba's growing impoverishment.

752 **Bitter Cuban sugar: monoculture and economic dependence from
1825-1899.**
Félix Goizueta-Mimó. New York: Garland, 1987. 287p.
Traces the emergence and consolidation of the Cuban sugar industry in 19th-century Cuba, in the context of the economic theory of monoculture. The author covers distortion of market conditions and social capital formation, dependence on British capital to finance Cuban railways and sugar technology. He extrapolates the lessons to be learned from the impact of monoculture on colonial Cuba in order to postulate projections for Cuba's economic independence in the year 2000. See also *The sugar planters of colonial Cuba: ideological and practical dilemmas of a dependent bourgeoisie* by Anton L. Allahar (Toronto: Two-Thirds Editions, 1982).

753 **Social and economic aspects of sugar production in Cuba, 1880-1930.**
César J. Ayala. *Latin American Research Review*, vol. 30, no. 1 (1995), p. 95-124.

Charts the transformation of sugar production at the turn of the century, with the expansion of sugar *centrales* and foreign ownership, decline in agricultural yields, labour difficulties, and ultimately sugar crash.

754 **The sugarmill: the socioeconomic complex of Cuban sugar, 1760-1860.**
Manuel Moreno Fraginals. New York: Monthly Review Press, 1976. 3 vols.

This study of sugar production in late 18th- and 19th-century Cuba deals with slavery, the character of the producing classes, production and manufacturing, economic development and trade. The third volume is in Spanish and provides an appendix with historical statistics, a glossary, and an extensive annotated bibliography. This is an abridged version of the author's seminal three-volume study in Spanish, *El ingenio: complejo económico-social cubano del azúcar* (Havana: Ciencias Sociales, 1978. 2nd ed. bibliog.).

Post-1959

755 **Cuba's international sugar trade.**
Gerry Hagelberg, Tony Hannah. In: *The fractured blockade.* Edited by Alistair Hennessy, George Lambie. London; Basingstoke, England: Macmillan Caribbean, 1993, p. 137-62.

The authors argue that the closure of the US market in 1960 actually shifted Cuban sugar exports from a declining to an expanding market. Their well-documented review follows the ensuing re-adjustment of the structure of international sugar trading and the fluctuations in Cuban production. A look at what Cuban imports from the USSR cost in terms of sugar suggests that the terms of trade became increasingly favourable to Havana in the 1970s, but probably worsened thereafter. They outline a probable scenario for the 1990s which is being confirmed by successive low harvests and billion-dollar revenue losses.

756 **Cuban sugar policy from 1963 to 1970.**
Heinrich Brunner. Pittsburgh, Pennsylvania: University of Pittsburgh Press, 1977. 163p. bibliog.

Brunner analyses Cuban planning and development strategies, looking at the origins of the theoretical guidelines, the application of the theory, and the specific relevance to sugar production. The work is particularly useful in elucidating the reasons for the débâcle of the attempt to achieve a sugar harvest of ten million tonnes in 1970.

757 **The economics of Cuban sugar.**
Jorge Pérez López. Pittsburgh, Pennsylvania: University of
Pittsburgh Press, 1991. 313p. bibliog.

Possibly the most comprehensive survey of the Cuban sugar industry in the years
leading up to, but not including, the period of change in Eastern Europe and the Soviet
Union. The approach is mainly quantitative and descriptive rather than analytical, but
the author had restricted access to information and was unable to check data at source.
This limits the book in certain respects, including lessening the credibility of Pérez
López's attempt to measure the so-called subsidy element in the preferential price the
USSR paid for Cuban sugar. However, until scholars have open access to Cuban
sources it remains a key work.

758 **Handbook of sugar cane derivatives.**
Cuban Sugar Cane Derivatives Research Institute (ICIDCA). Mexico
City: Group of Latin American and Caribbean Sugar Exporting
Countries (GEPLACEA), 1988. 239p. bibliog.

An edited English edition of a compilation in Spanish of developments in the use of
sugar cane derivatives, including technological and economic aspects and installed
capacity where applicable. The volume covers diversification of the sugar industry,
raw materials, and bagasse, molasses and other derivatives. A second updated edition
was published in 1990 in Spanish.

759 **El hijo alegre de la caña de azúcar: biografía del ron cubano.**
(Sugar cane's merry offspring: a biography of Cuban rum.)
Fernando G. Campoamor, introduction by Manuel Moreno
Fraginals. Havana: Editorial Científico-Técnica, 1988. 147p.

Campoamor presents a light, humorous, journalistic history of Cuban rum production
from the 16th century to the distilleries of the 1980s. He provides a wealth of facts,
figures and anecdotes on both the production process and the social and economic
aspects of rum-drinking, with illustrations of distillery machinery, canefields, rumshops
and the like.

760 **La industria azucarera en Cuba.** (The sugar industry in Cuba.)
Fernando Charadán López. Havana: Ciencias Sociales, 1982. 343p.
bibliog.

The first third of this study covers five centuries of Cuban sugar production, beginning
in the early 16th century and based on an exhaustive bibliography. The subsequent
analysis of the post-1959 industry probes the difficulties thrown up by the economic
blockade, and then looks in depth at the five-year periods 1971-75 and 1976-80, in the
context of Cuba's integration into the socialist trading bloc.

761 **Labour supply, harvest mechanization and the demand for Cuban sugar.**
Brian H. Pollitt, G. B. Hagelberg. Glasgow, Scotland: University of Glasgow, Institute of Latin American Studies, 1992. 27p. bibliog. (Occasional Papers, no. 54).

Discusses the nature and causes of the post-1959 agricultural labour shortage in the context of revolutionary development strategy; the early successes and failures of harvest mechanization and its implications for land tenure; and the mechanization trends in the 1980s. The authors argue that a different approach to analysis of data published by the sugar ministry in the 1980s shows that gains from mechanization were much lower than normally claimed. They also tackle the question of the sugar industry in the post-Soviet world and, prophetically, warn that reallocation of scarce resources by central command would lead to strains and incompatibilities.

762 **Mechanisation of sugar cane harvesting in Cuba.**
Charles Edquist. *Cuban Studies*, vol. 13, no. 2 (summer 1983), p. 41-64.

Deals with the mechanization of sugar-cane harvesting in Cuba from the late 1950s to the early 1980s, looking at issues such as the relation between plans and performance, costs and benefits, relative performance of harvesters, and technological capacity.

763 **Plantaciones cañeras.** (Sugar cane plantations.)
Andrzej Dembicz. Havana: Ciencias Sociales, 1989. 134p. bibliog.

The development of Cuban sugar cane plantations is examined in this monograph in the context of the plantation system in Latin America. It goes on to discuss the plantations as foci for population growth and includes a meticulous study of population structure in eastern Cuban sugar cane plantations.

764 **Revolution and the mode of production in the sugar-cane sector of the Cuban economy, 1959-80: some preliminary findings.**
Brian H. Pollitt. Glasgow, Scotland: University of Glasgow, Institute of Latin American Studies, 1981. 14p. (Occasional Papers, no. 35).

Claims that the mechanization of the sugar industry, which the government promoted in response to labour shortages, was feasible only because the Cuban sugar industry was able to absorb a level of costs unacceptable to sugar cane producers enjoying less favourable international trading terms.

765 **Rise and fall of Cuban sugar production in the post-war years.**
F. O. Licht. *International Sugar and Sweetener Report*, vol. 126, no. 33 (Nov. 1994), p. 727-34.

Prompted by the dramatic fall in Cuban sugar production in the 1990s, this report by international commodity analyst F. O. Licht provides a useful short review of the ups and downs of the Cuban sugar industry since the Second World War. It argues that, despite the halving of sugar output from 1992 to 1994, Cuba is still sufficiently important to have a substantial impact on world sugar prices.

766 **Sugar, dependency and the Cuban revolution.**
Brian H. Pollitt. Glasgow, Scotland: University of Glasgow, Institute of Latin American Studies, 1985. 44p. (Occasional Papers, no. 43).

Pollitt argues that the terms of trade in CMEA (Comecon) vitiated major objections to sugar's sustained predominance in Cuban exports and pushed to the sidelines proposals that Cuba should reduce the scale of its sugar exports to the USSR in the name of some 'greater economic independence'. The chronically depressed nature of the 'free' sugar market and the financial consequences of the expansion of trade outside the socialist bloc in the 1970s supported the continuation of a secure and profitable trade with Comecon.

767 **Transformation of the Cuban sugar complex.**
Miguel Alejandro Figueras. *Latin American Perspectives*, vol. 18, no. 2 (winter 1991), p. 86-94.

Figueras presents a brief analysis of the changing importance of sugar production to the Cuban economy, through a study of its historical role and more recent developments. He concludes that sugar production used to have a disproportionate influence on the economy, which, although still great, has decreased.

Tobacco

768 **Biografía del tabaco habano.** (Biography of the Havana cigar.)
Gaspar Jorge García Galló, prologue by Ernesto Che Guevara.
Havana: Comisión Nacional del Tabaco Habano, 1961. 2nd ed. 293p.

First published in 1946 and written by a Cuban cigar maker-turned-historian, this monograph discusses the importance of tobacco in Cuban history. It plays around with the picturesque, as well as social, economic and political history. There are eleven chapters on the tobacco economy (from leaf growing to the cigar machine), eight on sociology (from peasant uprising to tobacco union nationalism), and two concluding chapters on the psychology of both the cigar maker and the cigar smoker. The book also contains a glossary of tobacco vocabulary. Also of interest is the later work by Antonio Núñez Jiménez, *The journey of the Havana cigar* (Havana: Cubatabaco, 1988. 123p. bibliog.), and *Cuba: en las marquillas cigarreras del siglo XIX: as portrayed in 19th-century cigarette lithographs; dans les lithographes de cigarettes au XIXe siècle*, by Antonio Núñez Jiménez (Havana: Ediciones Turísticas de Cuba, 1985. 128p. bibliog.).

769 **Holy smoke.**
Guillermo Cabrera Infante. London: Faber & Faber, 1985. 329p.

This unorthodox chronicle of the Havana cigar begins in 1492, when Columbus first encountered tobacco in Cuba. The author, a well-known émigré Cuban novelist, cites a wealth of references from literature and film, including Oscar Wilde, Groucho Marx and Orson Welles, in this tribute to the best cigar in the world.

770 **Tobacco on the periphery: a case study in Cuban labour history, 1860-1958.**
Jean Stubbs. Cambridge, England: Cambridge University Press, 1985. 203p.

One of the few English-language texts on the history of Cuba's 'other' commodity, tobacco. This study traces the industry's promising beginnings, its successive crises, and the early form of de-industrialization it underwent with the impact of US capital, a certain exception to which was its internationally renowned, quality hand-rolled cigar. The work focuses on the impact of such changes on the labour force, its early unionization and politicization, and its strikes and other forms of action. This is used to help to explain the tobacco workers' traditionally high levels of class consciousness and nationalism.

771 **The world's best wrapper: El Corojo remains Cuba's greatest farm for shade-grown tobacco.**
James Suckling. *Cigar Aficionado* (summer 1995), p. 81-87.

While featuring one of Cuba's top tobacco farms, the article situates the farm and its history in the broader Cuban tobacco context. In its four years of existence, this New York-based magazine has become a key source of information on Cuban leaf and manufacturing, inside Cuba and abroad.

Energy

772 **CUPET: research and projects.**
Havana: Editorial Félix Varela, 1992. 12p.

The Petroleum Research, Development and Project Centre, groups together the Chemical Research Centre, Petroleum Research and Development Centre, and the Petroleum Engineering and Project Centre. One of several publications produced by the Centre, this provides overview information on CUPET research and projects.

773 **Energía nuclear y desarrollo.** (Nuclear energy and development.)
Fidel Castro Díaz-Balart. Havana: Ciencias Sociales, 1990. 382p. bibliog.

The then head of Cuba's nuclear programme (and son of Fidel Castro) outlines the history of developments in this sector and argues the case for a Cuban nuclear option. Also of interest may be 'Cuba's nuclear power program and post-cold war pressures' by Jonathan Benjamin-Alvarado and Alexander Belkin (*The Nonproliferation Review*, winter 1994).

774 **Nuclear power in Cuba after Chernobyl.**
Jorge Pérez-López. *Journal of Interamerican Studies and World Affairs*, vol. 29, no. 2 (summer 1987), p. 79-117.

This technical and economic analysis of Cuba's nuclear power dilemma provides a wealth of data on the island's energy requirements and its nuclear power capability, and discusses why Cuba is committed to nuclear energy.

775 **Oil and gas exploration in Cuba.**
G. Echeverría Rodríguez, et al. *Journal of Petroleum Geology*,
vol. 14, no. 3 (July 1991), p. 259-74.

A group of nine authors working for the Unión del Petróleo (Oil Union) outline their geological findings on oil exploration in Cuba over the last century. They conclude that the island has both oil and gas potential, especially offshore.

Mining

776 **Apuntes sobre la historia de la minería cubana.** (Notes on the
history of Cuban mining.)
Luis D. Soto González.   Santiago de Cuba: Editorial Oriente, 1981.
121p.

Reviews the history of mining in Cuba, beginning with what is known of the activities of the indigenous inhabitants and proceeding through the 1511-30 period when the prospect of gold drew Spanish colonizers to the island. Later chapters look at specific ores, such as iron, copper and gold, and consider separate areas of the island. There is also a discussion of the interconnection between mining and the struggles for emancipation from slavery and from Spain. The volume includes a guide to the documentation on mining held in the National Library of Cuba.

777 **Historia y desarrollo de la minería en Cuba.** (History and
development of mining in Cuba.)
Antonio Calvache.   Havana: Editorial Neptuno, 1944. 170p. maps.
bibliog.

A study of mining in Cuba from the pre-Columbian period to the early 20th century. It covers iron, manganese, gold, copper and nickel, with attention paid to Cuban efforts to regulate and supervise company mining.

778 **The international political economy of Cuban nickel development.**
Theodore H. Moran.   *Cuban Studies*, vol. 7, no. 2 (July 1977),
p. 145-65.

The Cuban nickel industry is analysed in the context of the international nickel trade, and with reference to US–Cuba relations.

779 **Iron mining and socio-demographic change in eastern Cuba,
1884-1940.**
Lisandro Pérez.   *Journal of Latin American Studies*, vol. 14 (1982),
p. 381-406.

This article details mining activity in a part of the island which is rich in deposits. Mining is looked at in conjunction with demography.

780 **Piedras hirvientes: la minería en Cuba.** (Burning stones: mining in
      Cuba.)
      Joaquín Oramas.   Havana: Editora Política, 1990. 124p.
An outline history of Cuban mining and oil exploration.

781 **Report on a geological reconnaissance of Cuba.**
      C. Willard Hoyes, Y. Wayland Vaughan, Arthur C. Spencer.
      Washington, DC: US Government Printing Office, 1901. 123p. maps.
Reports on a geological survey of Cuban mines and mineral resources, carried out at
the turn of the century and commissioned by the military government of Cuba.

782 **Report on the mineral resources of Cuba in 1901.**
      Harriet Connor Brown.   Baltimore, Maryland: Press of Guggenheimer,
      Weil, & Company, 1903. 121p.
A survey of mines and mineral resources made during the US military occupation of
1899-1902 with the purpose of providing information for investment in mining in
Cuba.

783 **Zeolita: el mineral del siglo.** (Zeolite: mineral of the century.)
      Lilia Excurra, C. Pérez Domínguez.   Havana: Centro de Información
      y Documentación Agropecuaria (Centre for Agricultural Information
      and Documentation), 1989. 34p. bibliog.
Discusses primarily the agricultural uses of this mineral, of which Cuba has vast
reserves.

Sixty years in Cuba.
See item no. 49.

**Travels in the west: Cuba with notices of Puerto Rico and the slave
trade.**
See item no. 52.

**Cuban rural society in the nineteenth century: the social and economic
history of monoculture in Matanzas.**
See item no. 129.

Sugar and social change in Oriente, Cuba, 1898-1946.
See item no. 138.

Social equity, agrarian transition and development in Cuba, 1845-90.
See item no. 475.

**Industrial Cuba: being a study of present and industrial conditions, with
suggestions as to the opportunities presented in the island for American
capital, enterprise and labour.**
See item no. 660.

Agrarian reform and the 'agricultural proletariat' in Cuba, 1958-66: some notes.
See item no. 784.

Dandy or rake? Cigar makers in Cuba, 1860-1958.
See item no. 791.

The greening of the revolution: Cuba's experiment with organic agriculture.
See item no. 826.

Cuban counterpoint: tobacco and sugar.
See item no. 1017.

ANAP.
See item no. 1120.

Ciencia y Técnica en la Agricultura. (Science and Technology in Agriculture.)
See item no. 1121.

Cigar Aficionado.
See item no. 1122.

Cubatabaco. (Cuba Tobacco.)
See item no. 1123.

Cuba Azúcar. (Cuba Sugar.)
See item no. 1124.

Revista Cubana de Ciencia Agrícola. (Cuban Journal of Agricultural Sciences.)
See item no. 1125.

Bibliografía botánica cubana, teórica y aplicada, con énfasis en la silvicultura (1900-67). (A Cuban botanical bibliography, theoretical and applied, with emphasis on forestry [1900-67].)
See item no. 1149.

Labour and Trade Unions

Pre-1959

784 **Agrarian reform and the 'agricultural proletariat' in Cuba, 1958-66: some notes.**
Brian H. Pollitt. Glasgow, Scotland: University of Glasgow, Institute of Latin American Studies, 1979. 22p. (Occasional Papers, no. 27).

Attempts to quantify certain pre- and post-revolutionary attributes of what is popularly conceived of as the 'landless agricultural proletariat', which is usually believed to have been the predominant agrarian class in 1959. The author deploys statistical data to partially correct this oversimplistic view, arguing that the landless rural proletariat was neither so landless nor so numerically predominant as previously assumed. He also shows the extensive and relatively swift socialization of the means of agricultural production accompanied by a contrasting 'de-proletarianization' of the labour force. Data from rural surveys conducted in 1966 are included. Occasional Paper no. 30 (1980) is a sequel article.

785 **Alfredo López: maestro del proletariado cubano.** (Alfred López: master of the Cuban proletariat.)
Olga Cabrera. Havana: Ciencias Sociales, 1985. 233p.

Alfredo López was the founder of the Workers' Federation of Havana and the National Workers' Confederation of Cuba, and a key anti-imperialist forerunner to labour in the 1920s. This biography, based on archival documentation and oral history, looks at his life work and action.

786 **Azúcar y lucha de clases, 1917.** (Sugar and class struggle, 1917.)
John Dumoulin. Havana: Ciencias Sociales, 1980. 284p.

A monograph on an important sugar workers' strike in 1917, at a moment of sugar market slump. The author, a US historian for many years resident in Cuba, brings to light new information and situates the strike in the context of the world sugar market and class struggle in Cuba, in the years of the developing bourgeoisie and labour movement. The book includes appendices of documents related to the strike.

787 **Carlos Baliño: documentos y artículos.** (Carlos Baliño: documents and articles.)
Edited by the Instituto de Historia del Movimiento Comunista y de la Revolución Socialista de Cuba. Havana: Departamento de Orientación Revolucionaria del Comité Central del Partido Comunista de Cuba, 1976. 277p.

This anthology of writings from the years 1865 to 1925 by the early Cuban socialist Carlos Baliño, covers diverse topics of national and international interest, including slavery, economic independence, the Russian revolution, and US imperialism. The book contains an introductory eulogy by Blas Roca and appendices of documents written by Baliño.

788 **Collapse of the house of labor: ideological divisions in the Cuban labor movement and the U.S. role, 1944-1949.**
Harold Dana Sims. *Cuban Studies*, vol. 21 (1991), p. 123-48.

This study of division in Cuban organized labour between the end of the Second World War and the Cold War challenges the assumption of US government backing for purging communist union leadership in Cuba. United States embassy personnel proved more concerned than the American Federation of Labor about corrupt anti-communist labour leaders.

789 **Cuban labor and the Communist Party, 1937-1958: an interpretation.**
Harold D. Sims. *Cuban Studies*, vol. 15, no. 1 (winter 1985), p. 43-58.

The article examines relations between the Cuban Communist Party and organized labour under different régimes, and the 26th July Movement of the 1950s.

790 **The Cuban working-class movement from 1925 to 1933.**
Fabio Grobart. *Science and Society*, vol. 39, no. 1 (spring 1975), p. 73-102.

An account of the Cuban labour movement from the formation of the Cuban National Workers' Confederation in 1925 to the 1933 general strike, with specific reference to working-class opposition to Gerardo Machado's régime (1925-33).

791 **Dandy or rake? Cigar makers in Cuba, 1860-1958.**
Jean Stubbs. London: University of London, Institute of Commonwealth Studies, 1982, p. 17-25. (Collected Seminar Papers, no. 29, Caribbean Societies, vol. 1).

This article seeks to dispel the aura of myth and legend in the historiography about cigar makers and cigar manufacturing in Cuba, portraying an industry and a labour force on the wane.

792 **Dos décadas de lucha contra el latifundismo: breve historia de la Asociación Nacional Campesina.** (Two decades of struggle against rural landowners: a brief history of the National Peasant Association.) José Mayo. Havana: Editora Política, 1980. 99p. bibliog.

An overview of peasant struggles fought by the National Peasant Association of Cuba against Batista and for land reform, complete with contemporary press accounts and photographs of the time.

793 **Esbozo biográfico de Jesús Menéndez.** (Biographical sketch of Jesús Menéndez.)
Gaspar Jorge García Galló. Havana: Editora Política, 1978. 217p.

Cuba's communist cigar maker-turned-historian writes about the black communist leader of the sugar workers, on the thirtieth anniversary of his assassination in the Cold War years. On the basis of documentary and testimonial evidence, García Galló reconstructs the life of Jesús Menéndez, as he rose to become a regional, provincial, national and international worker leader and key member of Cuba's Communist Party. One chapter deals in detail with January 1948, the month of his assassination in an anti-communist onslaught on the unions, and the book closes with a eulogy by Blas Roca and the poem 'Elegy to Jesús Menéndez' by the communist poet Nicolás Guillén.

794 **Historia del movimiento obrero cubano. 1865-1958.** (History of the Cuban workers' movement 1865-1958.)
Instituto de Historia del Movimiento Comunista y de la Revolución Socialista de Cuba. Havana: Editora Política, 1985. 2 vols.

The history of the workers' movement is divided into five periods: 1860-98, the period of the wars of independence against Spain, abolition of slavery and incipient labour organizations; 1899-1925, from the end of Spanish rule through US military occupation and economic investment, with a growing labour movement; 1925-35, the period of the Machado dictatorship, economic depression and failed 1933 revolution, with strikes building up to the general strike of 1935; 1935-46, a period of popular front and labour consolidation; and 1946-58, ushered in by the Cold War attack on organized labour and 'officialist' labour unions. Companion volumes contain reprints of documents and articles on labour organizations and leaders.

795 **Los que viven por sus manos.** (Those who live by their hands.)
Olga Cabrera. Havana: Ciencias Sociales, 1985. 382p. bibliog.

Traces the historical shaping of the Cuban working class in the context of the growth and formation of the Cuban labour movement, from the early mutual aid societies in the second half of the 19th century, through the anarcho-syndicalism of the early 20th century, to the foundations of a national trade union movement and Marxist-Leninist Party in the 1920s. The author documents anti-worker government policies, charts major strike action, and discusses the intertwining of class and national thinking in prominent labour leaders.

796   **Las luchas campesinas en Cuba.** (Peasant struggles in Cuba.)
       Antero Regalado Falcón.   Havana: Editora Política, 1979. 220p.
       bibliog.

The author was a grass-roots organizer who started out leading the Peasant Union in
the small town of San Antonio de los Baños in the 1930s. He joined the leadership of
the Havana Peasant Federation and the National Peasant Association in the 1940s and
was active in underground peasant struggles in the 1950s before spearheading the land
reform and National Association of Small Farmers in the 1960s and 1970s. This is an
account of the struggles in which he was involved.

Post-1959

797   **Castro and the Cuban labor movement (1959-1961).**
       Efrén Córdova.   Lanham, Maryland: University Press of America,
       1987. 341p.

Córdova tackles the question of Castro's intentions regarding the nature of the
revolution by analysing the events surrounding what the author calls the capture of
organized labour. He concludes that Castro was clearly familiar with communist
tactics for capturing political power and that intellectually he espoused Marxist
principles. He finds, nevertheless, that he was 'a new breed of communist dictator'.

798   **Collision course: labor force and educational trends in Cuba.**
       Sergio Díaz-Briquets.   *Cuban Studies*, vol. 23 (1993), p. 91-112.

Discusses the impact of the collapse of the Soviet bloc on the Cuban labour force,
highlighting the difficulties caused by closed factories and reduced facilities, in turn
the result of material and energy shortages. The author analyses the various measures
taken by the government to try and ease the crisis and questions whether they will
work when taking into consideration the relatively high levels of education in Cuba
and the tendency among workers to aspire to white-collar occupations.

799   **Economic significance of unpaid labor in socialist Cuba.**
       Carmelo Mesa-Lago.   *Industrial and Labor Relations Review*, vol. 22,
       no. 3 (April 1969), p. 339-57.

Examines the different types of unpaid labour in Cuba after the revolution, the way in
which Cubans are mobilized and labour is utilized, and the contribution of the unpaid
to the general labour input to the economy.

800   **Institutionalization and workers' response.**
       Marifeli Pérez-Stable.   *Cuban Studies*, vol. 6, no. 2 (July 1976),
       p. 31-54.

This study, based on a series of interviews with union leaders and rank-and-file
workers in 1975, covers worker–management relations, the role of the trade unions,
incentives, and women in the work force.

801 **The labor force: employment, unemployment, and underemployment in Cuba, 1899-1970.**
Carmelo Mesa-Lago.   Beverly Hills, California: Sage, 1972. 72p. bibliog.

The author traces developments in the Cuban labour force, in three periods: 1899 to the late 1920s; the early 1930s to the late 1950s; and 1960-72. An earlier study by the same author is *The labor sector and socialist distribution in Cuba* (New York: Praeger, 1968. 250p. bibliog.) Two related Spanish-language studies are: *El empleo en Cuba* (Employment in Cuba) by Raúl Lorenzo (Havana: Seoane, Fernández y Cía, 1987); and *Cuba: el movimiento obrero y su entorno socio-político 1865-1983* (Cuba: the workers' movement and its socio-political context 1865-1983) by Rodolfo Riesgo (Miami, Florida: Saeta Ediciones, 1985. 248p.).

802 **The labor union in the Cuban workplace.**
Gail Lindenberg.   *Latin American Perspectives*, vol. 20, no. 1 (1993), p. 28-39.

Considers the operation of labour unions in Cuba's socialist system, which does not allow room for many traditional union functions. Lindenberg explains how one of the primary roles of Cuban labour unions is to make sure state and private employers honour the rights granted in the Labour Code. They are also responsible for developing the workers' socialist consciousness, in order to increase production, fight corruption, and overcome inefficiency. The article is based in part on interviews conducted with workers at a Cuban textile plant in Ariguanabo.

803 **Labour and development in rural Cuba.**
Dharam Ghai, Cristóbal Kay, Peter Peek.   Basingstoke, England; London: Macmillan, 1988. 141p.

Part of a series of case-studies on developing countries, this work is based on a three-week visit made to Cuba by the authors in February 1985, and is designed for general readers. It begins with a discussion of the agricultural situation prior to the revolution, before analysing in detail the reforms that were instituted after 1959. The authors look in particular at the improvements that have been made in agriculture and the rural economy since 1970, considering wage reforms, living standards, work patterns, and labour markets. They examine the three main forms of production – state farms, co-operatives and private farming – and assess the general social and economic achievements of the revolutionary government.

804 **Memoria del XV Congreso.** (Documents of the 15th Congress.)
Central Confederation of Cuban Workers.   Havana: CTC, 1988. 286p.

Speeches, documents and resolutions of the 1984 National Congress are contained in this publication. Similar compilations exist for earlier congresses: *Memoria del XIV Congreso* (Documents of the 14th Congress) which took place in 1978 and was published 1980 (354p.); and *Memoria del XIII Congreso* (Documents of the 13th Congress) held in 1973 and published 1974 (206p.).

805 **Revolutionary politics and the Cuban working class.**
Maurice Zeitlin. Princeton, New Jersey: Princeton University Press, 1967. 306p. map.
For this study of working-class attitudes to the revolution, over 200 interviews were conducted in twenty-one factories in 1962. From these, the author correlates views with race, sex, skill, background and mobility. Greater support for the revolution is found among those who had not previously been in stable work.

806 **El salario: sus aspectos sociosicológicos.** (Salary: socio-psychological aspects.)
Pablo García Sehwerert. Havana: Ciencias Sociales, 1987. 88p. bibliog.
A short study outlining Cuban thinking behind the economic mechanism of salary in building socialism: distribution according to work (material as well as moral incentive) and elevation of production and well-being, drawing on technical, economic, legal, political and socio-psychological concepts. The study was written with the practical aim of informing Cubans, workers and managers alike.

807 **Socialismo, empresas y participación obrera.** (Socialism, business and worker participation.)
Haroldo Dilla Alfonso. In: *Cuba en crisis.* Edited by Jorge Rodríguez Beruff. San Juan, Puerto Rico: Editorial de la Universidad de Puerto Rico, 1995, p. 101-20.
The central issues in this article are worker participation and the role of the unions in the workplace in socialist Cuba, as they evolved over the 1970s and 1980s under the economic management and planning system (SDPE) and during the post-1986 rectification and special period. The author articulates the legitimacy of a Marxist viewpoint in the future challenge to labour as 1990s Cuba seeks a way out of economic crisis and adjusts to the world capitalist economy.

808 **Some notes on the development of the Cuban labor force 1970-1980.**
Claes Brundenius. *Cuban Studies*, vol. 13, no. 2 (summer 1983), p. 65-78.
The 1979 national demographic survey was the first source of hard data on the Cuban labour force after the 1970 census. The author analyses statistics from the survey and fills in gaps with his own estimates. He covers the labour force, employment, open unemployment, and the distribution of employment between state and private sectors.

809 **Work and democracy in socialist Cuba.**
Linda Fuller. Philadelphia, Pennsylvania: Temple University Press, 1992. 274p.
This is the only study of its kind to focus on attempts to democratize labour relations in the years from 1970 to 1985, a period which the author contrasts with both the pre-1970 command society and the post-1986 rectification. Based on field research in Cuba carried out between 1982 and 1983, and involving informal observation at eleven worksites, and open-ended, loosely structured, in-depth interviews with

twenty-nine workers, the book provides a largely procedural account of changing union and Party functions. These occur through the variables of economic/production decision-making, collective organization and action, worksite and supra-worksite arenas, the multiplicity of channels, and the size of enterprise and empowerment.

The population of Cuba: the growth and characteristics of its labour force.
See item no. 282.

El barracón y otros ensayos. (The slave yard and other essays.)
See item no. 287.

Azúcar e inmigración 1900-1940. (Sugar and immigration 1900-40.)
See item no. 289.

Caidije.
See item no. 290.

Jamaican migrants and the Cuban sugar industry, 1900-1934.
See item no. 291.

Chinese contract labour in Cuba, 1847-1874.
See item no. 293.

Idéologie et ethnicité: les chinois macao à Cuba, 1847-1886. (Ideology and ethnicity: the Macao Chinese in Cuba, 1847-86.)
See item no. 296.

Gender constructs of labour in prerevolutionary Cuban tobacco.
See item no. 366.

Código de trabajo. (Labour code.)
See item no. 545.

Labour supply, harvest mechanization and the demand for Cuban sugar.
See item no. 761.

Trabajadores. (Workers.)
See item no. 1075.

Statistics

810 **Anuario Estadístico de Cuba.** (Statistical Yearbook of Cuba.)
Comité Estatal de Estadísticas. Havana: CEE, 1914-89. annual.

The yearbook is the most comprehensive source of statistical data available on Cuba and follows on from its predecessor of the same name, published between 1914 and 1961 by the former Finance Ministry. Publication was suspended from 1989 to 1995, a period of severe economic crisis, and data began to appear again during 1995. Now, however, internationally recognized methodology was used to measure economic performance, rather than the Material Product System employed during the period of CMEA membership. The yearbook contains data on territory and climate, population, global indicators, work and salaries, agriculture, industry, construction, transport and communications, domestic trade, foreign trade, education, culture and art, sports and physical education, public health, tourism and leisure.

811 **Availability and reliability of statistics in socialist Cuba.**
Carmelo Mesa-Lago. *Latin American Research Review*, vol. 4, no. 2 (spring 1969), p. 53-91; vol. 4, no. 3 (summer 1969), p. 47-81.

Examines in detail the use and misuse of statistical data in Cuba after the revolution.

812 **Censo de población y viviendas.** (Population and housing census.)
Havana: Comité Estatal de Estadísticas, 1991. 196p.

A report on the 1981 census. this covers population, age, sex, rural/urban residence, and number of dwellings, cross-tabulated, and broken down by province and municipality.

813 **Cuba: a handbook of historical statistics.**
Susan Schroeder. Boston, Massachusetts: G. K. Hall & Co., 1982. 589p.

This is the most comprehensive statistical compilation on Cuba in English, from the early colonial period up to the revolution. It includes data on climate, population, politics, agriculture, industry, finance, labour, education, culture, sports and tourism.

814 **Cuba: handbook of trade statistics 1994.**
Washington, DC: US Central Intelligence Agency, Directorate of Intelligence, 1994. 108p.

Contains Cuban trade statistics for 1989-93, mainly compiled from data provided by Cuba's trading partners. This is a useful supplement to the *Cuban Statistical Yearbook*, whose publication was suspended during this period.

815 **Cuba 1968.**
Edited by C. Paul Roberts, Mukhtar Hamour. Los Angeles: University of California, Latin America Center, 1970. 213p. maps.

This supplement to the annual UCLA publication *Statistical Abstract of Latin America* provides statistical information on a wide variety of areas. Subjects covered include spatial characteristics, demography, education, health, transport, communication, agriculture, industry, foreign trade, domestic commerce, wages and employment.

816 **Estadísticas de migraciones externas y turismo.** (Statistics on external migration and tourism.)
Comité Estatal de Estadísticas. Havana: Editorial Orbe, 1982. 126p.

This collection of data on international migration is especially valuable for the period 1959-77. It takes the form more of an analytical report than a statistical compendium, seeking to explain trends since colonial times. Comprehensive data on the age, sex, occupation, province of origin and destination of migrants in the period 1970-77 are included.

817 **Las estadísticas demográficas cubanas.** (Cuban demographic statistics.)
Departamento de Demografía de la Dirección de Estadísticas de Población y Censos, Dirección Central de Estados de la JUCEPLAN. Havana: Ciencias Sociales, 1975. 169p.

This is a useful compilation of demographic information published by JUCEPLAN, the former central planning ministry.

818 **FAO Production Yearbook.**
Food and Agriculture Organization. Rome: Food and Agricultural Organization, Statistical Division, 1947- . annual.

This annual publication contains indices of food and agricultural production, statistical summaries of agricultural production, and indices of agricultural trade. It is updated every three months by the *FAO Quarterly Bulletin of Statistics*.

819 **Statistical Yearbook.**
United Nations Department of Economic and Social Affairs, Statistical Office. New York: United Nations, 1948- . annual.

A comprehensive statistical abstract, this deals with a wide variety of subjects, including population, labour, agriculture, forestry, fishing, industry, mining, manufacturing, trade, energy, transport, communication, balance of payments, finance, health, housing, education and culture.

820 **Yearbook of International Trade Statistics.**
United Nations Department of International Economic and Social
Affairs, Statistical Office. New York: United Nations, 1951- . annual.
Data on trade, by country and by commodity is presented here.

International historical statistics: the Americas 1750-1988.
See item no. 110.

Cuba: estadísticas culturales, 1987. (Cuba: cultural statistics, 1987.)
See item no. 923.

Environment

821 The Caribbean environment.
Mark Wilson. Oxford: Oxford University Press, 1993. 4th ed. 278p.

This is a general text which covers Caribbean Examination Certificate (CXC) geography requirements, with sections on human and physical geography and mapwork. There is an emphasis on the interaction between natural and man-made systems. While there is little specific reference, Cuba is referred to throughout in general terms.

822 Catálogo de plantas urbanas amenazadas o extinguidas. (Catalogue of threatened or extinct urban plants.)
Attila Borhidi, Onaney Muñiz. Havana: Editorial Academia, 1983. 85p.

Catalogues the scientific and vulgar names of plants and their state of conservation and geographical location by province. The work also contains tables showing families with ten or more species in danger; and numbers of species in various states of conservation.

823 Diez años de colaboración científica Cuba–RDA (en el campo de la protección de plantas). (Ten years of Cuban–East German scientific collaboration [in the field of plant protection].)
Santiago de las Vegas, Cuba: Instituto IFA Tropical A. de Humboldt, 1976. 100p.

A rundown of joint plant-protection programmes, with summaries in Spanish, German, Russian and English.

824 La erosión desgasta a Cuba. (Erosion is wearing Cuba away.)
Antonio Núñez Jiménez. Havana: Instituto Cubano del Libro, 1968. 79p.

A brief illustrated account of how erosion has altered the island's landscape, by a well-known geographer and ecologist.

825 **Geografía del medio ambiente: una alternativa del ordenamiento ecológico.** (Geography of the environment: an alternative to the ecological order.)
Edited by Miriam I. Arcia Rodríguez. Mexico City: Universidad Autónoma del Estado de México, 1994. 289p. maps.

Brings together essays on Cuban environmental policy and conditions. See also: *Desarrollo sostenible y enfoque geosistémico del medio ambiente cubano* (Sustainable development and a Cuban geosystemic environmental approach) by G. J. Cabrera (Havana: University of Havana, Centre for Demographic Studies, 1991).

826 **The greening of the revolution: Cuba's experiment with organic agriculture.**
Peter Rosset, Medea Benjamin. Melbourne, Australia: Ocean Press, 1994. 110p.

A report of Cuba's experiments with organic farming compiled by an international fact-finding mission which visited the island in late 1992.

827 **The poisoning of paradise: environmental pollution in the republic of Cuba.**
José R. Oro. Miami, Florida: Cuban-American National Foundation, 1992. 134p.

An indictment of the environmental record of socialist Cuba, this was published by the leading anti-Castro organization in the United States. It surveys the pollution record of heavy industry and includes useful appendices on pollution by region.

828 **Tomorrow is too late: development and the environmental crisis in the Third World.**
Fidel Castro. Melbourne, Australia: Ocean Press, 1993. 54p.

This slim volume opens with Fidel Castro's speech at the Rio de Janeiro Earth Summit in June 1992. It is followed by the full text of the document highlighting the threat posed by the appalling environmental destruction which, he argues, cannot be blamed on the Third World.

Education

829 **Alfabeticemos.** (Let's teach literacy.)
Havana: Ministry of Education, 1961. 98p.

Used to train those who volunteered as teachers in the 1961 literacy campaign, this manual provides a fascinating insight into the thinking behind the campaign, which was both educative and political. The manual contains general orientations on how to conduct oneself in the campaign and teach literacy, and short readings on key themes such as revolution, co-operatives, nationalization, industrialization, schools, racial discrimination, imperialism, internationalism and democracy, as well as religion, health, and recreation. It also contains the 1960 Declaration of Havana and a vocabulary of terms.

830 **The basic secondary school in the country: an educational innovation in Cuba.**
Max Figueroa, Abel Prieto, Raúl Gutiérrez. Paris: UNESCO, 1985. 47p.

This study of rural secondary schools, in which the majority of pupils aged between fifteen and seventeen are enrolled, describes the curriculum, administration, and structure of the system.

831 **Children are the revolution: day care in Cuba.**
Marvin Leiner. New York: Viking Press, 1974. 213p.

A New York educator spent over a year in Cuba at two different periods in the late 1960s and early 1970s, studying the country's education system, and in particular its day-care programme for over half a million children. A sympathetic evaluation, yet not without its critical eye, it compares the Cuban experience with developments taking place in the United States, Russia, England, China and elsewhere. Leiner combines an eye-witness account with a wealth of information and statistical data.

832   **Children of Che: childcare and education in Cuba.**
Karen Wald.   New York: Ramparts Press, 1977. 382p.
This account of nursery and primary education in Cuba is totally sympathetic to, and uncritical of, the concepts current in Cuban educational circles in the early decades of the revolution.

833   **Children of the revolution.**
Jonathan Kozol.   New York: Delacorte Press, 1978. 245p. bibliog.
This first-hand account of revolutionary Cuba's educational innovations ranges from the literacy campaign to adult education and the administration of the education system. The author travelled throughout the island, talking with Cubans in all areas of education.

834   **Cuba: territorio libre de analfabetismo.** (Cuba: a land free of illiteracy.)
Equipo de Ediciones Especiales.   Havana: Ciencias Sociales, 1981. 101p. bibliog.
A popular overview of the 1960-61 Literacy Campaign and the Literacy Museum, this also contains brief biographies of young literacy teachers who died in the campaign.

835   **Cuba's educational revolution.**
Arthur Gillette, foreword by Robert Márquez.   London: Fabian Society, 1972. 36p. (Fabian Research Series, no. 302).
Gillette looks at the achievements that had been made in the field of education after twelve years of revolution. He seeks to present the major highlights of Cuban education under the revolution and discusses critical issues emerging from the educational efforts. The conclusion draws lessons on what can be learnt from the Cuban experience.

836   **Cuba's schools: 25 years later.**
Marvin Leiner.   In: *Cuba: twenty-five years of revolution, 1959-1984.* Edited by Sandor Halebsky, John M. Kirk.   New York: Praeger, 1985, p. 27-44.
A reflective look over twenty-five years in which education was a national priority. The author assesses revolutionary policy and change, including the 1970s schools in the countryside movement, and outlines problems in teacher quality and curriculum delivery. See also the section on education by Richard Jolly (p. 161-280) in *Cuba: the economic and social revolution* (q.v.), edited by Dudley Seers. Also of interest is *Making a new people: education in revolutionary Cuba* by Theodore MacDonald (Vancouver, British Columbia: New Star Books, 1985).

837 **Cuban educational strategies.**
Pauline Sahoy. In: *Education in the Caribbean: historical perspectives*. Edited by Ruby Hope King. Mona, Jamaica: Special Issue of the *Caribbean Journal of Education*, vol. 14, nos. 1-2 (Jan.-April 1987), p. 178-95.

Reprinted from a 1978 issue of the journal, this article provides an overview of the Cuban education strategy after the 1959 revolution, with reference to adult education, rural education, school construction, teacher training and educational problems. See also: 'The revolutionary transformation of Cuban education, 1959-1987' by Alfred Padula and Lois Smith, in *Making the future: politics and educational reform in the United States, England, the Soviet Union, China and Cuba*. Edited by Edgar B. Humbert (Atlanta, Georgia: Center for Cross Cultural Education, 1988, p. 117-39); and 'Educational reform and social transformation in Cuba, 1959-1989' by Martin Carnoy, in *Education and social transformation in the Third World*. Edited by Martin Carnoy, Joel Samoff (Princeton, New Jersey: Princeton University Press, 1990).

838 **The Cuban university under the revolution.**
Eusebio Mujal-León. Washington, DC: Cuban-American National Foundation, 1988. 70p.

Mujal-León claims that Cuban higher education is designed to serve political aims and that no intellectual force opposed to the revolution could emerge from it. He criticizes the role of some US academics and institutions in bilateral scholarly relations. The account includes data on growth, enrolment, and faculty specialization.

839 **La educación estética del hombre nuevo.** (The aesthetic education of the new man.)
Graciela Montero Cepero, et al. Havana: Ciencias Sociales, 1987. 151p.

Four Cuban educators discuss the history of aesthetic education, the classical Marxist aesthetic, and aesthetic education in socialist Cuba.

840 **Educación sexual: selección de lecturas.** (Sex education: a selection of texts.)
Edited by Monika Krause. Havana: Editorial Científico-Técnica, 1987. 111p.

A compilation of articles published in Cuba by Cuban specialists on diverse aspects of sex education, ranging from the need for sex education; through biology, anatomy, health and contraceptive orientation; to socio-cultural issues such as virginity, promiscuity, the love triangle, divorce and equality for women.

841 **Education in revolution.**
Havana: Instituto Cubano del Libro, 1975. 233p.

Published when Cuba's educational revolution was at its peak, this work contains full-colour photographs accompanying texts taken from Fidel Castro's 1953 landmark defence plea 'History will absolve me' and various speeches between 1959 and 1973. The book stands as an eloquent testimony to a nation's determination to prioritize and invest in the education of its people.

842 **Education, society and development in revolutionary Cuba.**
Sarah Thomas. MEd thesis, Faculty of Education, Manchester
University, England, 1995. 80p. bibliog.
Reviews educational developments in Cuba prior to the 1959 revolution and during
the period 1959-90, and considers the efforts being made in the 1990s to preserve the
gains of the post-revolutionary period. Thomas concludes that these efforts have been
largely successful given the severe resource shortages and other difficulties following
the economic collapse experienced after 1989.

843 **La enseñanza artística en Cuba.** (Art education in Cuba.)
Ministry of Culture. Havana: Editorial Letras Cubanas, 1986. 160p.
A description of the system of art teaching in Cuba is followed by chapters on music,
the visual arts, ballet, modern and folk dance, drama, circus, and the training of
culture promoters.

844 **Higher education and the institutionalized régime.**
Eusebio Mujal León. In: *Cuban communism 1959-1995.* Edited by
Irving Louis Horowitz. New Brunswick, New Jersey; London:
Transaction, 1995, 8th ed., p. 365-86.
The author ascribes a new importance to higher education after the mid-1970s, claiming that it tightened the relationship between the state and the university, university
centres, higher polytechnics and worker-peasant faculties in consolidating communism. The Ministry of Higher Education was newly established in 1976 to oversee this
process, with measures taken to improve the political and ideological content of
education. The author includes tables on higher education enrolment and Cuban
students in Eastern European bloc countries, and final sections deal with the censorship of academic freedom.

845 **Historia de la Universidad de La Habana.** (History of the University
of Havana.)
Ramón de Armas, Eduardo Torres-Cuevas, Ana Cairo Ballester.
Havana: Ciencias Sociales, 1984. 2 vols. 917p. bibliog.
Volume one takes in the period 1728-1929, covering the university's founding, growth
and development as a colonial institution, first as the Real y Pontificia Universidad de
San Gerónimo de La Habana and then as the 19th-century Real y Literaria Universidad
de La Habana. It also discusses the early neo-colonial 20th-century Universidad de La
Habana. Volume two covers 1930-78, from the revolutionary years of the 1930s
through to the insurrectional 1950s. It ends with two pieces by Raúl Roa and Carlos
Rafael Rodríguez, two of its eminent communist leaders, thinkers and writers.

846 **Problemas de la formación de las nuevas generaciones.** (Problems
of shaping the new generations.)
Gaspar Jorge García Galló. Havana: Editora Política, 1986. 131p.
This monograph was published as Cuba was about to embark on the rectification
programme, which entailed a renewed emphasis on the importance of a social conscience and moral ethics. The author explains the ideas shaping the theoretical basis of
Marxism-Leninism and the vision of Fidel Castro in forging the new society and a
people building communism. Paradoxically, 1986 was a turning point in which Cuba

Education

started moving away from a Marxist-Leninist communism and back to a more autochthonous nationalist and socialist humanism. The book is, nonetheless, a clear exposition of many guiding principles which remain in Cuba today.

University students and revolution in Cuba, 1920-1968.
See item no. 172.

Collision course: labor force and educational trends in Cuba.
See item no. 798.

Educación. (Education.)
See item no. 1114.

214

Science and Technology

847 **Academia de Ciencias de Cuba, nacimiento y forja.** (The Cuban
Academy of Sciences: founding and development.)
Antonio Núñez Jiménez.   Havana: Academia, 1972. 357p.
A history of the founding and early years of the Cuban Academy of Sciences.

848 **Caribbean science and technology.**
Wallace C. Koehler, Aaron Segal.   *Caribbean Review*, vol. 14,
no. 3 (summer 1985), p. 11-15.
Koehler and Segal take a brief look at science and technology in Cuba in the mid-
1980s within a Caribbean context.

849 **Momentos y figuras de las ciencias en Cuba.** (Moments and
personalities in Cuban science.)
Havana: Cuban Academy of Sciences, [n.d.]. 128p.
An overview of some of the highpoints and leading personalities in the Cuban
scientific field, prepared under the auspices of the Carlos J. Finlay Centre for Research
in Science History and Organization.

850 **Notes on science in Cuba.**
Marcel Roche.   *Science*, vol. 169, no. 3,943 (July 1970), p. 344-49.
Examines science and scientific study in Cuba on the basis of personal travel and
interviews in Cuba. The article is particularly concerned with the place of science and
technology in the high school and university curriculum, research, and the status of
scientists.

851 **La polémica de la esclavitud: Álvaro Reynoso.** (The slavery controversy: Álvaro Reynoso.)
Francisco Díaz Barreiro. Havana: Ciencias Sociales, 1987. 91p.
Álvaro Reynoso (1829-88) was a prominent chemist who confronted the scientific establishment in Cuba with science as a weapon to change the slave system and modernize agriculture and industry.

Medical applications of high technology in Cuba.
See item no. 493.

Biociencias en Cuba 1994-95. (Life sciences in Cuba 1994-95.)
See item no. 714.

Diez años de colaboración científica Cuba–RDA (en el campo de la protección de plantas). (Ten years of Cuban–East German scientific collaboration [in the field of plant protection].)
See item no. 823.

Ciencia, técnica y revolución: Academia de Ciencias de Cuba. (Science, technology and revolution: the Cuban Academy of Sciences.)
See item no. 1051.

Biotecnología Aplicada. (Applied biotechnology.)
See item no. 1131.

Revista Cubana de Física. (Cuban Journal of Physics.)
See item no. 1132.

Revista de Investigaciones Marinas. (Journal of Marine Research.)
See item no. 1133.

Literature

Anthologies, general literary history and criticism

852 Breaking the silences: 20th century poetry by Cuban women.
Edited and translated by Margaret Randall. Vancouver, British
Columbia: Pulp Press, 1982. 293p.

Work from twenty-five contemporary women poets is produced in Spanish and
English in this bilingual anthology, with brief biographical sketches of the poets. An
introduction by Randall provides a background history to the better-known Cuban
women poets of the 19th and 20th centuries, and discusses the work of contemporary
female poets in detail.

853 Bridges to Cuba.
Edited by Ruth Behar, Juan León. *Michigan Quarterly Review*
(summer 1994), p. 399-638; (fall 1994), p. 639-900.

This double issue brings together personal essays, poetry, short fiction and painting,
book reviews, interviews and performance pieces. It also contains hybrid creations of
text and image exploring 'the uncertain, sometimes absurd, often tragic encounters of
individual lives with the violent polarized politics of U.S.–Cuban relations'.

854 Crítica cubana. (Cuban literary criticism.)
Cintio Vitier. Havana: Editorial Letras Cubanas, 1988. 570p.

Literary essays by a leading Cuban poet and literary scholar are contained in this
substantial publication, including an earlier lengthy study of 19th-century Cuban
literary criticism, and essays on Lezama Lima and others.

855 **Cuba.**
Amelia S. Simpson. In: *Detective fiction from Latin America.*
Cranbury, New Jersey: Associated University Presses, 1990, p. 97-122.

Simpson traces the history of Cuban detective fiction from the publication of the first novel in the genre in 1971 (written in 1968) up to 1985. She discusses cultural policy and censorship, gives a résumé of the basic formula for detective fiction in Cuba, and reviews various titles.

856 **Cuba and Hemingway on the Great Blue river.**
Mary Cruz. Havana: Editorial José Martí, 1994. 243p. bibliog.

Ernest Hemingway was one of the more famous foreign writers to be attracted to Cuba and it was there he wrote his novels *Islands in the stream* and *The old man and the sea.* This is one of the best critical studies of Hemingway to be written in Cuba and is particularly rich on what is Cuban in his work. Basing his work on extensive research, the author, a Cuban critic and novelist, contributes an approach often overlooked in English-language appreciations of Hemingway's writing. See also *Hemingway in Cuba* by Norberto Fuentes (Secaucus, New Jersey: Lyle Stuart, 1984).

857 **The Cuban condition: translation and identity in modern Cuban literature.**
Gustavo Pérez Firmat. Cambridge, England: Cambridge University Press, 1989. 185p. bibliog.

The author bases his examination of Cuba's cultural identity on the premise that Cuba, unlike Puerto Rico for example, has never suffered from cultural *insularismo* but has synthesized its own culture by drawing on exogenous sources. Agreeing with Jorge Mañach that 'the continuous influx and outflow of peoples and goods have made it difficult to hold the sustained intramural discussion required for national self-definition', Pérez Firmat examines this theory with particular reference to: *Contrapunteo cubano* . . . and other writings by Fernando Ortiz; Guillén's *Motivos de son*; Carpentier's *Los pasos perdidos*; and works by Eugenio Florit, Luis Felipe Rodríguez and Carlos Loveira. See also: *Cuban consciousness in literature, 1923-1974 (a critical anthology of Cuban culture)* by José R. de Armas, Charles W. Steele (Miami: Editiones Universal, 1978. 243p. bibliog.); and *Fundación de la imagen* (The founding of the image) by Nancy Morejón (Havana: Editorial Letras Cubanas, 1988. 294p.), in which twenty-three critical essays are collected together on Cuban and other Caribbean, Central American and Afro-American writers and artists. The process of transculturation is the common theme running through the collection, which examines aspects of the work of: Cirilo Villaverde; Anselmo Suárez y Romero, Gertrudis Gómez de Avellaneda, Martín Moruá Delgado, Ramón de la Sagra, Juan Marinello, Mirta Aguirre, Nicolás Guillén, José Lezama Lima and Manuel Mendive.

858   **El cuento de la revolución cubana: una visión antológica y algo
       más.** (The short story in the Cuban revolution: an anthological view,
       and something more.)
       Seymour Menton.   In: *El cuento hispanoamericano ante la crítica*
       (The Spanish-American short story faces the critics.)   Edited by
       Enrique Pupo-Walker.   Madrid: Editorial Castalia, 1973, p. 338-55.

Menton presents a survey of the principal short-story writers of the revolutionary
period, including Onelio Jorge Cardoso, Eduardo Heras León, Jesús Díaz, Samuel
Feijóo, Calvert Casey, Raúl González de Cascorro and Gustavo Eguren. The survey
includes an examination of the authors first published during the 1950s dictatorship
(Antón Arrufat, Casey, Edmundo Desnoes, Lisandro Otero, Cabrera Infante and
Ambrosio Fornet), and traces how the harsh reality of revolutionary struggle,
including the Bay of Pigs victory, increasingly influenced their subject matter. Menton
shows how from 1968 on, following the Padilla/Arrufat prize controversy, the
politically committed short story won out over the fantasy tale.

859   **Disidencias y coincidencias en Cuba.** (Dissidences and coincidences
       in Cuba.)
       Lisandro Otero.   Havana: Editorial José Martí, 1984. 132p.

The coverage of these fourteen essays includes: the ideas of Fernando Ortiz and Raúl
Roa; dissidence and subversion in the Cuban novel from the 19th century onwards;
literature and revolution; and a re-examination of the work of Lezama Lima. Two
articles criticizing the shortcomings of the exiled writers Heberto Padilla and
Guillermo Cabrera Infante are of historical interest.

860   **En el fiel de América: estudios en literatura hispanoamericana.**
       (At the fulcrum of America: studies in Spanish-American literature.)
       José Juan Arrom.   Havana: Editorial Letras Cubanas, 1985. 214p.

A collection of essays by a veteran Cuban-American academic giving a glimpse into
the vast range of his literary, linguistic, political and ethnographic interests. Arrom
discusses works by Nicolás Guillén, Alejo Carpentier and José Lezama Lima, and
reassesses José Martí alongside José Hernández, the author of *Martín Fierro*. He also
examines how the poetic image of Cuba as a nation has evolved from pre-Columbian
times to the present.

861   **Ensayo de otro mundo.** (Essay from another world.)
       Roberto Fernández Retamar.   Havana: Instituto Cubano del Libro,
       1967. 188p.

The collection includes chapters on José Martí, Rubén Martínez Villena, César
Vallejo, Frantz Fanon, Ezequiel Martínez Estrada, and Ernesto Che Guevara, as well
as chapters on themes concerning the intellectual, poetry and revolution. One
particular theme throughout is the underdeveloped 'other' world of the poor of the
earth as reflected in the writings of the revolutionary authors chosen.

862 **Ensayos de estética y de teoría literaria.** (Essays on aesthetics and literary theory.)
José Antonio Portuondo. Havana: Editorial Letras Cubanas, 1986. 470p.

A compilation of essays by one of Cuba's leading literary critics exploring the Cuban aesthetic in the context of a world revolutionary and Marxist-Leninist aesthetic.

863 **Escribir en Cuba, entrevistas con escritores cubanos: 1979-1989.**
(Writing in Cuba, interviews with Cuban writers: 1979-89.)
Emilio Bejel. San Juan, Puerto Rico: Editorial de la Universidad de Puerto Rico, 1991. 387p.

Cuban writers offer their views on a range of topics related to literature and history and the revolution: politics and the creative imagination; the generation of the 1950s; literary policy of the 1960s; the Lezama and Padilla cases; the 'grey years' of the early 1970s; the founding of the Ministry of Culture; the 1980 Mariel exodus; the 1989 changes in the socialist camp; as well as women, homosexuals and religion.

864 **Images of women in pre- and post-revolutionary Cuban novels.**
Lourdes Casal. *Cuban Studies*, vol. 17 (1987), p. 25-50.

Under scrutiny in this article is the portrayal of women in fifteen pre-1959 and fifteen post-1959 novels, which were overwhelmingly written by male novelists. The images depict a continuing upper- and middle-class value of female virginity and an ethos of machismo which spans the two eras, as women remain seriously under-represented as major and minor characters.

865 **Intellectuals and the Cuban revolution.**
Nicola Miller. In: *Intellectuals in the twentieth-century Caribbean: volume II Unity in variety: the Hispanic and Francophone Caribbean.*
Edited by Alistair Hennessy. London; Basingstoke, England: Macmillan, 1992, p. 83-98.

Miller briefly considers: the crises of the 1960s and early 1970s; the film *P. M.* in 1961; the Military Units to Aid Production in 1965-66; the case of Heberto Padilla in 1967-71; and adds a summary comment on the late 1970s and 1980s. Cultural policy is seen as a casualty of economic and political developments, especially increasing dependence on the Soviet Union. Also in the same volume (p. 58-82) is Antoni Kapcia's *The intellectual in Cuba: the national-popular tradition*.

866 **Literary bondage: slavery in Cuban narrative.**
William Luís. Austin, Texas: University of Texas Press, 1990. 312p. bibliog.

In this work, anti-slavery narrative and blacks are seen as counter-discourse to the European aesthetic in Cuban history. The study contains textual analysis of: Juan Francisco Manzano's *Autobiography*; Cirilo Villaverde's *Cecilia Valdés*; Francisco Calcagno's *Romualdo and Aponte*; Martín Murúa Delgado's *Sofía* and *La familia Unzuana*; Lino Novás Calvo's *El negrero*; Alejo Carpentier's *The kingdom of this world*; Miguel Barnet's *The autobiography of a runaway slave*; César Leante's *Los guerrilleros negros*; and Reinaldo Arenas's *Graveyard of the angels*. See also: *The black protagonist in the Cuban novel* by Pedro Barreda, translated by Page Bancroft. (Amherst, Massachusetts: University of Massachusetts Press, 1979. 179p. bibliog.); and *Black writers in Latin America* by Richard L. Jackson (Albuquerque, New Mexico: University of New Mexico Press, 1979. 224p.).

867 **Lo cubano en la poesía.** (The Cuban element in poetry.)
Cintio Vitier. Havana: Instituto Cubano del Libro, 1970. 585p.

This book was originally written as a series of seventeen lectures in 1957 at the Havana Lyceum. When it was published twelve years later, the author, a major Cuban writer and critic, reflected on how it had been conditioned by history – post-Machado Cuba, the Spanish Civil War, and the Second World War – and described it as a declaration of poetic faith in Cuba's destiny in times of despair. Vitier traces themes in the work of Cuban poets over the ages: the bucolic and the romantic; nationalism, Indianism and Africanism; foundations and frustrations.

868 **El negro en la novela hispanoamericana.** (The black man in the Latin American novel.)
Salvador Bueno. Havana: Editorial Letras Cubanas, 1986. 2nd ed. 294p.

Discusses narrative references to the exploitation of, and discrimination against, blacks in novels from Cuba, Colombia, Ecuador, Mexico and Peru. The chapters on Cuba look at early and late anti-slavery narrative, particularly slavery and race relations in the novel *Cecilia Valdés*, as well as the 'black' in the work of Alejo Carpentier.

869 **Neither golden exile nor dirty worm: ethnic identity in recent Cuban-American novels.**
Jorge Duany. *Cuban Studies*, vol. 23 (1993), p. 167-86.

The article discusses the various different attitudes towards Cuban immigrants in the United States, arguing that the Cuban experience is isolated from that of other immigrant groups. Duany analyses three novels by Cuban-American authors, looking at the concept of ethnic identity.

870 **La novela de la revolución cubana.** (The novel of the Cuban revolution.)
Rogelio Rodríguez Coronel. Havana: Editorial Letras Cubanas, 1986. 312p. bibliog.

The author examines the development of the novel genre in the first two decades following the revolution against the background of socio-political influences at home and abroad. Some discussion of the rise of detective and counter-espionage fiction is included and there is a useful appendix listing the novels published in Cuba between 1959 and 1979. See also *Narrativa cubana de la revolución* (Narrative prose of the Cuban revolution), edited by J. M. Caballero Bonald (Madrid: Alianza Editorial, 1968. 255p.), which constitutes a selection of twenty-four short stories and extracts from novels, all published in Cuba since 1959. Included are the most representative prose writers at the time of publication: Dora Alonso, Jesús Díaz, Jaime Sarusky, Lisandro Otero, Severo Sarduy, César López, Virgilio Piñera, José Lezama Lima, Guillermo Cabrera Infante, Edmundo Desnoes, Felix Pita Rodríguez, Onelio Jorge Cardoso and Gustavo Eguren. The volume includes a prologue and notes on the authors by the editor.

871 **Poemas al Che.** (Poems to Che.)
Edited by Ambrosio Fornet. Havana: Instituto Cubano del Libro, 1969. 243p. bibliog.

The death of Ernesto Che Guevara in 1967 in Bolivia guaranteed his place in history as a legend of almost mythical proportions. He was a popular hero, not only in his native Latin America, but the world over; he was the humanist and the romantic ready to fight and die for his ideals. In this volume, poets of Spain and the Americas pay tribute to Che's memory.

872 **Poesía cubana de la revolución.** (Cuban poetry of the revolution.)
Selection, presentation and notes by Ernesto Cardenal. Mexico City: Editorial Extemporáneos, 1976. 334p.

Cardenal, the poet-priest of the Nicaraguan revolution, paid tribute to Cuban revolutionary poetry in this collection of poets, both established and new. He rates among the best in the anthology, poems by the erstwhile shoeshine boy, who became professor of poetry and philosophy at the University of Havana, and the sausage factory worker, who became a poet working at the Union of Writers and Artists in Cuba. See also *En tiempos difíciles: la poesía cubana de la revolución* (In difficult times: poetry of the Cuban revolution) by J. M. Cohen, translated by Isabel Vericat. (Barcelona, Spain: Tusquets, 1970. 78p.) which looks at the work of twenty representative Cuban poets.

873 **Poesía social cubana.** (Social poetry of Cuba.)
Edited by Mirta Aguirre. Havana: Editorial Letras Cubanas, 1985. 574p.

The work of over 150 Cuban poets is included in this anthology of socially committed poetry from 19th- and 20th-century Cuba. See also 'The climate of current Cuban poetry' by Robert Pring-Mill, in *Collected Seminar Papers*, no. 29, Caribbean Societies, vol. 1 (London: University of London, Institute of Commonwealth Studies, 1982, p. 122-43).

874 **Poetisas cubanas.** (Cuban women poets.)
Edited by Alberto Rocasolano. Havana: Editorial Letras Cubanas, 1985. 355p.

A compilation of the work of Cuban women poets, starting from Gertrudis Gómez de Avellaneda in the mid-19th century. The anthology then traces the development of women's poetry through: the romanticism of Luisa Pérez de Zambrana and Julia Pérez Montes de Oca; the modernism of Mercedes Matamoros and Juana Borrero; the post-modernism of María Villar Buceta; the intimacy of Dulce María Loynaz, Mirta Aguirre and Rafaela Chacón Nardi; the neo-romanticism of Carilda Oliver Labra; the more contemporary Fina García Marruz, Georgina Herrera, Nancy Morejón and Minerva Salado; to Soleida Ríos, Reina María Rodríguez and Marilyn Bobes.

875 **Por la poesía cubana.** (For Cuban poetry.)
José Prats Sariol. Havana: Ediciones Unión, 1988. 2nd ed. 295p.

An eclectic collection of articles reviewing the work of young as well as established poets, celebrating the centrality and universality of contemporary Cuban poetry. See also the older *Nueva poesía cubana* (New Cuban poetry), edited by José Agustín

Goytisolo (Barcelona, Spain: Ediciones Península, 1970. 236p.) in which the work of twenty-seven contemporary poets is included, along with an introductory essay and biblio-biographical notes on each poet.

876 **Prose fiction of the Cuban revolution.**
S. Menton. Austin, Texas: University of Texas Press, 1975. 344p. bibliog.

Menton divides his study into five separate areas, covering the Cuban novel of the revolution; literature and revolution; the Cuban short story of the revolution; anti-revolutionary prose fiction; and foreign prose fiction of the Cuban revolution. He presents a chronology of the principal novels and short stories centring on this theme and concludes with twelve succinct summary points on the state of Cuban literature at the time. See also *Prose fiction criticism and theory in Cuban journals* by Terry J. Peavler (*Cuban Studies*, vol. 7, no. 1 [Jan. 1977], p. 58-118) which is a compilation of literature, literary criticism, literary theory and authors and titles in the first decade after the revolution. It also includes Cuban criticism of Latin American and United States literature.

877 **Reading Cuba, 1984.**
Edited by Phyllis Janik. *Another Chicago Magazine*, no. 13 (1985), p. 71-215.

Comprises English-language translations of poetry by Eliseo Diego, Nancy Morejón, Guillermo Rodríguez Rivera, Reina María Rodríguez, Pedro Pérez Sarduy, with photographs by Mario García Joya (Mayito) and María Eugenia Haya (Marucha).

878 **The repeating island: the Caribbean and the postmodern perspective.**
Antonio Benítez-Rojo, translated by James Maraniss. Durham, North Carolina; London: Duke University Press, 1992. 303p.

An original interpretative study of Cuba in the Caribbean context, this is written by a Cuban exile writer who draws heavily on history, economics, sociology, cultural anthropology, psychoanalysis and literary theory. He shows that by appropriating chaos theory as a metaphor, apparent disorder (different lands, colonial histories, ethnic groups, languages, beliefs, and politics) renders unexpected order and identity. Included are powerful re-readings of writers Nicolás Guillén and Alejo Carpentier and ethnologist Fernando Ortiz.

879 **Sugar's secrets: race and the erotics of Cuban nationalism.**
Vera M. Kutzinski. Charlottesville, Virginia; London: University Press of Virginia, 1994. 287p. bibliog. (New World Studies).

Cultural and feminist critical theories are used to construct a highly original interpretation of the *mulata* in Cuban and Caribbean literature. The author sets out to explore how and why Cuba's national identity has been cast in terms of cross-cultural *mestizaje* and considers the roles race, gender, sexuality and class have played in the construction of that synthesis in 19th- and 20th-century poetry, fiction and visual arts. She also examines the fundamental paradox of celebrating racial diversity yet refusing to acknowledge a historical reality of racial conflict in Cuban literature and popular culture.

880 **Writing in Cuba since the revolution: an anthology of poems, short
stories and essays.**
Edited and introduced by Andrew Salkey. London: Bogle
L'Ouverture Publications, 1977. 162p. bibliog.

Salkey argues that the combination of cultural invasions and nationalist visions has
produced a Cuban genius for adaptation, assimilation and innovation. This anthology
includes writing which is indicative of artistic experimentation and creative freedom
within the revolution and makes art a weapon of denunciation and accusation in the
hopes of a better society of tomorrow.

Literary criticism and selected translations of individual writers

Reinaldo Arenas

881 **Before night falls: a memoir**.
Reinaldo Arenas, translated by Dolores M. Koch. New York: Viking
Penguin, 1993. 317p.

The devastating autobiography of an unrestrained homosexual writer, who left a poor
rural background to fight in the revolutionary insurrection and then found himself at
odds with the revolution in power. Begun before he left Cuba in the 1980 Mariel
exodus, the book forms a compelling account of his experiences in Cuba and the
United States, where he remained every bit as much an exile. The work ends in New
York, as he takes his life in an advanced stage of AIDS.

882 **Reinaldo Arenas: the Pentagonía.**
Francisco Soto. Gainesville, Florida: University Press of Florida,
1995. 204p. bibliog.

This essay studies Arenas's *Pentagonía*, a five-novel sequence, in the context of the
general framework of a Cuban documentary novel. Soto analyses how Arenas's novels
explore history rather than fiction and sees *Pentagonía* as giving a voice to the
forgotten members of revolutionary society. A brief consideration of the same topic
can also be found in the author's earlier 'Reinaldo Arenas: the Pentagonía and the
Cuban documentary novel' (*Cuban Studies*, vol. 23 [1993], p. 135-66). Various
English-language translations of Arenas's work are available and these include: *The
palace of the white skunks* (London: Penguin, 1993); *The doorman* (New York: Grove
Weidenfeld, 1991. 191p.); and *The assault* (New York: Harley Viking, 1994. 145p.).
In addition, readers may be interested to find out about *Old Rosa*, a novel in two
stories, *Singing from the well*, *The ill-fated peregrination of Fray Servando*,
Graveyard of the angels, *El Central: a Cuban sugar mill*, and *Otra vez el mar* (Once
again the sea) (Barcelona, Spain: Editorial Argos Vegara, 1982. 420p.).

Miguel Barnet

883   **The autobiography of a runaway slave.**
Esteban Montejo, edited by Miguel Barnet, translated from the Spanish
by Jocasta Innes, introduction by Alistair Hennessy.   London;
Basingstoke, England: Macmillan, 1993. 248p.

Based on the oral testimony of a former slave, this mid-1960s classic documentary
novel (*Cimarrón*) has been translated into many foreign languages, appearing as an
English-language reprint. It provides a unique account of a slave's life before
abolition, the experience of being a runaway, life on the sugar plantations as a
freeman, as a soldier in the 1895 War of Independence, and as a poor black in 20th-
century Cuba.

884   **La fuente viva.** (The living source.)
Miguel Barnet.   Havana: Editorial Letras Cubanas, 1983. 241p.

A series of essays written between 1964 and 1981, in which the author of *Cimarrón*,
Canción de Rachel and other testimony novels, discusses the role of oral testimony as
a living literary source and then goes on to examine the mythical elements which have
contributed to the synthesis of a Cuban national identity. *Canción de Rachel*, written
after *Cimarrón* (Autobiography of a runaway slave), is also available in translation:
Rachel's song (Willimantic, Connecticut: Curbstone Press, 1991. 125p.). It is the story
of a famous showgirl from the once vibrant Alhambra Theatre as she herself told it to
Barnet, and through newspaper reports and other contemporary accounts. Barnet's
subsequent works, *Gallego* and *La vida real*, also follow the style of the testimony
novel.

Guillermo Cabrera Infante

885   **Major Cuban novelists: innovation and tradition.**
Raymond D. Souza.   Columbia, Missouri; London: University of
Missouri Press, 1976. bibliog.

Three trapped tigers, Cabrera Infante's controversial first novel, is selected for
detailed analysis, along with *Explosion in a cathedral* (Carpentier) and *Paradiso*
(Lezama Lima). The study as a whole provides a panorama of the Cuban novel's
development during the 19th and 20th centuries, with particular reference to the
tensions between innovation and tradition, as implied by the title. *Three trapped tigers*
was the early novel that established the author (London: Faber & Faber, 1989. 487p.).
Set in the 1950s world of Havana's seamy dockland, its wordplay has led it to be
described as a blend of metarealism and metaphysics as well as a nostalgic *adiós* to
the disappearing world of the author's youth. See also: *View of dawn in the tropics*; *A
twentieth century job*; *Rites of passage*; and *Infante's inferno* (London: Faber & Faber,
1984. 410p.).

Literature. Literary criticism and selected translations of individual writers.
Alejo Carpentier

886 **Mea Cuba.** (My Cuba.)
Guillermo Cabrera Infante, translated by Kenneth Hall with the author.
London: Faber & Faber, 1994. 503p.

Presents a collection of essays, articles and interviews by the author, published in the press and literary journals between 1968 and the 1990s, which lend coherence to the author's political and literary irreverence. Chapter headings are evocative in this respect: Perversions of history; Background to exile; Have a Havana; Men in iron masks; Patriots galore; As the media see her; Birth of a notion; Castroenteritus; and An exiledom by the Thames.

Alejo Carpentier

887 **Alejo Carpentier: the pilgrim at home.**
Roberto González Echevarría. Ithaca, New York: Cornell University Press, 1977. 307p. bibliog.

The first book-length study in English devoted to Carpentier's life and work, this discusses his relationship to the Latin American avant-garde, his role in the founding of the Afro-Antillan movement, his involvement with the surrealist group in Paris, and his writings of the 1940s and 1950s and in post-revolutionary Cuba. The author looks in particular at literary theory and modernity as well as fact and fiction in Carpentier's major novels: *El reino de este mundo* (The kingdom of this world); *Los pasos perdidos* (The lost steps); *El siglo de las luces* (Explosion in a cathedral); and *El recurso del método* (Reasons of state). Carpentier was a prolific writer, not just of fiction, and his other works include: *Ecué-yamba-O*; *La música en Cuba*; *Tientos y diferencias*; and *Guerra del tiempo*. See also: *Alejo Carpentier and his early works* by Frank Janney (London: Tamesis, 1981. 141p. bibliog.); *Alejo Carpentier: a comprehensive study* by Bobs M. Tusa (Valencia; Chapel Hill, North Carolina: Albatros Hispanofila, 1982. 48p.); and *Alejo Carpentier: bibliographical guide/guía bibliográfica* by Roberto González Echevarría, Klaus Muller-Bergh (Westport, Connecticut: Greenwood, 1983. 271p.).

888 **Explosion in a cathedral.**
Alejo Carpentier. London: Victor Gollancz, 1963. 351p.

This is the hugely successful sequel to *The lost steps*, in which the author reveals the existence of a neglected historical figure, Victor Hugues. Set in Guadeloupe, Venezuela and Barbados in the period of the French Revolution, it is a masterpiece which embraces the whole Caribbean. See also *The harp and the shadow* (El arpa y la sombra), a late work by Carpentier which demythologizes Columbus and the 'discovery' of America (London: André Deutsch, 1992. 159p.).

889 **The genesis of America: Alejo Carpentier.**
Gordon Brotherston. In: *The emergence of the Latin American novel.*
London: Cambridge University Press, 1977, p. 45-59. bibliog.

Discusses the work of Nobel Prize-winning author Alejo Carpentier, with particular reference to *El siglo de las luces* (Explosion in a cathedral). See also: *Towards a Caribbean literary tradition* by Lloyd King (St. Augustine, Trinidad: University of the West Indies, [n.d.]. 92p. bibliog.), which explores the portrayal of the Hispanic

Caribbean in the work of three writers, one of whom is Carpentier; *Carpentier: el reino de este mundo* by Richard Young (London: Grant & Cutler, 1983. 122p. [Critical Guides to Spanish Texts]); *Carpentier: los pasos perdidos* by Verity Smith (London: Grant & Cutler, 1983. 78p. [Critical Guides to Spanish Texts]); and *Carpentier's Proustian fiction: the influence of Marcel Proust on Alejo Carpentier* by Sally Harvey (London: Tamesis, 1994. 171p. bibliog. [Monograph Series, no. 156]).

890   **The kingdom of this world.**
Alejo Carpentier.   Harmondsworth, England: Penguin, 1975. 113p.

Perhaps the best-known of Carpentier's novels in translation, the story is woven around the late 18th-century Haitian revolution and the figure of Henri Cristophe. It is set against the backdrop of an island ravaged by struggle against slavery and French dominion, in the time of Napoleon Bonaparte. The novel was originally published in translation by Knopf (New York) in 1957 and is also available in a 1967 Gollancz version. Another of Carpentier's better-known works, also available in translation, is *The lost steps* (Harmondsworth, England: Penguin, 1968. 252p.), which deals with one man's disillusionment with modern life and his journey back to the primitive. For a more complete picure of Carpentier's oeuvre, see *Obras completas* (Complete works) (Mexico City: Siglo XXI, 1983. 9 vols).

891   **Reasons of state.**
Alejo Carpentier, translated by Francis Partridge.   London: Readers & Writers Publishing Cooperative, 1977. 311p.

El recurso del método (Reasons of state) is Carpentier's fascinating contribution to the Latin American sub-genre of the dictator novel. In it, he provides a penetrating retrospective of the career of the central character, an amalgam of some of the region's most notorious tyrants, as he finds himself the victim of a coup. See also: *Baroque concert* (Tulsa, Oklahoma: Council Oak Books, 1988. 135p.); and *The chase* (New York: Farrar, Straus & Giroux, 1989).

Manuel Cofiño López

892   **La novela de mis novelas.** (The novel of my novels.)
Manuel Cofiño López.   In: *Los novelistas como críticos* (Novelists as critics.)   Compiled by Norma Klahn, Wilfrido H. Corral.   Mexico City: Fondo de Cultura Económica, 1991, p. 326-34.

This is the text of a lecture in which the author recalls the post-revolutionary historical and social context which inspired him to write his novel *La última mujer y el próximo combate* and the short-story collection *Tiempo de cambio*.

Literature. Literary criticism and selected translations of individual writers.
Gertrudis Gómez de Avellaneda

Eliseo Diego

893 **Poems.**
Eliseo Diego, translated by Kathleen Weaver, Eliseo Diego.   New
York: Center for Cuban Studies, 1982. 96p.

A collection of Diego's poems in Spanish and English, selected by Diego and Weaver
for this limited edition.

Roberto Fernández Retamar

894 **Caliban and other essays.**
Roberto Fernández Retamar, translated by Edward Baker, foreword by
Frederic Jameson.   Minneapolis, Minnesota: University of Minnesota
Press, 1989. 139p.

The only English-language translation of Retamar's literary writing, this provides an
opportunity for a rethink of the relationship between poetry, literary criticism and
politics. A leading politico-literary figure of the revolution, Retamar argues that the
Calibanesque is at the heart of Cuba's rebellion. Retamar's poetic works include:
Buena suerte viviendo; *Alabanzas, conversaciones, circunstancias y Juana*; and *A
quien pueda interesar*.

Cristina García

895 **Dreaming in Cuban.**
Cristina García.   New York: Ballantine Books, 1992. 245p.

A haunting first novel by a Cuban American, written in a warm and gentle style, this
tells the story of three generations of Cuban women and their responses to the
revolution. The narrative is woven around a grandmother who is a Castro supporter,
her two daughters, one of whom retreats into Afro-Cuban religion and another who is
militantly anti-Castro and emigrates to the United States, and the latter's own
rebellious, punk artist daughter who goes in search of her grandmother and her Cuban
past.

Gertrudis Gómez de Avellaneda

896 **Gertrude the great: Avellaneda, nineteenth-century feminist.**
Beth Miller.   In: *Women in Hispanic literature: icons and fallen idols.*
Edited by Beth Miller.   Berkeley, California: University of California
Press, 1983, p. 201-14.

The article examines the feminist content and context of Avellaneda's writing, which
was primarily for and about women, and her own unconventional life. This included
editing the only Cuban women's journal of the time, arguing against marriage as an
institution, and being unsuccessful in her bid to be the first woman member of the

Spanish Real Academia. See also: 'Una feminista cubano-española: Gertrudis Gómez de Avellaneda ante la sociedad de su tiempo' (A Cuban-Spanish feminist: Gertrudis Gómez de Avellaneda in her times) by Brígida Pastor (*Journal of the Association for Contemporary Iberian Studies*, vol. 8, no. 1 [spring 1995], p. 57-62), which demonstrates Cuba's impact on the liberal ideas of Avellaneda, and how she in turn used literature to publicize her feminism.

897 Sab and Autobiography.

Gertrudis Gómez de Avellaneda, translated and edited by Nina M. Scott. Austin, Texas: University of Texas Press, 1993. 157p. bibliog.

A rare translation of two major works by the increasingly celebrated Spanish-Cuban feminist authoress of the 19th century. *Sab* is an anti-slavery novel about a passionate affair between a mulatto slave and a white woman, and predates the more famous American novel *Uncle Tom's cabin* by Harriet Beecher Stowe by eleven years. *Autobiography* was written in the same period and tells the story of a truly amazing woman for her time. 'I feel', she wrote, 'that true freedom is never enslaving yourself to anyone or anything.' See also: *Visión romántica del otro: estudio comparativo de Atalá y Cumaná, Bug-Jargal y Sab* (Romantic vision of the other: a comparative study of Atalá, Cumaná, Bug-Jargal and Sab) by Nara Araujo (Havana: Universidad de la Habana, 1993. 198p.), which situates the prose of Gómez de Avellaneda in a comparative cultural study of four romantic novels which arose out of the European presence in the Americas.

Nicolás Guillén

898 Nicolás Guillén: popular poet of the Caribbean.

Ian Isidore Smart. Columbia, Missouri; London: University of Missouri Press, 1990. 187p. bibliog.

Taking an Afro-Caribbean approach to Guillén's life and work, this study portrays the poet as the smartman, the hero-trickster-maroon, and the poet-intellectual of resistance, for whom *mulatez* is a quintessentially Caribbean area of conflict. See also: *The poetry of Nicolás Guillén: an introduction* by Denis Sardinha (London; Port of Spain: New Beacon Books, 1976. 80p.), which analyses Guillén's poetry and traces his literary development. The work includes an extensive selection of his poems with English translations. Also of interest, but not translated, are *Nación y mestizaje en Nicolás Guillén* (Race and nation in Nicolás Guillén) with a prologue by Nancy Morejón (Havana: Casa de las Américas, 1974. 429p.); and *Nicolás Guillén: notas para un estudio biográfico-crítico* by Angel Augier (Santa Clara, Cuba: Universidad Central de las Villas, 1962. 2. vols).

899 Nicolás Guillén's world of poetry.

Translated by Salvador Ortiz-Carboneres, introduction by Alistair Hennessy. Warwick, England: University of Warwick Centre for Caribbean Studies & Centre for Research in Ethnic Relations, 1991. 147p. bibliog.

Included in this 1990s bilingual anthology of selected poems, are: 'Sóngoro Cosongo', 'West Indies Ltd.', 'Sones para turistas', 'España', 'El son entero', 'Cities and

Literature. Literary criticism and selected translations of individual writers.
Nicolás Guillén

Tengo'. Hennessy in his introduction pays posthumous tribute to Guillén as a poet in a Cuban tradition of both black and communist politics of his times. See also: *Man-making words: selected poems of Nicolás Guillén* (Havana: Editorial Arte y Literatura, 1973. 214p.), another bilingual collection which includes some of Guillén's lesser-known poems; *¡Patria o muerte!*; *The great zoo and other poems by Nicolás Guillén* (Edited and translated by Roberto Márquez. Havana: Editorial Arte y Literatura, 1975. 223p.) which contains poems from the years 1925-69; and *The daily daily*, translated and with an introduction by Vera M. Kutzinski (Berkeley, California: University of California Press, 1989. 139p.).

900 **The poet's Africa: Africanness in the poetry of Nicolás Guillén and Aimé Césaire.**
Josaphat B. Kubayanda.   Westport, Connecticut: Greenwood, 1990.
176p. bibliog.

The author states that his primary reason for writing this book was to demonstrate that a more enlightened view of Africa and of things African has provided a united principle around which the poetry of Nicolás Guillén of Cuba and Aimé Césaire of Martinique has been constructed. He considers the genesis of Caribbean interest in Africa from the 1920s onwards and attempts to indicate the elements that constitute the originality of Guillén's and Césaire's poetic compositions. Kubayanda also examines the technical innovations of the two poets, such as Guillén's alteration of Spanish metrical systems by the introduction of African oral and musical forms. He concludes with a discussion of the place of Guillén and Césaire in Caribbean creative writing. See also: *Cuba's Nicolás Guillén* by Keith Ellis (Toronto: University of Toronto Press, 1985. 2nd ed. 251p. bibliog.); and *Un poeta y un continente* (A poet and a continent) by Mirta Aguirre, a fellow-poet and one of Cuba's best-known Marxist literary critics (Havana: Editorial Letras Cubanas, 1982. 139p.).

901 **Self and society in the poetry of Nicolás Guillén.**
Lorna V. Williams.   Baltimore, Maryland: Johns Hopkins University
Press, 1982. 177p.

This study attempts to fill a gap existing at the time in book-length studies on Guillén. Williams examines both his style and poetic technique and his portrayal of human experience, taking in both his early work and later poetry. To the same end, she examines the different understandings of various critics of Guillén's work, from those who concentrate on his use of musicality and *son* to those who focus on his depiction of blacks in his early verse. See also 'The African presence in the poetry of Nicolás Guillén' by Lorna V. Williams, in *Africa and the Caribbean: the legacies of a link*. Edited by Margaret E. Crahan, Franklin W. Knight (Baltimore, Maryland: Johns Hopkins Univeristy Press, 1982).

José Francisco Heredia

902   **Abufar-Abdala: aspects tragiques de la cubanité, 1820-1880.**
(Abufar-Abdala: tragic aspects of Cubanness, 1820-80.)
Maria Poumier.   Paris: L'Equipe de Recherche de l'Université de
Paris VIII, 1992. 145p.

Reproduces the text of José Francisco Heredia's *Abufar*, with a chronology of the
writer's life and an introductory essay situating the 19th-century tradition of literary
tragedy, as Cuban nationhood was forged out of slavery, racial bigotry and the mulatto
condition, through the work of Gómez de Avellaneda, Plácido, Manzano, Tanco,
Villaverde, Heredia and Martí.

José Lezama Lima

903   **José Lezama Lima: poet of the image.**
Emilio Bejel.   Gainesville, Florida: University Press of Florida, 1990.
178p. bibliog.

A rare study in English of one Cuba's greatest 20th-century Cuban writers, who is
little appreciated in languages other than Spanish but whose existential literary
philosophizing has captivated young Cuban writers of the 1990s more than any other.
A critical study of Lezama's monumental writings (his poetry, essays, novels and
short stories) forms the bulk of this work and situates his vision of the image as
creative power stemming from a fundamental lack of natural order, in relation to
universal artistic and philosophical currents. The author discusses image and subject,
subject in crisis, metaphorical and poetic history, complexity of language, and textual
and symbolic planes. See also *Lezama Lima: el ingenuo culpable* (Lezama Lima:
guilty naif) by Reynaldo González (Havana: Editorial Letras Cubanas, 1988. 164p.),
which is a collection of literary essays.

904   **José Lezama Lima's joyful vision: a study of *Paradiso* and other
prose works.**
Gustavo Pellón.   Austin, Texas: University of Texas, 1989. 151p.

Pellón examines the work of Lezama Lima in the context of not only Hispanic but also
world literature and current literary theory. Concentrating on the major works
Paradiso, its sequel *Oppiano Licario*, and *Essays*, this text seeks to highlight rather
than resolve the contradictions in Lezama's mystical quest for illumination through
obscurity, the calculated motivation of naïvety, cosmopolitan Americanism, Proustian
fascination with homosexuality and modernist narrative style. Lezama Lima's other
Spanish-language works include: *Tratados en La Habana, Fragmentos a su imán*;
Muerte de Narciso; *Enemigo rumor*; *Aventuras sigilosas*; *La fijeza dador* (poetry);
Cangrejos; *Golondrinas* and *Relatos* (short stories); *Analecta del reloj*; *La expresión
americana*; and *La cantidad hechizada*. There are also three volumes of *Obras
completas* (Complete works), volume one of which covers his novels, volume two his
poetry, and volume three literary criticism (Mexico City: Aguilar, 1975).

Literature. Literary criticism and selected translations of individual writers.
José Martí

905 **Paradiso.**
José Lezama Lima, translated from the Spanish by Gregory Rabassa.
Austin, Texas: University of Texas Press, 1978. 2nd ed. 466p.

Rabassa has produced the only English-language translation of Lezama's 1966 masterpiece, which tells the story of José Cemí, whose life begins at the turn of the 20th century in Cuba. From a childhood dominated by a colonel father, matriarch mother, and Hispanic-Cuban Catholic upbringing, Cemí goes on to find two adolescent intellectual and sexual male soul-mates. The intense, introspective literary style, and the themes of love and eroticism, including explicit male homosexuality, made this a classic and controversial novel. The book was originally published by Farrar, Straus & Giroux in 1974. Other works not translated into English include: *Cartas* (1939-76); *Muerte de Narciso*; *Antología poética*; *Relatos*; and *Imagen y posibilidad*.

Juan Francisco Manzano

906 **The autobiography of a Cuban slave.**
Juan Francisco Manzano, translated by Lloyd King.   St. Augustine,
Trinidad: University of the West Indies, [n.d.]. 66p. bibliog.

This is the first complete English translation of the Cuban slave Juan Francisco Manzano's rare autobiography. Originally published in English in 1836, the early edition was an incomplete translation used by the British abolitionist Richard Madden. King prefaces his translation with an insightful essay analysing the political, social and moral climate of 19th-century Cuba through the literature dealing with slavery and race relations by Domingo del Monte, Anselmo Suárez y Romero, Antonio Zambrana, Cirilo Villaverde and Martín Morúa Delgado. See also: *The life and poems of a Cuban slave: Juan Francisco Manzano, 1797-1854*. Edited by Edward J. Mullen (Hamden, Connecticut: Archon Books, 1981. 237p.).

José Martí

907 **The America of José Martí.**
José Martí, translated from the Spanish by Juan de Onís, with an
introduction by Francisco de Onís.   New York: Noonday Press, 1953.
330p.

A collection of prose, including the much-celebrated *Our America* (on Latin America) and writing spanning the other America (the United States) as well as Cuba. Among the famous figures who appear in the text are Carlos Manuel de Céspedes and Ignacio Agramonte from Cuba.

908 **Fundación de una escritura: las crónicas de José Martí.**
(Foundations of a literature: the chronicles of José Martí.)
Susana Rotker.   Havana: Casa de las Américas, 1992. 290p. bibliog.

A Casa de las Américas prize-winning study of the language and ideas of José Martí's historically and politically committed newspaper reports in the context of late 19th-century Modernism. Martí was a prolific writer on a wide number of topics. Among his works readers may be interested to find *La Edad de Oro* (The Golden Age) (Havana: Editorial Letras Cubanas, 1989. 131p.), which is considered the forerunner of modern Latin American writing for children.

909 **Major poems.**
José Martí, edited and with an introduction by Philip S. Foner, translated from the Spanish by Elinor Randall. New York: Holmes & Meier, 1982. 173p.

A bilingual anthology of poetry, this contains an introduction to Martí and his work, and a chronology. Collections included are: *Ismaelillo, Versos sencillos* (Simple verse); two poems from *La Edad de Oro* (The Golden Age); *Versos libres* (Free verse); and *Flores de destierro* (Flowers of exile). A political activist and prolific political writer, Martí declared that poetry was the friend after the strenuous tasks of the day.

Nancy Morejón

910 **Where the island sleeps like a wing.**
Nancy Morejón, translated by Kathleen Weaver. San Francisco: Black Scholar Press, 1985. 92p.

A selection of poetry by the leading contemporary black woman poet and literary scholar of Cuba is contained in this bilingual Spanish–English anthology. Readers may also be interested in: 'A womanist vision of the Caribbean: an interview', in *Out of the Kumbla: Caribbean women and literature*. Edited by Carole Bryce Davies, Elaine Savor Fido (Trenton, New Jersey: Africa World Press, 1990, p. 265-69. bibliog.). Other examples of Morejón's work, not in translation, can be found in: *Mutismos* (1962); *Amor, ciudad atribuida* (1964); *Richard trajo su flauta* (1967); *Parajes de una época* (1979); and *Cuaderno de Granada* (1984).

Heberto Padilla

911 **Cuba: revolution and the intellectual, the strange case of Heberto Padilla.**
Index on Censorship, vol. 1, no. 2 (summer 1972), p. 65-88, 101-34.

Provides a detailed account of what happened to Heberto Padilla after winning the 1968 poetry prize for a book that was subsequently condemned. The article includes poems from the book, ripostes of Padilla and Guillermo Cabrera Infante, international denunciation, Padilla's public self-denigration, and his discussion with leading Cuban writers at the time.

912 **Legacies: selected poems.**
Heberto Padilla, translated by Alistair Reid, Andrew Hurley. New York: Farrar, Straus & Giroux, 1980. 179p.

A bilingual anthology containing the controversial award-winning book of poems, *Fuera del juego*, that was branded counter-revolutionary and triggered the 'Padilla

Literature. Literary criticism and selected translations of individual writers. Severo Sarduy

Affair'. For an earlier English-language anthology which includes an introduction on the life and work of the writer and contextualizes the 'Affair' see: *Sent off the field: a selection of the poetry of Heberto Padilla*, translated by J. M. Cohen (London: André Deutsch, 1972. 127p.).

913 **Self portrait of the other: a memoir.**
Heberto Padilla. New York: Farrar, Straus & Giroux, 1990. 247p.

Broken into numbered, untitled chapters, this is the story of Padilla's return to Cuba from New York, after the triumph of the revolution, to work at the newly established Prensa Latina news agency. It follows the story through to his disenchantment, arrest and ultimate exile. Padilla reached the pinnacle of recognition as a writer in 1968 when his award-winning book, *Fuera del juego*, was deemed to be counterrevolutionary.

Pedro Pérez Sarduy

914 **Cumbite and other poems.**
Pedro Pérez Sarduy. New York: Center for Cuban Studies, 1990. 81p.

The author has assembled a bilingual anthology of his poetry that spans the major moments of a twenty-year period. The collection includes some of his early, unpublished poems which are full of social comment, as well as poems on international themes. See also his: 'Myth and history: literary reconstruction around the life of a maid in prerevolutionary Cuba' (*Notebook / Cuaderno, A Literary Journal*, vol. 6, no. 2 [1990], p. 64-79), in which he reflects on the fine dividing line that stands between fiction and non-fiction, myth and reality, in the genre of testimonial literature; and *Surrealidad* (Surreality) (1968).

Severo Sarduy

915 **The name game: writing / fading writer in De dónde son los cantantes.**
Oscar Montero. Chapel Hill, North Carolina: University of North Carolina, 1988. 149p. bibliog.

This study of Severo Sarduy's writing looks in part at his first novel *Gestos* (Gestures), published in 1963, and his later novel *Cobra*, published in 1975, but focuses mainly on *De dónde son los cantantes* (From where are the singers). This has been seen as a radical reworking of *Lo cubano*, as the writer travels from province to capital to metropolis, staking out a creative textual territory.

916 **Cobra.**
Severo Sarduy, preface and translation by Suzanne Jill Levine. New York: Ed Dutton & Co., 1975. 176p.

Little known and little translated, Sarduy was heralded as the great writer of modernity, who was removed from the novelistic realism of Latin American literature.

Literature. Literary criticism and selected translations of individual writers.
Cirilo Villaverde

Cobra has been seen as the culmination of the new Latin American novel. See also his anthology of four radio plays: *For voice*, translated by Philip Barnard (Pittsburgh, Pennsylvania: Latin American Literary Review Press, 1975. 136p.).

Cirilo Villaverde

917 **Cecilia Valdés or Angel's Hill: a novel of Cuban customs.**
Cirilo Villaverde, translated by Sydney G. Gest. New York: Vantage Press, 1962. 546p.

The classic historical novel of 19th-century Cuba, this is the tragic love story of a beautiful young mulatto woman living in the harsh times of Spanish colonialism and slavery.

918 **Contradanzas y latigazos.** (Contredanse and whiplash.)
Reynaldo González. Havana: Editorial Letras Cubanas, 1983. 296p. bibliog.

The novelist Reynaldo González presents a series of essays on Villaverde's novel *Cecilia Valdés*, which he uses to explore key themes of the early 19th century which are still of relevance in Cuba today. He embarks on a deconstruction of the colonial picaresque, explores the myth and reality of the mulatto woman, and re-characterizes the black problem as a white problem.

Inside the monster: writings on the United States and American imperialism by José Martí.
See item no. 154.

Our America.
See item no. 161.

Un análisis psicosocial del cubano, 1898-1925. (A psychosocial analysis of the Cuban, 1898-1925.)
See item no. 166.

Afro-Cuba: an anthology of Cuban writing on race, politics and culture.
See item no. 323.

Casa de las Américas. (House of the Americas.)
See item no. 1101.

La Gaceta de Cuba. (The Cuban Gazette.)
See item no. 1104.

Revista de la Biblioteca Nacional José Martí. (The José Martí National Library Review.)
See item no. 1105.

Revolución y Cultura. (Revolution and Culture.)
See item no. 1106.

Unión. (Union.)
See item no. 1107.

Diccionario de la literatura cubana. (Dictionary of Cuban literature.)
See item no. 1135.

Dictionary of twentieth-century Cuban literature.
See item no. 1137.

Alejo Carpentier, bibliographical guide.
See item no. 1153.

A bibliography of Cuban creative literature: 1958-1971.
See item no. 1154.

Culture and The Arts

General culture

919 **Autógrafos cubanos.** (Cuban autographs.)
Miguel Barnet. Havana: Ediciones Unión, 1990. 150p.

Barnet presents twenty-five essays on a wide range of historical and contemporary Cuban cultural figures. These include: writers such as Heredia, Carpentier, Guillén, Renée Méndez Capote, Carilda Oliver Labra and Nancy Morejón; folklore specialists Fernando Ortiz and Carolina Poncet; artists René Portocarrero and Manuel Mendive; and popular entertainers such as Rita Montaner, Bola de Nieve, Barbarito Diez, Esther Borja and Pablo Milanés. This is a useful and readable introduction to some of the essential icons of Cuban culture. A similar publication is *Conversar con el otro* (Conversing with the other) by Luis Álvarez (Havana: Ediciones Unión, 1990. 215p.), which contains eleven critical essays on literary and cultural figures, ranging from Félix Varela and José Martí to Onelio Jorge Cardoso, Nicolás Guillén and Ernesto Che Guevara.

920 **Casa de las Américas: an intellectual review in the Cuban revolution.**
Judith Weiss. Chapel Hill, North Carolina: Estudios de Hispanófila, 1977. 171p. bibliog.

Chronicles the work and changing role of the Casa de las Américas between 1960 and 1971. The main argument is that during the period 1960-65, the Casa de las Américas provided a literary forum for the Latin American avant-garde, but that from 1965 to 1971 its role changed to that of the ideological conscience of Latin American artists and intellectuals. This created major schisms and tensions between the fictional and ideological nature of the Casa's work, whereby the review became an ideological battlefield.

921 Changing the rules of the game.

Armando Hart Dávalos, interviewed by Luis Báez. Havana: Editorial Letras Cubanas, 1983. 124p.

In a question-and-answer format, the Cuban Minister of Culture provides an overview of revolutionary policy on education and culture and the provision of facilities, in the context of broad cultural and political debates. The questions answered encompass the role of artists and intellectuals in the revolution; errors of revolutionary cultural policy; cultural freedom and censorship; and the US- and Cuban American-driven anti-Cuba cultural human rights campaign.

922 Cuba: cultura y sociedad (1510-1985). (Cuba: culture and society [1510-1985].)

Francisco López Segrera. Havana: Editorial Letras Cubanas, 1989. 328p.

A periodization of Cuba's cultural history, providing an overview of the arts and with an extensive bibliography.

923 Cuba: estadísticas culturales, 1987. (Cuba: cultural statistics, 1987.)

Havana: Ciencias Sociales, 1988. 68p.

Statistics quantifying all aspects of Cuban cultural life are contained in this book: museum attendance; records, cassettes and sheet music produced; films made and cinema attendance; libraries and books published; theatrical performances and music festivals; and amateur movements.

924 Cultura afrocubana. (Afro-Cuban culture.)

Jorge and Isabel Castellanos. Miami, Florida: Ediciones Universal, 1988-94. 4 vols.

In the first three volumes of this series, the authors present a detailed history of the black Cuban from 1492 to 1959. They offer an in-depth study of the origins and development of the Afro-Cuban culture, which today is such a vital element of the Cuban nation. Volume one concentrates primarily on the historical processes that brought the African to Cuba; volume two looks at the history of Cuban 'people of colour' and volume three studies Afro-Cubanism and its influences on society and culture up to 1959. Volume four brings the story up to date, examining the position of blacks in Cuban society since the revolution.

925 Culture and the Cuban revolution.

Pedro Pérez Sarduy. *The Black Scholar*, vol. 20, nos. 5-6 (winter 1989), p. 17-23.

A personal reflection by a black Cuban writer of thirty years of cultural change under the Cuban revolution, in response to an attack by Cuban exile writer Guillermo Cabrera Infante.

926 **En las raíces del árbol.** (In the roots of the tree.)
Joel James Figarola. Santiago de Cuba: Editorial Oriente, 1988.
118p.

Figarola examines the relationship between popular cultural expression and the interpretation of local history. Chapters cover: the folkloric performances organized by Santiago's black lodges as a precursor to carnival; folklore and theatre in Cuban culture; and issues in the interrelationship between art, culture and history.

927 **Panorama de la cultura cubana.** (A panorama of Cuban culture.)
Havana: Editora Política, 1983. 205p.

Presents ten essays written mainly from a Marxist viewpoint, in which Alejo Carpentier, Mirta Aguirre, José Antonio Portuondo and other Cuban intellectuals review various aspects of Cuban literature, music, architecture and art.

928 **Política cultural de la revolución cubana.** (The cultural policy of the Cuban revolution.)
Havana: Ciencias Sociales, 1977. 140p.

Contains classic documents, including Fidel Castro's 1961 speech to the intellectuals, the 1971 declaration of the National Congress of Education and Culture, the 1975 Communist Party of Cuba statement on the role of culture, and section four of the 1976 Constitution on education and culture.

929 **Popular culture.**
Judith Weiss. In: *Cuba: twenty-five years of revolution, 1959-1984.*
Edited by Sandor Halebsky, John M. Kirk. New York: Praeger, 1985, p. 117-33.

Weiss examines the ways in which traditional popular culture, as distinct from élite culture, has been promoted since 1959. This includes the infrastructures of cultural promotion, cultural policy and such institutions as the Casa de Cultura (Culture House) and agit-prop theatre.

930 **Report from Cuba.**
The Black Scholar, vol. 8, nos. 8-10 (summer 1977), p. 2-96.

An entire issue of the journal, *The Black Scholar*, was given over to Cuba, with articles by Robert Chrisman on national culture, Samella Lewis on art, Phyl Garland on music, Jonetta Cole on Afro-American solidarity with Cuba, an interview with Afro-Cuban film-maker Sergio Giral and an Alice Walker short story.

931 **The state of cultural democracy in Cuba and Nicaragua during the 1980s.**
David Craven. *Latin American Perspectives*, vol. 17, no. 3 (1990), p. 100-19.

Craven considers the emphasis placed on art and cultural affairs by the Cuban and Nicaraguan governments as an example of their manipulation of social factors for political ends. He employs the theories of Ernesto Che Guevara and Paulo Freire as an ideological background and describes how through its state- and locally-funded cultural institutions Cuba hopes to educate and expose people to art, especially new forms that are a synthesis of the past and present.

932 Talking about culture.
Sandra Levinson. In: *The Cuba reader.* Edited by Philip Brenner, et al. New York: Grove Press, 1989, p. 487-97.

This is a short, thought-provoking piece on cultural life and cultural policy over three decades of socialist Cuba. It draws on interviews with Cuban writers Reynaldo González, José Rodríguez Feo, Nancy Morejón and Edmundo Desnoes, painter Raúl Martínez, singer-composer Silvio Rodríguez, and actor Sergio Corrieri.

933 Transculturación en Fernando Ortiz. (Transculturation in Fernando Ortiz.)
Diana Iznaga. Havana: Ciencias Sociales, 1989. 112p. bibliog.

Discusses the concept of transculturation as developed by Fernando Ortiz, whose pioneering work earlier this century laid the foundations for Cuban ethnographic and folklore studies.

Visual arts

934 Amelia Peláez: exposición retrospectiva, 1924-1967. (Amelia Peláez: retrospective exhibition, 1924-67.)
Caracas: Museo de Bellas Artes (5 May-16 June). 72p.

An exhibition catalogue which provides a valuable overview of Peláez's work. It was also published by Havana's Museo Nacional to accompany an exhibition at the Biblioteca Luis Angel Arango in Bogotá in March-April 1992.

935 Art of Latin America 1900-1980.
Marta Traba. Baltimore, Maryland: Johns Hopkins University Press, 1994. 196p.

The author sadly died in 1983 so never saw publication of this work. In it, she attempts to represent Latin American art as a coherent whole, dealing with its development throughout the region, and demonstrating how various movements spread from country to country. Although Cuba is not dealt with specifically, making it necessary to search for references throughout the book, a large number of Cuban artists are covered, some in more detail than others. In addition, for those not already familiar with contemporary Cuban artists, searching is facilitated by the inclusion of country names in brackets after artist names. There are many colour reprints. See also: *Handbook of Latin American art: comprehensive annotated bibliography 1942-1980* directed by Joyce W. Bailey (New York; London: Holmes & Meier, 1983).

936 **The art of revolution.**
Dugald Stermer, Susan Sontag.   New York: McGraw-Hill, 1970.
101p.

A richly illustrated volume on the 1960s boom in Cuban poster art. It contains posters produced by the Organization of Solidarity with Asia, Africa, and Latin America (OSPAAAL), the Commission for Revolutionary Orientation (COR), Casa de Las Américas, and the National Film Institute (ICAIC).

937 **La Bienal de la Habana.** (The Havana Biennial.)
Llilian Llanes.   *Third Text*, no. 20 (autumn 1992), p. 5-12.

The Havana Biennial of Third World art is one of the major activities of the Wifredo Lam Centre, founded in 1983 in honour of the late Cuban painter. The Biennial, and the Centre, situate Cuban art in the context of the extraordinary fusion of peoples and cultures in the history of the Third World that has made a major contribution to global art.

938 **Caraïbes-Caribbean.**
Revue Noire no. 6 (Sept.-Nov. 1992), special issue.

A special issue of this contemporary international African arts magazine on the Caribbean, featuring Cuba, Haiti, Jamaica, Martinique and Guadeloupe. The issue includes stunning full-colour reproductions of the work of lesser-known Cuban artists residing both in Cuba and abroad.

939 **La creación está en cualquier lugar.** (Creation can be found anywhere.)
Manuel García.   *Lápiz*, vol. 94, no. 11 (1993), p. 23-27.

An interview with the director of the 1994 Havana Biennial, considering the work selected for the exhibition, which was dominated by Third World artists. It also discusses the state of contemporary Cuban art.

940 **Cuba dos épocas.** (Two ages of Cuba.)
Raúl Corrales, Constantino Arias, introduced by María Eugenia Haya.
Mexico City: Fondo de Cultura Económica, 1987. 69p.

This is a book of quality reproductions of photographs by two major Cuban photographers. Arias's photographs show Cuba before 1959: the wealthy; entertainers; people in the streets; and poverty. Those by Corrales, in contrast, are mainly taken after 1959 and portray such diverse scenes as ordinary militia people in the 1960s and 1980s domestic settings. Haya, a photographer in her own right, was also an excellent photo-historian, as evidenced in her introduction.

941 **Cuba: la fotografía de los años 60.** (Cuba: photography from the 1960s.)
Edited by María E. Haya, introduction by Roberto Fernández Retamar.
Havana: Fototeca de Cuba, 1988.

Photographs taken by Raúl Corrales, Ernesto Fernández, Mario García Joya, Alberto Korda and Osvaldo Salas are included in this book of quality reproductions. The photographs reflect major phenomena of the 1960s, such as the militia and the literacy campaign, and prominent persons such as Fidel Castro, Che Guevara and Celia Sánchez.

942 **Cuban art and national identity: the vanguardia painters, 1920-1940s.**
Juan Antonio Martínez. PhD thesis, Florida State University, 1992. 299p. (Available from Dissertation Abstracts International. Order no. DA9222401).

Examines the relationship between modernism and nationalism in the context of Cuban history and culture. Martínez makes particular reference to the avant-garde artists who broke with the Academia de Bellas Artes in the 1920s to form a movement which integrated Cuban traditional art with European modernism. He concludes that the outcome was the creation of 'lasting, if mythical, symbols of national ethos'. See also Martínez's *Cuban art and national identity: the Vanguardia painters, 1927-1950* (Gainesville, Florida: University Press of Florida, 1995. 203p. bibliog.).

943 **Cuban photography: context and meaning.**
John Mraz. *History of Photography*, vol. 18, pt. 1 (spring 1994), p. 87-96. bibliog.

An examination of the status of photography in Cuba since 1959 which attempts to assess how it was influenced by the 1959 revolution. The author notes the popularity of photo-journalism and discusses the issue of censorship, both inside and outside Cuba.

944 **Cuban visual poetry.**
Pedro Juan Gutiérrez. *Visible Language*, vol. 27, pt. 4 (autumn 1993), p. 410-21. bibliog.

The author discusses the status of a genre which, he considers, has been important in Cuba since the 1920s. In the 1960s it melded with poster art to produce what he describes as visual art at its best. The style and use of the genre by several Cuban visual artists, including Félix Beltrán, Zaída del Río and Luis Miguel Valdés, is described.

945 **Esteban Chartrand: nuestro romántico.** (Esteban Chartrand: our romantic.)
Raúl R. Ruiz. Havana: Editorial Letras Cubanas, 1987. 85p. bibliog.

Chartrand was a major landscape painter of 19th-century Cuba. In this biography, Ruiz situates him in his times, and includes official documents and a list of his paintings.

946 **Exploraciones en la plástica cubana.** (Explorations in Cuban art.)
Gerardo Mosquera. Havana: Editorial Letras Cubanas, 1983. 472p.

The author is a leading Cuban art critic. In this anthology of essays, he broaches indigenous Amerindian art in Cuba and the work of modern Cuban painters: the nationally and internationally famous Servando Cabrera Moreno, Wifredo Lam, Manuel Mendive, and Tomás Sánchez, as well as the lesser-known Julio Girón, Jorge Rodríguez, Gilberto Frómeta, Luis Cabrera, Flavio Garciandía and José Bedia, among others. The essays testify to an explosion in the visual arts in Cuba in the 1970s and 1980s.

947 **Exposición antológica: 'homenaje a Wifredo Lam' 1902-82.**
(Retrospective exhibition: 'homage to Wifredo Lam' 1902-82.)
Madrid: Museo Español de Arte Contemporáneo, [1982]; Paris: Musée d'Art Moderne de la Ville de Paris, [1983]; Brussels: Musée d'Ixelles, [1983]. 180p. bibliog.

A catalogue for an exhibition of paintings and pastels by Lam shown in Madrid, Brussels and Paris, this contains extracts from previously published articles about Lam and the artist's own recollections of a meeting with Picasso in 1938. With 171 illustrations and a biography, the catalogue also includes lists of other publications by, or about, Lam.

948 **Herencia clásica: oraciones populares ilustradas por Zaída del Río.**
(Classic heritage: popular prayers illustrated by Zaída del Río.)
Edited by Carlos Alberto Cruz Gómez, presentation by Manuel Moreno Fraginals. Havana: Centro de Desarrollo de las Artes Visuales, 1990. 103p.

Del Río grew up in the 1950s in the central province of Villa Clara, where there was a local tradition of improvised prayer sheets that reflected the popular syncretic beliefs of the area, which were part Afro-Cuban, part-Catholic, and part-Spiritism. This compilation of prayers kept from those times is illustrated in full colour by her paintings. The end-product of textual and visual imagery is stunningly beautiful. The book has a glossary and brief biographical sketch of Del Río.

949 **Modernity & Africanía: Wifredo Lam in his island.**
Gerardo Mosquera. *Third Text*, no. 20 (autumn 1992), p. 43-68.

Counterpoises Eurocentric visions of Lam's work, by looking at it in the context of Africa in America and the intercultural dialogue implicit in the new mestizo cultures of the Caribbean. Lam is depicted as an artist whose painting is a 'primitive'-modern cosmogony, which recreates the Caribbean world but appropriates European techniques which are anti-colonial, polemical but not utopian. The author finds that, like the Yoruba's Elegguá, in art terms, he is the opener of pathways, the lord of knowledge and the crossroads.

950 **New art of Cuba.**
Luis Camnitzer. Austin, Texas: University of Texas, 1994. 432p.

Camnitzer takes a unique comprehensive look in the English language at the work of forty young Cuban artists, who received their education and art training after the 1959 revolution and whose work has been shaped by it. This New York-based artist sensitively captures the complexity of how his young Cuban counterparts have produced work which both celebrates and criticizes the revolution, and has provoked some fierce controversy as they move to more cosmopolitan concerns and art forms. The work contains over 200 black-and-white illustrations.

951 **Nuevos mapas y viejas trampas.** (New maps and old traps.)
Iván de la Nuez. *Lápiz*, vol. 12, no. 103 (May 1994), p. 34-39.

Compares the nature of Cuban art produced in exile with that of Cuban artists on the island. Nuez outlines the main characteristics of exile art, including homesickness and conflict with the new environment. Illustrations include works by Arturo Cuenca, Carlos R. Cárdenas, Juan Pablo Ballester and Ajubel.

952 **Outside Cuba: contemporary Cuban visual artists.**
Edited by Ileana Fuentes Pérez, Graciella Cruz Taura, Ricardo Pau
Losa. New Brunswick, New Jersey: Transaction, 1995. 366p.

This is the catalogue of the 1987/88 exhibition of the same name, which took to the United States and Puerto Rico the first major works of contemporary Cuban artists since 1944. It takes a chronological approach, commencing with the 1930s, and including, in the case of contemporary artists, those described as being in 'inevitable exile'. The catalogue draws on their lives, and includes full-colour reproductions of their work.

953 **Palmas reales en el Sena.** (Royal palms on the Seine.)
José Seoane Gallo. Havana: Editorial Letras Cubanas, 1987. 193p.

A series of interviews with the sisters of the leading 20th-century Cuban woman painter Amelia Peláez (1896-1968) and with Amelia herself.

954 **Pintores cubanos.** (Cuban painters.)
Havana: Editorial Gente Nueva, 1974. 66p.

An introduction to the rich history of 19th- and 20th-century Cuban painting by theme: landscape and seascape; town, house and square; portraits and places; history; and cubism and realism. The book is produced with full-colour illustrations.

955 **René Portocarrero.**
Graziella Pogolotti, Ramón Vázquez Días. Berlin: Editorial
Henschel; Havana: Editorial Letras Cubanas, 1987. 52p.

This beautifully produced book on the artist René Portocarrero (1912-85), contains an essay on his work, a chronology of his life, a bibliography, and twenty-six annotated reproductions of his paintings.

956 **A short guide to old Cuban prints.**
Emilio C. Cueto. *Cuban Studies*, vol. 14, no. 1 (winter 1984),
p. 27-42.

Some 200 prints covering over 400 years of colonial history are detailed in this article, with information on the location of originals and reproductions.

957 **Signs of transition: 80s art from Cuba.**
New York: Center for Cuban Studies and MoCHA, 1988. 48p.

Presents eighteen reproductions of paintings by young Cuban artists, which were shown in the 1988 exhibition of the same name at the Museum of Contemporary Hispanic Art. Also included are essays by Luis Camnitzer and Coco Fusco, a short biography and list of exhibitions for each artist, and cover art by Zaída del Río. Other artists include Consuelo Castañeda, Humberto Castro, Arturo Cuenca, Magdalena Campos, Carlos Alberto García, Rubén Torres-Llorca, Flavio Garciandía, Gustavo Pérez Monzón, Moisés Finale, Israel León and Gustavo Acosta. Earlier Center for Cuban Studies art catalogues include tenth and fifteenth anniversary editions, 'Retrospectives of Cuban photography 1959-1982', 'Cuban poster art 1961-1982', and 'Young artists of Cuba'.

958 **Temporada en el ingenio.** (A season in the sugar mill.)
Chinolope, introduction by José Lezama Lima. Havana: Editorial Letras Cubanas, 1987. 70p.

A photographic essay of work in a sugar mill, which contains present-day photographs interspersed with reproductions of prints during the period of slavery.

959 **Tomás Sánchez: the mysticism of landscape; recent works.**
Gerardo Mosquera, Giulio V. Blanc. *Art Nexus*, no. 10 (Sept.-Dec. 1993), p. 48-53, 181-83.

The Cuban landscape painter, Tomás Sánchez, was a member of the New Figuration movement from 1956 to 1975 before beginning to incorporate surrealist elements into his landscapes. This article analyses the evolution of his art and considers the ecological messages in his recent works. Illustrations are included.

960 **The visual arts since the Cuban revolution.**
David Craven. *Third Text*, no. 20 (autumn 1992), p. 77-102.

Traces the broad-ranging artistic praxis of the revolution, from the 1965-75 golden age of the Cuban poster and pop art (decentring Western trends) to the 1979-89 new generation of artists (assimilating yet combating Eurocentric art). The author explores in particular Cuban artists' renewed emphasis on ethnic hybridization which produces a diverse and variegated spectrum of art.

961 **Wifredo Lam.**
Madrid: Museo Nacional Centro de Arte Reina Sofía, 1992. 156p. bibliog.

This is the catalogue for an exhibition of Lam's paintings from the period 1930-70, which was shown at the Fundació Joan Miró in Barcelona and the Museo Nacional Centro de Arte Reina Sofía in Madrid in 1992. The publication includes ten poems by Severo Sarduy and five essays: 'Wifredo Lam at the Museo Nacional of Havana'; 'Lam in our century'; 'Modernity and Africa: Wifredo Lam in his island'; 'Lam in Spain (1923-38)'; and 'Spain and Wifredo Lam: a revelatory encounter'. There are also 108 illustrations and a biography of the artist.

962 **Wifredo Lam.**
Antonio Núñez Jiménez. Havana: Editorial Letras Cubanas, 1982. 280p. bibliog.

This book is based on an interview conducted by the Cuban Deputy Minister of Culture with Lam in Havana in 1980. The introduction contextualizes the artist's Afro-Chinese Cubanness, as well as his universality. This is followed by a 1950 tribute to Lam's work by Fernando Ortiz. The remainder of the book comprises five parts: Lam's childhood; the painter and combatant in the Spanish Civil War; Lam in Paris; the painting *The jungle*; and Lam's return to Cuba. The work ends with a bibliography of books, monographs and press articles on Lam.

Music and dance

963 **Adolfo Guzmán: apuntes y testimonios.** (Adolfo Guzmán: notes and testimonies.)
Leonardo Depestre Catony.   Santiago de Cuba: Editorial Oriente, 1988. 54p.

This is a slim volume with a short biography of the conductor, performer and composer of Cuban popular music, Adolfo Guzmán (1920-76), and a testimony by people who knew him.

964 **La africanía de la música folklórica de Cuba.** (The African origins of Cuban folklore music.)
Fernando Ortiz.   Havana: Editorial Cárdenas, 1965. 2nd ed. 492p.

Although dated, this detailed and wide-ranging work is still of great value for the study of the African origins of Cuban music, a little-studied area at the time this book was first written (1950). Ortiz considers: the origins and different varieties of Cuban music and dance; musical and oral expressions of African blacks in Cuba; the origins of poetry and song among Afro-Cubans; rhythm and melody in African music; and the instrumental and choral music of blacks. A number of reproductions of musical pieces and a bibliography are included. See also Ortiz's *Los instrumentos de la música afrocubana* (The instruments of Afro-Cuban music) published in four volumes between 1952 and 1955, by Cárdenas y Cía in Havana.

965 **Alicia Alonso: the story of a ballerina.**
Beatrice Siegel.   New York: Frederick Warne & Co., 1979. 182p.

Written for high-school students, this biography of Cuba's prima ballerina begins with a description of Alonso being taught ballet by a Russian in Havana in 1931. It traces her career in Cuba, the United States and Europe, and discusses her role in the creation of both the American Ballet Theatre and the National Ballet of Cuba in 1955 (which she closed in 1957 under Batista and built to fame under the revolution). The book contains a fine selection of photographs of Alonso and other dancers.

966 **Caribbean currents: Caribbean music from rumba to reggae.**
Peter Manuel, with Kenneth Bilby, Michael Largey.   Philadelphia, Pennsylvania: Temple University Press, 1995. 272p.

In this wide-ranging survey of the richly diverse forms of Caribbean music, Cuba is covered, along with Puerto Rico, the Dominican Republic, Haiti, Jamaica, Trinidad, Suriname, Martinique and Guadeloupe. The book spans genres such as salsa, merengue, bachata, reggae and calypso and explores the music in relation to issues of race, regional diversity, gender and socio-political conflicts.

967 **Catálogo de música popular cubana.** (Catalogue of popular Cuban music.)
Eliseo Palacios García. Havana: Editorial Pueblo y Educación, 1987. 277p.

A rare catalogue of individual entries on contemporary Cuban popular musical groups, soloists, composer-musicians, and composer-singers, under the rubric of the Centre for Research and Development of Cuban Music. A short introduction provides an overview of Cuban musical history evolving out of African and European influences and generating autochthonous Cuban forms from the 19th century onwards: *son*; danzón; rumba; mambo; cha-cha-chá; jazz; feeling; and protest. The entries are organized alphabetically, by province, providing an easy-reference panorama of the modern-day Cuban musical explosion.

968 **Cuba: dos siglos de música (siglos XVI and XVII).** (Cuba: two centuries of music [16th and 17th centuries].)
Gloria Antolitía. Havana: Editorial Letras Cubanas, 1984. 109p. bibliog.

The author traces the 16th-century evolution of musical forms and instruments, from the initial blend of drum, trumpet and bell, to the wind family, and through religious and popular influences. She portrays musical expression as intrinsic to the emerging 17th-century identity, as the popular black influence brings new instruments into the mainstream.

969 **Dance and diplomacy: the Cuban National Ballet.**
Aaron Segal. *Caribbean Review*, vol. 9, no. 1 (winter 1980), p. 30-32.

The story of the Cuban National Ballet is traced throughout the 1960s and 1970s under its director and leading ballerina Alicia Alonso. The author highlights its role in presenting a positive image of Cuba abroad.

970 **Del bardo que te canta.** (Of the bard who sings to you.)
Margarita Mateo Palmer. Havana: Editorial Letras Cubanas, 1988. 329p. bibliog.

An in-depth study of the traditional Cuban song movement, the *trova tradicional*, based on interviews with performers and on song lyrics which cover love, politics, landscape, humour and satire.

971 **Del canto y el tiempo.** (Of song and time.)
Argeliers León. Havana: Editorial Pueblo y Educación, 1984. 319p. bibliog.

A history of Cuban music, tracing the various African and Hispanic influences, from earliest colonial times to the *son*, rumba, guaracha and bolero of the present. The author, a respected musicologist and composer, attempts to place developments in their sociopolitical context. He includes the words and music of many songs, as well as attractive line-drawings of instruments and historical illustrations.

972　**La Diane Havanaise, ou la rumba s'appelle Chano.** (Havana reveille, or the rumba is called Chano.)
　　　Mayito and Marucha (Mario García Joya, María E. Haya). Havana: Editorial José Martí, 1985. 104p.

This is a book of 63 period photographs of traditional musical groups and people dancing the rumba. It includes introductory articles by the musicologist Leonardo Acosta and the novelist Jesús Díaz, and brief histories of typical Cuban instruments.

973　**From the drum to the synthesizer.**
　　　Leonardo Acosta, translated by Margarita Zimmerman. Havana: Editorial José Martí, 1987. 134p.

Also published in Spanish (1982) and French (1985), this collection of seven essays by a well-known performer and musicologist, covers various aspects of contemporary Cuban music including the origins of the mambo, instrumental formats, and music in film.

974　**Ignacio Cervantes y la danza en Cuba.** (Ignacio Cervantes and dance in Cuba.)
　　　Solomon Gadles Mikowsky. Havana: Editorial Letras Cubanas, 1988. 332p.

A scholarly study of the major Cuban composer Ignacio Cervantes (1847-1905).

975　**Música colonial cubana: tomo I (1812-1902).** (Cuban colonial music: volume I [1812-1902].)
　　　Zoila Lapique Becali. Havana: Editorial Letras Cubanas, 1979. 295p.

The first in a series of volumes on Cuban colonial music, this reproduces various pieces of music from the colonial period. Providing an insight into the history of 19th-century Cuban music, the author emphasizes the changes and developments in style which took place throughout that time. Another work by the same author is *Una tradición litográfica* (A lithographic tradition) published in Havana in 1969 by Editorial Consejo Nacional de Cultura.

976　**La música de las sociedades de tumba francesa.** (The music of the 'tumba francesa' societies.)
　　　Olavo Alén. Havana: Casa de las Américas, 1986. 271p. bibliog.

Alén presents a study in the musicology of the Haitian-origin 'tumba francesa' (literally French drum), which was brought to the coffee plantations of eastern Cuba in the aftermath of the 1791-1804 Haitian revolution. The text provides the background to the French and Haitian immigration and the growth and development of the societies through Cuba's 19th-century independence wars and 20th-century republic. The bulk of the work consists of a description of the fiestas, instruments, chants, melody and rhythm, with appendices containing musical scores and tables of values.

977   **La música en Cuba.** (Music in Cuba.)
      Alejo Carpentier.   Havana: Editorial Letras Cubanas, 1988. 346p.
An account first published in 1945, of the history of popular and 'highbrow' Cuban music. Known best as a novelist, Carpentier was himself a pianist and composer.

978   **La música, lo cubano y la innovación.** (Music, Cubanness and innovation.)
      Leo Brouwer.   Havana: Editorial Letras Cubanas, 1989. 2nd ed. 117p.
A lengthy essay by Cuba's most renowned living composer and musicologist who, in theory and performance, has built bridges between classical and Cuban popular music. The publication contains eight pages of plates.

979   **La música y la danza en Cuba.** (Music and dance in Cuba.)
      Odilio Urfé.   In: *Africa en América Latina.*   Edited by Manuel Moreno Fraginals for UNESCO.   Mexico City: Siglo Veintiuno Editores, 1977, p. 215-38.
A leading musicologist and pianist traces the African roots and evolution of Cuban music and dance, from that of the African societies or *cabildos*, through ritual, ceremonial and profane music, to modern dance and popular musical forms. The article documents the Afro-Cuban stamp of Cuban musical nationalism, including the work of classical Cuban composers written in a more European vein.

980   **La Nueva Trova: written and sung poetry in Cuba.**
      Rigo Vásquez.   *Third Text*, no. 20 (autumn 1992), p. 69-76.
The Cuban song movement of over two decades is explored by Vásquez in the context of the fusion of orality, poetry and music plus the developed mass media in Cuba. The aesthetic strength deriving from fusing literature and music is highlighted with specific reference to the works of singer-composers Pablo Milanés and Silvio Rodríguez.

981   **Presencia y vigencia de Brindis de Salas.** (Presence and relevance of Brindis de Salas.)
      Selection, introduction and notes by Armando Toledo.   Havana: Editorial Letras Cubanas, 1981. 193p. bibliog.
The introduction to this collection traces the history of Brindis de Salas, the black virtuoso violinist of early 19th-century Cuban musical salons. At a time when slavery was at its height, he belonged to Havana's sizeable free coloured community, which was strong in the skilled trades and the arts and crafts. Dubbed the 'black prince of the violin' and the 'black Paganini', he conquered musical circles in Europe and the Americas. The collection includes a piece by Nicolás Guillén written in 1935, press articles over the years and from around the world, and a chronology of his life.

982   **Rita la única.** (The one and only Rita.)
      Aldo Martínez Malo.   Havana: Editora Abril, 1988. 164p.
This is a collection of journalistic articles on the singer Rita Montaner (1900-58) by Nicolás Guillén, Alejo Carpentier and others. The volume also contains poems written in her honour, photographs and a chronology of her life.

983 **Salsa guidebook for piano and ensemble.**
Rebeca Mauleón.   Petaluma, California: Sher Music Co., 1993. 259p.

This guidebook provides basic background information on salsa. It focuses on certain technical aspects and fundamentals of salsa (such as the rhythmic structure), and includes musical examples, excerpts of musical scores, a discography and recommended listening list, a glossary of terms, and photographs of musicians.

984 **Salsa! Havana heat, Bronx beat.**
Hernando Calvo Ospina, translated by Nick Caistor.   London: Latin America Bureau, 1995. 151p.

Salsa is the generic term for a range of dance music rhythms originating in the Hispanic Caribbean, especially Cuba (and its musical form *son*) and Puerto Rico, but also the Dominican Republic, Colombia and Venezuela. This book traces salsa from its Cuban roots to the synthesis of musical genres brought about by New York's Hispanic communities, and its subsequent rise to worldwide popularity.

985 **Salsiology: Afro-Cuban music and the evolution of salsa in New York City.**
Edited by Vernon W. Boggs.   New York: Excelsior Music Publishing Company, 1992. 386p.

The Cuban presence in the United States is perhaps at its most pervasive in music, and the musical impact was nowhere greater than in New York, starting with the rumba in the 1920s and merging with other Latin rhythms into the generic salsa. In this richly informative book the story is told in a collection of interviews, biographical sketches, celebrity reminiscences, analysis and history of the development of salsa in New York, from nightclubs and dance venues; disc jockeys, musicians, arrangers and composers; to the record industry and business of Latin music.

986 **Silvio: que levante la mano, la guitarra.** (Silvio: let the guitar raise its hand.)
Víctor Casáus, Luis Rogelio Nogueras.   Havana: Editorial Letras Cubanas, 1988. 287p.

Presents the story of the popular Cuban singer-composer Silvio Rodríguez, with the lyrics of his songs and many photographs.

987 **El son cubano: poesía general.** (Cuban *son* and poetry.)
Samuel Feijóo.   Havana: Editorial Letras Cubanas, 1986. 496p.

An in-depth study of the Cuban musical and poetic form, and of its antecedents and dissemination throughout the Caribbean. A leading Cuban folklorist, the author delves into the roots of the word *son*; Spanish dance and music antecedents (fandango, cahacona, guineo) and Cuban developments (Ma Teodora, *son*, sucu-sucu); literature and lyrics (Spanish, Cuban, Amerindian, Afro-Latin, Afro-Caribbean); and the influence of the *son* on black Cuban poetry (Crespo, Benítez del Cristo, Guillén).

Theatre and film

988 **Alea: una retrospectiva crítica.** (Alea: a critical retrospective.)
Edited by Ambrosio Fornet. Havana: Editorial Letras Cubanas, 1987.
353p.

A singular collection of reviews of the work of Cuba's leading film-maker Tomás
Gutiérrez Alea, with an introduction as well as interviews, articles and texts by Alea
himself, published in Cuba and abroad. The book covers a period of over a quarter of
a century, beginning in 1960, and includes a chronology of his life, a filmography and
a list of awards he has received.

989 **Los bailes y el teatro de los negros en el folklore de Cuba.** (Black
dances and theatre in the folklore of Cuba.)
Fernando Ortiz.   Havana: Editorial Letras Cubanas, 1985. 2nd ed.
588p. bibliog.

Described by musicologist Argeliers León in his prologue as a companion volume to
another seminal work by Ortiz, *La africanía de la música folklórica de Cuba*, this
volume traces, with a wealth of detail, the historical development and social
significance of the performance arts brought to Cuba by Africans and preserved by
their descendants. It includes historical engravings and the words and music (voice
and *batá* drum parts) to many of the traditional chants dedicated to African deities.

990 **Cinema and social change in Latin America.**
Edited by Julianne Burton.   Austin, Texas: University of Texas Press,
1986. 302p.

The volume includes interviews with Cuban film-makers Tomás Gutiérrez Alea, Julio
García Espinosa and Humberto Solás, and with Cuban film critic Enrique Colina.

991 **Le cinéma cubain.** (Cuban cinema.)
Edited by Paulo Antonio Paranagua, translated into French by Nicole
Canto, François Maspero, Monique Roumette.   Paris: Editions du
Centre Georges Pompidou, 1990. 198p. bibliog.

This attractively illustrated book reviews the history of Cuban film from the days of the
silent movies, through the early talkies, to the first thirty years of the revolutionary period.
Trends in Cuban film-making are discussed as well as the interaction between cinema,
culture and society in this nation of avid cinema-goers. A directory of Cuban film-makers
together with profiles of four leading personalities – Santiago Álvarez, Tomás Gutiérrez
Alea and Humberto Solás, and animator Juan Padrón – and an index of films, make
this a valuable reference work. This is the most complete guide to Cuban cinema.

992 **Cinema in revolutionary Cuba.**
Nissa Torrents.   In: *Collected Seminar Papers*, no. 29.   London:
University of London, Institute of Commonwealth Studies, 1982,
p. 8-16. (Caribbean Societies, vol. 1).

A dynamic and prolific revolutionary film industry has grown up in Cuba and this
article provides an interpretation of films as a weapon in revolutionary Cuba.

Documentary work, fiction and animation are intended to educate and entertain, and imaginatively and didactically pick up issues important to Cuba's past and present.

993 Les cinémas de l'Amérique latine. (Latin American cinema.)
Guy Hennebelle, Alfonso Gumacio-Dagrón, with Paulo Antonio Paranagua, René Prédal. Paris: L'Herminier, 1981. 543p. bibliog.

The history and structure of Latin American film industries is covered in this work, with reference to film-makers and their films, on a country-by-country basis. The Cuba chapter (54p.), by Julianne Burton, provides an overview of pre-revolutionary Cuban film, from rebel cinema to the National Film Institute in the 1960s, and the film production of the revolution, and is illustrated with stills.

994 Cuba: a view from inside: short films by and about Cuban women.
Center for Cuban Studies. New York: Center for Cuban Studies, [n.d.]. 49p.

Twenty-four photographs are included in this catalogue, along with essays by Jean Stubbs, Catherine Benamou and Coco Fusco. There is a homage to Sara Gómez and descriptions of eighteen short films by and about Cuban women. All of the films were made in Cuba and the catalogue contains interviews with the directors: Guillermo Centeno; Rebeca Chávez; Gerardo Chijona; Sara Gómez; Fernando Pérez; Miriam Talavera; Marisol Trujillo; Oscar Valdés; and Mayra Vilasís.

995 Cuban cinema and the Afro-Cuban heritage.
Interviewed by Julianne Burton, Gary Crowdus. In: *Film and politics in the Third World.* Edited by John D. Druming. Westport, Connecticut: Praeger, 1985, p. 267-77. (Reprinted from *The Black Scholar*, vol. 8, nos. 8-10 [summer 1977]).

In interview the Afro-Cuban film-maker Sergio Giral talks about his life, as a child and adolescent in Cuba, as a young man in New York, and working in film in Cuba in the 1960s and 1970s. During those years, he made political documentaries and produced his trilogy of feature films reconstructing slavery in Cuba.

996 The Cuban image: cinema and cultural politics in Cuba.
Michael Chanan. Bloomington, Indiana: Indiana University Press, 1985. 314p. bibliog.

This is possibly the single most important text on revolutionary Cuban film. It is both an exploration of Cuban film history and Cuban history through film, with discussion of individual films, film-making and cultural politics, directors, and actors. Published in the same year was 'Film and revolution in Cuba: the first 25 years' by Julianne Burton, in *Cuba: twenty-five years of revolution, 1959-1984.* Edited by Sandor Halebsky, John M. Kirk (New York: Praeger, 1985, p. 134-53).

997 Delirios y visiones de José Jacinto Milanés. (Delirium and visions of José Jacinto Milanés.)
Tomás González. Havana: UNEAC, 1988. 95p.

This is the script for a play with a highly personal interpretation of the 19th-century Cuban romantic poet José Jacinto Milanés, himself an enigmatic figure in the world of

Cuban drama. Milanés has his first nervous breakdown after his first play and teeters between obscurity and lucidity, until he becomes a mute in the last eleven years of his life.

998 **10 años del nuevo cine latinoamericano.** (10 years of the new Latin American cinema.)
Teresa Toledo. Madrid: Verdoux, SL, 1989. 725p.

Toledo has compiled a complete listing, for the period 1979-89, of all film and video features and documentaries entered in the Latin American Film Festival held every December in Havana, and in which Cuban productions feature prominently. There is also a listing of production and distribution companies represented at the festivals.

999 **Fresa y chocolate.** (Strawberry and chocolate.)
Senel Paz. Navarra, Spain: Txalaparta, 1994. 63p.

Originally published as *El lobo, el bosque y el hombre nuevo* (The wolf, the forest and the new man), this short story won its author the prestigious Franco-Mexican Juan Rulfo Prize. Paz then adapted it for the theatre, and later for the screen. Under the title *Fresa y chocolate* it was the first ever Cuban production to receive an Oscar nomination (in the Best Foreign Film section). Described by Paz and the film's directors as a plea for tolerance, it was hailed internationally for championing gay rights and recognized in Cuba as heralding a relaxation of public attitudes towards gays and lesbians. See also *Conducta impropia* (Improper conduct) by Nestor Almendros, Orlando Jiménez Leal (Madrid: Editorial Playor, 1984). The script for Almendros's controversial film about the repression of homosexuality in Cuba consists mainly of interviews with Cuban exiled homosexuals, many of whom left in the 1980 Mariel boatlift. Their testimonies paint a poignant story of anti-homosexual conformity but in the end fail in the attempt to attribute this entirely to the repressive nature of the revolution and Castro.

1000 **Magical reels: a history of cinema in Latin America.**
John King. London: Verso, 1990. 266p. bibliog.

Included in this comprehensive analysis of Latin American cinema is a chapter on film-making in revolutionary Cuba. This covers: the early years of the Cuban Film Institute, 1959-69, and the early debates on revolutionary cinema; and the 1970s and 1980s move away from imperfect cinema to features and entertainment films.

1001 **Memories of underdevelopment and Inconsolable memories.**
Tomás Gutiérrez Alea, Edmundo Desnoes, with an introduction by Michael Chanan. New Brunswick, New Jersey: Rutgers University Press, 1990. 258p. bibliog.

Memories of underdevelopment remains the film classic of the Cuban revolution, and Alea its most celebrated film-maker. This volume contains the script of Alea's film and the text of the novel *Inconsolable memories* by Edmundo Desnoes on which the film was based, as well as press reviews and commentaries. The introduction places the film in context and is followed by a biographical sketch of its maker. The filmography of Alea is listed as an annex.

1002 **Monólogos teatrales cubanos.** (Monologues of Cuban theatre.)
Selection and prologue by Francisco Garzón Céspedes. Havana:
Editorial Letras Cubanas, 1989. 524p.

A collection of monologues from Cuban plays before and after 1959 which make their
statement on the human condition.

1003 **Perspectives on Cuban theatre.**
George W. Woodward. *Revista / Review Interamericana*, vol. 9,
no. 1 (spring 1979), p. 42-49.

Woodward discusses state policy and support for the theatre in Cuba, and the condition of playwrights.

1004 **Repertorio teatral.** (Theatrical repertory.)
Prologue by Amado del Pino. Havana: Editorial Letras Cubanas,
1991. 421p.

The prologue sets the scene for this collection of scripts of six plays by contemporary
Cuban playwrights. *El esquema* (The scheme) by Freddy Artiles pokes fun at
caricature, prototype, and paradigmatic personalities ('the bold', 'the conservative',
'the optimist', 'the orthodox'). *Mónica* by Gerardo Fernández is about how money
corrupts, in this case two 'macho' characters, the factory manager and the party
secretary. *La querida de Enramada* (The Enramada Street mistress) by Gerardo Fulleda
León centres on Santiago de Cuba's historically famous Enramada Street and a local
politician, his family and his mistress. *Los juegos de la trastienda* (Backroom games)
by Tomás González is an improvised story of a young man and a young woman active
in the late 1950s underground movement against Batista. *Weekend en Bahía* by Alberto
Pedro became the theatre hit of the 1980s, and portrays a young Cuban American who
returns on a visit and spends the whole night talking with an old flame. Finally, *Sábado
corto* (Free Saturday) by Héctor Quintero is a humorous look at everyday
neighbourhood ups and downs on a Saturday off work. Also of interest are: *Algunos
dramas de la colonía* (Colonial dramas) by Gerardo Fulleda León (Havana: Editorial
Letras Cubanas, 1984. 307p.) which contains the scripts of three plays; and *Dramas de
imaginación y urgencia* (Dramas of imagination and urgency) by Nicolás Dorr
(Havana: UNEAC, 1987. 340p.) containing eight plays written between 1960 and 1980.

1005 **Revolutionary Cuban cinema.**
Jump Cut, no. 19 (1979), p. 17-33; no. 20 (1980), p. 13-20.

Presented in a special section, this is a two-part feature on Cuban cinema, including an
introductory overview by Julianne Burton; reviews of documentaries ('Simparele',
'With the Cuban women', 'Life in Cuban boarding schools') and feature films (*Lucía*;
One way or another; *A woman, a man, a city*; *The adventures of Juan Quin Quin*);
interviews with Humberto Solás, Manuel Octavio Gómez; and an English translation
of Julio García Espinosa's 'For an imperfect cinema'.

1006 **Seeing, being seen: 'Portrait of Teresa', or the contradictions of
sexual politics in contemporary Cuba.**
Julianne Burton. *Social Text*, no. 4 (fall 1988), p. 79-95.

A perceptive analysis of Pastor Vega's 1979 feature film about a woman textile
worker whose involvement in the trade union amateur theatre movement brings her

marriage to an end. In the context of a board debate taking place in Cuba, the film graphically tackles the dual standards of work and morality, the socialization of children, and a female subject in her own right.

1007   **Socialist ensembles: theater and state in Cuba and Nicaragua.**
        Randy Martin.   Minneapolis, Minnesota: University of Minnesota
        Press, 1994. bibliog. (Cultural Politics, vol. 8).

This study of the ethnography of theatre and political culture draws the focus away from the state and political leaders to civil society, homing in on the dynamics of change in daily life. Theatre is used as the privileged object of analysis in two countries experiencing disruptive external forces and internal policies. There are specific chapters on sources of political culture in Cuba and Cuban theatre under rectification.

1008   **Teatralización del folklore y otros ensayos.** (The theatricalization
        of folklore and other essays.)
        Ramiro Guerra.   Havana: Editorial Letras Cubanas, 1989. 157p.
        bibliog.

A discussion of the process by which various folk traditions became theatrical manifestations. There are chapters on the *trinitarias*, traditional dances of the city of Trinidad; the *parrandas* of Remedios, which involve mass participation by the town's inhabitants; and the Spanish roots of Cuban dance.

1009   **Teatro Alhambra: antología.** (Alhambra Theatre: anthology.)
        Edited by Eduardo Robreño.   Havana: Editorial Letras Cubanas,
        1979. 706p. bibliog.

A collection of eleven of the most representative works of the *teatro bufo* burlesque genre popular in Havana in the first three decades of the 20th century. A prologue is provided by the editor along with a historical study by Álvaro López placing it in its historical and social context.

1010   **Teatro Escambray.** (Escambray Theatre.)
        Compiled by Rine Leal, foreword by Graziella Pogolotti.   Havana:
        Editorial Letras Cubanas, 1990. 395p.

Includes the scripts of plays performed by the Escambray Theatre: *Y si fuera así* (And if it were thus), based on Bertolt Brecht's *Mother Courage*; Albio Paz' *El paraíso recobrado* (Paradise regained), versions one, two and three (1976); and Sergio González' *Las provisiones* (The provisions) from 1975. The extensive foreword situates the emergence of the Escambray Theatre Group in the context of developments in Cuban theatre in the 1960s. A final chapter on the inclusion of a visual arts dimension, and a chronology of significant dates for the theatre group complete the book.

1011   **Theater and political criteria in Cuba: Casa de las Américas awards, 1960-1983.**
Paul Christopher Smith.   *Cuban Studies*, vol. 14, no. 1 (winter 1984), p. 43-47.

This article looks at the awards that were made over the years in the context of changing ideological developments and artistic modes of expression. See also 'Theater and cinematography' by Julio Matas, in *Revolutionary change in Cuba*. Edited by Carmelo Mesa-Lago (Pittsburgh: University of Pittsburgh Press, 1971, p. 427-45).

1012   **The viewers' dialectic.**
Tomás Gutiérrez Alea, translated and introduced by Julia Lesage.
Havana: Editorial José Martí, 1988. 89p.

Cuba's leading film-maker and film theorist discusses media–spectator relations, the aesthetics of cinema, and theories of Aristotle, Brecht and Eisenstein.

Folklore and festivals

1013   **Los animales en el folklore y la magia de Cuba.** (Animals in folklore and the magic of Cuba.)
Lydia Cabrera.   Miami, Florida: Universal, 1988. 208p.

This is one of the more recent works by the prolific Cuban-American folklorist. Another by the same author which may also be of interest is: *Supersticiones y buenos consejos* (Superstitions and good advice) (Miami, Florida: Universal, 1987).

1014   **El carnaval santiaguero.** (Santiago carnival.)
Nancy Pérez Rodríguez.   Santiago de Cuba: Editorial Oriente, 1988. 2 vols.

Presents a compilation of municipal decrees, press articles and correspondence, chronologically arranged, documenting the history of Santiago de Cuba carnival from the 17th century to 1958. This incorporates and builds on the author's earlier work documenting Cabildo Carabalí Isuama in Santiago de Cuba, from its African nation origins in the early 19th century, through its evolution as an Afro-Cuban mutual aid society, to the carnival *comparsa* of the present day.

1015   **Carnival and festivals in Cuba.**
Judith Bettelheim.   In: *Caribbean festival arts*.   Edited by John W. Nunley, Judith Bettelheim.   Seattle: University of Washington Press, 1988, p. 137-46.

This entry in the catalogue accompanying a major 1988 exhibition of Caribbean festival arts provides a vivid description of carnival and festivals in three major Cuban cities: Havana; Matanzas; and Santiago de Cuba. Bettelheim considers their history and some of the costumes associated with them. Another study by Bettelheim of carnival in Santiago de Cuba is: 'Ethnicity, gender and power: carnival in Santiago de Cuba', in *Negotiating performance, gender, sexuality and theatricality in Latin*

America. Edited by Diana Taylor, Juan Villegas (Durham, North Carolina; London: Duke University Press, 1994, p. 176-212).

1016   **Chago de Guisa.**
Gerardo Fulleda León.   Havana: Casa de las Américas, 1989. 145p.
Contains the script of the 1989 Casa de las Américas award-winning play which is inspired by a *patakín* (legend) of Yoruba origin. It concerns the story of a young man who seeks out the path which will reveal the secret of wisdom behind avarice, envy, pride, greed, ingratitude, disobedience, death and love.

1017   **Cuban counterpoint: tobacco and sugar.**
Fernando Ortiz, introduction by Fernando Coronil.   Philadelphia,
Pennsylvania: Temple University Press, 1995. 416p.
A timely new edition of the classic 1940 work by Cuba's prolific leading ethnographer, which skilfully blends elements of the economy with folklore, social custom and popular culture. One of the more important treatises about the two principal sectors of the economy of Cuba, the work's main thesis is that tobacco signified freedom and independence, while sugar spelled slavery and dependence. Ortiz also elaborates on his theory of transculturation, as opposed to acculturation, whereby cultures fuse and transpose rather than assimilate one to the other.

1018   **Cuban festivals: an illustrated anthology.**
Edited by Judith Bettelheim.   New York: Garland Press, 1993. 261p.
This unique anthology includes the first English-language translation of Cuban ethnographer Fernando Ortiz's classic 1920s study of the old Havana festival 'Day of the Kings', with an annotated glossary. It also contains a contemporary glossary and personal recollections of popular festivals by Cuban scholars, the editor's account of Haitian-Cuban festivals, and forty illustrations.

1019   **Diálogos imaginarios.** (Imaginary dialogues.)
Rogelio Martínez Furé.   Havana: Editorial Arte y Literatura, 1979.
283p. bibliog.
By now a classic work, this text is divided into two dialogues, one with Africa and one with Cuba. The first half of the book engages with old and contemporary figures in the world of African arts and civilizations, while the second half looks at the peoples, cultures and legends of African origin that shaped Cuba. The author, one of Cuba's leading contemporary Afro-Cuban folklorists, an arts adviser and a singer, ends with an imaginary dialogue with his mentor, the late Cuban ethnographer Fernando Ortiz. In it, he situates Cuba firmly in a broader Pan-Caribbean culture.

1020   **Grupos folklóricos de Santiago de Cuba.** (Folklore groups of
Santiago de Cuba.)
José Millet, Rafael Brea.   Santiago de Cuba: Editorial Oriente, 1989.
178p. bibliog.
Two researchers of the Casa del Caribe in Santiago de Cuba document the strong folklore tradition of the city and of eastern Cuba. The book is divided into five sections: the *cabildos* Carabalí Izuama and Carabalí Olugo; the French-Haitian *tumba francesa* and Paseo El Tivolí; the Santiago carnival groups, *comparsas* (Los Hoyos, El

Guayabito, San Agustín, Paso Franco, San Pedrito, and El Alto Pino), and *paseos* (La Quimona, La Placita, Heredia, Sueño, El Comercio, and Los Textileros); the re-vitalization of folklore and theatre groups (Cabildo Teatral Santiago, Conjunto Folklórico de Oriente, Conjunto Folklórico Cutumba, Grupo Caribe and others); and a vocabulary of festivals.

1021 **The *ibelles* and the lost paths.**
Pedro Pérez Sarduy, translated by Jean Stubbs. In: *Under the storyteller's spell: folk-tales from the Caribbean.* Edited by Faustin Charles. London: Penguin, 1991, p. 75-84.

In this folk-tale, *ibelles* (male twins) are sent by the gods Oludumare and Olorun to an old African couple on a tumbledown estate in western Pinar del Río. When they are grown, they follow the path of all their older brothers who left home never to be seen again. As identical twins, they are able to trick the devil-figure, Okurri Boroku, re-open the paths and bring back all those who had been lost. To this day, twins are very special in Cuba.

1022 **Mitología cubana.** (Cuban mythology.)
Samuel Feijóo. Havana: Editorial Letras Cubanas, 1986. 496p.

An extensive compilation of tales displaying the strong creative fantasy and humour in mythology which originates from Indians, Spaniards, Africans and Cuban creoles striving for a national identity. Extraordinary animals, fireballs, enchanted places, headless horsemen, mysterious lights, flying witches and horrible apparitions make up the panorama of the nation's folklore.

1023 **El negro en la literatura folklórica cubana.** (The black man in Cuban folk literature.)
Samuel Feijóo. Havana: Editorial Letras Cubanas, 1987. 315p.

This anthology of oral traditions, refrains, stories, myths and fables evidences the African influence in Hispanic-American culture. Based on both library research and extensive fieldwork recordings, it introduces the reader to oral tradition in the Americas and Cuba, with an emphasis on that which has been documented and/or passed on during the 19th and 20th centuries. The author details sayings, song lyrics, and a wealth of Afro-Cuban stories told over generations.

Architecture

1024 **Apuntes para una historia sobre los constructores cubanos.** (Notes for a history of Cuban builders.)
Llilian Llanes. Havana: Editorial Letras Cubanas, 1985. 84p. bibliog.

Deals largely with developments in the provision of professional training for Cuban architects and builders in the 19th and early 20th centuries, and the relationships between the two groups. The work includes engravings, photographs and blueprints of representative buildings of the period.

1025 **Architecture and the building industry in contemporary Cuba.**
Howard Glazer.   In: *Cuba: a different America.*   Edited by
Wilber A. Chaffee, Jr., Gary Prevost.   Totowa, New Jersey: Rowman
& Littlefield, 1989, p. 76-101. bibliog.

Traces the history of home building in Cuba from the idealistic early days of the 1959 Housing Law, which led to the replacement of the worst shanty towns by apartment blocks. Glazer looks at state-sponsored housing programmes in rural areas; self-help housing, in particular the microbrigades; the first major urban redevelopment schemes in the 1970s; and the 1984 Housing Law, passed following the realization that plans were over-optimistic. The account includes a useful explanation of ownership patterns.

1026 **La arquitectura colonial cubana del siglo XIX.** (Cuban
19th-century colonial architecture.)
Joaquín E. Weiss.   Havana: Junta Nacional de Arqueología y
Etnología, 1960. 126p.

A survey of Cuban public and commercial premises and private dwellings built in the late colonial period.

1027 **La arquitectura de hoteles en la revolución cubana.** (Hotel
architecture in the Cuban revolution.)
Raúl González Romero, et al.   Havana: Ministry of Construction,
[n.d.]. 201p.

The author provides an overview of the history of hotel construction in Cuba, detailing works that were completed in the 1970s, and projected works, and including photographs, ground plans and specifications. The emphasis in this period was on catering to a new kind of tourism, looking not only for sun, sand and sea, but also to learn about revolutionary developments. Hotel architecture sought to use low-cost local materials, maximize climatic conditions and respect the surrounding nature.

1028 **Arquitectura y urbanismo de la revolución cubana.** (Architecture
and town planning in the Cuban revolution.)
Roberto Segre.   Havana: Editorial Pueblo y Educación, 1989. 254p.
bibliog.

Contextualizes the modernism which informed the ideology and culture of Cuban architecture between 1930 and 1958, by way of a prologue to two revolutionary periods: 1959-69 and 1970-85. The first covers early rural–urban territorial redefinition, experimental construction and prefabrication. The second focuses on Havana, Old Havana in particular, as well as public works such as mass housing and school building. The work is meticulously researched and illustrated.

1029 **La ciudad de las columnas.** (The city of columns.)
Alejo Carpentier.   Havana: Editorial Letras Cubanas, 1982. 84p.

A lyrical and informative essay in which one of Cuba's foremost novelists conjures up the atmosphere of the streets and thoroughfares of Havana's oldest districts. Evocative photographs by Grandal are included.

1030 **Continuità e rinnovamento nell'architettura cubana del XX secolo.** (Continuity and renewal in Cuban 20th-century architecture.)
Roberto Segre.   *Casabella*, vol. 45, no. 466 (Feb. 1981), p. 10-19, 61-62. bibliog.

A short history of Cuban architecture from colonial times is followed by a discussion of the conceptual problems faced by Cuban architects since 1959, including those arising from early attempts to apply socialist ideology to design. In particular, the author stresses the dialectic between the avant-garde and popular expression. There is a summary in English and thirty-one illustrations.

1031 **Cuba: architecture in countries in the process of development.**
Havana: Union of Architects of Cuba, 1963. 118p.

Provides an overview of the rich colonial and modern architecture of Cuba prior to the revolution, and considers the country's architecture as a reflection of its development. Illustrated with ground plans and photographs, the text focuses on major architecture of the early years of the revolution: rural and urban schools; hospitals; factories; farms; and housing. The book details the development of building techniques, pre- and post-1959.

1032 **La Habana y la crisis urbana, desafíos y propuestas.** (Havana and the urban crisis, challenges and proposals.)
Gina Rey.   *Convenio*, no. 2 (1994), p. 3-7. (University of Zurich, Centre for Scientific Research and Documentation for Latin America and the Caribbean; Havana: University of Havana Faculty of Philosophy and History).

Rey offers a short discussion, which places Cuba in the context of the generalized urban crisis, and notes that while Havana is suffering from a high degree of accumulated physical deterioration it has not been subjected to indiscriminate demolition of its architectural heritage. She discusses aspects of the city's conservation and development strategy, including popular participation in planning and execution.

1033 **Para un análisis histórico y de la tipología arquitectónica de la Ciudad de Remedios.** (Towards a historical analysis and architectural typology of the city of Remedios.)
A. Sánchez Cepero, L. Torres Manso.   *Islas*, no. 73 (1982), p. 123-65.

The authors link changing architectural styles in the city of Remedios, which has an interesting selection of buildings from the colonial period, to various historical factors.

1034 **Sobre la marea de los siglos.** (On the tide of the centuries.)
Regino Pedroso. Havana: Editorial Letras Cubanas, 1987. 82p.
bibliog.

A series of brief historical sketches, written in poetic vein, in which one of Cuba's foremost contemporary writers looks at twenty of Havana's best-known colonial buildings.

1035 **Unos que otros.** (A bunch of people.)
Ernesto Fernández. Havana: Editorial Arte y Literatura, 1978.
unpaginated.

This is a photographic essay of the experience of a construction minibrigade which started in 1972. The minibrigade comprised thirty-three writers, photographers, journalists, designers, print workers and students who were given a crash course in construction work.

1036 **La urbanización de las murallas: dependencia y modernidad.**
(Urbanization of the walled city: from colonial dependence to modernity.)
Carlos Venegas Fornias. Havana: Editorial Letras Cubanas, 1990.
129p. bibliog.

In this study the author traces how, in successive historical periods, socio-political, economic and cultural developments have influenced city planning and architecture in the area of Old Havana formerly occupied by the city walls.

1037 **Vida, mansión y muerte de la burguesía cubana.** (Life, mansions and death of the Cuban bourgeoisie.)
Emma Alvárez-Tabío Albo. Havana: Editorial Letras Cubanas, 1989. 104p.

Presents an illustrated account of the ostentatious dwellings built by the *nouveaux riches* of Havana in the period 1900-30, with a socio-political and cultural profile of those who lived in them.

Old Havana, Cuba.
See item no. 9.

Un análisis psicosocial del cubano, 1898-1925. (A psychosocial analysis of the Cuban, 1898-1925.)
See item no. 166.

The African presence in Cuban culture.
See item no. 322.

Cómo surgió la cultura nacional. (The birth of a national culture.)
See item no. 325.

Flash of the spirit: African & Afro-American art and philosophy.
See item no. 327.

Culture and The Arts

El folclor médico de Cuba. (Medical folklore of Cuba.)
See item no. 485.

La Habana: salas del Museo Nacional de Cuba, Palacio de Bellas Artes.
(Havana: in the halls of the National Fine Arts Museum of Cuba.)
See item no. 1055.

Arquitectura Cuba. (Architecture Cuba.)
See item no. 1092.

Cine Cubano. (Cuban cinema.)
See item no. 1102.

Del Caribe. (From the Caribbean.)
See item no. 1103.

Revolución y Cultura. (Revolution and Culture.)
See item no. 1106.

Anales del Caribe. (Annals of the Caribbean.)
See item no. 1115.

Temas – Cultura, Ideología, Sociedad. (Themes – Culture, Ideology, Society.)
See item no. 1119.

Diccionario de la música cubana. (Dictionary of Cuban music.)
See item no. 1136.

Sport and Leisure

1038 All about Cuban cookery.
Josefina Alvarez. Los Angeles, California: AACC Publisher, 1991. 168p.

The scarcity of Cuban cookbooks makes this a collector's item, with the added bonus that it is in both English and Spanish. Written by a culinary art teacher, the book includes a variety of Cuban recipes, selected to represent the finest and simplest cooking from all parts of the island. These are organized by food type, with a brief description of their origin. Drinks recipes are also included, with a list of US market outlets for the ingredients.

1039 Baseball in Cuba.
Eric A. Wagner. *Journal of Popular Culture*, vol. 18, no. 1 (1984), p. 113-20.

Surveys the history of baseball in Cuba and the continued popularity of the sport since Castro's rise to power. See also: 'Cuban baseball' by Bruce Brown (*Atlantic*, vol. 253 [June 1984]); and *El béisbol: travels through the Pan-American pastime* by John Krich (New York: Atlantic Monthly Press, 1989).

1040 Cars of Cuba.
Essay by Cristina García, photographs by Joshua Greene, created by D. D. Allen. New York: Harry N. Abrams, 1995. 64p.

Cuba in the 1990s is famed for its old American cars of the 1940s and 1950s. These 53 photographs, with an essay by Cuban-American novelist Cristina García, offer a delightful taste of the living car museum that is Cuba.

1041 The connoisseur's book of the cigar.
Z. Davidoff. New York: McGraw-Hill, 1967. 92p.

Produced in an outer and inner cover made to resemble a box of cigars, this collector's item on the know-how of the smoking, choosing and keeping of cigars, is complete with after-dinner cigar quotes and anecdotes originating from suitably eminent sources. The Havana cigar is accorded pride of place and the author, himself from a major European retailing family, divulges his personal love of the cigar. A centre section comprises illustrations of famous cigar-smoking figures, along with cigar artefacts, labels and cartoons.

1042 **The Cuban sports program.**
Raudol Ruiz Aguilera. *Cuba Review*, vol. 7, no. 22 (June 1977), p. 10-20.

Considering sport within the context of the physical education and recreation programme of the revolution, the author offers reflections on sport and politics, including mass access to sport, the power of ideology for athletes representing their people and country, and sports excellence. An edited version appears in *The Cuba reader: the making of a revolutionary society*, edited by Philip Brenner, et al. (New York: Grove Press, 1989).

1043 **Fidel Castro and the quest for a revolutionary culture in Cuba.**
Julie Marie Bunck. University Park, Pennsylvania: Pennsylvania State University Press, 1994. 237p.

Examines the forces resisting efforts to mould the new *conciencia* that was one of Fidel Castro's revolutionary goals, focusing on youth, women, labour and athletes. It emphasizes the success in sports more than any other field, attributing it less to patriotism and socialism than the fact that sport offers a means to individual expression, a way to compete, and a new sports élite. This is a somewhat shallow and simplistic study, but it is not entirely devoid of interest.

1044 **Havanas: a unique blend of sun, soil and skill.**
Sergio Morera, Simon Chase, Bill Colbert. London: Hunters & Frankau, 1993. 22p.

A beautifully illustrated, full-colour publication, extolling the attributes of the tobacco growing, processing, manufacture, presentation and marketing of the Havana cigar. It contains quality reproductions of twelve famous Havana cigar labels and many more cigar bands, as well as tips on how to keep, cut, light and smoke a Havana. The book accompanies a video.

1045 **The place of sport in Cuba's foreign relations.**
Trevor Slack, David Whitson. *International Journal*, vol. 43, no. 4 (autumn 1988), p. 596-617.

Cuba's use of sport to gain international prestige is analysed in this article, which picks up on the way in which the government portrayed the nation's sporting successes as a symbol of progress. The authors also look at sport as part of aid packages to other countries.

1046 **The politics of sports in revolutionary Cuba.**
Julie Marie Bunck. *Cuban Studies*, vol. 20 (1990), p. 111-31.

Discusses Cuba's heavy emphasis on sports, the costs involved, the international successes, and the incorporation of sports stars within the country's élite.

1047   **Sport in Cuba: the diamond in the rough.**
Paula J. Pettavino, Geralyn Pye.   Pittsburgh, Pennsylvania:
University of Pittsburgh Press, 1994. 301p.

Despite the obvious success and importance of sport in Cuba, little has been written in English on the subject. This book attempts to fill that gap. On the basis of personal interviews as well as archival and secondary sources, the authors study the development of Cuban sport before 1959, paying particular attention to the national sport, baseball. They analyse how sport became such a high priority in revolutionary Cuba that the country moved from being an international sports backwater to a world sports power by the mid-1970s. They also explore the impact of both mass and élite sports on Cuban society, and raise questions for the future of Cuban sport in the crisis 1990s.

1048   **Sport in revolutionary societies: Cuba and Nicaragua.**
In: *Sport and society in Latin America: diffusion, dependency, and the rise of mass culture.*   Edited by Joseph L. Arbena.   Westport, Connecticut: Greenwood, 1988, p. 113-36.

Describes and analyses the social aspects of sport in Cuba and Nicaragua, concentrating primarily on baseball as the dominant sport in both countries. !t is argued that contemporary sport has two main emphases – mass involvement and the winning of international prestige – and that political leaders have channelled it in ways supportive of their revolutionary goals.

1049   **Sport: the people's right.**
John Griffiths.   In: *Cuba: the second decade.*   Edited by John Griffiths, Peter Griffiths.   London: Writers and Readers Cooperative, 1979, p. 247-60. bibliog.

Presents a sympathetic account of the place of sport in Cuban society, tracing the methods used to make sports facilities more widely available and to involve large sections of society in sporting activities.

Libraries, Museums, Archives and Publishing

1050 **Casa natal de José Martí.** (José Martí's birthplace.)
Armando O. Caballero. Santiago de Cuba: Editorial Oriente, 1987.
98p.

A museum guide to the house in which Cuba's independence leader José Martí (1853-95) was born. Martí's life is summarized and pictures show the contents of the house as well as portraits of Martí at various moments in his life.

1051 **Ciencia, técnica y revolución: Academia de Ciencias de Cuba.**
(Science, technology and revolution: the Cuban Academy of Sciences.)
Havana: Editorial José Martí, 1988. 143p.

A description in text and pictures of the activities and history of the Cuban Academy of Science.

1052 **Cuba: Biblioteca Nacional José Martí.**
Israel Echeverría. In: *Encyclopedia of library and information science.* Executive editor Allen Kent. New York: Marcel Dekker, 1985, vol. 39, supplement 4, p. 98-105.

Echeverría was for many years one of the key librarians at Cuba's National Library. In this piece he presents a synopsis of the library's 100-year history, from what was described as a deplorable and shameful state to the 1950s construction of its present building. Reference is made to the library's directors and holdings.

1053 **Cuban academic publishing and self-perceptions.**
Peter T. Johnson. *Cuban Studies*, vol. 18 (1988), p. 103-24.

Analyses what is being published and read in Cuba amid the drastic reductions that have taken place in recent years in the amount of material appearing. Johnson identifies five different market levels and considers the insights that can be gained from them into the Cuban situation.

266

1054 **Guía de bibliotecas de la República de Cuba.** (Guide to libraries of the Republic of Cuba.)
Consejo Nacional de Cultura, Dirección Nacional de Bibliotecas.
Havana: Biblioteca Nacional José Martí, Departamento Metódico, 1970. 101p.

A directory listing forty-three libraries and reading rooms throughout the country. Some of these are new libraries, whilst others are old, reorganized and with new names.

1055 **La Habana: salas del Museo Nacional de Cuba, Palacio de Bellas Artes.** (Havana: in the halls of the National Fine Arts Museum of Cuba.)
Havana: Museo Nacional de Cuba, 1990. 184p.

More than 100 superbly printed colour plates accompany a text on art history and short biographies of the artists whose work is housed in the Havana Fine Arts Museum. The Museum spans the main schools of Western art, and has a remarkable collection of Cuban painting and sculpture.

1056 **Libraries in Cuba.**
Carmen Rovira. In: *Encyclopedia of library and information science.* Executive editors Allen Kent, Harold Lancour. New York: Marcel Dekker, 1971, vol. 6, p. 312-32.

This is a comprehensive summary of the provision of library services in Cuba from the 1700s to the present day. It contains sections on the National Library as well as academic, special, government, public and school libraries, and also discusses training for librarianship, librarian associations, legislation and library science publications.

1057 **Patrimonio cultural e identidad.** (Cultural heritage and identity.)
Marta Arjona. Havana: Editorial Letras Cubanas, 1986. 142p.

In this selection of periodical articles and reports to international forums, the director of cultural heritage for the Ministry of Culture shares her thoughts on museums and society, and Cuba's endeavour to preserve and exhibit objects of cultural value.

1058 **Publishing and libraries in Cuba.**
R. W. Howes. *International Library Review*, vol. 14, no. 2 (July 1982), p. 317-34.

Howes reports on an official visit to Cuba by a librarian of the British Library Reference Division. The report covers the main publishing houses and booksellers, periodicals and newspapers, public libraries and library schools, with specific entries on the following: Biblioteca Nacional José Martí; Casa de las Américas; Academia de Ciencias de Cuba; Instituto de Literatura y Lingüística; Archivo Nacional; Instituto de Documentación e Información Científica y Técnica; and others. See also: 'Cuban libraries: 30 years after the revolution' by R. J. Chepesink (*American Libraries*, vol. 21, no. 10 [Nov. 1990], p. 994-97).

Libraries, Museums, Archives and Publishing

Revista de la Biblioteca Nacional José Martí. (The José Martí National Library Review.)
See item no. 1105.

Directory of vendors of Latin American library materials.
See item no. 1138.

Mass Media

1059 **Agression over the airwaves.**
National Information Agency. Havana: National Information
Agency, 1989. 32p.
This is a collection of articles by Cuban journalists on the history of anti-Castro US
broadcasts. There are bibliographical references at the end of each chapter. See also
Cuban-American radio wars: ideology in international communications by Howard H.
Frederick (Norwood, New Jersey: Alex Publishing Corporation, 1986. 200p. bibliog.),
which looks at both sides of the argument.

1060 **The CIA's war against Cuba.**
Havana: National Information Agency, 1988. 102p.
Prepared by the National Information Agency (AIN), this work was based on the
television series of the same name shown on Cuban television in 1987.

1061 **Cuba en la prensa norteamericana: la 'conexión cubana'.** (Cuba in
the North American press: the 'Cuban connection'.)
Alfredo Prieto González. *Cuadernos de Nuestra América*, vol. 7,
no. 15 (July-Dec. 1990), p. 223-57.
A Cuban academic examines the US media's treatment of Cuban issues, focusing in
particular the reporting of the Ochoa drugs trial in 1989.

1062 **Cuban telecommunications systems: confronted by global
political and technological change.**
Hopetun S. Dunn, Felipe Noguera. In: *Globalization,
communications and Caribbean identity*. Edited by Hopetun S.
Dunn. Kingston, Jamaica: Ian Randle, 1995, p. 185-96.
The constraints and possibilities facing Cuba in the telecommunications field are
considered here from a Caribbean perspective, arguing that operations are restricted
by continuing US economic sanctions.

1063 **Un desafío al monopolio de la intriga.** (A challenge to the monopoly of intrigue.)
María Begoña Arostegui Uberuaga, Gladys Blanco Cabrera.
Havana: Editora Política, 1981. 108p. bibliog.

Presents a history of the Prensa Latina news agency, which was founded in Havana in 1959 under the directorship of Argentinian journalist Jorge Ricardo Masetti, to disseminate an alternative Cuban/Latin American view of news.

1064 **La guerra oculta de la información.** (The secret information war.)
Rogelio Gárciga Marrero. Havana: Ciencias Sociales, 1986. 426p.

The author studies how information is used by transnational companies in the Third World, and the role of UNESCO, the new information order and the United States. Although this work does not deal specifically with Cuba, much of its content is of relevance.

1065 **Llorar es un placer.** (The joy of crying.)
Reynaldo González. Havana: Editorial Letras Cubanas, 1988. 355p. bibliog.

A rare analysis and critique of *radio-* and *telenovelas*, Latin America's version of 'soap operas', which are hugely popular in Cuba. Among the themes he considers, González explores the concept of soaps as broadcasting an endemic evil or cultural message and alludes to Cuba's war of the airwaves.

1066 **The mass media: their functions in social conflict.**
John Spencer Nichols. In: *Cuba: internal and international affairs.* Edited by Jorge I. Domínguez. Beverly Hills, California: Sage, 1982, p. 71-111.

In this piece the mass media are viewed as an essential channel for mass mobilization and control, management of domestic conflict and maintenance of the Cuban revolutionary process. The author argues that the leadership recognized this fact and therefore placed heavy emphasis on the role of the media, an emphasis not matched in scholarship on the media, either in Cuba or abroad. The chapter looks at the system, ideology, and economic and technological constraints through an analysis of national daily newspapers and the weekly *Bohemia*, and by studying the key events of the years 1970, 1975 and 1980. It concludes that the press was not monolithic and changed significantly over the decade.

1067 **Medios de comunicación: Cuba también se bloquea.** (The media: Cuba blockades itself.)
María López Vigil. *Envío-UCA*, no. 153 (Oct. 1994), p. 44-55.

Arguing that the Cuban body politic needs a plurality of opinion more than a multi-party system, the author suggests Cubans should put their own media on trial. Having discussed the debate on Cuban problems in the context of the Americas as a whole, the author presents a perceptive analysis of the Cuban media.

1068   **El periodismo: una misión histórica.** (Journalism: a historic
        mission.)
        Nydia Sarabia.   Havana: Editorial Pablo de la Torriente, 1987. 150p.

A collection of articles on journalists who have entered rebel-held areas in Cuba, from
James O'Kelly in the 19th-century wars of independence to Herbert Matthews in the
1950s insurrection. It also includes articles on the journalistic activities of Fidel
Castro and Ernesto Che Guevara.

1069   **'Radio Martí': una nueva agresión.** ('Radio Martí': a new attack.)
        José Cabañas.   *Cuadernos de Nuestra América*, vol. 1, no. 1
        (Jan.-July 1984), p. 174-204.

The US decision to establish a radio station aimed at Cuban listeners is described, in
typical Cuban fashion of the time, as an act of aggression.

1070   **The selling of Fidel Castro: the media and the Cuban revolution.**
        Edited by W. Ratliff.   New Brunswick, New Jersey: Transaction,
        1987. 197p.

A critical examination of the media's treatment of Fidel Castro, with chapters on: the
New York Times and the Cuban revolution; the world according to *Granma*; the press
in Cuba, 1952-60; covering Cuba (a guide based on interviews with journalists); Fidel
Castro and the US press; and Cuba's fickle friends: the verdict of the European press
on the Cuban revolution.

1071   **'Tele Martí': una nueva escalada.** ('TV Martí': a new escalation.)
        Arnaldo Coro Antich.   *Cuadernos de Nuestra América*, vol. 6, no. 12
        (Jan.-June 1989), p. 6-23.

Traces the antecedents to TV Martí, which was transmitted from offshore Florida to
Cuba, and considers its function, its violation of international agreements ratified by
the US government and its impact on US–Cuba relations.

1072   **Television Martí: electronic invasion in the post-Cold War.**
        Laurien Alexandre.   *Media, Culture and Society*, vol. 14 (1992),
        p. 523-40.

Considers the debate in the international arena over TV Martí, the US-financed
television station which attempted to broadcast into Cuba. Alexandre examines
international law and argues that at the core of the conflict there is a fundamental clash
between national sovereignty, communications technology and US ideology.

Newspapers and Periodicals

Newspapers

1073 Granma.
Havana: Central Committee of the Communist Party of Cuba, 1965- .
daily.

Articles and editorials reflecting the opinion of the Communist Party on various topics are printed in this paper, with major speeches and declarations, national and international news coverage, and regular sections. Replacing previous papers, *Hoy* and *Revolución*, when it began in 1965, this paper was the only remaining daily at the time of publication, due to economic circumstances. Since 1990 it has only been published Tuesday to Saturday. Also published on a weekly basis (1966-) is *Granma International* which contains a selection of features from the daily *Granma*, as well as specially commissioned articles, major speeches and events, national and international news coverage and regular sections. It is published in English, French, Spanish, Portuguese and German editions.

1074 Juventud Rebelde. (Rebel youth.)
Havana: Union of Young Communists, 1965- . weekly.

Provides general national and international coverage of news and events, with articles, features, interviews and regular sections on topics of interest to young people. A daily paper until 1990, this now appears on a weekly basis on a Sunday.

1075 Trabajadores. (Workers.)
Havana: Central Organization of Cuban Trade Unions, 1970- .
weekly.

The official organ of the Central Organization of Cuban Trade Unions, this contains articles on a broad range of topics of interest to Cuban workers, with news and feature coverage related to the Cuban and international labour movement. Before 1990 it was published on a daily basis.

General-interest periodicals

1076   Bohemia.
Havana: Bohemia, 1908- . weekly.

A general-interest magazine covering current topics related to politics, culture, the economy and industry, with photo features, interviews and reviews, and regular national and international sections. Since February 1995 a monthly international version has been available, containing a selection of articles from the weekly publication.

1077   Bulletin of Latin American Research.
Oxford, 1982- . tri-annual.

The journal of the UK Society for Latin American Studies, primarily intended for longer articles reflecting original research but also including shorter contributions on topics of interest.

1078   Caribbean Insight.
London: West India Committee, 1978- . monthly.

Contains regular sections on Cuba, with an emphasis on economic and political developments.

1079   Caribbean Studies.
Río Piedras, Puerto Rico, 1968- . quarterly.

The publication of the Institute of Caribbean Studies at the University of Puerto Rico, this disseminates the work of Caribbeanists, from a multi-disciplinary and multicultural perspective.

1080   El Correo de Cuba. (The Courier of Cuba.)
Havana: Foreign Ministry, 1995- . quarterly.

This is a new publication aimed at Cubans living abroad.

1081   CubaInfo.
Washington, DC: Johns Hopkins University Press, Paul H. Nitze School of Advanced International Studies, 1989- . three-weekly.

A newsletter with particular emphasis on Cuban–US relations.

1082   Cuba Internacional.
Havana: Prensa Latina, 1959- . bi-monthly.

A general-interest magazine published in Spanish, this publication contains articles, features and interviews on developments in Cuba and international events from a Third World perspective. A monthly English-language edition was published between 1983 and 1990. It has also been published in French, Portuguese and Russian. It was originally entitled *Revista INRA* (Journal of the National Agrarian Reform Institute).

1083 **CubaNews.**
Miami, Florida: Miami Herald Publishing Company, September
1993- . monthly.
Focuses mainly on the Cuban economy, and publishes signed contributions from
Cuba-watchers.

1084 **Cuba Update.**
New York: Center for Cuban Studies, 1980- . quarterly.
This is an informative magazine covering Cuban current affairs, culture and society,
which, while sympathetic to Cuba, often focuses on a single issue or group of issues
from several perspectives.

1085 **Cuban Review.**
Havana; Amsterdam: International Press Service, 1995- . monthly.
Written in Havana, this Cuban current affairs tabloid covers similar ground to *Granma
Internacional*.

1086 **Cuban Studies.**
Pittsburgh, Pennsylvania, 1971- . annual.
This is the journal founded by Carmelo Mesa-Lago and the University of Pittsburgh
group of Cuban-American academics. It is the established journal for the academic
field of Cuban Studies, and publishes articles from academics, mainly but not
exclusively based in the United States. A recent feature of the journal is to publish
thematic issues by guest editors and this includes work by academics based in Cuba
and elsewhere.

1087 **Latin American Perspectives.**
Beverly Hills, California, 1974- . quarterly.
A journal of radical thought, providing a forum for discussion and debate on the
political economy of capitalism, imperialism and socialism in which revolutionary
voices active in Latin America can be heard. Special issues on Cuba include: vol. 20,
no. 1 (spring 1993), 'Cuba: labour, local politics and internationalist views'; and
vol. 18, no. 2 (spring 1991), 'Cuban views on the revolution'.

1088 **Latin American Research Review.**
Pittsburgh, Pennsylvania, 1965- . quarterly.
The journal that provided the impetus for founding the US Latin American Studies
Association, whose membership now runs to some 4,000.

1089 **Prisma Latinoamericano.** (Latin-American Prism.)
Havana: Prensa Latina, 1974- . monthly.
Published in Spanish and also in English between 1985 and 1990, this news magazine
contains reports and features on Cuban and international issues.

1090 **Revista Bimestre Cubana.** (Cuban Bi-monthly Review.)
Havana: Sociedad Económica de Amigos del País, 1995- .
semi-annual.

This is a modern revival of a prestigious and historically influential publication dating from colonial times. The first edition of what was labelled the third epoch carried articles discussing the history and contemporary aims of the publication, and short articles on political, economic and historical issues.

1091 **Verde Olivo.** (Olive green.)
Havana: Ministry of the Revolutionary Armed Forces of Cuba,
1960- . weekly.

Contains articles, interviews and photo-features on general cultural, sports and recreational activities, including national and international events, with special emphasis on issues related to the military.

Specialist periodicals

Architecture

1092 **Arquitectura Cuba.** (Architecture Cuba.)
Havana: Construction Information Centre. tri-annual.

Offers information on projects, completed works and technology for construction design, planning, and architecture, with special emphasis on Cuba and the problems of socialist developing countries. Summaries in English and French are provided.

Business and trade

1093 **Business Latin America.**
New York: The Economist Intelligence Unit, 1966- . weekly.

This weekly report to managers of Latin American operations is paying growing attention to Cuba.

1094 **Business Tips on Cuba.**
Havana: Cuban Office of the Technological Information System,
United Nations Development Programme, 1992- . monthly.

Published as a newsletter between 1992 and 1994 and as a magazine since March 1994, this contains short news items on companies, initiatives, ventures and events as well as advertisements by Cuban enterprises seeking investment or trade partners. It is published in English, Spanish, French, Russian and Portuguese.

1095   **Contactos.** (Contacts.)
      Havana: Chamber of Commerce of the Republic of Cuba,
      June 1993- . monthly.

A magazine aimed at the business reader, with news of investment and trade developments, and features on business opportunities.

1096   **Country Report: Cuba, Dominican Republic, Haiti, Puerto Rico.**
      London: The Economist Intelligence Unit, 1986- . quarterly.

A publication aimed mainly at businesses, monitoring and analysing political and economic events. It includes economic data, two-year outlooks, and a guide to the political structure of each country.

1097   **Cuba Business.**
      London: Cuba Business Ltd, English edition, 1987- ; Spanish edition,
      1995- . 10 issues a year.

Bi-monthly until 1993, this is a well-informed publication providing reports on, and analysis of the Cuban economy, business and finance. It offers an invaluable briefing for those doing business in Cuba.

1098   **Cuba: Foreign Trade.**
      Havana: Chamber of Commerce of the Republic of Cuba. irreg.

This glossy promotional publication, published in both Spanish and English, is supposed to appear on a quarterly basis but in practice appears only sporadically. It contains articles and general information relevant to foreign trade and investment.

1099   **The Cuba Report.**
      Miami, Florida: Cuba Publications Inc., 1992- . 11 issues annually.

A newsletter covering Cuban business activity.

1100   **Opciones.** (Options.)
      Havana: Juventud Rebelde, January 1994- . weekly.

A newspaper aimed mainly at the foreign business community in Cuba, it contains Cuban and international commercial and financial news.

Culture and the arts

1101   **Casa de las Américas.** (House of the Americas.)
      Havana: Casa de las Américas, 1960- . monthly.

Publishes articles, fiction, poetry, literary criticism, interviews, book reviews, art criticism and cultural news from Latin America and the Caribbean.

1102   **Cine Cubano.** (Cuban Cinema.)
      Havana: Cuban Film Institute, 1960- . quarterly.

Cuban and other Latin American film-makers and film critics contribute features, articles and interviews to this journal, on the politics and aesthetics of film.

1103   **Del Caribe.** (From the Caribbean.)
Santiago de Cuba: Casa del Caribe, 1984- . quarterly.
A journal reflecting research into the culture of Cuba and the broader Caribbean.

1104   **La Gaceta de Cuba.** (The Cuban Gazette.)
Havana: Union of Writers and Artists of Cuba, 1962- . bi-monthly.
Founded by Nicolás Guillén in 1962, this tabloid covers literature, art, performance arts and politics, with articles, interviews and comment on current national and international topics.

1105   **Revista de la Biblioteca Nacional José Martí.** (José Martí National Library Review.)
Havana: Biblioteca Nacional José Martí, 1950- . tri-annual.
Contains major research articles on Cuban history, literature and the social sciences, along with bibliographical and library information.

1106   **Revolución y Cultura.** (Revolution and Culture.)
Havana: Ministry of Culture, 1971- . monthly.
An illustrated magazine with cultural articles, features, interviews and reviews, this also contains excerpts from unpublished work by Cuban authors, information on Cuban culture, and colour reproductions of Cuban art.

1107   **Unión.** (Union.)
Havana: Union of Writers and Artists of Cuba, 1964- . quarterly.
A literary journal disseminating the work of writers and artists, including Cuban fiction and criticism and articles from abroad on aesthetics and the philosophy of art.

Economics

1108   **Boletín de Información sobre la Economía Cubana.** (Bulletin of Information about the Cuban Economy.)
Havana: Centre for Research on the World Economy, Jan. 1992-monthly.
Compiled by one of Havana's most important think-tanks, this bulletin presents original academic articles side-by-side with news on the Cuban economy and short summaries of current economic research.

1109   **Country Profile: Cuba.**
London: The Economist Intelligence Unit, 1986- . annual.
Background information on the country's history, politics and economic affairs, with six-year series of macroeconomic data.

1110 **Cuestiones de la Economía Planificada.** (Questions of Planned Economy.)
Havana: Central Planning Board, 1978- . bi-monthly.

This is a theoretical journal with articles on the economy and planning by Cuban economists. It contains a selection of articles from specialized publications of former socialist bloc countries and also provides abstracts in English.

1111 **Economía y Desarrollo.** (Economics and Development.)
Havana: University of Havana, Faculty of Economics, 1970- . bi-monthly.

Contains articles on international economic issues and provides abstracts in both English and French.

1112 **La Sociedad Económica.** (The Economics Society.)
London: La Sociedad Económica, 1991-94; Paris, 1995- . irreg.

These are occasional bulletins on Cuban economic, legal and political issues, usually focusing on a single issue.

1113 **Tribuna del Economista.** (The Economist Tribune.)
Havana: National Association of Cuban Economists, 1989- . monthly.

An outlet for the opinions of Cuban economists, as well as the association's official analysis of issues of economic interest.

Education

1114 **Educación.** (Education.)
Havana: Ministry of Education, 1971- . quarterly.

Covers the main areas of Cuban educational policy, and includes reprints of articles, translations and general information on education, as well as publishing the findings of educational research.

History, politics and society

1115 **Anales del Caribe.** (Annals of the Caribbean.)
Havana: Centre for Caribbean Studies, Casa de las Américas, 1980- . annual.

A digest of essays on historical and cultural topics by Caribbean intellectuals.

1116 **Anuario del Centro de Estudios Martianos.** (Yearbook of the
Centre for Martí Studies.)
Havana: Biblioteca Nacional José Martí, 1978- . annual.

An annual compilation of essays on Martí's philosophy, ethics and politics, with a
bibliography.

1117 **Cuadernos de Nuestra América.** (Notebooks of Our America.)
Havana: Centre for American Studies, 1984- . semi-annual.

Contains essays on political and economic themes relevant to the Americas.

1118 **Cuba Socialista.** (Socialist Cuba.)
Havana: Central Committee of the Communist Party,
Sept. 1961-Feb. 1967. monthly; 1980- . irreg.

This was an important journal during the early years of the revolution. It promoted
party policy and recorded the experiences of Cuba and other countries, of socialism,
labour, communist organizations, national liberation movements, revolutionary theory
and research. Early issues were especially informative on the great debates of the early
1960s. Abstracts in English and French are provided.

1119 **Temas – Cultura, Ideología, Sociedad.** (Themes – Culture,
Ideology, Society.)
Havana: Revista Temas, 1995- . quarterly.

A fresh attempt to provide a platform for Cuban intellectuals to discuss contemporary
cultural, ideological and social questions.

Industry and agriculture

1120 **ANAP.**
Havana: National Association of Small Farmers, 1961- . monthly.

This is a Cuban farming magazine, containing human interest stories and tips on the
application of agricultural science and technology. See also item no. 738.

1121 **Ciencia y Técnica en la Agricultura.** (Science and Technology in
Agriculture.)
Havana: Ministry of Agriculture, Information and Documentation
Centre, 1978- . semi-annual.

Constitutes several series of journals publishing the results of Cuban agricultural
research, with abstracts in English. The journals in the series cover a large number of
technical topics and include titles such as: *Café y Cacao* (Coffee and Cacao);
Mecanización de la Agricultura (Mechanization of Agriculture); *Pastos y Forrajes*
(Pasture and Fodder); *Suelos y Agroquímica* (Soils and Agrochemistry); *Tabaco*
(Tobacco); and *Veterinaria* (Veterinary Medicine). They have varying publication
frequencies.

1122 **Cigar Aficionado.**
New York: M. Shanken Communications, Inc., 1992- . quarterly.

The glossy magazine for lovers of fine cigars, this caters for the up-market audience of those who can afford a 'good smoke' and are fighting an anti-anti-smoking campaign. The magazine carries full-colour consumer articles and advertisements, provides cigar quality ratings, and is a mine of information on companies and personalities in the cigar world. Since the Havana cigar still reigns supreme, there are many articles on Cuban tobacco growing, manufacture and consumption in Cuba and abroad, especially the Dominican Republic, Honduras, Mexico, Jamaica, and Florida.

1123 **Cubatabaco.** (Cuba Tobacco.)
Havana: Ministry of the Food Industry, Ministry of Agriculture and the Tobacco Export Enterprise of the Ministry of Foreign Trade, 1972- . quarterly.

Articles, features and interviews on the Cuban tobacco industry are published in this journal, which provides abstracts in English and Russian and a special issue in English.

1124 **Cuba Azúcar.** (Cuba Sugar.)
Havana: Ministry of the Sugar Industry, 1966- . monthly.

A technical journal containing articles and information by Cuban specialists in the development of sugar production. It includes abstracts in English and French.

1125 **Revista Cubana de Ciencia Agrícola.** (Cuban Journal of Agricultural Sciences.)
Havana: Agricultural Sciences College of Havana, Institute of Animal Sciences, 1967- . tri-annual.

Contains articles related to tropical livestock raising and reports of Cuban and foreign specialists working on the development of livestock farming in Cuba. An English version is available.

Law

1126 **Revista Cubana de Derecho.** (Cuban Journal of Law.)
Havana: National Union of Cuban Jurists, 1972[?]- . quarterly.

This journal contains articles in the field of law, and helps publicize the main laws decreed by the Cuban government. It includes abstracts in English, French and Russian.

Medicine

1127   **Avances Médicos de Cuba.** (Cuban Medical Advances.)
        Havana: Prensa Latina, 1994- . quarterly.

A magazine aimed at medical professionals abroad, with reports on developments in Cuban medicine, news of medical conferences, and general health articles. Summaries in English are provided.

1128   **Revista Cubana de Administración de Salud.** (Cuban Journal of
        Health Administration.)
        Havana: Ministry of Public Health, National Medical Sciences
        Information Centre, 1975- . quarterly.

The official organ of the Cuban Society of Health Administration, this journal contains articles on general health administration as well as statistics and data on population growth, cybernetics, the economy, medical education, sociology and other related subjects. Abstracts are provided in English, French and Russian.

1129   **Revista Cubana de Medicina.** (Cuban Journal of Medicine.)
        Havana: Ministry of Public Health, National Medical Sciences
        Information Centre, 1962- . bi-monthly.

Covers topics of a general nature, as well as including articles on more detailed medical matters, mainly by Cuban specialists. Abstracts in English and French are provided.

1130   **Revista Cubana de Medicina Tropical.** (Cuban Journal of Tropical
        Medicine.)
        Havana: Ministry of Public Health, National Medical Sciences
        Information Centre, 1966- . tri-annual.

This is the official publication of the Cuban Society of Tropical Medicine and the Dr Pedro Kourí Institute of Tropical Medicine. It specializes in tropical medicine, particularly parasitology, but also treats epidemiology, microbiology and other related areas. Abstracts are provided in English, French and Russian.

Science

1131   **Biotecnología Aplicada.** (Applied Biotechnology.)
        Havana: Sociedad Iberolatinoamericana de Biotecnología Aplicada a
        la Salud, 1984- . quarterly.

A professional publication which includes articles discussing biotechnology research in Cuba.

1132 **Revista Cubana de Física.** (Cuban Journal of Physics.)
Havana: University of Havana, Scientific-Technical Information
Department, 1981- . tri-annual.

This journal documents the evolution and development of physics in Cuba. It is sponsored by the Cuban Society of Physics, the Academy of Sciences of Cuba and the Ministries of Education and Higher Education. Abstracts in English are provided.

1133 **Revista de Investigaciones Marinas.** (Journal of Marine Research.)
Havana: University of Havana, Scientific-Technical Information
Department, 1980- . tri-annual.

Publishes articles on marine and fisheries research, ecology, oceanography, physics, chemistry and conservation.

Dictionaries, Encyclopaedias and Directories

1134 **The Cambridge encyclopedia of Latin America and the Caribbean.**
Edited by Simon Collier, Thomas Skidmore, Harold Blakemore.
Cambridge, England: Cambridge University Press, 1992. 2nd ed.
479p. maps.

This one-volume encyclopaedia makes reference to many aspects of Cuban life and culture.

1135 **Diccionario de la literatura cubana.** (Dictionary of Cuban literature.)
Instituto de la Literatura y Lingüística de la Academia de Ciencias de Cuba. Havana: Editorial Letras Cubanas, vol. 1, 1980; vol. 2, 1984.

Providing brief, concise information, this dictionary of authors, movements and organizations connected with literature, was begun in 1966.

1136 **Diccionario de la música cubana.** (Dictionary of Cuban music.)
Helio Orovio. Havana: Editorial Letras Cubanas, 1981. 442p.

Provides a detailed listing of Cuban music, musicians, musical terms and groups, with pictures and excerpts from pieces of music.

1137 **Dictionary of twentieth-century Cuban literature.**
Edited by Julio A. Martínez. Westport, Connecticut: Greenwood, 1990. 537p. bibliog.

This one-volume companion to contemporary Cuban literature provides concise information, in dictionary format, on both island and exile writers, as well as literary genres and movements. Longer sections are included on: literary criticism since 1900; the novel, 1900-69; the novel of the Cuban revolution, 1960-85; poetry since 1900; the short story since 1900; and the theatre since 1900. Bibliographies are provided for many of the entries.

1138 **Directory of vendors of Latin American library materials.**
Howard L. Karno, Beverly Joy-Karno. Albuquerque, New Mexico:
University of New Mexico, 1993. 4th ed. 42p. (Bibliography and
Reference Series, no. 32).

Provides an alphabetical listing of vendors supplying Latin American library materials
throughout the world. Many have a general Latin American and Caribbean coverage.

1139 **La enciclopedia de Cuba.** (Encyclopedia of Cuba.)
Edited by Vicente Báez. San Juan, Puerto Rico: Enciclopedia y
Clásicos Cubanos, 1977. 14 vols.

Contains broad information on all major aspects of Cuban history, geography, arts,
education, politics, society and literature.

1140 **Political and economic encyclopaedia of South America and the
Caribbean.**
Edited by Peter Calvert. Harlow, England: Longman, 1991. 363p.

General information on Cuba can be found in this encyclopaedia (under Cuba, Castro
etc.), although it is scattered and not always easy to locate.

1141 **Who's who in Latin America: part VII, Cuba, Dominican
Republic and Haiti.**
Edited by Ronald Hilton. Stanford, California: Stanford University
Press, 1951. 77p.

This volume contains a substantial section on Cuba, providing information on
important national and international figures before the revolution.

Encyclopedia of Latin American history and culture.
See item no. 108.

Historical dictionary of Cuba.
See item no. 121.

Cuban commercial directory 1993/94.
See item no. 727.

Bibliographies

Regional

1142 **The complete Caribbeana, 1900-1975: a bibliographic guide to the scholarly literature.**
Edited by Lambros Comitas.   Millwood, New York: KTO Press, 1977. 4 vols.
Over 2,000 pages provide coverage of the humanities, social sciences, natural sciences and business.

1143 **Handbook of Latin American Studies.**
Hispanic Foundation, Library of Congress.   Cambridge, Massachusetts: Harvard University Press, 1935-51; Gainesville, Florida: University Press of Florida, 1952- . annual.
An annual annotated guide to the general sources on Latin America.

1144 **Latin America and the Caribbean: a critical guide to research sources.**
Paula H. Covington, with David Block, Dan Hazen, Peter T. Johnson, Barbara Valk.   New York; London: Greenwood, 1992. 924p.
This work updates and expands the 'standard' Griffen guide, emphasizing works published since 1960. It is intended as a research guide and teaching bibliography, and for identifying major Latin American collections in the United States. There are fifteen sections, each with an introductory essay or essays, indexed according to subject, author and title.

Cuba

1145 **Bibliografía de bibliografías cubanas.** (Bibliography of Cuban
      bibliographies.)
      Tomás Fernández Robaina.   Havana: Editorial Organismos, 1973.
      340p.

This is a comprehensive guide to bibliographies relating to Cuba, published in Cuba
and abroad. The work is divided into general and specialist bibliographies, newspaper
guides and library catalogues and is grouped under 19th- and 20th-century
publications.

1146 **Cuba: an annotated bibliography.**
      Compiled by Louis A. Pérez, Jr.   Westport, Connecticut:
      Greenwood, 1988. 301p.

With a total of 1,120 annotated entries on a broad range of topics, this bibliography is
especially strong on history and is the best of its kind for Cuban Spanish-language
publications. A major criterion for inclusion was the availability of the publications
outside of Cuba, specifically in libraries in the USA.

1147 **Cuban serials and primary source collections: a bibliography of
      microfilm negatives.**
      Peter Johnson, Francsico J. Fonseca.   *Cuban Studies*, vol. 22 (1992),
      p. 231-50.

Identifies, as part of the activities of the Intensive Cuban Collecting Group, a list of
US microfilms of serials and collections of primary sources not commercially
available.

1148 **A guide to Cuban collections in the United States.**
      Louis A. Pérez, Jr.   New York: Greenwood, 1991. 179p.

The first in the Greenwood series of reference guides to archival and manuscript
sources in world history, this was prepared to assist researchers in locating collections
in the United States. The work has detailed indexes according to collection and
subject.

Specialized bibliographies

Flora

1149 **Bibliografía botánica cubana, teórica y aplicada, con énfasis en la silvicultura (1900-67).** (A Cuban botanical bibliography, theoretical and applied, with emphasis on forestry [1900-67].)
H. Samkova, V. Samek. Havana: Cuban Academy of Sciences, 1967. 35p.
A bibliography of material on the subject published between 1900 and 1967.

Foreign relations

1150 **A bibliography of United States–Latin American relations since 1810.**
David F. Trask, Michael C. Meyer, Roger R. Trask. Lincoln, Nebraska: University of Nebraska Press, 1968. 441p.
Many of the entries in this compilation deal with US–Cuba relations. A sequel publication was *Supplement to a bibliography of United States–Latin American relations since 1910*, compiled by Michael C. Meyer (1979).

1151 **Cuba–U.S. relations: a survey of twentieth century historiography.**
Louis A. Pérez. *Inter-American Review of Bibliography*, vol. 39, no. 3 (1989), p. 311-28.
A historiographical essay on the relations between the United States and Cuba since the 18th century. The author evaluates the significant periodical and monographical literature in terms of general studies and specific periods as well as other important topics. The bibliography includes works in both Spanish and English, largely by Cuban and North American scholars and the citations on the 1959 revolution and subsequent relations are particularly extensive.

History

1152 **Historiography in the revolution: a bibliography of Cuban scholarship, 1959-1979.**
Louis A. Pérez, Jr. New York: Garland Publishing, 1982. 318p.
A listing of books and articles on Cuban history published during the first two decades of the revolution, organized chronologically and thematically.

Literature

1153 **Alejo Carpentier, bibliographical guide.**
Compiled by Roberto González Echeverría, Klaus Muller-Bergh.
Westport, Connecticut: Greenwood, 1983. 271p.

Over 3,000 publications on and by Carpentier are included in this work.

1154 **A bibliography of Cuban creative literature: 1958-1971.**
Lourdes Casal. *Cuban Studies Newsletter*, vol. 2, no. 2 (June 1972),
p. 2-29.

This is a compilation of novels, short stories, plays and poetry published by Cuban
authors in Cuba and in exile in the early years of the revolution.

Overseas population

1155 **Bibliography for the Mariel-Cuban diaspora.**
Thomas D. Boswell, Manuel Rivero. Gainesville, Florida:
University of Florida, 1988. 92p.

Provides a comprehensive listing of articles in the US press and the Cuban *Granma
Weekly Review* on the exodus of approximately 125,000 Cubans to the United States
in 1980 through the Cuban port of Mariel. An introductory chapter provides an
overview of the Mariel-Cuban diaspora, including motivational factors, demographic
characteristics and resettlement experiences. The extent and suddenness of the boatlift
were without precedent, with emigrants going to a Miami, Florida that was totally
unprepared for them, as is reflected in this documenting of a process of trial and error.

1156 **Cubans in the United States: a bibliography for research in the
social and behavioral sciences, 1960-1983.**
Compiled by Lyn MacCorkle. Westport, Connecticut: Greenwood,
1984. 227p.

Lists 1,600 entries on education, economics, public administration, psychology,
health, politics, sociology and demography in connection with Cubans living in the
United States.

Race

1157 **The blacks in Cuba: a bibliography.**
Rafael Fermoselle-López. *Caribbean Studies*, vol. 12, no. 3
(Oct. 1972), p. 103-12.

The books and articles included in this compilation are organized thematically under
sections including slavery and abolition, race relations, folklore, literature and
language.

Religion

1158 **Religion and politics in revolutionary Cuba: a bibliographical guide.**
John M. Kirk. *Inter-American Review of Bibliography*, vol. 37, no. 3 (1987), p. 327-43.
Considers the relationship between the Church and the state in Cuba from the 16th century to the present, emphasizing the recent revolutionary period, 1959-87. The author provides an extensive bibliographical essay and pays particular attention to Cuban studies produced under the régime of Fidel Castro. He notes that in recent years there have been numerous studies of religion and the role of the Catholic Church in Cuban politics. This suggests a normalizing of relations between the Marxist government and Church officials.

Revolution

1159 **Cuba, 1953-1978: a bibliographical guide to the literature.**
Ronald H. Chilcote. White Plains, New York: Kraus International Publications, 1986. 2 vols. 1,387p.
Almost 20,000 entries are contained in this massive work, including citations of books, articles, and newspapers from a total of some fifty countries. They cover the twenty-five-year period after the 1953 attack on the Moncada Garrison.

1160 **The Cuban revolution of Fidel Castro viewed from abroad: an annotated bibliography.**
Gilberto V. Fort. Lawrence, Kansas: University of Kansas Libraries, 1969. 140p.
Lists books, pamphlets and general studies, with at least one complete chapter on an aspect of the revolution, which appeared in English, Spanish and Portuguese between 1959 and 1967.

1161 **The Cuban revolution: a research-study guide (1959-1969).**
Compiled by Nelson P. Valdés, Edwin Lieuwen. Albuquerque, New Mexico: University of New Mexico Press, 1971. 230p.
This is a detailed compilation for the first ten years of the revolution of works on politics, international relations, economy, society and culture.

1162 **The Cuban revolutionary war, 1953-1958: a bibliography.**
Louis A. Pérez, Jr. Metuchen, New Jersey: Scarecrow Press, 1976. 225p.
A reference guide to written material published during the years 1953-75 which is housed at five US institutions: the University of Miami; University of Florida (Gainesville); Library of Congress (Washington); Center for Cuban Studies (New York); and the Hoover Institution on War, Revolution and Peace (Stanford). Topics covered range from the 26th July Movement and the attack on the Moncada Garrison

to the armed forces, students, women, peasants, labour, the Church, journalism, medicine, and the United States and the revolution.

1163 **Cuban Studies since the revolution.**
Edited by Damián Fernández. Gainesville, Florida: University Press of Florida, 1992. 318p.
This volume of papers was commissioned for a 1990 dialogue held at Florida International University. Leading specialists in the field of Cuban Studies, cutting across the political spectrum but all based in the United States, reviewed thirty years of scholarship since the revolution and identified promising areas for future research. Carmelo Mesa-Lago and Anthony Maingot provide overviews of the situation; Louis Pérez, Rebecca Scott and Gerald Poyo review the history; Jorge Domínguez, Marifeli Pérez-Stable, Rhoda Rabkin and Damián Fernández look at political science and international relations; Jorge Pérez-López, Susan Eckstein and Sergio Roca discuss economics; Roberto González Echeverría, Gustavo Pérez-Firmat and Isabel Castellanos comment on the humanities; Silvia Pedraza and Lisandro Pérez focus on Cubans in exile; and Rosa Mesa and Peter Johnson document bibliographical resources.

1164 **Human services in postrevolutionary Cuba: an annotated international bibliography.**
Larry Oberg. Westport, Connecticut: Greenwood, 1984. 433p.
An annotated bibliography of over 2,000 titles in English and Spanish covering education, housing, public health and medicine, the elderly, ethnic minorities, women and the family from 1959 to 1982.

1165 **Revolutionary Cuba: a bibliographical guide.**
Compiled by Fermín Peraza Sarausa. Coral Gables, Florida: University of Miami Press, 1966-68. 3 vols. 262p.
This is a thorough compilation of publications, in Cuba and abroad, on the early years of the revolution.

Social conditions

1166 **Analysis of research on the Cuban family 1970-87.**
I. Reca, M. Álvarez, M. C. Caño. Havana: Ciencias Sociales, 1990. 233p.
This is a guide to published and unpublished research on the Cuban family with summaries of the most significant findings. Problems which have not yet been studied are identified and the methodological and theoretical deficiences of the studies conducted in the period under review are discussed.

1167   **Annotated bibliography on the topic of the family.**
       Havana: Cuban Academy of Sciences, Centre for Psychological and
       Sociological Research, Family Research Group, 1987. 126p.

Provides information on the content and location (in libraries and documentation
centres) of approximately seventy studies on the Cuban family and related themes,
such as the incorporation of women into the workforce, and fertility.

Women

1168   **Bibliografía de la mujer cubana.** (Bibliography of the Cuban
       woman.)
       Tomás Fernández Robaina.   Havana: Ministry of Culture, Biblioteca
       Nacional José Martí, 1985. 210p.

Robaina lists sources available in the National Library on the history of Cuban
women, including items relating to women's congresses held since 1923, annotations,
and author and subject indexes.

Electronic sources

1169   **Info-South.**
       Coral Gables, Florida: University of Miami, North-South Center,
       1988- .

A database with bibliographical citations and abstracts from journals, news magazines, newsletters and newspapers from Latin America and the rest of the world.
These include *The Miami Herald* and *El Nuevo Heraldo* as well as the Cuban *Bohemia*
and *Granma*.

1170   **Latin American Data Base (LADB).**
       Albuquerque, New Mexico: University of New Mexico, 1986- .

Contains the full text of articles focusing especially on Cuban national policy and
foreign relations.

1171   **Latin American Studies.**
       Baltimore, Maryland: National Information Services Corporation,
       1993. vol. 1.

This CD-Rom provides access to citations from the *Nettie Lee Benson Latin American
Collection catalogue*, the *Handbook of Latin American Studies*, and the *Hispanic
American Periodicals Index* (HAPI).

1172 **PAIS International.**
New York: Public Affairs Information Service, 1991- . annual.

Provides bibliographical access to public and social policy materials that will be of use primarily to legislators, government officials, the business and financial community, policy researchers and students. Publications issued all over the world, in any of the six major languages (English, French, German, Italian, Portuguese and Spanish), are covered. Subjects covered include: economics; political science; public administration; international law and relations; the environment; demography; law; education; and social work. All types of publication are included – periodical articles, government documents, serials, pamphlets, and reports – and short annotations are provided. Available on CD-Rom and in print.

Phytogeographic survey of North America; a consideration of the phytogeography of the North American continent, including Mexico, Central America, and the West Indies, together with the evolution of North American plant distribution.
See item no. 79.

Bibliografía comentada de estudios lingüísticos publicados en Cuba, 1959-1980. (Annotated bibliography of linguistic studies published in Cuba, 1959-80.)
See item no. 410.

Indexes

There follow three separate indexes: authors (personal and corporate); titles; and subjects. Title entries are italicized and refer either to the main titles, or to other works cited in the annotations. The numbers refer to bibliographical entry rather than page numbers. Individual index entries are arranged in alphabetical sequence.

Index of Authors

301

302

Index of Titles

311

315

317

M

Machos, maricones, and gays: Cuba and homosexuality 529

Magical reels: a history of cinema in Latin America 1000

Main currents in Caribbean thought: the historical evolution of Caribbean society in its ideological aspects, 1492-1900 111

Major Cuban novelists: innovation and tradition 885

Major poems 909

Making the future: politics and educational reform in the United States, England, the Soviet Union, China and Cuba 837

Making a new people: education in revolutionary Cuba 836

Male and female in Latin America 403

The Mambí-Land, or, adventures of a Herald correspondent in Cuba 48

Man and socialism in Cuba: the great debate 682

Man-making words: selected poems of Nicolás Guillén 899

Manual de historia de Cuba 123

La Manuela: arqueología de un cafetal habanero 105

Markedness and a Cuban dialect of Spanish 424

The marks of birth 575

Maroon societies: rebel slave communities in the Americas 333

Marriage, class and colour in nineteenth century Cuba: a study

of racial attitudes and sexual values in a slave society 368

Marxistas de América 505

Mea Cuba 886

Measuring Cuban economic performance 675

Mechanisation of sugar cane harvesting in Cuba 762

La medicina popular en Cuba 494

Médicos y medicinas en Cuba: historia, biografía, costumbrismo 495

Medios de comunicación: Cuba también se bloquea 1067

Memoria del XIV Congreso 804

Memoria del XV Congreso 804

Memoria del XIII Congreso 804

Memoria histórica de Cienfuegos y su jurisdicción 137

Memorias de un juez y periodista cubano 554

Memorias: V Congreso ANAP 742

Memories of underdevelopment and Inconsolable memories 1001

Methodism's first fifty years in Cuba 443

Mi hijo el Che 267

Mi tesoro es Cuba: joyas de la ciencia y la naturaleza 78

Miami 313

The Miami Herald 1169

Middle America, its lands and peoples 14

The missiles of October: the declassified story of John F. Kennedy and the Cuban Missile Crisis 594

Mitología cubana 1022

Modernity & Africanía: Wifredo Lam in his island 949

Momentos y figuras de las ciencias en Cuba 849

Moncada: memories of an attack that launched the Cuban revolution 187

Moncada Tania the unforgettable guerrilla 187

Monetary problems of an export economy: the Cuban experience, 1917-1947 711

Monólogos teatrales cubanos 1002

Los monopolios norte-americanos en Cuba: contribución al estudio de la penetración imperialista 661

El Monte: Igbo, Finda, Ewe Orisha, Vititi Nfinda 450

The motorcycle diaries: a journey around South America 274

Muerte de Narciso 904-5

La mujer en los cien años de lucha, 1868-1968 369

La mujer en Cuba: familia y sociedad 377

La mujer rural y urbana: estudios de casos 392

Mujeres en empleos no tradicionales 393

Música colonial cubana: tomo I (1812-1902) 975

La música de las sociedades de tumba francesa 976

La música en Cuba 887, 977

La música, lo cubano y la innovación 978

Mutismos 910

Myth and history: literary reconstruction around the life of a maid in prerevolutionary Cuba 914

321

Index of Subjects

Mariel exodus (1980) 310,
314-15, 527, 576,
863, 881
marine life 32, 84, 86
maritime resources 22
maroons 330, 333, 335
Martí, José 142, 147, 149,
154-58, 161, 167,
205, 214, 236, 304,
362, 631, 860-61,
919
birthplace museum
1050
literary works 902,
907-09
Martinique 938
Marx, Groucho 769
Marxism 213, 228, 236,
238-39, 253, 387,
430, 505
mass media 1059-72
see also newspapers;
periodicals
Matanzas 51, 127, 129
Mayarí people 92
mechanization of sugar
harvest 761-62,
764
medical folklore 485
medicinal plants 80, 450,
459, 494
medicine 216, 481
see also specialist
periodicals
Mella, Julio Antonio 177,
505
Menéndez, Jesús 793
Methodism 443
Mexico 79, 363, 528, 636,
868
Miami 32, 307-08, 312-13,
317, 428
microbrigades 463, 469,
472, 1025, 1035
Middle East
Cuban policy in 586,
649-52
see also individual
countries by name
migration 96
routes 104
statistics 816
military affairs 124

mineral resources 19, 663,
701
foreign involvement
552
see also mining
mining 16, 52, 660, 687,
723, 776-83
Missile Crisis (1962)
235-36, 250, 504,
589-94
modern architecture 1028,
1030-31
Moncada Garrison attack
182, 186-87, 189-90
monetary policy 687, 693
monetary system 721, 730
monoculture 752
Monroe Doctrine 169
Montaner, Rita 982
Morejón, Nancy 857, 874,
877, 910, 919, 932
mortality 356, 488-90
municipal elections (1986)
540
Museum of Contemporary
Hispanic Art 957
museums 103
see also individual
museums by name
music 39, 963-64, 966-68,
970-71, 973, 975-87
education 843

N

Namibia 644
National Archive 1058
National Association of
Small Farmers 390,
738, 742, 796
National Ballet of Cuba
965, 969
National Congress of
Education and Culture
928
National Demographic
Survey (1979) 398
National Film Institute
(ICAIC) 936, 993,
1000
National Institute of
Tourism 35

National Library of Cuba
1052, 1056, 1058
National Museum of Cuba
1055
National Peasant
Association 792, 796
national security 625
national symbols 12
National Union of Cuban
Jurists 557
National Worker
Federation of Cuba
785, 790
nationalism 106, 112, 205,
215, 236-37, 247, 621
natural resources 17, 22,
654
see also maritime
resources; mineral
resources; soil; water
management; water
resources
New Jewel Movement 634
newspapers
daily 1073
weekly 1074-75
Nicaragua 249, 251, 262,
308, 376, 510, 585,
630, 636
Non-Aligned Countries,
Movement of 261,
576, 584, 646
North America 79
see also Canada; United
States of America
North American Free
Trade Agreement
(NAFTA) 701
novels 864, 866, 868-70,
876, 882, 885, 892,
895, 904, 915, 918
see also translations of
literary works
nuclear energy 773-74
nursery education 832
nutrition 216, 488, 496,
750

O

Ochoa, Arnaldo 249, 544,
1061

333

vegetation 22
  see also flora; forestry
Venceremos work brigade 210
Venezuela 87, 636
veterinary regulations 729
Vietnam 585, 696
Villaverde, Cirilo 857, 866, 917-18, 902, 906
Virgin Islands 104
visual arts 934-62
vocabulary 411, 426

W

water management 19
water resources 22
watersports 32

Welles, Orson 769
West Germans in Cuba 38
West Indies 79, 517
whales 32
Wifredo Lam Centre 937
Wilde, Oscar 769
wildlife 74
  see also fauna
windsurfing 32
women 206, 216, 530, 669, 672, 994
  family and fertility 397-402
  images in literature 864, 896
  pre-1959 363-71
  post-1959 372-88
  sexuality and sex education 403-04
  work 389-96, 800
  see also bibliographies

women slaves 364
women's clubs 363
women's labour movement 366
women's movement for legal reform 365
Worker Federation of Havana 785
worker participation 807

Y

yellow fever 494
youth 62, 460, 462, 466

Z

zoology 20
  see also fauna

Map of Cuba

This map shows the more important towns and other features.

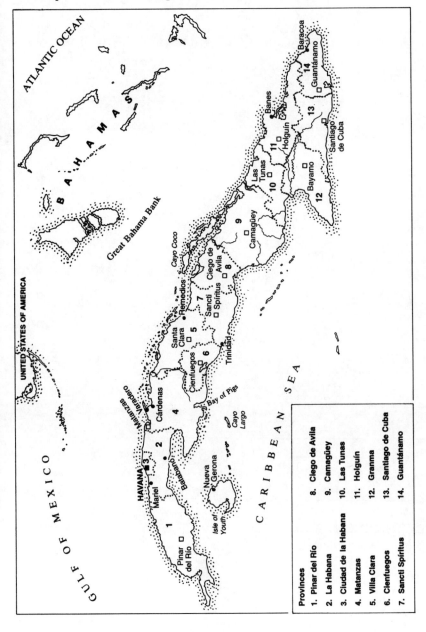

ALSO FROM CLIO PRESS

INTERNATIONAL ORGANIZATIONS SERIES

Each volume in the International Organizations Series is either devoted to one specific organization, or to a number of different organizations operating in a particular region, or engaged in a specific field of activity. The scope of the series is wide-ranging and includes intergovernmental organizations, international non-governmental organizations, and national bodies dealing with international issues. The series is aimed mainly at the English-speaker and each volume provides a selective, annotated, critical bibliography of the organization, or organizations, concerned. The bibliographies cover books, articles, pamphlets, directories, databases and theses and, wherever possible, attention is focused on material about the organizations rather than on the organizations' own publications. Notwithstanding this, the most important official publications, and guides to those publications, will be included. The views expressed in individual volumes, however, are not necessarily those of the publishers.

VOLUMES IN THE SERIES